November

November

LINCOLN'S ELEGY AT GETTYSBURG

Kent Gramm

Indiana University Press
BLOOMINGTON AND INDIANAPOLIS

This book is a publication of
Indiana University Press
601 North Morton Street
Bloomington, IN 47404-3797 USA

http://iupress.indiana.edu

Telephone orders 800-842-6796
Fax orders 812-855-7931
Orders by e-mail iuporder@indiana.edu

The paper used in this publication meets the minimum requirements of American National Standard for Information Sciences—Permanence of Paper for Printed Library Materials, ANSI Z39.48-1984.

MANUFACTURED IN THE UNITED STATES OF AMERICA

Library of Congress Cataloging-in-Publication Data

Gramm, Kent.
November : Lincoln's elegy at Gettysburg / Kent Gramm.
p. cm.
Includes bibliographical references.
ISBN 0-253-34032-2 (alk. paper)
1. Lincoln, Abraham, 1809–1865. Gettysburg address. 2. Gramm, Kent—Journeys—Pennsylvania—Gettysburg National Military Park. 3. Anniversaries—Social aspects—United States. 4. Memorials—Social aspects—United States. 5. November. 6. United States—Civilization—Philosophy. 7. Heroes—United States. 8. National characteristics, American. 9. Postmodernism—Social aspects—United States. 10. Gramm family. I. Title.
E475.55 .G73 2001
973.7′092—dc21
2001002228

1 2 3 4 5 06 05 04 03 02 01

It is for us . . . to be dedicated.

—Abraham Lincoln, November 19, 1863

When a civilization is in crisis, to preserve is to create.
—Jacqueline Kennedy Onassis

I know who I am,
and who I may be if I choose.
—Cervantes

Four score and seven years ago our fathers brought forth on this continent a new nation, conceived in Liberty, and dedicated to the proposition that all men are created equal.

Now we are engaged in a great civil war, testing whether that nation, or any nation so conceived and so dedicated, can long endure. We are met on a great battle-field of that war. We have come to dedicate a portion of that field as a final resting place for those who here gave their lives that that nation might live. It is altogether fitting and proper that we should do this.

But, in a larger sense, we can not dedicate—we can not consecrate—we can not hallow—this ground. The brave men, living and dead, who struggled here, have consecrated it far above our poor power to add or detract. The world will little note nor long remember what we say here, but it can never forget what they did here. It is for us the living, rather, to be dedicated here to the unfinished work which they who fought here have thus far so nobly advanced. It is rather for us to be here dedicated to the great task remaining before us—that from these honored dead we take increased devotion to that cause for which they gave the last full measure of devotion—that we here highly resolve that these dead shall not have died in vain—that this nation, under God, shall have a new birth of freedom—and that government of the people, by the people, for the people, shall not perish from the earth.

—Abraham Lincoln, Gettysburg, November 19, 1863

CONTENTS

CONTENTS

November

NOVEMBER

November 1637

A young man named Edward King dies in the Irish Sea when his ship, passing between England and Ireland, strikes a submerged rock. Seawater gushes in through an explosive wound in the hull. In minutes, the ship settles to the waterline like the *Titanic.* No strong wind is blowing; the ocean is calm. The elements cannot be blamed. Blame for these imminent deaths will have to be laid to human error, fate, chance, or the will of God.

"Life is unfair," John F. Kennedy would say years later, himself a victim of a shipwreck, though luckier. The young Kennedy knew how to swim, but Edward King and most passengers and sailors in 1637 did not. Nevertheless, some of the crew saved themselves by diving into the water and taking hold of flotsam. These remembered seeing King kneeling in prayer on the flooded deck.

At first, his dying was calm under that clear, empty sky. But soon he must have felt cold water streaming along the deck, soaking the knees of his trousers, rising, until the planks were gone and he knelt in the sea as it washed around his waist, then his chest. Had he looked, he would have seen the ship's rail, the mast, a litter of barrels, a spar, clothing, people here and there foundering—but his eyes were closed, or he looked fixedly into that clear sky. Water reached his neck and splashed his mouth and now, cold and salty, it enclosed him; he gasped upwards, perhaps unconsciously trying to stand as the deck slid away beneath him, water over him now, and now thrashing, gulping, swallowing.

One of his friends imagined it well. In November of that year, John Milton wrote an elegy for Edward King, which he titled *Lycidas* after a shepherd in Greek mythology. It is the greatest elegy in English—or was, until Abraham Lincoln delivered the Gettysburg Address in his November—but for Milton it was no mere literary exercise. He saw and felt too well the agonized struggle of his friend. His poem transmits that agony; the part that describes the sinking of King's body is in no sense consolatory.

"Why?" Milton cries in *Lycidas.* What had doomed this gentle friend?

But grief is not assuaged by answers to the question, "Why?" Elie Wiesel, a Holocaust survivor with what he calls a "wounded faith," claims that the great questions have no intellectual answers. The answer to grief is hope. Milton's elegy, like Lincoln's, moves from the past to the future, begins by plunging into the deeps of sorrow and dismay but then rises with hope. Some literary critics have charged *Lycidas* with lack of unity, with mixing in one element after another in seeming randomness, but its complex and flexible design bears the essential unity of all elegies: lament and hope. One grief suggests another, but all griefs are addressed by a single hope. The voices change in *Lycidas,* tenses change, and we become as confused as the sufferer. But in the end, the poem itself is evidence of things unseen: the "real world" of the last few lines is a made world—language only—meaning either that we have been fooled, or that there really can be more than one world.

By the time John Milton wrote *Paradise Lost,* he had become not only a representative of his age, but a citizen of several. In this he was a "modern," though an early one. Permeated by the Christian faith, he was partly medieval; he knew both biblical languages, and his great epic was biblical in origin. But the language of that epic was heavily Latinate in vocabulary and syntax; the poetry he wrote as a teenager, he wrote in Latin. *Paradise Lost* is dense with classical mythology:

> . . . Men call'd him *Mulciber;* and how he fell
> From Heav'n, they fabl'd, thrown by angry *Jove*
> Sheer o'er the Crystal Battlements: from Morn
> to Noon he fell, from Noon to dewy Eve,
> A Summer's day; and with the setting Sun

> Dropt from the Zenith like a falling Star,
> On *Lemnos* th' *Aegean* Isle . . .
> (I 740–46)

Milton was a man of the Renaissance, one foot in the old worlds—ancient and medieval—and one stepping toward the modern. Like a modern, he had a certain faith in human progress: things would get better; invention would thrive, the politics of nations like England would reject royal despotism and legislatures would govern, learning and art would increase to the benefit of humankind. Even epic poetry would improve. With his role in the latter development came a nascent modern sense of Self.

Modernism believes in human progress. If you and I read that sentence with detachment and irony, it is because we are at least partly "postmodern." Like Milton, we have roots in previous worlds, particularly the modern one. But to feel wry or skeptical about progress is to be postmodern. A Victorian Englishman or a soldier's mother in Civil War America would not have found the idea of progress futile or ironic. Abraham Lincoln staked his life on it, as did three hundred thousand Union dead.

We may question the meaning of those deaths as Milton lamented and questioned the death of Edward King.

> Where were ye Nymphs when the remorseless deep
> Clos'd o'er the head of your lov'd *Lycidas*?

That kind of question, which made the modern world, would also break it.

November 1863

Abraham Lincoln steps off a train in Gettysburg, Pennsylvania, carrying two or three carefully prepared pages of manuscript written on White House stationery. He has been asked to dedicate a cemetery but intends to dedicate a nation. The greatest battle on the North American continent has left thousands of men dead; now more mothers, sisters, and wives are wearing black all across the United States, more vacant chairs stand in darkened parlors all across the North, more fathers will never come back to their little sons and daughters again, and Abraham Lincoln must tell them why.

On the speakers' platform up on Cemetery Hill, Lincoln looks out over the soldiers' graves, over the crowd of ten thousand people who have come to listen and to mourn: he sees fields where the red battle flags of the Confederacy waved in the summer sunshine. They are not far away now. The war is still on. What the young men who defended Cemetery Hill did then, he must do now—but with words, and he must put them into the hearts and minds of men and women who have been devastated by death. His strong hands unfold the sheets of paper he has brought; he glances down at the first words, then looks at the people standing expectantly; and he speaks the most beautiful, memorable words of comfort, courage, and hope ever to have arisen from death, ever to have risen in the clear November air.

November 1918

The belief in reason and humane progress which we call modernism—and which found its perfect representative, American-style, in Abraham Lincoln—will not survive this November. Modernism will indeed affect people's minds for decades, even generations, more; but the world war ending this November has struck a deathblow to modernity. No single death symbolizes this more than that of Wilfred Owen, a promising young man like Edward King, already on his way to becoming a great poet—but who, with the absurd blackness of "postmodern" reality, has been killed only a week before the Armistice in a heroic little battle which, full of sound and fury, signified nothing except futility. No John Milton exists to write Wilfred Owen's elegy. That is altogether fitting and proper, because an elegy, though ancient in origin, is a modern thing in that it relates the past to the future, insists on the reality of hope, believes that things can make sense; but this war has made no sense, and the intellectual life of the Western World will no longer believe in sense. Fittingly, Wilfred Owen wrote his own elegies—for all those who were to be drowned in "the eucharist of their own blood"—but, as he said, those elegies "are in no sense consolatory." Yet they will survive not only him but also the devastation of the Great War, and the postmodern world itself. By what they remember, and by what they believe and do, future generations will write their anthems for the doomed youth of Owen's generation. They will do it in a world that is either a "long twilight struggle," or a new birth of freedom—or both.

November 1938

Kristallnacht, "night of broken glass": Nazi Germany breaks the windows of Jewish businesses and defaces synagogues in a massive "chastisement" of the Jews. It is the unmistakable prelude to the Holocaust. Where is God? Where is Reason? Where is Humanity?

November 1963

The last genuinely modernist president—a handsome young man who had seemed the brilliant apotheosis of reasoned hope—is shot in the head and killed in Dallas, Texas, by nobody in particular. Americans, collectively, are as disoriented and disheartened as Lincoln's people had been exactly one hundred years ago, and considerably more horrified. We have Kennedy's assassination on tape, and can replay it in color, the spraying red of his blood enough to make anyone with feelings wonder what it all means, and perhaps even ask, "Where was God?" Where indeed. Kennedy had just delivered a speech echoing the same Declaration of Independence that Lincoln's speech at Gettysburg had echoed, and not only did Kennedy use biblical phrasing, as Lincoln had, the young president had alluded to the coming season of Advent. But now hope is dust under the wheels of the flag-draped caisson (an imitation of Lincoln's funeral), as it slowly rolls past the stunned and weeping people waiting by the thousands along Pennsylvania Avenue. A decade of death and disillusionment is beginning.

On the same day, in Oxford, England, a strange man with long effects dies. He is Clive Staples Lewis, a man of reason who discovered the shortcomings of reason, a conservative who came to the most radical of conclusions and published them. People now read his books more than they reread the speeches of John F. Kennedy. He represents the oldest of worlds, but points toward a newer one. He was both modern and postmodern, and he was looking forward to Advent, too.

November 1965

Ia Drang, Vietnam. The armed forces of the United States fight their first major battle in a losing war that opposes enlightened self-interest to the dark urgencies of nationalism—one idea of liberty against another. This war will symbolize horror and futility, America's own small version of the First World War. As did the Civil War a hundred years earlier, this war will divide Americans against Americans, and bring tragedy to every household—right into the living rooms during the evening news, and into the streets, starting with Memphis and Los Angeles.

* * *

November is personal. If it were not, Lincoln's words would not have meant much at the time. Each listener had suffered some kind of personal loss, or knew someone who had. The modern world, in fact, raised the personal to the highest level. "I think; therefore I am." *We hold these truths to be self-evident, that all men are created equal, and are endowed by their Creator with certain unalienable Rights, that among these are Life, Liberty and the pursuit of Happiness.* Modern literature puts the first person at the forefront—call him Ishmael or Daedalus—and while postmodern theory takes the Self away, in theory, it also places the person of the observer at the focal point of scientific and historical observation, and whenever one scrambles literature according to postmodern specifications, one hears the postmodern theorist himself perched at one's ear, like one's own personal Mephistopheles, a puny inexhaustible voice always talking. That voice is gnawing away the world we know, chewing the planks—and water is rushing in; the deck is awash and tilting; the titanic civilization we took for granted is foundering; we look out on a wilderness of seawater.

That, at any rate, is my rationale for speaking, now and then, in the first person, and for interweaving my own private Novembers with the public ones, beginning with the following:

November 1917. A cemetery on a hill, shaded by old trees. A Norwegian immigrant named Martin buys a section of four plots near a row of Civil War graves. His younger brother is with the American army in France, fighting a strange, horrible, and vast war. But the site is not for his brother. Martin has lost his wife, Ingeborg, my grandmother whom I never met, a kind young lady of refined tastes and high social standing. She had married this blacksmith for love and followed him to the new world.

His brother Karl will never rest in that family plot. He will return from the war alive, but he will go to the far north and spend the rest of his days in the woods alone, a lumberjack, hale and blunt, keeping his Pershing moustache into old age. Like many of his comrades, he lies now in an unvisited soldier's grave—but it is in northern Minnesota, not in France. To his niece Ruth, Martin and Ingeborg's daughter, Karl wrote from time to time the tender letters of a brave and solitary mind.

Many Novembers later, Ruth taught her son the Gettysburg Address. Between my halting recitations and slovenly pronunciations ("Do not pronounce 'new' as though it were a bearded quadruped"), she recalled her town's Civil War veterans standing stiff and straight in their old uniforms before that row of their comrades' graves, near her mother's grave. Each year they marched up to the cemetery, and people from town came to see them and to hear the speeches. Ruth knew how to pronounce "Gettysburg" not the way northerners usually do, but as soldiers who had been there did.

November 1999. The gravesite adjoining Ingeborg's, bought so many years ago, is open today. This is our father's world, built stone by stone with their heavy hands; but we live from mother to mother.

There are two kinds of elegies: one is a melancholy contemplation, such as Gray's "Elegy Written in a Country Church-Yard"; and the other is lament and praise for the dead, ending with comfort and hope—such as Milton's *Lycidas* or Lincoln's Gettysburg Address. Both kinds are conceived in the fragile, passing beauty of time and dedicated to the mystery of eternity. Each kind of elegy blooms in sorrow from the soil of the past; its beauty remains for tomorrow.

November is nature's elegy. Let the month itself stand for grief and faith, a gray month of blank sky and cold winds, beginning in remembrance and ending in expectation—a month through whose strange beauty we all must pass and whose alien work must truly be our own.

* * *

"The world is different now," John F. Kennedy said on a clear, cold day in 1961, taking the oath of office as president of the United States. The rest of that decade would demonstrate the difference. How eras respond to tragedy shows what those eras are made of, and how one differs from another. The 1860s and the 1960s were very different.

In November of 1863, when Abraham Lincoln delivered his Address, the United States had been struck by tragedy at Chancellorsville, Gettysburg, and then Chickamauga, where a ghastly defeat reversed the entire progress of the war. The response of the Union can be phrased in three syllables: U. S. Grant. Not a week after the president left Gettysburg, Grant broke the siege at Chattanooga, stormed Missionary Ridge and Lookout Mountain, and in short order Sherman's boys were on their way to Atlanta and the sea.

But America responded to the tragedies of the 1960s with confusion. The reason for the difference might be easy to find. Lincoln's America stood squarely in the modern world. For better or worse, America knew where it had been and where it was going. Modernism synthesized the Enlightenment and Christianity, reason and religion, into a faith in progress and human effort "under God," who ordains, blesses, and aids whatever we do justly and according to what John Milton called Right Reason. But 1960s America had entered the postmodern world—and, characteristically for postmodernism, did not know it.

But we know it now. Our heritage includes both modernism and postmodernism; it includes the medieval world, the ancient world, the philosophies of India and China—all things that have gone before. We can be choosers of our faith. One of our tragedies is postmodernism itself, which embraces all possibilities and chooses none; for which all the past is present, and for which the past is illusion.

But choosing a faith is necessary because faith is a means of survival. Tragedy is calamity that must be explained. Explanations are sought, however, not for themselves but as a means of going on, of overcoming the paralysis that would be death—of ourselves, or of a nation. Ultimately, faith is not how we explain catastrophe but what we do about it. It is how we act when appalled. If we do nothing, we are overwhelmed; we drown.

It has been said that faith is believing what you know ain't so; but on the contrary, faith is believing what we know is true. It is certainty in action. Faith is less what we think than what we do. But we are in danger now of paralysis, or, equally fatal, of repeating the methods of old worlds here in a new world. For because we think so, the world is different now. Postmodernism eliminates all belief in truth, and because it is itself a half-truth, it appears to be the only game in town. But it is no mere game, no mere theory to be refuted: postmodernism is the way we live.

Never before have people been surrounded by alternatives, all of them in principle equally valid, therefore all equally invalid. The world is poured into our monitor. Similarly, postmodern thinking pours all the past into the present—at the expense of draining everything. The past no longer exists; it is an emptied-out intellectual category.

If we lose the past, we lose the future. Faith is passed to others. There are good faiths and bad faiths, faiths that sustain and faiths that destroy. Therefore, what we do about faith is a matter of life and death. If survival depends on keeping the faith, what faith shall we keep?

Lycidas and the Gettysburg Address are verbal encounters with tragedy. Such elegies try to give us back our past. *Four score and seven years ago, our fathers brought forth a new nation, conceived in liberty and dedicated to the proposition that all men are created equal.* People must hope. That nation must endure. What we think and what we believe change; but what we remember together endures. What we remember together tells us who we are, and what we may be if we choose.

* * *

An elegy mourns and hopes; it is an expression of faith whose means is memory. Bleak with cold, death, and dry vestiges of a summery world which is over and done, November nevertheless reveals an austere beauty. This beauty must come from something greater than our sorrow and confusion, greater than the evidence of dead leaves and brown fields.

Therefore November is a month not only of grief but also of promise. That promise is written on the leaves of memory. Jacqueline Kennedy Onassis, like Mary Todd Lincoln one of the most underestimated persons of her time, said, "if we don't care about our past, we can't have very much hope for the future."

Mrs. Jacqueline Kennedy seemed to be a living elegy, a beautiful emblem of intelligent, purposeful dignity. The murdered president's brother, a religious man, his world shattered, lived his own active elegy. Turning to the Greek tragic poets for help, he worked out an energetic faith that combined old verities with his consciousness of absurdity and horror. From them, as well as from Abraham Lincoln, we can seize a light to bear through the November of our postmodern world. What resource does this spent generation still have? The past.

We must believe in our history in order to believe in ourselves.

* * *

Modernism discovered the Self. When the individual, personal Self came to the forefront, the values of humanism arose and transformed the world: freedom, democracy, material welfare, the arts, humane learning, destruction of superstition and oppression. But the price was prohibitive. The locus of faith shifted from heaven to earth. Now, with postmodern thought, the Self has been lost as the reality of the past has been questioned. It had to be, for we lost the world in our modern self-absorption; it had become meaningless and absurd. But what will happen now? What paradise will be regained, and what lost? Will freedom be destroyed or expanded if humanism and enlightenment perish from the earth? Are we witnessing Liberty's death, or her new birth? Are humane values passing into selfish violence? Will we abandon learning, which has disappointed us, for technology, which gratifies us? Will we regain the world but lose our Self?

* * *

November is a calendar that marks both what has passed and what is to come. We watch between the modern world, grieving its unthinkable death, and the unknown world ahead. Modernity was ripe in November 1863 when Abraham Lincoln stated for all time the high hope and sheer faith of his world. One hundred years later, by the time of John F. Kennedy's assassination in November 1963, that world was clearly gone. Despite their differences, the 1860s and 1960s were mirror decades: both times of civil war, of passions and politics and violence, of leaders like meteors who burnished the skies and were shot dead. And exactly in between, November 1918, the turning point had been reached: The modern world had fought a civil war with itself and lost.

But my generation, apparently the weakest in American history, was not built and crippled by historical forces alone. We were made and unmade by our parents, that "heroic generation" which survived the Great Depression and won the Second World War. They conveyed to us the hopes and faith of Lincoln's America, housed in the material boredom of a parodied American Dream. Our parents pampered us, themselves devoted to duty and sacrifice, thinking to teach us an ideal of progress that had really been destroyed in 1918. "Our ancestors sinned; they are no more, and we bear their iniquities." Lincoln's dream was modern, but modernism was shelled to pieces on the Western Front, and can exist now only as irony. Our generation came trailing clouds of glory, but that glory has been spent. Still, we can pass our memories and our parents' memories through to the next generation, hoping that the natural strength in them can blossom in a better place and time—that the faith of our fathers can pass to our children transformed but untarnished—and that government of the people, by the people, and for the people shall not perish from the earth.

* * *

The two wars which bounded the century behind us and to which we are inevitably connected were the war between the Union and the Confederacy of the 1860s; and the war on the streets and campuses—really in our hearts and minds—of the 1960s, whose external emblem was the civil war in Vietnam. To call that hundred years a century of grief would not be an exaggeration. Certainly it was a century of death, violence, disillusionment, chaos, and brutality—perhaps the worst century in recorded history. It hasn't simply gone away; it is in us.

Though our generation always starts with the first person singular, the confusions we suffer and enact spread in ever-widening circles: self, family, our narrow era. Beyond that, November days are marked in black with shadows of the just-passed century: war, Holocaust. History enlarges these circles: this month, Abraham Lincoln turned his steps toward Gettysburg, where America received a new birth from the dead of the battle and the words of a president. Enclosing all of these November anniversaries, the circle of life and death turns silently, and we glimpse the constellations of time and eternity. We are back to ourselves and mortality. May we expect something, someone, to break into the sphere and offer us new birth? Will November end?

Our brightest political lights were extinguished like the Enlightenment itself. In the latter days of November we must look elsewhere after all for our last, best hope.

* * *

The month begins with things that perish. But ultimately, November is a journey of hope, as was Lincoln's journey to Gettysburg. So too I will journey to Gettysburg in these pages. Like Lincoln's fellow citizens, I go there to assuage personal griefs, to find answers; and I hope, for me as for them, that my personal sorrows become a vehicle for larger answers and a larger purpose. Lincoln addressed their grief, why not mine? He gave his generation purpose, why not ours? We are all Americans. To find Mr. Lincoln's hope, I will follow Mr. Lincoln's footsteps, though I know that we must make our own way at the end. I will stay in Gettysburg during the whole month of November, each day noting what Abraham Lincoln did on the corresponding date in November 1863, and hoping to meet him where he spoke his immortal elegy.

Because the exact spot where the president actually delivered the Address is not known, I will try to find out. It will give me something to do. True, I will be forced to remember the many sad anniversaries of this month as they come up on the calendar, and if I finish the month without becoming clinically depressed and wanting a new car, it will not be my fault. It will be because the steady undertone of hope in this month will have finally gotten to me in spite of myself. This danger and that hope I now propose to share with you, who are reading this book.

* * *

The month begins with memorials. Its days go past with the sharp-edged clarity of late-year light, as if we were passing one by one the distinct white stones marking places of the dead in the soldiers' cemetery at Gettysburg. We are part of all we have met, says Tennyson—which, if true, means we can neither evade our heritage nor escape our place in history. "We will be remembered in spite of ourselves," President Lincoln said. Our past floods through us to our posterity. We think we are drowning in the confusion of the present, but it is the gush of the past that threatens to overwhelm us. *Si recte calculum ponas, ubique naufragium est,* reads the motto of the memorial volume in which Milton's *Lycidas* appears: "If you reckon rightly, shipwreck is everywhere." The weight pressing us today is the dark flood of a dire century. We and our children may face the most difficult of tasks: to wrest a new vision from modernism and postmodernism; defeat the enlarged, monsterized Self; and find our own and our country's identities. Let us rally around our memories. This weak generation must find strength to grieve, if it wishes to hope.

"Who would not sing for Lycidas?" Milton cried. One writes an elegy because one must, because nature weeps, and because beauty is a high comfort. An elegy is our gift to the dead, and an investment in hope. "A thing of beauty is a treasure forever." *Who would not sing for Lycidas?*

* * *

Earth abides, and with it the mystery of death and rebirth. *He watereth the hills from his chambers: the earth is satisfied.* . . . November's sky is cold and gray; leaves are dead on the ground, the flowers of the witch hazel wither. At the end, snow comes, and the world can begin again. November begins in grief and ends in hope. It is the drear month of faith. November courage runs in the blood of saints. These are the days of November.

NOVEMBER 1

Years Ago

(All Saints)

Hell is hopelessness.
—Juergen Moltmann

Chaplain Horatio Howell was shot to death on the steps of Christ Church, Gettysburg, at around four o'clock on July 1, 1863. Thousands of young men belonging to Robert E. Lee's Army of Northern Virginia poured into town that afternoon pursuing Union troops. Several veteran Confederate units had been decimated by the Union First Corps, which was jamming the streets and alleys of Gettysburg. The Southerners were not only hot and tired, they were excited, angry, and jumpy. When what looked like a Federal officer appeared on the long, high steps of a church on the main street into town, a group of Confederate boys shouted at him to raise his hands. The church was being used as a hospital, but the Southerners might have seen healthy Federals running up the steps looking for a safe place.

The Union "officer" did not throw up his hands but commenced instead an explanation of some kind. Whereupon, not feeling like taking any jaw from a Yank officer, one of the young fellows pulled his trigger. The man in blue fell across the steps. The young Rebel who shot him had somehow crossed an invisible line between soldier and assassin.

The distinction between soldier and criminal might seem to some people who came of age during the 1960s to be without a difference, but this is because that generation has been infected with something alien to the modern world. The shooting of Chaplain Horatio Howell at Gettysburg on July 1, 1863, was an extremely unusual happening in the Civil War. Like the assassination of President Lincoln two years later, it did not properly belong to the Civil War era.

The Civil War has been called the first modern war, but it was actually the last modern war. Trench warfare, submarine warfare, and war against civilians—not to mention assassination—introduced contemporary war, a monstrosity that came to fruition in the world wars. These aspects of battle are not properly called modern warfare because they do not belong to the modern world. They are "postmodern."

Modern and *postmodern* are terms still seeking final form. Though many think of *modern* as referring to anything from art deco onward, the term can refer to a set of values including Reason, Progress, and Self which formed much earlier than the twentieth century—and has not fully expired yet. But its exact definition is problematical, as is that of *postmodern*. That we can use these terms, especially the second, in a variety of our own ways shows that we are standing knee-deep in postmodernism, which values diversity, as the following pages are meant to illustrate. (For further descriptions of modernism and postmodernism, see Appendix I.)

Modernism is a way of thinking and acting that was born during the Enlightenment. In warfare it meant the very short era during which armies moved and fought in what we would consider a quaintly if not foolishly logical, rational, even formal manner. Men in long ranks maneuvered at a walk, according to precise drill geometry, and fired, loaded, wheeled, retreated, and advanced in unison according to orders. Along with this, the key elements of modern warfare followed: the declining to make war on civilians, refusal to allow combat to degenerate into uncontrolled and purposeless killing zones, unwillingness to take unlimited advantage of the tools or chances of war. Until Gettysburg, volunteers who fought the Civil War intended to fight honorably, fairly, courageously, with restraint and for good Enlightenment reasons.

However, as John F. Kennedy said in his inaugural address, "The world is very different now." The murder of Chaplain Howell is as fitting a place as any to note the difference.

Today, a bronze Bible commemorating the slain chaplain stands on the steps of Christ Church. If you want to go inside, you have to pass it.

* * *

Abraham Lincoln entered the month of November wearing a black armband for his son Willie. The president renewed his grief every morning as he put on his clothes. Today he would have to think of many more sons because today, November 1, 1863, Mr. Lincoln would draw up another order concerning the draft. Gettysburg had been the last decisive battle fought entirely by volunteers.

The draft is a phrase that still carries considerable impact to men and women who were young during the Vietnam War. Lincoln's draft was both different from and the same as the one known in the 1960s. There was no such thing as a student deferment, but you could get out of the service if you had money:

> It is ordered that every citizen who has paid the $300 commutation shall receive the same credit therefor [*sic*] as if he had furnished a substitute, and is exonerated from military service for the time for which he was drafted, to wit, for three years.

Such a system seems blatantly unfair now only because we aren't about to be drafted into the Union army. In the 1960s, parental greenbacks, or the government itself, got draft-eligible young men into college or graduate school. Among prominent politicians against the war, only Robert Kennedy called the student deferment unfair.

Back in 1863, plenty of people—particularly the poor Irish in New York City—called the system unfair. In July, not two weeks after the Battle of Gettysburg, veterans from the Army of the Potomac were rushed to New York City to put down a draft riot in which hundreds of people were killed. After three days during which mobs shattered the police force, looted, and in drunken rages lynched black people and burned an orphanage for children of color, trains arrived carrying men who had faced Robert E. Lee's infantry on the fields of Gettysburg.

> We saw the grim batteries and weatherstained and dusty soldiers tramping into our leading streets. . . . There was some terrific fighting between the regulars [that is, soldiers] and the insurgents. . . . men were hurled, dying or dead, into the streets by the thoroughly enraged soldiery; until at last, sullen and cowed and thoroughly whipped and beaten, the miserable wretches gave way at every point and confessed the power of the law.

Nevertheless, the president knew that the war could not be won if the government had to put down, as his secretary of state said, "a riot and mob in every ward of every city." There had been civil unrest all across the

North that summer, from New Hampshire to New Jersey and Pennsylvania, and even as far as Kentucky and Milwaukee, Wisconsin. Some reasons had to be given for all the dying, for the draft, for the empty chairs in grieving homes throughout the Union states. Tomorrow, November 2, President Lincoln would get a letter he would see as an invitation to explain these things to the country, but today he just needed to order more men to their deaths.

Why people must suffer and die at all was beyond even Abraham Lincoln. He left it to the theologians. But theologians have had little success in explaining why a good God does not prevent holocausts, world wars, or even the murder of a saint on the steps of His own Christ Church.

* * *

November first is All Saints' Day. In Christ Church in Gettysburg today, well over a hundred years after Lincoln, one could sit in on an All Saints' Day service and think for a few moments that nothing much has changed. The same prayers are still said, the same hymns are sung, and we are as perplexed as Lincoln's people were. The polished floor we are standing on is not spotted with soldiers' blood today, but it is slippery and it feels like it is shifting.

That is because we question the very past which All Saints' Day relies upon. The shooting of Chaplain Howell, for example, probably did not happen in the way commemorated. In Gregory Coco's *On the Blood-stained Field* we find several disagreeing stories—all told by eyewitnesses. According to one, Chaplain Howell stopped on the steps to look toward the Confederates coming up the street and was "struck in the forehead by one of their bullets." Another witness says a group of mounted Rebels rode up to the steps and one fired his pistol at Howell. Still another says a sharpshooter fired at a doctor, wounding him, and the same bullet killed Howell. Another says the chaplain ascended the steps amid a "rain of bullets." The man whose memoir refers to the last witness concludes, "Now the tablet at the foot of the steps says he was 'Ruthlessly shot down while kneeling in Prayer.' You form your own conclusion." "You form your own conclusion" sounds like democracy but is really more like despair.

* * *

Today I am listening to the sermon in Christ Church and I am not very happy. I miss my children. The minister's English accent makes things worse because it reminds me of the past summer, which we all spent together in the British Isles. The minister is speaking of his own English father. We moderns and postmoderns never seem able to escape speaking of ourselves. If my children were here, I would be telling them about my father—their grandfather—who died thirty years ago tomorrow.

Outside after the service, I walk up to the Soldiers' Cemetery. The wind is raw; the streets are blown with dry leaves. *You see, my children, Abraham Lincoln is one of our fathers, too, like the saints of the Church, like your grandfather, like the "fathers" of the country, whom Lincoln referred to at the beginning of his speech. But we have forgotten this father, Lincoln. We can't even remember where he stood to deliver his speech. The Gettysburg Address needs to be explained again, just as we need to find again the spot where Lincoln spoke.*

But my daughters and son are not here. As it sometimes seems with America as a whole, I am living without parents and without children, which is to say, living without faith.

The minister's cadences linger in my mind. There is something wonderfully *civilized* about the English. They will line up—queue up—and wait their turn, where Americans will try to jockey for a shorter line or a place farther in front, and Germans will simply plow in ahead of you. This is a trivial example, but everyone notices it. The very inflections of Oxford English bespeak civilization and that premodern virtue, or collection of virtues, *courtesy.* Refined by learning—that is, run through the Enlightenment—and depleted of its profounder medieval meanings, courtesy has taken on a deceptively light quality that nevertheless embodies some of the finest elements of modern civilization.

One cannot help admiring that quality of the British soldier about to go over the top into barbed wire and machine-gun fire. It could perhaps be called "heroic unconcern." This splendid cultivated trait is by no means limited to soldiery. One bright afternoon in Oxford, I was sitting on a bench reading material for a lecture I was about to give on World War I, when an older English lady sat down next to me.

"What are you reading?" she inquired.

"World War One poetry."

"Wilfred Owen?" she asked. "Pity that he died, isn't it? And the last week of the war, did you know that? Makes you wonder what God was doing, doesn't it? Whether He cares about us at all."

* * *

Today is All Saints' Day; tomorrow will be All Souls' Day. Known saints and unknown saints; one day public heroes, the next day private heroes.

You judge the former by the latter. How do we know what heroes are anymore? The month starts with confusion and discouragement: maybe the idea of heroes is out of date.

The cemetery is windy and bleak. It is hard to imagine Lincoln ever having been here.

* * *

My hunch is that the present authorities are wrong about where Lincoln delivered the Gettysburg Address.

The National Park Service has placed a new marker tablet in the Soldiers' National Cemetery, which says, in effect, that the traditional site, where the tall column now stands, was a mistake. The place where Lincoln stood was not in the National Cemetery at all.

The question matters. If we Americans can't find Lincoln, we are lost.

NOVEMBER 2

Our Fathers

(L. L.)

It is not so much sin that plunges us into disaster, as rather despair.

—Saint Chrysostom

All Souls' Day—a day for commemorating the unknown men, women, and children who died in the faith.

On November 2, 1863, President Lincoln received a letter from Judge David Wills of Gettysburg, Pennsylvania, chairman of the committee for the establishment of the Soldiers' National Cemetery. Though the address for the occasion would be delivered by the distinguished orator Edward Everett, Wills and the committee wished the president to have a symbolic role in the ceremony: "It is the desire that, after the oration, you, as Chief Executive of the nation, formally set apart these grounds to their sacred use by a few appropriate remarks." But Abraham Lincoln saw his role differently. Gettysburg would be the place to tell the people why.

Lincoln had never been in any doubt as to the reason; he did not have to search his imagination or measure public opinion. He had said it years ago: the American experiment in government by the people was "*the last, best hope of earth.*" This time, he must say it better than he ever had before.

He must say it plainly; he must say it memorably. Over the next seventeen days, Lincoln called in the best speechwriter, the greatest literary artist, and the most profound political theorist: he did it by ushering everyone out and closing the door.

Judge Wills had signaled Lincoln that some people thought of him as a buffoon. Some were afraid the yarn-telling president from the prairies would embarrass the United States from this solemn platform. The *remarks*—not speech—should be *few* and *appropriate.* Well, that might be an insult, and it might sting, but what the president was dealing with was too vast for private feelings. Old Wills was probably right anyhow, more than he knew. If the speech is short it will be remembered. And it must be appropriate, not merely to the solemnity of the occasion, but to the great work we are in. Yes, in a larger sense these words must be altogether fitting and proper.

What the soldiers *did* there at Gettysburg must somehow be made into what the president *said,* so that it would remain something we *remember,* and therefore become something we *do.* The vehicle for this multiple transformation must be hope. That hope must be more than comfort for people who are suffering, for mothers and wives who are grieving. Like the expectation behind the religion Abraham Lincoln grew up with, *that hope* transfers deed to deed. In saying the speech, Lincoln must make word and hope and deed *one*—which is to say, he must make them *faith.* He must define the American faith.

So the message, on this solemn occasion, this dark November day, must be one of hope. Not false hope, not something manufactured. Real hope must be based on something real. As Juergen Moltmann wrote in the 1960s, hope "can overstep the bounds of life, with their closed wall of suffering, guilt, and death, only at the point where they have in actual fact been broken through." So where, *in actual fact,* have the boundaries of tyranny been broken through? By whom? Is it humanly possible, as the modern world believed, at all? If not, does the postmodern awareness we have gained at the cost of ghastly wars convince us, with Camus, that we can only "think clearly, and hope no more"?

Sometimes Americans might forget to care whether representative democracy lives or dies; but there is one tyranny most of us do care about: Death. Our own. A little hope would be a good thing in this matter.

On an anniversary of the letter Abraham Lincoln received from the judge, in a larger sense a similar letter was sent to my father. On a November 2, he died.

* * *

I also had an appointment with a cemetery on this second of November. I had made arrangements to meet the superintendent of Evergreen Cemetery, across the fence from the Soldiers' National Cemetery, this morning. Evergreen is the older burial ground in Gettysburg, the one that had been there during the battle. The famous Cemetery Ridge and Cemetery Hill were named for it. There, the defeated but unvanquished Union brigades had rallied on July first; there, gunners with clubbed rammers had defended the key to the Union position on the wild evening of July second; Confederate gunners had trained their artillery on that cemetery, making the Yankees dodge behind tombstones for protection. The Union was preserved in a cemetery.

Next to Evergreen, Solders' National Cemetery is arranged like a ground level, semi-circular amphitheater. The dead, ordered by states, fill concentric rows of graves. The focal point is a tall column, until recently said to mark the place where the speakers' platform stood and therefore the place where Lincoln delivered the Address.

In the 1960s, a letter written by a man named Selleck turned up. Selleck was a member of the cemetery's commission and sat on the platform with President Lincoln. His letter, with accompanying drawing, states unequivocally that the speakers' platform had been erected off to one side and somewhat downhill from the graves, not at the focal point of the semicircular layout. This letter opened a wide crack in what we thought we knew, because its premise made sense: nineteenth-century Americans would not have crowded in to trample on graves. *Behind* the soldiers' graves would be plenty of room for the mounted procession, and for the estimated five thousand to ten thousand listeners. There was no such room at the traditionally accepted site.

But why *down* the hill? Why not farther *up* the hill? Exactly that question was asked in the 1980s by the chief historian at Gettysburg National Military Park, Kathleen Georg Harrison. Examining two old brown photographs and various written sources, she concluded that the speech was given up the slope in Evergreen Cemetery, not down in the new Soldiers' National Cemetery. There would have been room for both the spectators and the processional uphill from the fresh military graves. So the Park Service has now placed a new marker, saying that the old site is incorrect. Then why the century-old certainty that the platform stood where the column is today? Why did eyewitnesses state that the column is in the right place?

I had come to Evergreen Cemetery to try to answer these questions. I had come here to inspect the ground. It seemed altogether fitting and proper that I should do this. And yet . . .

There was a note for me on the gatehouse door. The superintendent of the cemetery had been called away for at least a week by a serious family illness. "Sorry," he wrote, but as I was going to be in town all month, surely we could reschedule. "Hope deferred maketh the heart sick," I mused.

* * *

So on this day, President Lincoln had received his invitation to—Ms. Harrison says—this cemetery. Mine had been postponed for a time. Walking out through the gatehouse, I kept thinking that this was November second, the day my father had received his summons. Again I imagined that my children were with me.

You should know, children, what your grandfather was like:

* * *

On the morning of his stroke, he had been shaving. Shaving was very difficult for him because he was afflicted with Parkinson's disease. His whole right side was crippled. He used his left hand to guide his right, and so the shaving process was as fragile as trying to roll a BB around the edge of a glass. The stroke must have hit like a sledgehammer inside his head. *"Massive cerebral hemorrhage" is written as cause of death on your grandfather's death certificate.* But that was not what finally did it; he actually died of pneumonia. That was brought on by three months of lying in the hospital unable to move. He could never fill his lungs with air and clear them. Then they carried him out into thirty-degree weather to move him from the hospital to a nursing home. . . .

He had suffered for a long time. At seventy, Len was prematurely aged. Small and slight to begin with, he had been shrunk by the stress of his life to a stoop of less than five feet. He weighed about a hundred pounds. His hair was almost white. Parkinson's disease had reduced his walk to a shuffling limp.

But he had been quite different. Energetic—"peppy," in the phraseology of his contemporaries—he had built a very successful practice. For forty years he maintained his office in the center of the city's downtown, in prime space. He had earned much more than enough to buy a house; first in one well-heeled suburb, then, at the request or insistence of my mother, farther out in an even more exclusive area. But he never learned to drive—was too nervous, he said, and he was—so he took the bus early in the morning, returning late in the evening, eight or nine o'clock.

All this hustling undermined his health. Sundays at the second house brought not rest but physical labor on our three-quarter acre lot, all solid clay and Canadian thistle. And health was his profession. He had gone to Washington University Medical School, but quit near the end of his program to go into drugless therapy. With the indefatigability of an insecure person, he had pursued degree after degree, probably always wanting to outdo the "MDs" he detested. They were his enemies, recognized by the public, the insurance companies, the state legislatures—while chiropractors, back then, were not. People could not even pronounce *chiropractor* correctly. In self-mockery, partly, he referred to himself as a "cheeropractor."

His other titles were even more difficult. The marbled, translucent glass on his door was stenciled with a daunting list of gold letters: "P.T.," "D.C.," and other esoteric initials, signifying Physical Therapist, Doctor of Chiropractic, Doctor of Osteopathy, Doctor of Naturopathy. He had attended schools all over the country and taken state board exams here and there like an itinerant small knight so as to be certified wherever he might want—or need—to go.

He attended all the national chiropractic conventions. Everyone was acquainted with him because he was unusually knowledgeable, intense, driven—but mostly because he loved people. One of his oldest friends maintained, "there wasn't a malicious bone in his body." He believed in being cheerful and optimistic. A natural politician, "L. L." was elected treasurer of the national organization a couple of times and vice president once. Today there is a plaque in his memory at the National College of Chiropractic, about two miles from where—after traveling the country and the world—I am employed now. Even a rotten apple does not fall far from the tree.

I certainly do not remember a malicious moment concerning him—and only an instance or two of what a person might call anger. I knew he was angry only if, somewhat crossly, he would say my actual name instead of a nickname.

But he was not around much, and probably, except in the long run—the only run he believed in—he was not a particularly good father. Yet I remember once sitting in the same room with him reading. I looked up and was mildly startled, but not surprised, at his resemblance to Abraham Lincoln in the photograph of the president reading with Tad standing beside him. L. L., prematurely aged like Lincoln, reading glasses a bit far forward, once-black hair a bit unruly at the top, hands rather too large, high cheekbones and gaunt face, somewhat aquiline nose, same brow, same jaw, same expression. "The long and short of it," both might have said.

* * *

Len had belonged to a large family—five brothers and two sisters—all of whom except the next older brother he completely turned his back on. The family suffered a devastating division—a family which had been a house divided in the first place.

His father was a tailor. He had come from pioneer stock, Germans who moved all the way up the Baltic to what became East Prussia, rough land they settled and made German, though it was as far away from the Fatherland as Poland, Lithuania, and Russia. Probably Prussians but possibly northwest Austrians, the family was part of that restless hardworking tide of Germans which moved out in all directions: east to Russia, northeast up the Baltic, southwest to Latin America and Australia, west to the United States. Civil unrest in the mid-nineteenth century was one of the causes.

My paternal grandmother, whom I never knew, was "very mild-tempered," Len told me in the only description he ever gave of his parents. It almost sounded like an unstated contrast to his father—a tailor who moved to the United States around 1880. Their youngest son was born in 1899.

I never heard anything about Len's childhood, except for a story about fishing. Seems they took little Leonard out in a boat all day; he burned to a second-degree crisp and never went fishing again. His brother Louis owned a cabin in northern Wisconsin, so I assume the father was to some degree an outdoorsman. The youngest boy, Leonard, very small and always looking even younger than he was, must have been the special care of his mother.

She was probably a Masurian, that is, an East Prussian who spoke Polish, her people having moved into Protestant Prussia from Catholic Poland two or three hundred years previously. The Masurians were enemies of Roman Catholicism and considered themselves Germans, but their names—like Ludvika, my grandmother's—remained Polish. Assuming the father was Prussian, he was Lutheran. Len always detested Roman Catholicism: "the greatest superstition ever invented." But his relationship to Lutheranism was complicated—another story in itself. At any rate, people in the family took sides over something, and Len and his brother Louis walked out and never came back. They even changed the spelling of their name.

But Len never bought a suit that was ready-made.

* * *

Like many children of immigrants, and like Abraham Lincoln, Len tried to put as much distance between himself and his origins as he could. During World War I the German-language newspaper in Milwaukee was banned, and in some places schoolchildren with German parents were shunned and abused. Fortunately this latter was not the case for Len, who grew up in one of the large German neighborhoods. But his parents were still immigrants who spoke German at home. Years later, I never heard Len speak one word of German. He had determined to make something of himself, something different.

But he retained some of the old characteristics. He pronounced "Lincoln" like a German, with both l's sounded. He retained a residue of an unconventional English education. This man who had nearly five advanced degrees still used the double negative ("doesn't have no"). And, like a typical Milwaukee German, "L. L." (Leonard Lawrence) was mortally neat and clean, keeping everything orderly, everything in its place. The past had its place, too. Like Lincoln, Len seldom opened the door to that place—except perhaps in his sleep.

* * *

L. L.'s tidy office was very interesting and a little frightening. There was a partial skeleton in one of the rooms—a real human spine dangling on the wall. I have a photograph of Len in his student days, showing him standing with his classmates behind a cadaver; the young L. L. is the short one with the intense stare.

That office contained many odd and merciless-looking devices. The treating tables, first of all, were hard and cold as slabs, and too high up. There was a slit up at the head, and when you had to lie facedown my father would slice through a square of tissue paper with the knife of his hand. You put your face down, seeing the floor and smelling the twenty-five-year-old leather and wood—a substantial, if faintly musty, smell.

The rooms housed an aroma impossible to define in everyday terms. It combined clean linoleum, old walls, leather tables and desk chairs, carbon lamps, ozone lamps, Unguentine ointment, fresh linen, and mystery. What he knew about things unseen was part of the mystery. And where he had been and what he had done as a young man were part of a deep story of which I heard only the sparsest fragments.

Many treating apparatuses populated the rooms. One room contained a gleaming chrome traction machine, with heavy brown leather manacles and straps. I hoped never to deserve that one.

But I did have to go in during hay fever season, or when I caught colds. In one of the treating rooms there waited a thick black disc, the size of a discus or pie plate, extending on a tensile arm from a powerful machine on the floor. It was heat. You held a pad over it, and you sat on the edge of the hard treating table with the side of your face pressed against the disc, firmly enough for the pad not to slide off. Sitting on the cold table with your shirt off, fifteen minutes on a side, at age eight or ten, you learned the viscera, the very soul, of boredom.

Worse was the Hood. Black and thick like the disc, it was also heat for the sinuses. But it was a long rectangle in three hinged parts. You lay on the table and let pads be put on your face; then the Hood was lowered onto you and closed around your whole face—eyes, shutting off the light, nose, and part of the mouth. Burial alive, and hot as hell. In my early years I could not bear to have that hood clamped over me, lying cold and shirtless on the table. I suppose Len thought I did not trust him.

These contrivances might seem like quackery to you, but I always went away from them with my sinuses feeling better. Of course, after that kind of punishment, any Lutheran would have felt better.

I loved the "colors." Each treating room featured a carbon lamp. It looked like a squared megaphone on a stand about shoulder height. You lay on the table and the lamp was rolled over to you. My father turned on the current and moved two carbon sticks close enough together to ignite a small flame back in the base—a fascinating procedure. Then he would choose one or two squares of thick, bubbly glass and slide them over the front. He directed the face of it toward you and all you had to do in the world for the next twenty minutes was look at the burning glow in the deep blue. In a few minutes he would return and add perhaps green, or yellow, or take out the blue and put in a lovely ephemeral turquoise, or a graceful violet, or slide in a dark red and a profound blue to make an exquisitely deep purple. He would turn the carbons closer for more light, or separate them for a dimmer, smaller light. I do not know what effect these colors had on my outlook or my psychological makeup, but they relaxed me so much that some guy could have come in and cracked all my vertebrae and I would have been blissfully limber and indifferent. When I was very small my father said to look in, and I would see ballerinas.

The treating rooms contained all kinds of other things, too. In the corners, on rolling tables, stood machines with knobs, switches, dials, and timers, and cords connected to heated, rubberized pads. You would wait for that timer to peter out before the pad burned a square through you.

In another room stood the Plumb Line. From the top of what looked like a scaffold, a string ran down from the center almost to the base, suspending a small, cone-shaped weight. You stood in front of the line, and the doctor could tell how out of whack your spine was. Body English did not help; here was absolute final objectivity, the Book of Life. The thing was a late addition to the office and, I am persuaded, was inserted by redactors.

Best of all, absolute best of all, were the desks. Two rooms had desks. They were large, heavy desks of solid wood, with inlaid leather surfaces—and inside? Pens! Fountain pens, ballpoints, pencils, some with that black-and-green mottling, some of the fountain pens with levers. Paper, stationery. Compartments for paper clips, different sizes of rubber bands, and the smell of deep, deep desk. What an aroma. (A Pisces has a well-developed sense of smell, Len might have observed.)

The waiting room was frightening because sometimes there were sick people in it. Fortunately, I almost never saw people in the changing cells, behind whose doors hung fresh, clean, ironed smocks for the women to put on. A nurse would supervise, I suppose, until the patient learned the ropes. The early nurse, Catherine, was mild and humane; the subsequent ones always seemed severe and bigger.

Down the hall outside the lettered doors was where you went if you had to go. The men's room was behind a door to a storage area, which was very dark. Inside—assuming you did not rattle the door and get a harsh "Next!" hollered at you by a frightening optometrist—was a royal and ancient toilet—called a "throne" by my father—with its tank way up on the wall. To flush it you pulled a flat-link chain and held your ears as fast as you could.

Back near the elevators plunged a glass mail chute. Sometimes from invisible places far above, blurred messages would come fleeting on their way down. It was wonderful to be able to be lifted up to drop in a letter. The return address would be stamped, "L. L. Gramm, D.C., PH. T."

Down the marble steps, with the wider-than-your-hand rounded marble railing, you found the lunchroom, second floor, presided over by a short, round, red-haired woman my father blandly referred to as "Little Fatty." She always seemed to have the ball game on the radio. Pennants of the National League teams lined the walls. It was in the days when one of them read "Cincinnati Redlegs" instead of Reds. On rare mornings we went in there for breakfast. I would order pancakes, which were never available at home. My father would always order buckwheat cakes, and get me to taste the pungent, harsh things. Now, of course, they are my favorite.

Then the walk back to the office, past the glass doors, the familiar alien smell, the hard treating tables, and the solid desks. From down below, the faint, removed, obeisant mechanical downtown traffic cast dim colored reflections on the ceilings at certain times of the day, moving like shadows on the water, gliding like images and illusions. On the walls had been fastened old, framed poems, like "It Couldn't Be Done":

> Somebody said that it couldn't be done,
> But he with a chuckle replied
> That "maybe it couldn't," but he would be one
> Who wouldn't say so till he'd tried.
> So he buckled right in with the trace of a grin
> On his face. If he worried he hid it.
> He started to sing as he tackled the thing
> That couldn't be done, and he did it.

Late in the day, twilight filled the west corner room with depth and new texture. The last patient was gone. Outside it was summer evening.

For these score and more of years that have passed now, the lettering has been gone; but the same windows are still there, far up above the street, the corner rooms—a great ring of pure and endless light, while down beneath in hours, days, years, driven by the spheres, the world and all her train are hurled.

* * *

After nearly three months in a hospital, Len was moved. My mother found a nursing home—a very attractive one—and on a Friday L. L. was carried out into the cold air, put into an ambulance, transported to the north side of town, carried out into the cold again, and put into a private room. Cold was not his friend.

He was susceptible to "The Chills." One late fall night when I was a child, my father came in from the bus stop, shaking uncontrollably. Doubled over in agony, he was nearly helpless, unable to get a heating pad for himself, barely able to sip a cup of hot water. The exquisite torture of those Chills struck at any time, cause unknown, like a stroke of fate, not necessarily in frigid weather, no matter what Len tried to do to prevent them. I get them myself now and I know that they make one virtually surrender the will to live. The Chills hit my father every few years. That final November, Len was too weak to shiver; instead he got pneumonia. On Saturday the prognosis was plain.

November in Wisconsin is gray, cold, and wet. It offers neither the stupendous colors and clear blue sky of October, nor the snow and festivity of December. It is a month to be endured. On Sunday morning we got the telephone call. Arriving at the nursing home, we found a Hawaiian luau going on in the large lounge, leis draped over fragile aged people propped in wheelchairs, loud cheap music from the speakers—a schlocky setting for Len, and for his death. In his younger days, L. L. had been a musician.

He lay on his bed, eyes—gray like Lincoln's—not completely closed. He had been propped up on pillows, his arms partly outspread. Now he belongs to the ages.

Or rather, once again the ages might belong to him. He believed that we live many lives, moving like a glimmer from one body to another, down through time, building our own futures, creating the Karma that names us. Truly, in this scheme, the only investment that never fails is goodness.

My father's Lutherans believe in salvation by grace through faith, and he would not have disagreed with them. No, no. It is by grace that we are given chance after chance. But what for? Certainly not simply for one's own salvation.

I believe that L. L.'s sense of duty and his compassion did not guarantee for him an escape from the wheel of birth and death—not without help, anyway. A hero is not perfect. One who heals others cannot always heal himself. Len's good works were countered by the futility of his labor for wealth and security; his faith was constrained by his despair.

He would not have opted for salvation anyway. Sit in heaven, fishing, all day? No, no. Got to step right along. There's a lot to do; many more people need help. The world has to be straightened out; there's work to be done.

You can't find the living among the dead.

NOVEMBER 3

Brought Forth

(Pen and Sword)

> Hope alone is . . . "realistic," because it alone takes seriously the possibilities with which all reality is fraught.
>
> —Juergen Moltmann

Today it rains and rains. This morning few visitors came to the Visitors' Center to look at Civil War artifacts. I went in only to get out of the rain. November is a lousy month. Just so no one is fooled by there still being some colorful leaves lingering on a few of the trees, a cold wind with driving rain comes to knock them off. It is as if the dark sky and rain tell us: "This is 1999. The millennium is ending. It's over. Now what?"

I stood looking out the large windows toward the Soldiers' Cemetery. The pavement in between glistened black. A few cars sliced past. I wonder whether it rained on this date about 135 years ago, November 3, 1863. Abraham Lincoln knew he was coming here—right across the street, to that cemetery. Very likely he started writing his speech today.

Four score and seven years ago. The beginning is the most famous part. Repeat those words, and people know what you are referring to. The next words are not well known. They are strange, but more important. *Our fathers brought forth.* Everyone knows, more or less, what "four score and seven" means, but fathers bringing forth is another matter. I wonder whether Mr. Lincoln thought of that odd phrase today.

It would make sense if he did, because one way to look at the Gettysburg Address is as a definition of heroes. It is an elegy, of course, but to whom? To Lincoln's heroes—but what are heroes? That question was Lincoln's first problem in the speech. Were the Union dead more than mere victims? Their families might have wondered, might have thought most of all that their dead sons and husbands were simply to be mourned. Lincoln could not let that go on. Grief is necessary; Lincoln would refer several times to "these" dead here in these graves in front of him, but he could not allow the Union dead to remain victims. They must be seen as heroes.

Heroes have always inspired people. Lincoln and the United States had a war to win. But you could not simply declare the dead to have been heroes and tell the people to go out and do likewise. What are heroes?

The more I have studied the Civil War, the more convinced I have become that leadership made the difference between defeat and victory. For the past generation and more, it has been fashionable to emphasize the role of the common person. The idea arose in France with studies of medieval peasants, and it is altogether fitting and proper for countries in which equality is an ideal to remember that the common person bears the burdens of history, works the fields, and marches into battle. But in the American Civil War, both North and South mustered good soldiers into their armies. Abraham Lincoln knew that. Nevertheless, he was declaring the living and dead of one side, not the other, to be heroes. Why?

We would be naive to think that Lincoln imagined heroes—the Founding Fathers, the Union soldiers—to have been perfect. It is we, the sophisticated hotshots who refuse to consider someone a hero if faults have been discovered about him or her, who are childish. (Consider the reputation of JFK.) But Lincoln understood that heroes are made, not born, and to a degree they are made by us. They become heroes when we distill and use what was heroic from their imperfect lives.

Again, people must be inspired by leaders, who are themselves inspired by heroic examples. The great civil war in which the country was engaged on November 3, 1863, was in doubt and could turn out either way. That was not only because both sides had good soldiers. Both sides possessed resources equal to their goals, too. Later, the country would come to believe that it had been inevitable that the North would win because the Union had more men, money, railroads, and factories. But the South lost no battles for lack of hardware. The North assumed an immense task: subdue, control, and *convert* a hostile area larger than that which Napoleon had conquered. You need more men, more everything—especially *more will*—to stay on the offensive in a war whose benefits are not material nor clearly evident. That is why a year later, in 1864, the Union came close to losing. In the summer of that year, with the costly stalemate in Virginia, the president himself thought the November election would go to the peace candidate. The people's will was faltering. A Wisconsin soldier wrote correctly that in voting for Lincoln's reelection, "I was doing my country as much service as I have ever done on the field of battle."

So Lincoln must somehow inspire his people. But he could not do that himself. He knew that too many people thought of him as a buffoon, a mediocrity. Besides, what had he done that was heroic? Was Abraham Lincoln a hero? If he was, people did not realize it yet. In fact, what Lincoln would say at Gettysburg is essential to our translating his private heroism into public heroism. But right now, November 3, 1863, Abraham Lincoln must transfer not his heroism but his soldiers' heroism to the hearts and wills of the American people. He must assuage their grief and confusion and turn them toward resolve, effort, and triumph. The way to do that is through heroes. How to describe what heroism is?

Lincoln took the most natural course: he recalled who his own heroes were. Lincoln's statement to this effect is very, very brief, but the whole Address comes from it: *our fathers brought forth.* In that phrase is both *who* and *why.*

First, the heroes are "our fathers," that is, the fathers of the country: the writers and signers of the Declaration of Independence. The Declaration created the country and established what the new nation essentially was to be. Its composers had made it all with words. In such a nation, governed by laws, words are more important than bullets. Here in America, the pen was at first and always must remain mightier than the sword. Lincoln would follow this example, and he knew it was no merely idealistic wish. Lincoln was the ultimate practical idealist. He knew that right words were absolutely necessary to produce winning actions on the fields of battle and in the homes of the North. The Emancipation Proclamation and the Gettysburg Address—both *words*—were Lincoln's greatest *acts.* They had immense practical results.

Lincoln would have to find a way of saying that the Union soldiers somehow had been doing the same thing that the Fathers of the country had done. What had the Fathers done? That is, why were they heroes?

The answer is in Lincoln's bluntly feminine description of what they did: *brought forth.* The phrase means to give birth. If the Fathers were heroes, their heroism consisted in performing the role of mothers. How would the brave men and the people at home now do likewise? They would give the nation *new birth.*

Essentially, the people must decide what they wanted to be, and then bring it about. Lincoln had done this for himself. A poor man's son, mauling rails at a few cents a day, he had determined on a new birth for himself. Now such a man was about to do the same kind of thing for his country, according to a higher ideal, the ideal of Fathers who became something they had not been. They were most heroic in offering themselves—pledging their lives, fortunes, and sacred honor—that we might be what they imagined we could be.

* * *

On November 3, Abraham Lincoln wrote a note to his secretary of state, William Seward, who was away from Washington due to the serious illness of his son: "Nothing new. Despatches up to twelve last night from Chattanooga show all quiet and doing well. How is your son?"

Lincoln's law partner, William Herndon, wrote that in general, Abraham Lincoln's life was cold. He meant primarily his relationship to romance, to women, to his wife. In Springfield, Mary Todd Lincoln had said, "I'd love him more if he were home more." Of course it is reasonable to wonder which came first, absence of love or absence of Lincoln. In any case, even back in Illinois the Lincolns had slept in separate bedrooms, not an unusual arrangement among well-off people then. The picture of Lincoln going to his room in the White House at night is a bleak one, a lonely one. But if you want real coldness, go forward a hundred years to that same bedroom, not at night but one afternoon: "When two foreign service advisors bearing a batch of secret cables knocked on the door of the Lincoln Bedroom one summer afternoon, Jack angrily flung the door wide open, revealing a woman in bed. The president quickly cooled down, read the dispatches, made his decisions, and returned to his guest."

With little warmth in the relationship with his wife, and no close friends, Lincoln's life was lonely, but not cold. He suffered too much to live coldly; his compassion was enough to age him quickly during the agonizing war years. And there were his children. In November 1863, he is thinking of Willie. He asks Seward, "How is your son?"

In a sense, Lincoln's sons were dying by the thousands. "We are coming, Father Abraham, three hundred thousand more," they had sung last year. Before the end of the war, more than six hundred thousand, North and South, would be dead. Like a father, he felt responsible for them. His election had brought about secession, and his maneuvering with Fort Sumter had touched off the shooting. But more than that, Abraham Lincoln was president of the United States, with an oath "registered in heaven, to preserve, protect, and defend" the Constitution. He was the one human being most responsible for everything. Even the "erring" sons and daughters of the South were his; he never accepted the existence of the Confederacy as a separate nation. Photographs of the president, particularly from November 1863 onward, show a man who understood, felt, and accepted his responsibility. Its weight did not kill him or drive him mad, or induce him to surrender, because he had hope. The Fathers' many sons and daughters would bring something to life: "a new nation." The president believed in a Union not merely restored but reborn.

* * *

One hundred years later, another American president lost a child. The loss seemed to have touched him somewhere where he did not know he had a place. Before his election, John Kennedy had been asked by a friend if he had ever been in love. Considering for a moment—he had certainly had many "lovers"—Kennedy looked at his friend and said no. It was a tragic admission, for how does one who has never loved ever hope? Was Kennedy really optimistic, or did he merely *appear* to be optimistic? If the latter, we would have the great critique of Kennedy: he raised false hope.

Kennedy's model was not Lincoln, but rather another great mid-century president, Franklin Delano Roosevelt. Kennedy's resemblances to FDR might seem uncanny. Both Roosevelt and Kennedy came from wealthy, famous families; both were extraordinarily good-looking and charismatic; both were attractive to women; both courageously fought debilitating physical conditions and kept them out of the public eye; both appealed to those who had lost hope. But differences come to view quickly. Roosevelt, like Lincoln, faced huge crises. Kennedy manufactured crises in order to win the election, and maintained a crisis atmosphere where, by comparison to the Civil War, the Great Depression, and World War II, there was no crisis. Behold, he cried, War! War! But there was no war. The crisis of race was not foremost to the early Kennedy administration. There was, in short, little connection between word and fact.

Symptomatic of this, though by no means characteristic of JFK in particular among modern politicians, is that with the exception of a small part of his first inaugural address, Lincoln wrote all his own speeches; and with the exception of parts of his inaugural, Kennedy wrote virtually none of his speeches. ("Why not a little less profile, and a little more courage," someone said in reference to the book Kennedy had not written but for which he accepted a Pulitzer Prize.)

Kennedy's inaugural speech, which still pulls at the hearts of many who remember the Kennedy years, rings false now. It looks like an attempt to make a memorable speech, when the occasion for one was not there. By contrast, Lincoln honestly said, "I have never done an official act with a view to promote my own personal aggrandizement"; and when Franklin Roosevelt said, "The only thing we have to fear is fear itself," he was speaking to a paralyzed nation as a person who understood paralysis. Churchill said about Roosevelt that meeting him was like opening your first bottle of champagne. Maybe meeting John F. Kennedy felt like already having drunk the bottle.

In any case, the connection between word and world is different now. On November third, Lincoln was writing to Seward to ask about his son, and I was walking Cemetery Hill in the rain. Meanwhile, on still another November third, I had been in Boston for a conference on the theory that would tolerate putting all three November thirds together in the subjective present of this page.

It had been cold and rainy then, too. I was out in it, looking not for Mr. Lincoln, but for my own president, John F. Kennedy. Cold, stern, and indifferent, the New England wind itself seemed rocky. However, one can face a lot when one is fighting for freedom—as I was that raw, bleak early November Saturday in the late 1980s. I was supposed to have been in a lecture hall.

But as the first presentation opened that Saturday morning I was happily and independently freezing my keester in a blasting wind coming off the southern fringe of Boston Harbor. The complicated, screwed-up system of trains and buses that I had ridden in from the outskirts had fizzled out two miles from the Kennedy Library, and I was on foot. Like a Katzenjammer Kids device, Boston's public transportation system had impressed, intimidated, frustrated, conveyed, and impeded me all at once.

I had never been to Boston before. New England and its heroes, however, had been on my mind for many years: Thoreau and Walden Pond; the stolid mysticism of that first Thanksgiving which we learned as schoolchildren in those orange, clear autumns; Lexington and Concord, the Battle of Bunker Hill, the ride of Paul Revere; way down to the Irish precincts of Boston voting for young Jack Kennedy in the washed 1950s. I had been to Walden Pond, Concord, and Lexington, but never to the tart, pretty city itself: Boston.

I tramped along the roadway against the driving, pneumonic mist, looking across at university buildings and hoping that somewhere on the other side of them was the black-and-white John F. Kennedy Library I had seen pictures of. The library architecture certainly seemed modern rather than postmodern, as it should, because John F. Kennedy was an image of the modern age. During the Kennedy years, when I was a boy, the days were sunshine and light, things were going forward, the world was reasoning and muscling its way against its problems—against ignorance, tyranny, prejudice, and want—and though we (or rather they, for I was too young) had only just said, "Let us begin," a beginning implied an ending, a finishing, a satisfying completion of a newer world.

The world was different now, almost thirty years later. It was cold and cloudy and the darting, saturating fine rain drove into the folds and openings of my raincoat. I would have brought a winter parka, had I known what to expect. But you do not know what to expect in a postmodern world. Though this was Saturday and young President Kennedy had been killed on a Friday—just yesterday, as it might seem—not only the present but also the past had changed.

The past used to be reliable. We used to think we could know what happened in the history of our country, the world, or our own lives. The postmodern world is like a person suddenly discovering, after thirty years of family-man thinking—of history as sparkling clean as the surface of the 1950s—that his father had been divorced and, what is more, might never have particularly wanted a kid. We wake up to find one morning that President John F. Kennedy was really Jack Kennedy, and had never been what we had imagined all that time. He had not written the text of *Profiles in Courage.* He had not won the 1960 election fair and square. But Jim Bishop, saying in his *A Day in the Life of President Kennedy* that the man was an unusually hard-working president, had been right—tediously, disillusioningly right: our Pepsodent-smiling, idealistic, eloquent president was working with indefatigable persistence behind the scenes and under the covers, and given enough time there would not have been one virtuous female left this side of fundamentalism (if they count). That sentence mirrors the move from modern to postmodern world. It was a short nine years from young John-John saluting his father's passing caisson (coached, as we now "know," by Jacqueline Kennedy) to the callously moral, flippantly serious question, "What color are Richard Nixon's undershorts?" Answer: "You should know; he's been screwing you for four years." That was not how it had started in 1961.

The main topic of the conference I had been attending was postmodernism and deconstruction. I had left it to go out into the November rain and visit the John F. Kennedy Library, but I was postmodernizing and deconstructing in spite of myself.

I made it to the presidential library about midmorning, running on sheer grit, determination, and sin. The film they show inside brought back the one thing I had come for. The days came back: the winning smile, the glamorous self-effacing wit, the capacity to learn despite his weaknesses, the carefully falsified image, and the real darkness of that November day, the real end to something in life and in the world. Leaving, I bought a campaign poster—not of JFK, but of his brother, Robert F. Kennedy, which still hangs on my wall as a symbol that continues to live somewhere, even after the massy lead door slammed on the modern age that November in 1963: a symbol of living hope. Somewhere in the dark streets perhaps the everlasting light still shines. But wistful wishes are not enough anymore. It is time for *spes quarens intellectum,* in Moltmann's words: hope seeking understanding.

John F. Kennedy now prompts disillusionment more than hope. But we are fooled by the spirit of our own times if we admit defeat, if we imagine there is enough knowledge in the universe to destroy hope, the impulse of that universe. Hope, in some form, the Kennedys seem to have given us, and it was worth considerable disillusionment. We are angry at Kennedy for our disillusionment. We are angry because we realize he was never disillusioned and we are; maybe he was never disillusioned because he never hoped. We feel like suckers. I think we are angry also because we realize, perhaps instinctively, that John Kennedy hastened the end of the world his image symbolized.

Outside, on the lawn of the Kennedy Library, rests his sailboat. That sailboat was a playboy's toy. We were to believe that JFK read poetry while lounging against the gunwale. The monument, very personal and immediate, so immediate that you can touch Jack Kennedy's sailboat as it lies out in the weather, is poignant. The clearest picture I retain from the library is of that boat, not many yards from the rocks and water, alone and forever unused now, out there in the weather.

As I left the library with the RFK poster rolled up inside my raincoat, the sky began to clear. The wind off the harbor was still raw, but didn't have real rain in it. From the main road I looked back at the Kennedy Library jutting up among the waves, rocks, and dark university buildings, with the Boston skyline in the background. Was the black-and-white building striking, or merely out of place?

A few hours later, having marched more miles and grappled with the confounded buses and trains, I walked along a line painted on the sidewalk toward "Old Ironsides." The weather had turned even better; the sun was out a little, and the constant spray had stopped. I opened my raincoat. White seagulls wheeled and squawked, dipping from blue to blue. There, tied to the pier, black and white, the USS *Constitution* lay at anchor.

I got into line. The long day waned. Guards came up the column of people strung out along the dock and said there would be only one more tour—room enough for only the front half of the line. I remained, feeling it was better to stay here and be turned away than to do anything else in the world. I knew, despite the fact that I was well back in the queue, that I would get on board. I had glimpsed the future.

The only predictable outcome was for the line to be cut off just ahead of me. But that did not happen. The column in front dwindled away in a slow but inexorable, inevitable etherealization. I was let on board. I felt as if I were entering a holy place. The light of the universe cascaded, radiated all around me. It was a ship, but the ship was only a vessel. Below decks, the huge beams and masts lived like solid light and spirit. The *Constitution* moved in a sea of light.

I have no explanation. I had never been particularly interested in Old Ironsides, but now it was the culmination of some spiritual aspiration I did not even know I had. I must have looked like a maniac. I was surrounded by the timbers, beams, ropes, lines, cannons, and decks of heaven. Mystical experience conveys certainty, but it cannot be described or explained.

As I walked the gangplank off the ship, I was wrung out, full of fragile energy. I had left all my breath on the ship, and I hope to get back with it someday. All the rest of Boston was relatively unreal. So were past and present.

* * *

Today, up on Cemetery Hill, I thought I felt a similar inspiration despite the soaking rain. Perhaps more than inspiration, it was a vague suspicion.

I was looking up at the Jenny Wade statue in Evergreen Cemetery when a kind of puzzlement struck me. Miss Wade's grave is only a hundred feet or so from the Brown mausoleum, which sits on the knoll at the center of Evergreen Cemetery; it is the highest place, or nearly so, on Cemetery Hill. It is the place where Ms. Harrison says the speakers' platform stood when Abraham Lincoln delivered the Gettysburg Address.

I looked at the knoll, now shaded by evergreens, occupied by the small, square mausoleum. I looked back at Miss Wade's grave. Mid-nineteenth-century Americans would not have trampled graves. Certainly not solders' graves. But least of all the grave of Jenny Wade, the young woman—the only civilian—killed during the Battle of Gettysburg. This grave is awfully close to the platform site.

Clutching my umbrella, I commenced making a circuit of the Brown memorial. First the north side. There, of course, was the Wade family. On the east side, toward the wrought-iron fence of the Solders' National Cemetery, some old, very old headstones: 1850s, 1830s, even 1820s. On the south side, more old graves. But on the east and northeast, close to the Brown mausoleum, the oldest markers of all. They were ancient stones, full-length, lying flat over the whole gravesite, like the ones in Boston or England, like the ones in Thomas Gray's country churchyard. They are quaint, morbid designs reminding us of our mortality, with old script, very worn and some unreadable. But the dates are legible: 1754, 1731, and so on. And clinching the matter, here was the grave of a Revolutionary War veteran. No American of the 1860s would have considered stepping on that grave.

The Brown mausoleum is surrounded by over a hundreds years' worth of graves, all previous to November 1863. I need to think this out, and to investigate more carefully when it is not raining. Measure distances. I just might be on the verge of a significant discovery.

* * *

Nevertheless, a gnawing sense of futility overtakes a person when he is slogging in the mud. It reminds me that tomorrow is the anniversary of the death of a heroic young man—not one of Lincoln's soldiers, but someone caught up in the larger civil war fought by the Western World in 1914–1918. Wilfred Owen, who fought in the wet trenches and on the muddy fields of the western front, helped to preserve democracy, like Lincoln's soldiers, but at the same time he saw the whole enterprise as being ironic. One might think it is easier to be a hero in a romantic era like the American Civil War than in an ironic one like World War I, but I doubt it. In one age there is inflation of the heroic currency, in the other depression; but in the long run, heroism rises above such fluctuations.

In the rain at Gettysburg one can wish to bid a farewell to arms, but the effect of the place and its memories is to remind one of all war, and "the pity of war," as Owen phrased it. Warfare is an image of our present mental confusion, and is also merely an acceleration of the wheel of birth and death that we are all riding. It shows starkly the weaknesses and virtues in all of us. We study war and learn about ourselves.

From Cemetery Hill at Gettysburg we can see into the early twentieth century, when Lincoln's boys, by then old men, paraded in cemeteries back in their hometowns, and their grandsons slung on rifles and packs and marched toward the mud of France and Flanders. It was only fifty years from one war to the other. Would Americans have helped win either world war if the Union had not held in the 1860s? The Civil War's significance is understood better from the standpoint of the twentieth century and its wars. What Lincoln said was at stake really had been at stake. And his definition of heroes should stand the test of the end of Lincoln's world, which World War I brought about. If Lincoln's words can help us now, we have to pull them straight through World War I, the Holocaust and World War II, Vietnam, and the rest, because that is where we have been. We are part of all that we have met; we are made of all our parents' experiences. We are elegies. There is no avoiding it: we will remember, in spite of ourselves. The Civil War's rain and the Great War's rain still fall. November has to be walked through, day by day, before the dirty rain will turn to December snow.

NOVEMBER 4

In Vain (Lycidas)

For *Lycidas* is dead, dead ere his prime.
—John Milton, November 1637

November was a month of anniversaries for Lincoln, none of them particularly cheerful. He won both his presidential elections in Novembers. He delivered the Address. And, on November 4, 1842, he had gotten married. Dressing himself in unwonted fine clothing just before the wedding, which had not been publicized, Lincoln was asked by his landlord's son, *Where are you going?* "To hell, I suppose," Lincoln answered.

Twenty-one years later, November 4, 1863, was moving day for the Lincolns: they moved back into the White House. During the warm months—the airless, muggy, unhealthy summer—President Lincoln and his family lived in the Soldiers' Home, out of the central city. Washington City in those days was generally looked upon as a dirty jumble of government buildings, hovels, and brothels: pigs running in the ruts of traffic; soldiers and politicians roiling about the streets—a pleasant place compared to today, but uncomfortable in summer. Each day for half that year, President Abraham Lincoln had gone back to the Soldiers' Home in the evening, sometimes late at night. (Judging by yesterday's note to Seward, he had not gone home before midnight on the second.) Lincoln now moved with a small cavalry escort to and from the Soldiers' Home. Riding alone, he had been shot at more than once, on one occasion having a bullet hole in his hat to show for it. The picture almost would be amusing: the ungainly man in tall hat, stirrups comically low to the ground, shot at and suddenly galloping off holding the hat—except the bullet hole was so close to the site of the actual assassination wound. Walt Whitman would see the president on these escorted rides, regularly enough that eventually each man would acknowledge the other with a nod of the head. The poet observed that no photograph could ever capture the mobility and the deep, canny expression of Lincoln's mysterious face.

The rides ended for a few months this day. Except for the nineteen loads of furniture ferried into the White House—probably to Mr. Lincoln's embarrassment, if he stayed around to watch—it was an uneventful day, perhaps an opportunity to brood over the speech—a day like the previous, which he had described to Seward as "nothing new," in which it was "all quiet" on all fronts.

One reads those phrases with a thrill of foreboding today. They have become bitterly ironic. A tall man in black, sad and anxious, moves into the house of his mortality, while the fatal combinations twitch into place. In Washington the phrase "all quiet" already carried an ironic undertone. A sentimental, tragic song enlisted a common headline of the early phase of the war—"All Quiet Along the Potomac: A Picket Shot"—to lament the death of a lone soldier, "moaning out all alone the death rattle."

Both phrases Lincoln wrote in his note to Seward would be used for an even more horrible war. Erich Maria Remarque's *All Quiet on the Western Front* was titled in the original German *Im Westen Nichts Neues* (In the West, Nothing New). It was that war, World War I, which riddled the body of modernism, and blasted away the hopes of our fathers' world, preparing the way for the Second World War's devastation.

Like the orphans who are here twenty-five years after leaving Vietnam, the people of the Western World are still groping the unfamiliar landscape of the post–World War I world. And just as Vietnam affected one generation—eroded its trust in government and reverence for traditional ideas—so the Great War has affected us all personally, whether we know it or not. If we have lost confidence in the human race, its institutions, and its reason; if we have little reverence for the ideas and ideals of three thousand years of Western civilization—it is in part because the First World War stunned the world of our grandmothers and grandfathers. It happened to the Europeans initially, of course, but the effects increasingly filtered into American thought during the twentieth century.

Anyone who teaches the poetry of Wilfred Owen to students of British literature maunders in a no-man's land between instruction and lament. Owen reminds us of everything the West has lost, and stands for why we lost it. Lieutenant Owen is the Modern World at war with itself. That civil war is our civil war; his loss is our loss; we are Wilfred Owen's orphans.

* * *

The pocked, moonlike no-man's-land of the First World War became the bony grave of the Modern World, for the countries at the forefront of Europe's intellectual and cultural life. The shock was in some ways greater than that of World War II because Europe had not seen a major war for a century. The Western Front, 1914–1918: from the steely shore of the English Channel, across ripped-up Flanders fields, down five hundred fatal miles of France to the Swiss frontier, a generation of the Enlightenment's heirs slugged it out in the Western mind's most momentous civil war since the seventeenth century. France, Germany, and England machine-gunned millions of each other's sons across the blistered front—wise men, fools, poets, priests, and plumbers all together chopped like mutton, onions, spuds, and dumped out upon the squishy blank fields—our intellectual fathers clawing for each other's guts like weasels in a hole.

We have forgotten why the First World War brought people face-to-face with futility. Our view is obscured by World War II because we know its veterans. Similarly, Vietnam is the experience of today's middle-aged men and women. But compare the British death lists: In World War II, 244,000 British soldiers died. On the *first day* of the Somme offensive, July 1, 1916, the British lost 19,000 killed. By the time the Somme fighting ended on November 18, the Germans, French, and British had lost 1,250,000 killed, wounded, and missing. Britain lost 743,000 killed in the war. The Western Front devoured a generation of English men. Of course, America's losses in the Civil War were proportionally much higher. America had "seen the elephant" already.

But features of the 1914–18 Western Front were inseparable from the war's effects. Men lived in a gray, muddy, brutal landscape, devoid of trees (blasted by artillery) and holed with craters (stinking pools of settled poison gas and the stench of corpses); barbed wire bristling, artillery and small arms sounding a constant routine of death. "Some 7000 British men and officers were killed and wounded daily, just as a matter of course. 'Wastage,' the Staff called it." Trench warfare: solid lines facing each other for four years. The attacks: artillery barrage for hours or days, then "over the top" into the devastated landscape suddenly exploding in shells, mines, and machine-gun bullets. Lines of men would be killed, blown apart as the attacks, wave after wave, poured out into no-man's-land. It was not glorious: "Pervading the air was the smell of rum and blood." (Someone said later, "Had it not been for the rum ration I do not think we should have won the war.") The great battles were unbelievable by previous standards. About seven thousand men were killed at Gettysburg, a three-day battle. Waterloo, one day, was similar. But Verdun lasted months, killing about three hundred thousand German and French young men. By the fall of 1917, two and one-half million young men were dead on the Western Front. People became immersed in the belief that the war would never end. Ivor Gurney kept on writing war poems in his mental hospital until he died in 1937, thinking the war was still going on, which in a sense it is.

The causes and meaning of the war are still unclear. The "peace" dictated to Germany included Germany's admission of war guilt, but not everyone agrees Germany alone was responsible for the war. Woodrow Wilson appears to some as an idealist who could have established a just and lasting peace, but others see his willingness to enter the war as the factor which prevented a reasonable peace in 1917, due to the Allies' raised expectations of a war of conquest—a purpose for the war which Germans denied for themselves at the time. Even the large strategic concepts are uncertain. It had been generally accepted that the Germans did not win the war in August 1914 because they weakened the Schlieffen Plan, which called for a massive right-wing sweep across Paris. But this has been termed a "myth" for good reasons. Winston Churchill said the Germans lost the war because of two things: the invasion of Belgium and unrestrained submarine warfare. Propaganda arising from these brought America into the war—but was the propaganda mythology, too? Apparently there is insufficient proof of the stories of German atrocities in Belgium.

The war was begun partly because of an assassination, because of a complex of written arrangements which the powers had made with each other, and because a few people made bad decisions. It was neither inevitable, unavoidable, nor necessary. The word at the end was that this had been the war to end wars, but of course the "peace" invited World War II, with 55 million casualties, military and civilian, and the invention of nuclear weapons. So the millions of young men who were killed from 1914–1918—lost to themselves, their families, and the world, it seems—died in vain. Such futility made the intellectual damage of World War I more severe than that of the Civil War, which was given purpose in the North by Abraham Lincoln at Gettysburg, as well as by the causes of Union and emancipation.

* * *

A photograph of Wilfred Owen in his British infantry officer's uniform, taken in July 1916 before he went to the front, shows a calm, sensitive, intelligent young man. He wears a thin moustache. His eyes themselves are photographs: the meaning of everything they have seen is recorded in their expression. His uniform is an element of the eyes—the uniform worn by a million men on the Western Front. The traditions of four thousand years of Western thought, the lovely lanes of England, the promises of the King James Bible, are in those eyes: steady, sad, ironic, seared, noble, young—the eyes of a poet with conscience who has killed and knows he will be killed in the vast machine of a futile war.

But that is the look of his eyes in our eyes. Actually, Wilfred Owen had this look before the Great War. His brother Harold called it his "dark smile . . . an assured diffidence."

> This gravity of approach, which remained always in advance of his years, coupled as it was with his attractive appearance (not to be confused with good looks), his thick dark brown hair and small delicacy of build—perhaps a lack of robustness even—gave him an air of over-adultness.

Wilfred began writing poetry very early, and he was drawn to a poet (small in height like the five-foot-five Owen) who achieved greatness in his early twenties. Harold wrote: "Keats was ever-present in his mind, and he was given to this absorption in the life and work of men in all the arts who had died young." Owen worshiped Keats "in an almost religious sense," says a biographer. The aspiring poet read a biography of Keats and wrote afterward: "I never guessed till now the frightful travail of his soul towards Death; . . . Rosetti [the Keats biographer Owen had been reading] guided my groping hand right into the wound, and I touched, for one moment the incandescent Heart of Keats." He knew. He had known all along. He wrote to his brother Harold, "I know I shall be killed. But it's the only place I can make my protest from." The Great War was Owen's tuberculosis, just as it was the consumption of the modern mind. Keats, reclining like a mortally wounded angel, hollow eyes bright, the incandescent heart becoming a dream—these passed into Wilfred Owen's mind, hung in his eyes, and bloomed in his dark smile.

* * *

Owen brought "unseen voices" with him to the front. That of Keats was dominant, but there was also Gray's "Elegy," whose suggestions supplied material for the young poet's brooding mind. In 1911, at age eighteen, Owen had written:

To eastward, too
A churchyard sleeps, and one infirm old yew,
Where in the shadows of the fading day,
Musing on faded lives, sate solemn Gray.
. . . he is gone, and his high dignity
Lost in the past . . .

Echoes of Gray's "Elegy" emerge more than once, with irony, in Owen's war poems:

And I heard a voice crying
This is the Path of Glory.
(Gray: "The paths of glory lead but to the Grave.")

There is also a shadow of the "swain," or countryman, who in the "Elegy" one day misses the young poet whom he had been accustomed to seeing on the "upland lawn." The countryman has entered our century and become a loiterer among the luggage carriers at the station where troops are departing for France:

Dull porters watched them, and a casual tramp
Stood staring hard,
Sorry to miss them from the upland camp.
. . . .
Shall they return to beating of great bells
In wild train-loads?
A few, a few, too few for drums and yells

May creep back, silent, to village wells,
Up half-known roads.

The world they knew is gone, "half-known" now. The soldiers have brought a new England back from the war. Owen has lost Gray's country and churchyard at the front.

In Owen's "Elegy in April and September," the ancient yew tree of Gray's country churchyard emerges from a strangely discordant harmony, with words and sounds too carefully balanced, the mood a dark mixture of mockery, anger, skepticism, and a theological question:

Brood, wood, and muse, yews,
The ways gods use we have not understood.
Muse, yews, and brood, wood . . .

Gray defers judgment of all things and all people to the bosom of God, but Owen can no longer trust.

IN VAIN (LYCIDAS)

God for his glittering world
Seeketh our tears.
Prayers show as eyelids pearled.
God hath no ears.

* * *

Wilfred Owen had "a fine heroic feeling" when he arrived in France at the end of December 1916. He was a brand-new second lieutenant with a sound English education behind him. He had endured a brief and abortive tenure as a vicar, or ministerial understudy. Following that, he had spent some time in France as a tutor, and now the war had brought him back. Educated and intelligent, young Owen had received his commission, uniform, and the brief training customary for the short-lived officers of his grade. (Second lieutenants were first over the top in assaults.)

In a few days he was experiencing "the real thing, Mud." The men on the Western Front had the appearance of "expressionless lumps," a look he would later compare to persons wearing blindfolds.

On January 7, 1917, he heard the guns for the first time. "It was a sound not without a certain sublimity." But the suffering had begun. Though he wrote, "I cannot do a better thing or be in a better place," he also said, "There is nothing in all this inferno but mud and thunder." The front is "like the eternal place of gnashing of teeth," and he alludes to "the keen spiritual cold." On January 16, he tells his mother:

> I can see no excuse for deceiving you about the last 4 days. I have suffered seventh hell.
>
> I have not been at the front.
> I have been in front of it.

Trapped with twenty-five men in a dugout with two feet of water and "say 4 feet of air," they had remained fifty hours. "I nearly broke down and let myself drown in the water that was now slowly rising over my knees."

Sentries over the dugout were "blown to nothing. One of these fellows was my first servant whom I rejected. If I had kept him he would have lived, for servants don't do Sentry duty."

Second Lieutenant Owen kept his platoon's sentries partly in the dugout "during the more terrific bombardments," but still one of them was blinded by an exploding shell. This is described in Owen's poem "The Sentry":

> ... thud! flump! thud! down the steep steps came thumping
> And sploshing in the flood, deluging muck,
> The sentry's body . . .

The soldiers hastily stumble out and "dredge" not "him" but "it" up "for dead." Then the wounded sentry speaks, or rather—significantly—"whines":

> "O sir—my eyes—I'm blind,—I'm blind,—I'm blind."

The soldier recalling this story marshals the great emblem of modern civilization: portable fire. He produces a match or lighter, the symbol of modern technology and the leading motif of the Enlightenment:

> Coaxing, I held a flame against his lids
> And said if he could see the least blurred light
> He was not blind; in time they'd get all right.
> "I can't," he sobbed.

Here is the final modern situation. Our own small enlightenment makes no impression against the great irrational flash, part technological, part savage.

The nightmare in that dugout will not go away; the poet's mind will not "get all right":

> Eyeballs, huge-bulged like squids',
> Watch my dreams still,—yet I forgot him there . . .

There are other casualties, or, put more plainly, "other wretches . . . bled and spewed." One of them "would have drowned himself for good,—"

> I try not to remember these things now.

But the poet must stay in the story anyway; he must go on with telling it, though history has become a nightmare with no meaning but "dread."

> Through the dense din, I say, we heard him shout
> "I see your lights!"—but ours had long gone out.

Their modern, Enlightenment hope had been a delusion. On the Western Front, among such soldiers as this poet, such light, all light—except in the flashes of artillery—has gone out.

* * *

An early title for Owen's first collection of poems was "English Elegies." But his poems have little in common with the elegiac tradition of the previous generation. For Owen no rational labor "forms the firmer mind," and no spiritualistic experience assuages grief, as in the most popular elegy of the Victorian Age, Tennyson's *In Memoriam.* Even Tennyson's doubts seem captive to the Enlightenment. The Romantic, Keats, with his ability to endure skepticism, remains Owen's dominant influence. The Victorian mind is the epitome of the modern view of the world; this view has been shelled to pieces.

All we have left is the ironic, faint, wry smile of "assured diffidence." There is no evidence, to the modern mind, of anything that transcends the pointless mayhem that is destroying that mind.

For Owen, as for Keats, beauty could have a kind of saving power: "Every Spring the Narcissus do enough to save a man's soul, if it be worth saving." But other sights overwhelm the attention:

> I suppose I can endure cold, and fatigue, and the face-to-face death, as well as another; but extra for me there is the universal pervasion of Ugliness. Hideous landscapes, vile noises, foul language and nothing but foul, even from one's own mouth (for all are devil-ridden), everything unnatural, broken, blasted; the distortion of the dead, whose unburiable bodies sit outside the dug-outs all day, all night, the most execrable sights on earth. In poetry we call them the most glorious. But to sit with them all day, all night . . . and a week later to come back and find them still sitting there.

In any event, spring is not quiet enough for Narcissus; our pensive gaze is always jerked outward to the war. On Easter Sunday, 1917, Second Lieutenant Owen witnessed "a German Aeroplane come shuddering down the sky." He writes his brother Colin:

> The Pilot—well I need not horrify you without need . . .
>
> I could not stay to see the engines & guns dug out of the soil, because I am so frightfully busy.

Not many days later Owen's platoon went to the front line, being ordered "over the top" to attack twice in one day.

> The reward we got for all this was to remain in the Line 12 days. For twelve days I did not wash my face, nor take off my boots, nor sleep deep sleep. For twelve days we lay in holes, where at any moment a shell might put us out. I think the worst was one wet night when we lay up against a railway embankment. A big shell lit on the top of the bank, just 2 yards

> from my head. Before I awoke, I was blown in the air right away from the bank! I passed most of the following day in a railway Cutting, in a hole just big enough to lie in . . . My brother officer of B Coy, 2/Lt Gaukroger lay opposite in a similar hole.

He began not to function properly. In a letter to his mother he confesses some unsoldierly thoughts: it had been "curious and troubling" to come upon a town the enemy had just evacuated and "pick up his letters where he had left off writing in the middle of a word!"

Only after another week passed could he allude, in a letter to his sister, to the worst of it all:

> You know it was not the Bosche [Germans] that worked me up, nor the explosives, but it was living so long by poor old Cock Robin (as we used to call 2/Lt. Gaukroger), who lay not only near by, but in various places around and about . . .

Second Lieutenant Owen was sent back from the front lines, diagnosed with Neurasthenia, "shell shock"—what would be called "battle fatigue" in the next war.

* * *

Back in Britain, he was transported to a rehabilitation facility, Craiglockhart, in Edinburgh.

In the days and months following, Owen struggled to retain his sense of humor. He wrote a long parody of King James English: "But he, stooping down, began to tie the latchet of his shoe. Now because of the new wine and the old leather, it came to pass that the same was rent in twain. And he stood up and cursed them." He referred to himself in a letter as the poet, "Wilpher d'Oen" and described his "Mood: highest of jinks." But he had not stopped considering his own experience, the war, and his duty.

The ambiguous point of view of a "conscientious objector with a seared conscience" ripened into a new sense of duty during the long months at Craiglockhart. While in Scotland, Owen met the poets Siegfried Sassoon and Robert Graves. He edited a poetry magazine, and began to study German. ("It is a vile language to learn.") "Disastrous dreams" continued to ride upon his sleep, and he worked and reworked his poems. Through it all he had the firm sense that he must go back to the war: "As for myself, I hate washy pacifists as temperamentally as I hate whiskied prussianists. Therefore I feel that I must first get some reputation of gallantry before I could successfully and usefully declare my principles."

His intent was to protest war through his poetry, written "as from the trenches." His work was being recognized already, particularly by Sassoon and Graves—who wrote to him: "Don't make any mistake, Owen, you are a—fine poet already, & are going to be more so. . . . Puff out your chest a little, and be big for you've more right than most of us. . . . You must help . . . to revolutionize English Poetry. So outlive this war."

But his first duty was toward the young men in the trenches, and those about to go—a duty to "prepare them for the eucharist of their own blood." He had, as he wrote, "sympathy for the oppressed always."

Before leaving, he wrote of a night walk in Scotland:

> It was already darkening when we reached Colinton and had tea, and quite dark when we took the Edinburgh road; and so we took it in good style with songs and dancing, whistling and halloing. Until the meteors showered in heaven; and we fell calm under the winter stars, and some of us saw the pale pathway of the Spirits for the first time.
>
> And seeing it so far above us, and feeling the good road so firm beneath us, we worshipped God in our hearts; and knew we loved one another as no men love for long.
>
> That was my way of spending Sunday.

On the Eastern Front, the situation was so "stupefyingly catastrophic" that some wondered whether "the whole of civilization is extremely liable to collapse." At the very least, Owen was living through "the ebbing tide of the Victorian Age." The Modern World was ending. There is no comfort. Owen will not numb himself to the catastrophe: "I quite see the origin of Theosophy. It is the same as that of heaven, and Abraham's bosom . . . : desperate desire."

But we have our duty. "I am started," he wrote. "I feel the great swelling of the open sea." His pathway led back to the war, the infinite, unending war:

> Last year, at this time . . . I lay awake in a windy tent in the middle of a vast, dreadful encampment. It seemed neither France nor England, but a kind of paddock where the beasts are kept a few days before the shambles. I heard the reveling of the Scotch troops, who are now dead, and who knew they would be dead . . .
>
> But chiefly I thought of the very strange look on all faces in that camp; an incomprehensible look, which a man will never see in England. . . .

> It was not despair, or terror, it was more terrible than terror, for it was a blindfold look, and without expression, like a dead rabbit's.
>
> It will never be painted, and no actor will ever seize it. And to describe it, I think I must go back and be with them.

In August 1918, Owen was given orders sending him to the front. He wrote his mother that he was "unreluctant." From the fields of France in October, in command of a company, he would explain, "I came out in order to help these boys—directly by leading them as well as an officer can: indirectly, by watching their sufferings that I may speak of them as well as a pleader can."

* * *

> It seemed that out of battle I escaped
> Down some profound dull tunnel, long since scooped
> Through granites which titanic wars had groined.

So begins Owen's "Strange Meeting," written in 1918. The speaker finds that he is surrounded by prone figures groaning. He reaches down to touch them, but they do not respond—"Too fast in thought or death to be bestirred"—until one springs up and, staring, "with piteous recognition in fixed eyes,"

> Lifted distressful hands, as if to bless.
> And by his smile, I knew that sullen hall, —
> By his dead smile I knew we stood in hell.

The figure speaks:

> I am the enemy you killed, my friend.
> I knew you in this dark: for so you frowned
> Yesterday through me as you jabbed and killed.
> I parried; but my hands were loath and cold.
> Let us sleep now . . .

Young men on both sides were fighting to defend the modern world, but they all woke up in the strange hell of the postmodern world.

* * *

Perhaps something uncanny was behind Owen's imagining of "that other" in "Strange Meeting." The Owen family had gone to Ireland on holiday in

1902, where a peculiar event took place. They had been walking in a dark wood when they came out into an open field (as Harold related it):

> for the first and only time in my life I heard her [their mother] give a stifled scream. This spun us all around to see, standing ten yards or so from us, the shadowy figure of a tall man. . . .
> My father . . . at once addressed this sinister looking person, I have no doubt with some apology for our trespass if we were committing one. The sound of my father's voice had the unexpected effect of contorting the man into a frenzy of fury, and he raised the heavy stick he was carrying with such ferocious intent that attack from him seemed unavoidable. The surprise perhaps silenced my father and immediately the figure relaxed to its original stationary position.
> . . . the figure . . . was suddenly not there any longer . . .

That evening the parents told their story to a local couple. The two froze into an "immediate and astounding" stony silence, and Tom Owen (Wilfred's father) realized that this was a subject not to be talked about. Finally the local couple told the Owens that nothing about this should be said to anyone. It is perhaps a final irony—but what is final when it comes to irony, and what is still deferred?—that this kind of strange meeting stands at the end of the story of Wilfred Owen's life.

* * *

From September 30 to October 2, Second Lieutenant Owen was engaged in heavy fighting, about which he wrote his mother: "I lost all earthly faculties, and fought like an angel. . . . Of whose blood lies yet crimson on my shoulder where his head was—and where so lately yours was—I must not now write."

The year before, when Owen was shell-shocked, some of his superiors had wondered whether he was fit to command. Now, he received the Military Cross—a fine, ironic oxymoron for him, no doubt, a "military cross." The citation read: "For conspicuous gallantry and devotion to duty in the attack on the Fonsomme Line on 1st/2nd October 1918. On the Company Commander becoming a casualty, he assumed command and showed fine leadership and resisted a heavy counter-attack. He personally manipulated a captured enemy machine gun in an isolated position and inflicted considerable losses on the enemy. Throughout he behaved most gallantly."

He wrote to Siegfried Sassoon in early October: "the boy by my side, shot through the head, lay on top of me, soaking my shoulder, for half an hour." He went on: "Photograph? Can you photograph the crimson-hot iron as it cools from smelting? That is what Jones's blood looked like, and felt like. My senses are charred."

* * *

In September 1918, French premier Clemenceau had delivered a speech reported in the London *Times,* where it was read by Wilfred Owen. Its subject was victory and the end of the war. With his faint, cool, and by now tragic smile, Owen set down the words of a poem, "Smile, Smile, Smile," titled from a popular song at home and brought with helpless irony to the front.

> Nation?—The half-limbed readers did not chafe
> But smiled at one another curiously
> Like secret men who know their secret safe.
> (This is the thing they know and never speak,
> That England one by one had fled to France.
> Not many elsewhere now, save under France.)

He perceived that the former England had nearly died out, probably not only because a generation of its men were interred in French ground. England had lost its way of thinking, as had the other nations. What was left of old Blighty now? Not the country they had set out to save. Once you start thinking the old thoughts ironically, they are dead. The enlightened, humane hopes of the modern world were finished.

Clemenceau's words remind one of the Gettysburg Address:

> All are worthy of victory, because they will know how to honor it. Yet, however, in the ancient spot where sit the fathers of the Republic we should be untrue to ourselves if we forgot that the greatest glory will be to those splendid *poilus* [the French equivalent of Doughboys or GIs] who will see confirmed by history the titles of nobility which they themselves have earned. At the present moment they ask for nothing more than to be allowed to complete the great work which will assure them of immortality. What do they want and what do you? To keep on fighting victoriously until the moment when the enemy will understand there is no possible negotiation between crime and right.

Such a goal—finishing the work which they who fought here have thus far so nobly advanced, or, as Lincoln put it in his Second Inaugural, to "finish the work we are in" and to establish a "just, and a lasting, peace, among ourselves and with all nations"—such a goal would strike Wilfred Owen, well, just the way it did. Smile, smile, smile.

> Pictures of these broad smiles appear each week,
> And people in whose voice real feeling rings
> Say: How they smile! They're happy now, poor things.

The "poor things"—the corpses "under France"—smile, grins frozen on their rotting skeletal faces. How happy they must be, knowing we are continuing the work they have thus far so nobly advanced. For the American Civil War, the goals and accomplishments were real; therefore so was the rhetoric. But in the "Great War," the rhetoric was false because any results would be meaningless.

The Great War was futile, if not worse. This in no small part because Clemenceau, the one who preached about "crime and right"—who as a young man had been in Richmond, Virginia, when "Unconditional Surrender" Grant's victorious troops had marched into the city—vengefully pushed Germany into an intolerable position after the war. There is irony enough to go around and, perhaps someone like Owen might say, nothing but irony came out of that war, except eight and one-half million dead soldiers and the end of modern thought.

* * *

The Great War changed our language so that words like Lincoln's can be read ironically. The twentieth century has deconstructed the nineteenth—and earlier centuries as well. Few poetic lines are as bitter as the way Owen's metrics force us to read the last lines of his "gas poem."

> Gas! GAS! Quick, boys!—an ecstasy of fumbling . . .

One man fails to get his mask on in time:

> If in some smothering dreams you too could pace
> Behind the wagon that we flung him in,
> And watch the white eyes writhing in his face,
> His hanging face, like a devil's sick of sin;
> If you could hear, at every jolt, the blood
> Come gargling from the froth-corrupted lungs,
> Obscene as cancer, bitter as the cud
> Of vile, incurable sores on innocent tongues, —
> My friend, you would not tell with such high zest

To children ardent for some desperate glory,
The old Lie: Dulce et decorum est
Pro patria mori.

The Latin phrase is from Horace, *Odes,* III.ii.13, and means "It is sweet and seemly to die for one's country"—or, to be more literal with the word *patria,* "fatherland." To die for one's fatherland is as "sweet and seemly" as blood gargled from a gassed soldier's lungs.

What would Wilfred Owen think of a war to stop a slave power? He might smile that doomed smooth smile, perhaps, and recite the words

Dulce et decorum est pro patria mori.

He was acquainted with the Kaiser. That fine jewel, England, and its laws, culture, democracy—civilization, as the Allies saw it—were threatened by the host of the Hun, the Prussian machine—Athens overwhelmed by a savage, sausage-grinding Sparta. Nevertheless Owen, still the soldier with his most desperately heroic fighting not far ahead of him, wrote,

> I am more and more Christian as I walk the unchristian ways of Christendom. . . . One of Christ's essential commands was: Passivity at any price! suffer dishonour and disgrace; but never resort to arms. Be bullied, be outraged, be killed; but do not kill. It may be a chimerical and an ignominious principle, but there it is. . . .
>
> Christ is literally in no man's land.

If all of history has become a shell-pocked foreground, if all the past becomes our simple noisy surface, perhaps the death of Christendom's divinity happened in the stinking fields of France—Gethsemane and Golgotha extended through four years and along five hundred miles of trenches. The blood of one, the blood of many, shed for nothing, soaking our shoulders, percolating through the uneasy floors of our own graves.

* * *

Owen's last poem is called "Spring Offensive." A group of soldiers, "knowing their feet had come to the end of the world" at the base of a ridge, rest "marveling" at the soft, fresh springtime meadows around them:

. . . watched the long grass swirled
By the May breeze . . .

But a "little word" of command tightens them like a "cold gust." With "only a lift and flare of eyes that faced / The sun, like a friend with whom their love is done," they shoulder their rifles and go up.

> . . . instantly the whole sky burned
> With fury against them; earth set sudden cups
> In thousands for their blood; and the green slope
> Chasmed and deepened sheer to infinite space.

In running to that "last high place" (the ridge), they are going to a place of sacrifice.

"Some say," we read, that those who "plunged and fell away past the world's verge" after going over that last ridge,

> Some say God caught them before they fell.

At first glance what "some say" is sheer rot. But there is a darker possibility. God's catching them even before they fell suggests God's acquiescence or even His dooming them to fall. God failed to "catch" them, or God caught them and fed them to the machine guns. Which is worse?

Owen wrote in an unfinished preface to his poems:

> . . . these elegies are to this generation in no sense consolatory. They may be to the next. All a poet can do today is warn. That is why true poets must be truthful.

The ones who really know something about this double offense, this spring offensive, are not civilians at home but soldiers who were in it and survived—but these have acquired a fallen knowledge. They "plunged and fell" like the biblical Adam and Eve, who ate of the Tree of the Knowledge of Good and Evil. Their knowledge is demonic—how reliable is it?—but who else has any knowledge of this at all?

> The few who rushed in the body to enter hell,
> And there out-fiending all its fiends and flames
> With superhuman inhumanities,
> Long-famous glories, immemorial shames . . .

These crawl "slowly back" and, as before, find themselves in "cool peaceful air in wonder"—bliss of a kind, seemingly, but in silence. What these soldiers know of "what happened" is nontransferable, if they know anything. Perhaps the knowledge gained by eating of the Tree of the Knowledge of Good and Evil is not knowledge at all.

Why speak not they of comrades that went under?

Language has been killed. Prophetically, this poem studies the plunge from modernism to postmodernism. (Wilfred Owen did not need to read Jacques Derrida, a French philosopher—another irony—to know that he and his "friends" and "enemies" were *deconstructing* the modern world by hand.) Modernism, the maker of these very weapons, is dead—shot, dumped, and left to rot. Who will next be sacrificed on one of the "high places"? Perhaps it is for us, the living, to be dedicated.

The Modern World's most prized element, progress, has been its own forbidden fruit.

As killing as the canker to the Rose.

* * *

The last attack Wilfred Owen participated in exemplifies the courage, fatality, and futility of the Great War. In command of his company due to its captain still being in the hospital, Owen led his men forward with the other companies of the 2nd Manchester Regiment. It was raining and cold the night of November 3, 1918; as midnight passed the rain ceased, replaced by a thick mist shrouding both the Manchesters and the German positions across the Sambre and Oise Canal. To the right of the Manchesters, two more regiments—Lancashire men—quietly, mechanically, moved into the small fields three hundred yards west of the canal. They waited for 5:45 A.M.

The men had time to think of the German position across the fields, across the canal, through the sunken mist. The dug-in enemy were waiting with their machine guns. They would wait underground while the British artillery barrage pounded the east side of the canal to pieces—an old tactic, an old, useless tactic that seemed to make so much sense. Then, knowing there would be several minutes between the cessation of the barrage and the arrival of the attackers at the canal itself, the Boche would rush out of their dugouts carrying parts of machine guns, fit them together, and open fire. The same thing again. We will fall like sheep, but there's nothing for it. Will there be wire this side of the canal?

Three things had to be done in the foggy gray dawn before the Tommies could actually close with the enemy. First, all three regiments would move forward through the fields as the barrage began exploding on the enemy side of the canal. They would then have to cross a three-foot-deep ditch before reaching the canal itself. Across the fifteen yards of land between ditch and canal, they would wait exposed to German fire while the Royal Engineers carried into the water the components of their bridge—an affair of wood and wire whose parts must be assembled in the canal.

At exactly 5:45 the officers blew the whistles which all during the war had signaled an attack. Immediately the artillery far behind them opened up and the scream, shriek, and rush of shells coming over ignited a steady line of explosions three hundred yards in front, across the canal. Second Lieutenant Owen led his men forward with the rest. He was a very good officer. One of his men had written home, "Do you know the little officer called Owen who was at Scarborough; he is commanding my company, and he is a toff I can tell you. No na-poo." ("Na-poo" means nonsense.)

After five minutes of walking forward, they were exposed in abrupt silence as the barrage ceased. Perhaps not complete silence—perhaps through the eerie mist, as they covered the last field, they could hear the metallic clacking together of German machine-gun parts. The Manchester men dropped planks and boards over the ditch and ran across. Getting up onto the wet towpath, they felt the first bullets. Men splashed backward into the ditch or dropped to the earth as the machine gunners found them. The other side of the canal came alive with the continuous spark and rattle of fire; the air streamed with bullets.

Nearby, one of Owen's heroes—if the word is appropriate and it probably is not quite—Maj. J. N. Marshall, was deploying Lancashire troops, as acting lieutenant colonel of his battalion. Marshall had not had to enlist, but in fact had joined the Belgian army already in 1914, selling off his highly conspicuous and successful stock of thoroughbred horses and becoming a lieutenant. The man, wrote Owen, was "the most arrant utterly soldierly soldier I ever came across." A lion of a man, apparently, wounded ten times, including a severe wound in the lung and a bayonet wound to the face, Marshall had received from the Belgian army an order of officers, an order of knights, the Croix de Guerre, the Medaille Militaire, and as a British officer in the Irish Guards, the Military Cross. He was, Owen said, "Bold, robust, dashing, unscrupulous, cruel, jovial, immoral, vast-chested, handsome-headed, of free, coarse speech." Owen's biographer, Jon Stallworthy, concludes that it must have been the contrast to such dominating men as these that caused the lieutenant to receive the (I think not disrespectful) nickname "The Ghost"—quiet, even-tempered soldier that he must have been.

Now they were all ghostly in the mist, facing a ghostly enemy. The engineers ran into it almost instantly. German artillery, probably pre-sighted on the canal, began their "deep cursing" and shells exploded in among the engineers and cut up segments of the bridge they were trying to assemble. At the same time, the German machine gunners concentrated upon them:

> the Engineers set to work to repair it, while bullets splintered the wood in their hands and struck sparks from the wire binding the floats. One by one they fell, on the bank, in the water, until all but two were killed or wounded.

This was the kind of heroism, and mortality, that the young men of First World War, and indeed also their successors in the Second, gave and received. We can hardly imagine it, sitting in our chairs. Wilfred Owen was one of these soldiers. Like the young GIs on Omaha Beach twenty-five years later, someone took responsibility and put forward his life. A nineteen-year-old Manchester second lieutenant, James Kirk, picked up a machine gun and bolted for the water. Throwing the gun and himself onto a raft, he paddled through the fire to "within ten yards" of the Germans, brought the barrel around, and opened up. The Germans threw themselves down and Kirk kept on shooting while the last two engineers—who received the Victoria Cross afterward—finished the bridge.

> Then Kirk's machine-gun stopped firing. The last of his magazines was empty. He was wounded in the arm and in the face, but more magazines were paddled out to him, and again he opened fire from his tilting raft. Behind him the bridge was pushed out and two platoons scrambled across.

This moment does not come to the Hollywood ending we are expecting. This is World War I:

> Almost at once, as a lucky shell severed the pontoons, they [the two platoons] were cut off, and James Kirk fell forward over his gun, shot through the head.

The 16th Lancashire Fusiliers, fighting on the Manchesters' right, were in the same killing zone. Their temporary commander was the man Owen so admired, J. N. Marshall. Seeing his battalion's bridge shot apart like that of his former comrades in the Manchester regiment, Marshall called in his loud voice for volunteers. A group of men rushed over the towpath and onto the bridge fragments, frantically trying to lash the thing together. Machine-gun bullets and shells tore the gray air around them, and in a few minutes every one of them was down. Marshall stood over their bodies, a large and conspicuous target for the Germans thirty or forty yards away, and "for a moment turned his broad back on the enemy and bellowed for another party of volunteers. Again they came forward and he cursed and encouraged them as they went to work." Again the Germans let them have it, but "miraculously," as Stallworthy puts it, "enough survived to repair the bridge and push it out over the whipped water." Marshall, still unhit, charged across the bridge with his men, but there was no miracle as they reached the canal's bank, where Marshall was shot down with what proved to be a mortal wound this time.

While this happened, Wilfred Owen, a small, calm figure in a misty hell of bullets and exploding shells, walked back and forth among his men, "patting them on the shoulder, saying 'Well done' and 'You're doing very well, my boy.' " At the water's edge he leaned toward a duckboard to help a man put it onto the water. It was approximately 6 A.M., November 4, 1918.

* * *

Who would not weep for Lycidas?

He must not lie upon his bier unwept. We knew him; we were nursed upon the self-same hill, we fed the same flock, we walked these same fields together. In the morning of our days we went out—but now the heavy change! Now you are gone; you are gone. Never will you return. The dry trees themselves seem to mourn, the brown willows and hazel copses, the myrtles and the laurels crisp and sere, for time has turned the season. Time, as killing as the canker to the rose, has run into this cold November. The frost is on the white thorn.

Where were the arts, the Muses, when those shots rang out? Foolish thought—as if they could have saved you. As if they could have hushed the guns on the Western Front. Poetry prevents no sudden death.

What, then, is the use of this lament? November could as easily turn to summer as I stave off the tragedies of long ago by mourning them. But to turn and tend our pleasures in the shade leaves the heart sorrowful and cloyed. *Who would not sing for Lycidas?* What else can I do? What else could Lycidas do but try to change his world? He is dead, that we know; but we will never know while we are in this world how things would have been—had he not touched his hand to the lyre of our souls. The beauty of his spirit draws a keening beauty from our own.

What caused his death? What steered the bullets to him, or drove the nations mad in 1914, or conspires against our dreams?

Grief ripens our rage at villainy. Shall we sit mute in tears while wolves rip the lambs of God, while children have no milk or bread? From beyond these times a sword comes, gleams like singing in a cold night, flashes truth like words struck in silver: we can read its righteous sentence by these dim and flaring lamps.

Place quietly your flowers here—the bells and florets of a thousand hues, the primrose and the jasmine, the pansy freaked with jet, the glowing violet, the musk-rose and the woodbine, daffodils and cowslips here, and last the never-fading amaranth; and with them now that one last sprig of lilac from the empty dooryard. Place them on the broken skull, the upturned eyes: Is it really Lycidas that in this coffin lies?

* * *

His children would be with us now, the sons of Wilfred Owen, and his daughters, filled with power and prophecy—that deep, cool look in their eyes. When I remember that Wilfred Owen was born in the same year as my father, I understand that the graves of young men are the graves of our fathers.

What candles may be held to speed them all?
    Not in the hands of boys but in their eyes
Shall shine the holy glimmers of goodbyes.
    The pallor of girls' brows shall be their pall;
Their flowers the tenderness of patient minds,
And each slow dusk a drawing-down of blinds.

(from "Anthem for Doomed Youth")

NOVEMBER 5

The Living and the Dead (Character)

> A thing is alive only when it contains contradictions within itself.
>
> —Juergen Moltmann

On November 5, 1863, Abraham Lincoln conferred with a former Louisiana congressman about how to restore state government there, and followed up with a letter to the general whose work overseeing the process had been, thus far, unsatisfactory. A little later he met with a committee of the African Civilization Society who had come to ask for a grant of $5,000 toward solving the problems of race and slavery by sending former slaves to Africa. He collected his October salary voucher ($2,022.33). In the afternoon he rode to Georgetown Heights with John Hay, one of his secretaries. Meanwhile, John Nicolay, his other secretary, a native German, returned healthy from the Rockies, where he had been taking a cure.

We, not Lincoln, seem to be in the position today of deciding which, if any, of these activities was important. Already there is an incurable divide between Lincoln and us. History is different from life: Among events that have already happened, historians filter the interesting from the uninteresting. We select History—we make History—from the standpoint of its consequences.

Even the consequences change. What one historian finds interesting today, such as Lincoln's attempts to send African Americans out of the country, others might dismiss tomorrow. Even today we disagree about Lincoln's intentions, motives, and judgment. Is the African Civilization Society important because it shows Lincoln's understanding of black and white Americans, or because it symbolizes his lack of understanding? Either way, a hundred years of subsequent events creates the backward look. When one considers that Lincoln was a modern and we are postmoderns, the sense of how little we know, or *can* know, begins to dawn.

We cannot go back to Abraham Lincoln any more than I can wish away the First World War and grasp Wilfred Owen's hand. It is our own minds we cannot go through; it is our own knowledge we cannot dissolve. We have lost an innocence that no absolution can restore. The Modern World is dead, and with it any mind that could know where Lincoln stood and hear the man talk. All I can do is make a Lincoln with my bits of knowledge; but to believe that my construction is actually Abraham Lincoln would be foolish. He is gone; he is dead. Perhaps I should go back to my books and leave the world I cannot know in peace. *For lo, between us and you a great chasm has been fixed.* But his world will not leave us in peace. We will listen, in spite of ourselves. His words are enough. Verily, if we do not believe what he said here then, we will not believe though the man should come back from the dead.

There is only one way to find him and to hear his voice. It is through the imagination—and there is no way rationally to verify the imagination. The modern mind rejects it; the postmodern mind mistakes it for desire and fantasy. It is for poets to accept it—those we recognize only after time and wars and tides have come and gone.

Shall we let the man rest, with his soldiers in their graves? The world is different now.

History is not a record of the acts of the dead. It is a struggle between the living and the dead. The living are like Jacob wrestling the angel: To receive the blessing of the past, we must fight it for our lives; we must not let it go. It is stronger than we are, and by it we are named. In History we ask why. Why do human ashes drift over the ruins of time? To ask why is to wrestle with God.

The imagination works by analogy. One thing is like another. The human heart beats the same in all of us. Thus the living understand the dead.

* * *

Up in Evergreen Cemetery again today, I find that the superintendent is still away. I must have a look at the burial records to verify my theory.

Tomorrow, perhaps. Meanwhile, I again remember the past, and imagine my children:

Your grandfather was an earnest man, too earnest probably, and what little of his humor I knew as a child usually presented him as a somewhat comical victim of other people's odd habits. Still, he had a kind *of vanity about him.* It was a sort of fragile pride, perhaps. He had to take his lumps. The first patient that came to his office took one look at him and informed him that she would not be treated by a boy. (He was thirty.) A few years later, hoping a moustache would make him look older and more distinguished, he let it grow. His hair was coal black; the moustache came out red. Comical. Scratch that one. During World War II he tried to enlist in the navy but was told he was too small. In fact, he bought most of his clothing, except suits, in the boys' department. He wore size 7½ AAA shoes.

His shoes were interesting to me because he took such good care of them. In late spring, he brought out his summer shoes—a couple of dozen two-tone models. In the fall he put the trees back into them and took out the solid-color winter shoes. He must have had almost four dozen shoes—but he had bought them all in the 1940s. I never knew him to buy a pair of shoes. They were all in perfect condition, and they were all out of style. But until he became shrunken in his clothes, he always looked dapper. I doubt whether he owned two sport shirts, and certainly not one pair of jeans.

When he became stricken with Parkinson's disease he ceased going out in public, except to work. We used to go out to dinner twice a week with his business partner and former friend. This stopped. Of course, additional reasons developed: for one thing, the business had become a war, and for another, my father no longer had money for going to restaurants. My mother would go out—she needed an escape from the house and her nursing duties at that time—but I was inflamed by the humiliation this must have caused him. I was always invited, but I would not budge. He and I never spoke about it.

Then my grandfather became ill and my mother, Ruth, took the Greyhound up to see him. This left father and son on their own for a week. Ruth had managed, over objections no doubt, finally to get me baptized at age eight and to make a churchgoer out of me. (In a neat twist that perhaps mildly relieved my father, the day I was baptized was not only Easter Sunday but also April Fools' Day.) I had bicycled to Sunday School every Sunday, regardless of the weather, while my mother got a ride to church with a friend. Then I graduated to the High School Youth Services. Finally I began sliding into the regular services. Every Sunday.

Len was pretty much through with the church, an institution for which he had little respect. And of course now he would not be seen in public, limping, shrunken, looking ninety years old.

That Sunday when my mother was gone, he got up at his usual weekday hour. As long as I had known, Len had slept very late on Sundays. When I got up, he was already in his suit and tie. We were going to church.

* * *

In a manner of speaking, he came back to that church only one more time, about sixteen months later. His funeral, on a fifth of November, was for my mother's benefit; it was not anything my father would have wanted. The proceedings were conducted in the rich, syrupy tones of my mother's pastor, in a Lutheran church. The reading was the famous passage from Ecclesiastes:

> To every thing there is a season,
> and a time for every purpose under heaven:
> a time to be born, and a time to die . . .

In meaning, this passage is grim comfort indeed—a flat observation on the cold cyclicism of existence. But in terms of emotion, or sentimentality rather, the sound of the passage can be consolatory.

I had requested that a gold-plated cross of mine be cremated with him. It may have been sentimental but he had had too little of that. Of course, the symbolism of a gold cross was sadly appropriate, as was the fact that Len's favorite color was gold. He had worked furiously to be prosperous for a season—and then his income fell back below the poverty line. L. L. had enjoyed the worst of both worlds, belonging in neither, racing to escape the devils he at last fell into the arms of. Vanity, vanity, saith the Preacher, all is vanity and a chasing after wind.

"Oh, why should the spirit of mortal be proud?"

* * *

Abraham Lincoln was elected by the American public chiefly for his party's ideology, not for his personal character, although his supporters publicized the nickname "Honest Abe." His major opponent, Stephen A. Douglas, was defeated on ideological grounds, though many also distrusted him due to his apparent shiftiness. To have elected the less honest candidate would have avoided Civil War, at least for the time being. But the job of freeing the slaves and killing more than six hundred thousand Americans did not want Douglas, it wanted Lincoln.

The "Question of Character" is not simple. Is character merely a configuration of personality that relates us to the pleasures and pains of a brief existence? Or is character entirely different from personality?

One might assume character to be something you come here with, something you are born with. Lincoln's early life is examined as an unfolding of his character, even while his early experiences are studied for their possible effects upon his characteristics. On one hand, his biographer Herndon discusses the superstitions of backwoods Indiana with a view to their formative effects on the mature president. On the other hand, tendencies toward compassion, satire, storytelling, and quiet thought are displayed as unfoldings of the true Lincoln. In this double procedure there is as much bafflement as explanation, and the question of what character itself is, is left unexamined, remaining mysteriously underneath it all. In studying Lincoln, what are we trying to find out? Are we trying to find out what made him, or explain how he was made?

Lincoln was both a fatalist and a believer in Providence. His life and death seemed to fulfill the terms of literary tragedy. His unlikely career and election, no less than his strangely choreographed death, suggest to some people an inexorable plan. Perhaps character is a tragic dynamism, an interior civil war: It is the drama inside us of fate or circumstances and duty struggling with desire. It is a war between what we want and where we are.

We are beggars. We come to the door empty-handed, with only the simple clothes on our backs, and knock softly. We are given an envelope. And that is us. Some of us, who expected to go to Hollywood or Broadway or Paris—like the nation itself, perhaps—get an envelope with an address scrawled in pencil: "Gettysburg."

* * *

Like many who fought their way through the Great Depression, L. L. was always concerned about money and craved security. He lost a great deal of money trying to get rich quick, and he wrecked what little remained of his health and happiness by making the one financial investment that paid in the long run.

His brother Louis, a plumber, had stood by Len through his schooling, and helped him pay his bills—so Len knew something about salvation by grace. But Len also worked hard and ate little. He had cut hair while in school, and eventually bought his own barbershop. (It must have been an ideal occupation for him; he loved to talk to people. One day, perhaps about nine or ten months after his son was born, he took him out in the stroller, and stopped halfway around the block to talk to someone. Quite a while later, our Norwegian nanny/housekeeper came out to see what had become of them and found Len still talking. "And the kid—*you,*" as she told me years later, "vas yust *blue* vid the cold.")

He was indeed a musician, though I never heard him play a note. He had played violin, banjo, melodeon, and I am not sure what else. He played a lot of ballrooms but he still went hungry. "I used to fill the belly up with water," he said. When I knew him, he would use his paper napkin for days if he could get away with it. He carried one neatly folded tissue. I grew up being admonished always to turn out the electric lights, so as not to be "working for the Electric Company."

But he was shamelessly generous. Every so often an effusively grateful old acquaintance would come out of the woodwork, someone in town for a meeting, or someone we would visit on a trip to a National Chiropractic Convention; somebody Len had helped out, given a lot of money to, back in the tough times.

He was also very interested in helping himself. Having pulled himself up by the bootstraps, he did not want to slip back down again. He made catastrophic investments. Absolutely, unfailingly, inevitably honest himself, he could never imagine that the sincere person with the gleaming scheme might simply disappear with the money. Which is what happened several times.

Two schemes involved unconscious teaching systems. One was "sleep teaching"—a canard of which Len must have bought every expensive record ever produced, for himself and his patients. The other method had been sold to him a decade or two in advance of "sleep teaching." It was elaborate and expensive, involving speakers in every treatment room, special machinery to make special sounds, and of course the recordings had to be made. It cost $75,000, back in the thirties. The fast-talking entrepreneur took the money and disappeared. Based upon what I was told by other people, I estimate the total loss in these investments to have been around $300,000. That would be well over $1 million in today's money.

What it assured L. L. of was having to work like a dog to get money back into the bank. Then the next smooth-talking salesman would come along. When Len died he had no savings account whatsoever, and just $300 in checking.

Of course he had signed up for life insurance policies—which he was forced to borrow against. He had also taken out two policies on me, for college, the year I was born. Thirty-eight years later I dissolved both of those worthless scraps, sick of paying the premiums. (I rolled them over for a better, much improved policy.) Some of Len's most loyal friends were his insurance agents.

By the mid-1960s, Len's practice had dwindled down to a faithful remnant. The advancing disease was taking strength out of his muscles and control from his nerves, steadily reducing his ability to perform the chiropractor's stock-in-trade spinal adjustments. Sometimes a strong and skillful pair of hands can move the vertebrae and other bones back where they belong and tone the muscles to keep them there. Well, Len could not jerk necks anymore, for which I was grateful, but his income fell to under $3,000 per year. And we lived in an exclusive suburb. We were the only people there who did not have a car.

Len's get-rich-quick investments had ruined it all. But his most catastrophic investments had been for education. He always felt he should elevate his patients. Why waste the time they spent under heat treatment, or light treatment, or traction? Play them records. Give them the opportunity to lift themselves, as he had lifted himself. Some of the records were about finances, about investing, about getting rich. Some reassuringly described ways to develop a healthful frame of mind. His most valued records lectured on spiritual growth. Len believed the mind and body were a unit.

He did not neglect his own education. We borrowed money and bought a car—a Chrysler as big as the Brandenburg Gate, always needing repairs—and I drove him to seminars and classes. He was developing a way to adjust the spine without using force. "Never force nothing," he said. Eventually he came up with a technique of using small wooden blocks and wedges, slipping them under the hips, targeted vertebrae, and so on, then slowly moving the patient's leg or arm. You could feel the vertebrae move. And it would not stress the joint.

Most patients missed that satisfying, heart-stopping crack. I did not. In spite of myself I respected what he kept on doing, long after many people would have given in—and today I think any bone-cracking chiropractor is a cave man.

He never considered retirement. The morning of his stroke, at age seventy, he was getting ready to go to his office. But to continue working he had been compelled to sustain the worst defeat of his life. Long before, he had quit medical school and devoted his life to the idea that the body must be, and could be, cured naturally. "The body cures itself." No drugs. No drugs whatsoever. He would not even take aspirin.

I became a spectacular hay fever sufferer at about age seven. From then through high school I was chronic. Every August brought a carnival of sneezes, vociferous muscle-developing jolts, along with tearing eyes. I was in utterly inescapable misery. My mother remembered sitting by my bedside in fear that I would stop breathing. But no antihistamines for this boy. "Beats up the linings of the sinuses. You'll pay for it in the long run." So, except when my mother sneaked out to her M.D. and smuggled me back a prescription, it was "natural" remedies only.

The worst remedy I can remember was a kind of grain that was supposed to build up my immunity to pollen. Eat it every morning instead of cereal, starting six months before hay fever season. And no quarter. The stuff was like BB-sized rubber pellets, virtually impervious to milk, time, or misery. I would have to commence breakfast early, and stand the course late, gnawing on those leathery brown things filling my bowl. I need not mention what impact that stretch I did, from January to July, had upon the season's hay fever.

But one thing he did do: He bought me a Puritron, a machine to filter the air. Not the base model, but the two-compartment version. A conservative, I always used only one side, wanting to save the second filter and fan for the long run, for when I would be forty, or eighty. In August and September, demonstrating Newton's Second Law a hundred times an hour practically to the point of tears of frustration and rage, I could turn on the machine next to my bed at night. In a while I would be better. Not free, but better. The mind and body are one.

That machine gave off a faint smell that duplicated the clean, lifting fragrance emitted by one of the light treatment machines in my father's office. It came from a chicory-blue bulb inside, and the machine in the office had a very large circular coiled bulb of the same color. The fan of the machine humming unfailingly beside me, the lovely small blue light, and the clean, clean fragrance that lifted the heart were unspeakably comforting. I knew I would be better soon, and would stay better through the night. Each year I almost looked forward to hay fever season, when I could take the precious white machine down from the highest shelf in my closet and turn it on at night—no admonitions regarding the electric company—and have it running tranquilly beside me. And for years, even into adulthood, it has been the same comfort. I use it seldom now, but it runs quietly and faithfully still, the light is still a pale chicory-blue, and the clean, clean fragrance still consoles and lifts the heart.

* * *

Len must have loved music as a child, but as a young man he used it as a means of earning money. Like Lincoln, he believed that if one worked hard, educated oneself, and worked harder, one could "better his condition in life." But Len's life is an illustration of how certain aspects of modern thought can end in futility. For Len, all was vanity and a chasing after wind. So it will always be for some, no matter how smart they are, no matter how hard they work. And many will have sold the beauty in their souls to buy the dream. Providence, fate, or circumstance sometimes decrees that some lives must be failures; some will never "better their conditions in life." Fundamentally, this is true for all of us. *Naked came I from my mother's womb, and naked shall I return.*

If there is nothing but pecuniary economics in Lincoln's American Dream, then we are all headed on a course of ultimate futility. There must be something deeper. Behind the dream is a vision of justice, and beyond that, equality. But if we are equal, it is not because we have made ourselves so. Ultimately it makes no difference whether a man or woman is driven by an overseer with a lash, or whether that slave driver is oneself. "It is the same tyrannical principle." We will never prove anything. We have been "created equal," or we have not. Glorious though it is, the American Dream cannot prove one side or the other.

* * *

Wilfred Owen and my father did their duty, and duty means putting the interests of others before your own. Overruling oneself seems to be the first quality of a hero. That is why so often we study war when we want to learn about heroes: courage is the first thing demanded of a hero.

But there must be more to heroism than dutifulness. That is the *sine qua non,* but only the beginning. Why do we single out a few from the thousands, millions, who do their duty? A soldier, a father, a mother—each learns the economy of life: you give of yours, so others may have theirs. Heroism, as a durable good, must have an element of love in it somewhere. But the heroic requires still more, and I intend to tramp through this month to find it.

The rains of the past few days have ended. It is about time. Why interrupt or distract from the severity of the month?

> The Willows and the Hazel Copses green
> Shall no more be seen.

I will spend the next three days walking in silence. The route from World War I to the next horror is nasty, brutish, and short. People who fought the first war led the second. But despite the terrible fighting of the soldiers in

World War II, what that war did to civilization and modernism involved civilians. For the first time in Europe since perhaps the Thirty Years' War, civilian deaths outnumbered soldier deaths. The proportion was roughly three to one. The essence of that horror was the Holocaust. To that anniversary, the sere pages of November lead.

NOVEMBER 9

Never Forget (Nights of Broken Glass)

Remembering is the same thing as hoping.
—Paul Ricoeur

Between Lincoln's time and the new millennium stretches a century of barbed wire and broken glass. Sixty years ago the Nazis burned, defaced, and destroyed businesses and synagogues all across Germany. Shattered windows of businesses owned by Jews gave November 9, 1938, the name *Kristallnacht,* "night of broken glass."

As leaves cease falling in November, the forest floor becomes a pale brown uniform. Like ghostly soldiers, gray tree trunks spread their battalions across the swales of sweet-smelling, crisp decay. Skies are gray and sunsets are bloody. Farmers burn bonfires; into the night their shreds of smoke rise and cross, making broken crystal of the cold November heavens.

It is difficult to fix a date for the end of the Modern World, but since the Holocaust we have known it was over. The world we knew might have vanished on November 11, 1918, when the Western Front's eerie silence ended the vast nightmare that shelled to pieces the illusion of human progress. The old world might have ended in November 1914 as Albert Einstein finished work on his General Theory of Relativity, which showed that the universe cannot be like anything the human mind is capable of imagining.

Or perhaps for the present generation of American leaders the Modern World, with its belief in reason and progress, ended on November 22, 1963, perishing as the body of John F. Kennedy lay under electric lights in Parkland Memorial Hospital. Maybe it perished in Vietnam. Many of that generation have never trusted reasonable explanations since those days, nor can they think of "progress" without irony. The world they grew up in has become a childish fantasy.

But the evaporation of what human beings over centuries have learned to rely upon from day to day did not begin with us. It is possible that modernism was struck its death-wound during the American Civil War. The time since has been a long, slow dying, a steady darkening of the modern era. Now we are engaged in "a long twilight struggle."

Modern ideas do not seem to work anymore. With the ideas have gone the beliefs. Law, poetry, history, and theology have been deconstructed into free-floating nets of language with no connections to anything else—mere *words, words, words.* We are left

> . . . as on a darkling plain
> Swept with confused alarms of struggle and flight,
> Where ignorant armies clash by night.

Some people are happy that the Modern World is gone, because modernity meant complacent belief in material, artistic, scientific, political, and social progress on human terms, in human hands. Modernism bypassed our spiritual nature and proceeded as if there were no God. After the grass of the field was thrown into the ovens, and human smoke ascended into vacant skies, no Word of the Lord has remained.

Those who rejoice over the end of the Modern World and its mistaken glories need to think about what comes after an age that assumed human beings were valuable and that certain happy truths about them were self-evident. The bright days of looking into the human mirror may be gone; now we wander alone through nights of broken glass.

As darkness drops, a clamor rises, climbing, winding around the ascending ashes. The gloom is all the more nightmarish and deep for its interlocked and blinking technology, its absorbing surface of information. Our brains got us into this; perhaps memory can help us get out. We need to reconnect the past to the future. Vietnam and Gettysburg can be forgotten if we agree to abandon the duties they impose on us. History's effects on us can never be escaped, and what we forget will descend upon our children.

The children. If the Holocaust is unthinkable, then how men and women could do what they did to children is unimaginable. If our rights to life, liberty, and the pursuit of happiness came from God, where did the SS get their right to kill, confine, and destroy children? I think Mr. Lincoln knew where it came from. He saw it clearly. It was not simply in *the enemy,* it was in all his people; it appeared more stridently but certainly not exclusively in the South. It was a principle.

This principle is rooted in what, not where, we are. Hitler's Germans had no monopoly on it. Saint Paul saw it; Augustine saw it; Luther saw it; the Founding Fathers saw it and their program was to limit it. Lincoln understood that it festered in America. There is, as he might have put it, a difference in purpose between the Almighty and ourselves. It is beyond our own curing. *None can keep alive his own soul.*

The world believed otherwise until the children died. Our hand parted from God's then; our cherished beliefs were liquidated. One child seized from her apartment, marched through the streets, crowded into a boxcar, ordered out where the train stopped, pulled from her mother's grasp, pushed into line before a gas chamber—her fate is enough to destroy all modern beliefs. The Modern World left us nowhere to stand but beside her ashes. Her flesh and blood have turned to powder, cold as the colorless sky.

Our idea of God was only flesh and blood: a pattern in our pumping brains. Ideas are words and words are wind. God has come down from omnipotence, omniscience, justice, and all the high and lofty thoughts he inhabited before: all has crashed to flesh and blood. Flesh and blood burn. Such stuff has been transformed to putrid smoke.

Faith is fire. Beliefs are faith's fuel: it burns them.

Elie Wiesel's words stand etched on a wall inside the Holocaust Museum in Washington, D.C. In a darkened room where exhaust fans continuously and ineffectively draw off air laden with the odor of deteriorating leather, hundreds of pairs of shoes taken from Jewish families at the extermination camps lie piled and spread: business shoes, workmen's shoes, high heels, and the shoes of children.

On the wall across from these shoes is written an excerpt from this passage in Wiesel's *Night:*

> Never shall I forget that night, the first night in camp, which has turned my life into one long night, seven times cursed and seven times sealed. Never shall I forget that smoke.
>
> Never shall I forget the little faces of the children, whose bodies I saw turned into wreaths of smoke beneath a silent blue sky.
>
> Never shall I forget those flames which consumed my faith forever.
>
> Never shall I forget that nocturnal silence which deprived me, for all

> eternity, of the desire to live. Never shall I forget those moments which murdered my God and my soul and turned my dreams to dust. Never shall I forget these things, even if I am condemned to live as long as God Himself. Never.

After speaking to the National Press Club in 1997, Mr. Wiesel was asked whether his experience during the Holocaust destroyed his faith, as this passage seems to say. No, he answered. I have a wounded faith.

Faith cannot die; it is not of our making. It is the only evidence of God when all the evidence is shattered. Faith cries out to God: "Why?" But *God hath no ears.* All we know is our cry. The rest is silence.

Today we are lost, so we go looking for Mr. Lincoln. What would Abraham Lincoln say if the children who died in the camps were his own? Perhaps here at Gettysburg he said it to the World War II generation—those of our fathers and mothers who helped save the world from Abraham and Sarah's killers. Lincoln's words had made civilization unsafe for inequality. The grandchildren of Lincoln's brave men kept the faith; they did not accept a world without rights and justice. They ventured their flesh and blood in the crucible of a war that to them was necessary. They entered war's evil, shed their security, and accepted a naked mortality. Whoever or whatever gave Nazis the power to segregate and kill, our parents hated and resisted. For their part, they would deny evil any right to the world. They were Lincoln's children, believing that all people are created equal.

The Civil War and World War II are directly related. The principle behind the idea of "master race" and the principle behind the man who says, in Lincoln's words, "you earn the bread, and I'll eat it," are "*the same tyrannical principle.*" But the relationship between the two wars was also a very practical one. With two nations here, possibly hostile to one another and neither as strong as the United States combined, who would have helped England survive? Who would have opened a second front to relieve the Russian army? Who would have produced more ships, planes, tanks, and guns than the Germans and Japanese? Who would have landed at Omaha Beach?

We cannot answer the question made by the Holocaust's horror. We cannot account for one child sacrificed to Moloch. Let Lincoln's answer suffice for now; let Lincoln's answer stand.

NOVEMBER 11

Long Endure
(Armistice Day)

The superintendent has been gone a week. Doesn't he know that people die, waiting? Down in a newer part of the National Cemetery a small ceremony is taking place. Today is Veterans Day—what used to be called Armistice Day.

On November 11, 1918, the Armistice silenced the ancient guns on the Western Front. Wilfred Owen's parents, in the English town of Shrewsbury, had not received any news from the front in more than a week. They had no knowledge of the 2nd Manchesters' attack on the Sambre and Oise Canal. At about eleven o'clock, as church bells in Shrewsbury pealed out the unfathomable relief, a very small bell rang at the Owens' front door. They were handed a telegram from the War Office.

On the same day, Harold Owen also got a message. Harold was at sea half a world away. Since the two brothers had been very close throughout Wilfred's life, it was with a certain irony—not a bitter irony, but a strange irony—that Harold had found himself assigned to the cruiser *Astraea*, "whose launching the *Times* had reported on 18 March 1893, the day Wilfred Owen was born." This is Harold Owen's description of what happened on the day of the Armistice:

NOVEMBER 11

We were lying off Victoria. I had gone down to my cabin thinking to write some letters. I drew aside the door curtain and stepped inside and to my amazement I saw Wilfred sitting in my chair. I felt shock run through me with appalling force and with it I could feel the blood draining away from my face. I did not rush toward him but walked jerkily into the cabin—all my limbs stiff and slow to respond. I did not sit down but looking at him I spoke quietly: "Wilfred, how did you get here?" He did not rise and I saw that he was involuntarily immobile, but his eyes which had never left mine were alive with the familiar look of trying to make me understand; when I spoke his whole face broke into his sweetest and most endearing dark smile. I felt no fear—I had not when I first drew my door curtain and saw him there; only exquisite mental pleasure at thus beholding him. All I was conscious of was a sensation of enormous shock and profound astonishment that he should be here in my cabin. I spoke again. "Wilfred dear, how can you be here, it's just not possible . . . " But still he did not speak but only smile his most gentle smile. This not speaking did not now as it had done at first seem strange or even unnatural; it was not only in some inexplicable way perfectly natural but radiated a quality which made his presence with me undeniably right and in no way out of the ordinary. I loved having him there: I could not, and did not want to try to understand how he had got there. I was content to accept him, that he was here with me was sufficient. I could not question anything, the meeting in itself was complete and strangely perfect. He was in uniform and I remember thinking how out of place the khaki looked amongst the cabin furnishings. With this thought I must have turned my eyes away from him; when I looked back my cabin chair was empty. . . .

I felt the blood run slowly back to my face and looseness into my limbs and with these an overpowering sense of emptiness and absolute loss. . . . I wondered if I had been dreaming but looking down I saw that I was still standing. Suddenly I felt terribly tired and moving to my bunk I lay down; instantly I went into a deep oblivious sleep. When I woke up I knew with absolute certainty that Wilfred was dead.

"Dead"?

* * *

L. L. had got to the point where painstakingly rocking himself out of bed in the morning was a ten-minute procedure. He could no longer dress himself. The last thing—going to the office to see patients—was almost gone. At this point he finally accepted crucifixion: he began taking a drug for the Parkinson's.

He had always preached that in the long run, a drug will do you more damage than good. He might have been right about this drug: it might have brought on the stroke. But he made the Achillean trade: an earlier death for the ability to do his work. It was a sensible, if harsh, bargain; the exquisite torture of it was that he had to do, and admit to doing, what his life's work had stood against. He surrendered, body if not soul, to his nemesis, his personal devil. Character occurs at the intersection of love, duty, desire, and circumstance. It is a crossroads town in Adam's county.

The name of the drug was humiliating: "aldopa." Sounded like El Dopa; might as well have been El Druggo. Let us make the very sound of it advertise the defeat. As a result of this Mephistophelean bargain, as necessary as fate, my father's mobility was partially restored. Shaving still took a half hour. (Afterward his electric razor was hot as a coal.) But he could dress himself. He had to get up at 5:30 to be ready by seven, when he rode downtown with our neighbors, but he could do it on his own again. Until *wham,* the shot in the head.

As we stood in his room the Sunday he died—the associate pastor had arrived and the body had not been removed yet—my mother, looking at the ashen face, the arms somewhat outstretched, said, "He looks like Christ on the cross." The pastor agreed, quite evidently feeling he ought to agree with whatever the distraught, irrational widow said. Of Norwegian descent himself, he understood, or thought he understood, that this woman was as hysterical as a Scandinavian gets.

Norwegians handle things by not talking about them. Their language is as subtle as the old Norse sagas, seeming to remark about one thing, but actually revealing an entire world to those who have learned the grammar of reserve. The only mention Ruth ever made of Len's years of humiliation, the agonized mornings and evenings, the inexorably dwindling practice, the poverty, the surrender to the enemy (to drugs, the Father of Lies)—was the comment, "He looks like Christ on the cross."

The pastor had another problem because Len had wanted nothing—or almost nothing—to do with the church. He had never joined a church, and had little use for organized Christianity. His attitude verged to the left of distaste, toward contempt. Only once did I hear him describe his religious classification. An old friend of Ruth's asked him where he stood on religion, and he answered that he was a "freethinker." The word stuck with me. Now I believe a free thinker is the only kind of thinker anyone ought to be, the only kind of faithful person there is.

But I did not think so in high school. He entertained notions any self-respecting adolescent who had read Bertrand Russell's history of philosophy would not take seriously for a minute.

In the first place, he was a Rosicrucian. Every month there arrived a thick packet of reading material from California, mixing ancient astrology, modern science, psychology, mystic symbolism, Eastern philosophies, and whatnot. He also believed in "psychic phenomena"; he was a spiritualist of sorts. Shortly after his death one of his innumerable old friends called me. "Has L. L. crossed over? I saw him. I felt a terrible physical hunger—terrific pangs."

In this bizarre way I learned something about his suffering. Len had been fed intravenously for over two months. His hunger had never occurred to me. But it should have; it was only logical.

This physician had not been able to heal himself. His was a drawn-out agony. "Like Christ on the cross." And mental agony? He had not been able to move at all. For two months he had been unconscious. Then one day his eyes were open, and could follow you around the room. Closed again. But when we shaved him, he puffed out his cheeks.

He could form words, barely, after another week. One afternoon he looked "deep in thought," and my mother bent close to him to ask what he was thinking about. This man on his cross, who I thought had basically ignored me all my life, pronounced, carefully and distinctly, the name of my college.

About six weeks after that call, I suddenly knew my father was in the room where I was sitting and reading. I did not see him, as Harold Owen saw his brother, but I was as certain of his presence as I was of my own name. Some might say that the father was teaching something important to his son. As a modern, I merely report an experience. As a postmodern, I merely connect this text about L. L. to another text:

> Look homeward Angel now . . .
> For *Lycidas* your sorrow is not dead . . .

* * *

The Killer Angels, a 1976 novel about the Battle of Gettysburg, was written because its author, Michael Shaara, believed that Generals Robert E. Lee and James Longstreet had spoken to him—across one hundred years, across the gulf of life and death. The film based upon the book, in turn, was made as its director *felt* the ghosts of Gettysburg, including Michael Shaara, who died four years before the filming but who seemed present on the battlefield. Some of the reenactors who did the movie say they saw ghosts on the field during their encampment/production in the summer of 1992. But I, who read the book, saw the film, and visit the battlefield, have seen no ghosts there. Clearly, the ghosts are afraid of me. With good reason. I am a living, breathing citizen of the United States at the turn of the millennium. I am therefore a hazard to myself and others.

Take, for instance, my reaction to a photograph in a news magazine a few years ago. It showed the battered, punctured, near-naked dead body of a U.S. serviceman being triumphantly dragged down a street in an African country. That night on the news a U.S. senator was explaining how the deaths proved that we should pull out of that region. I could not fathom that way of thinking. How the country has changed. In 1860, such a photograph—in fact, considerably less—might have sent the North or South to war. I felt our honor had been violated. Were I younger, I might have volunteered to go myself. Actually, were I younger, I might have had more sense. I had reacted more rationally to Vietnam twenty-five years previously.

The National Cemetery at Gettysburg contains the graves of U.S. servicemen who died in Vietnam. As I walk past them today, as I stop to read the names, I must decide what to think—about men who were my college acquaintances, and about myself. Do we ever know enough to make the decisions demanded of us? Are we sound enough in ourselves to use our knowledge rightly, even when it suffices?

"You are your own worst enemy," my father used to tell me. (I do not recommend talking this way to little boys.) His statement is not a bad description of Christian theology on the subject of human nature, nor would it be out of place as a caution pertaining to what we think we know. It certainly accords with the "perennial philosophy"—the combination of mysticism and Eastern thought to which Len more or less subscribed. Chance, illness, and other people—maybe even devils—can injure our bodies, but only we ourselves can hurt ourselves "in the long run"; only we can injure our souls. But we can befriend that inner Self, too.

Len occasionally took me to the zoo on Sundays—by bus, of course. With his perennial facility for liking people and their liking him in return, Len struck up an acquaintanceship with a zookeeper who worked in the giraffe building. This resulted in the ineffable experience of me, a five year old, feeding the tallest giraffe, whom my father called "Looie."

The zookeeper lifted me up on his shoulder. So, for starters, I was seven feet off the ground. I wobbled up there, so high off the ground that my stomach spun as I grabbed onto the man's head—but then he lifted a slice of white bread up to me and I had to use one hand to hold it. (The white bread made an impression because we never had it at home. I was troubled that the giraffe received poor nutrition.) Then came the fright that washed away all those fears.

The huge giraffe worked its legs toward us. Down out of the precipitous heights came a huge, alien face, descending down, down, down toward me, larger and larger. I held up the tasteless, non-nutritious bread. The great unearthly face, its parchment skin and large leather-brown patches, the huge, intent, soft eyes that saw me and saw through me into my fear and awe—an inscrutable look that comprehended and transcended me: he took the offering. Out of the great face, past parting lips and big, long teeth, emerged a great tongue. I was absolutely transfixed by terror and wonder. The rough, grayish tongue wrapped partly around the bread, barely touching my hand, feeling leathery and harshly adhesive, and withdrew into the long mouth. Chewing down and around, down and around, the eyes at first still looking at me but then moving off, the great face slowly moved back up to the heights. Exhausted, I was lowered onto wobbly legs.

I did not realize it then, but the name by which my father addressed the giraffe, "Looie," was his own brother's name.

* * *

My father also took me to some ball games. Milwaukee won the World Series around the time we first went, so I thought that Milwaukee would always have Warren Spahn, Henry Aaron, Eddie Mathews, and Lew Burdette; that the National Anthem ended with "the land of the free, and the home of the Braves"; and that we could have heroes in our own hometown. But we always sat in the lower grandstand, because Len had a phobia about heights. He said that if he went higher, he would have the terrible urge to throw himself down.

Len was not made of many heroic materials, perhaps, but he gave what he had, and that was heroic enough. He was "peculiarsome" all right, with his phobias, physical frailties, obsessions, and poor financial judgment. He was no Oliver Cromwell, Thomas Gray might have observed—but in this country we can all be a little like Abraham Lincoln. We can work hard for ourselves and give our best away. Heroes in a democracy are not supermen or saints, but men and women who do not believe that futility is an excuse for doing nothing. We need not invent fantastic images, Napoleons and Caesars, nor believe their lies. It is for us, the living, rather to draw from ordinary men and women like our own parents the qualities that we wish to enact ourselves. Our heroes teach us what we are, and what we may be. Heroes in "that nation" of Lincoln's help us to be better than we were born to be.

* * *

One gray, dull day I drove my father to a doctor for an examination. The specialist was a hale, solid man, intelligent and masterful, in his early fifties. As Len laboriously removed his suit coat and shirt in another room, this doctor nodded toward the door and said, “I’ve known your dad for many years.” He paused, giving me a casual, sidelong look. “You’re a lucky young man.”

Me?

“I wish I had had a father like yours.” He nodded again toward the door. “That’s a great man in there. He’s done so much for so many people. If it weren’t for your father, I don’t know where I’d be.”

We cannot save ourselves. If America forgets its history, it forgets its mothers and fathers, and therefore no longer knows itself. The mid-November trees are bare. All the fathers, mothers, Lincolns, and gods are dead; all we know of spring must come from memory, hope, and faith.

NOVEMBER 14

The Brave Men (Ia Drang)

Today, Mr. Lincoln's speech must be nearly finished. He has to go to Gettysburg in four days, on the eighteenth, to deliver the speech on the nineteenth. I wonder if he held the sheets of paper in his hand and gazed out the White House window—I wonder if he saw anything of his children's children's vague forms—the combat fatigues, web gear, helicopters over their heads. Might he have heard them asking why? Did he know that his words on that White House stationery would be needed for other wars, for *our* wars?

Somewhat fewer than sixty thousand soldiers were killed in Vietnam; approximately ten times that many died in the Civil War. Figuring numbers of enrollments alone—about three million during Vietnam and four million during the Civil War—one had not quite ten times more likelihood of being killed fighting in the 1860s than in the 1960s.

At Ia Drang, November 14–17, 1965, only a fraction of Gettysburg's killed were lost by the 1st Air Cavalry Division: 7,000 killed at Gettysburg, 305 at Ia Drang. But 150,000 Americans were engaged in Pennsylvania, only somewhere around 1,000 at Ia Drang. The 2nd Battalion, 7th Cavalry, took about 450 men into the landing zone in the Ia Drang Valley, and came out with about 100: 150 had been killed, 130 wounded, others missing. The killed-to-wounded ratio was incredible by Civil War standards—which were about 5 or 6 wounded for each man killed. The 24th Michigan of the Iron Brigade lost 73 percent of its 496 men on the first day at Gettysburg, a higher loss, but fewer killed. The 2nd Wisconsin lost 77 percent going in with 300 men.

In the Army of the Potomac you might be in the war for three, or even four, years. In Vietnam the tour of duty was twelve months. A combat regiment in the Union or Confederate army at Gettysburg would stand a good chance of losing nearly all its original men during the course of its enrollment. At Appomattox, Pickett's whole division (six thousand strong before the charge at Cemetery Ridge) was down to sixty men. The comparisons mean nothing as comparisons, but the numbers make the point that war is all hell, as Sherman said.

Aeschylus wrote that truth is the first casualty in war. But we can afford to bury only so much truth. Take the figures above, for instance. In *Dispatches,* Michael Herr wrote that reporters covering the aftermath of the Ia Drang battle believed that not three hundred Americans, but maybe three times that many, had been killed. It would seem that the numbers engaged, along with army records, cast doubt on the reporters' estimates, but army figures are not exactly reliable. They were meant to look reliable, though. The "estimate" of North Vietnamese dead at Ia Drang is 3,561. Pretty exact for an estimate. The Vietcong and North Vietnamese Army did suffer hundreds of thousands of killed by the stupendous American firepower during the war, but one can never be sure of numbers. The nightly news reported ridiculous figures fed to it by the U.S. government. I talked to a soldier who served in an information job, sent out regularly to photograph "supply dumps" (small piles of rice) and "body counts." He had no belief in official army estimates.

As to Gettysburg, there can be no certainty of Confederate numbers engaged or of killed and wounded. What the Army of Northern Virginia headquarters reported, adding numbers given it from down the chain of command, was lower than what civilian burial parties found on the field during the long disinterment period, and perhaps a thousand have never been found.

So comparisons cannot be made, and perhaps should not be made. But a connection can be made. On November 17, 1965, Larry L. Hess was killed at Ia Drang. The twenty-year-old second lieutenant was from Gettysburg, Pennsylvania.

Someday people will be as far from the Vietnam War as we are from the Civil War. Someday both wars will be so far back that they will come together, like the Crusades, like the Punic Wars, like the battles of the Third Dynasty. Vietnam and Gettysburg will meet in any mind that hears or reads the stories.

But they are also meeting in the America we are making today. “This story is about time and memories,” begins the book about Ia Drang, *We Were Soldiers Once . . . and Young.* “The time was 1965 . . . when one era was ending in America and another was beginning. . . . The class of 1965 came out of the old America, a nation that disappeared forever in the smoke that billowed off the jungle battlegrounds where we fought and bled. The country that sent us off to war was not there to welcome us home. It no longer existed.”

Whether what soldiers faced in Vietnam was worse than Korea, World War II, or other wars is debatable. In each war, soldiers do what they were taught by churches and mothers not to do. In every war, this could be written:

> I guess deep down in my head now I can’t really believe in God like I did because I can’t really see why God would let something like this happen. . . .
>
> . . . I’ve talked to chaplains, talked to preachers about Vietnam. And no one could give me a satisfactory explanation of what happened overseas.
>
> But each year since I’ve been back I have read the Bible from cover to cover, I keep looking for the explanation.
>
> I can’t find it. I can’t find it.

* * *

Many young people at that time thought the answer—the evil—was in ourselves. Therefore they believed that the war should be ended and, to that purpose, the draft resisted. Had the American public changed so much—had *human nature* changed so much—that by 1968 we were a generation full of cowards? I doubt it. It is one of the characteristics of youth to throw aside fear in patriotic fervor. Why not during Vietnam?

Now, looking back, we might see Vietnam simply as a war between freedom and totalitarianism. But at the time, a lot of young people were not so sure.

The young people who were not so sure were in college. They were not so sure not simply because they enjoyed their pot-smoking ease in college more than they thought they would like it in the jungles of Southeast Asia, but because they had access to information about Vietnam, about what war is like, about the objections to Vietnam. They also had access to the 2S draft-deferment classification. Combine doubts concerning a war with the ability to stay out of it, and you have a lot of *other guys* going in. Why didn't the college students simply accept their 2Ss then, along with their free-loving, long-haired Woodstock women and Jimi Hendrix records, and keep quiet—if all they wanted was to stay out?

Because of the 1960s idealism which seems so foreign today. A lot of idealists stayed out for a purpose. To this group, the war was *wrong;* it was simply that. If it was enough for Lincoln, in 1858, that slavery was simply *wrong,* then it was enough in 1968, if the war was simply *wrong,* to oppose it and to resist it—for one's own sake, for America's sake, perhaps for God's sake. Every patriotic American was obligated to do *right* and not *wrong.*

For many others, their obligation was not arrived at by figuring it out in their own minds, with unreliable and biased information, but by answering the call of *duty.* This call was issued by the country, and one's duty was to answer the call. One side believed that the call could not be questioned by each individual, because at a certain point we must rely on our duly elected leaders, and the call then came from a transcendent entity: the United States of America. The other side saw the call not as coming from a transcendent entity, or in any sense from the traditional, historic United States of Lincoln and Washington, but from some specific individuals: from Lyndon Johnson, a murderous yokel; or from Richard Milhous Nixon, worse beyond description. Both of these politicians were seen as hypocrites (a conclusion which subsequent developments and revelations have not entirely contradicted), and hypocrisy is one thing not tolerated by youth.

As a youth, I probably should have consulted my father. But I did not. I could not imagine him having an opinion on the subject. Or maybe I did not want to hear what I was afraid he would say. But ultimately I felt it was a decision I had to make on my own. Ultimately, it was up to me; the issue was in my mind and my conscience alone. And this is just the essence of the late-sixties mentality: I must decide for myself; no reliable authority existed, no authority that I was obligated to. Except one. That one authority was God. (This might not have been part of the essence of 1960s thinking.) Presidents and draft boards were under Him also. How could one know what God wanted? The only way was to sound out one's own conscience. Thus "God" is co-opted into the small circle. But there was no alternative. No authority represented Him reliably: not the Church, not the Bible, not—certainly not—the state. The 1960s was a "decade of disillusionment." The educated, or partly educated, young people were both idealistic and disillusioned—a perhaps unique combination that characterized the 1960s.

Meanwhile, on the other side—for this was America's second civil war—the war ground on and, like it or not, we had to go. Most of us were poor and ignorant. We were eighteen years old, and when the 1A classification came, and then the draft notice, we simply went because no alternative ever came into our heads. Some of us said, Hell no, I don't want to go—but we went anyway because it was the law. If there is a war and you are drafted, you have to go. Others of us were idealistic about it: We went because America was fighting for freedom over there. Just as my father went when his turn came, so it is my duty to go. I don't ask that the cowards join me over there, just that they keep their unpatriotic mouths shut and don't shoot me in the back with their demonstrations and votes. We, too, were disillusioned—with the war itself, and with the America that sent us over there to do its killing.

Sixty thousand American soldiers and vets are dead, and so are several hundred thousand Vietnamese. And this month, American companies are negotiating with the Vietnamese to sell cola and automobiles there. You see; we were *all* right to be disillusioned.

There is a distinction between veterans and *combat* veterans. David Regan, a marine combat veteran of two tours of duty in Vietnam, wrote about his day of discharge: "I had no goodbyes to make, no addresses to write down, no promises to keep. There was only a vague feeling that what I had done was wrong. I had relegated myself to the level of a beast; a mindless, soulless animal, capable of committing unspeakable violations of human dignity." One does not recover from this "vague feeling" with time, any more than from cancer.

Well, what followed the Vietnam War, like the Civil War, was a "gilded age," as Mark Twain called it—a binge of materialism and corruption. A lot of guilty hands getting and spending.

Meanwhile, about nine thousand comfortless combat veterans (a number comparable in percentage to other wars) were turning weapons on themselves, as if they had internalized Victor Charlie and the thing in baggy black was their own unforgiven life. But the great majority found their way back into what they called over there, with good reason, "the World."

But there were others. Regan again: "Of course, everybody knows a 'Johnny down the block' who is making good despite his wheelchair. The trouble is that the only people we ever see are the Johnnys who make good. We never, ever, see the Sams and Freds who are still in the back ward at the VA hospital, getting washed and turned once a day."

Have we forgotten what a lousy war Vietnam was? Have we forgotten that it ate the guts out of Lyndon Johnson's Great Society program, stunted Martin Luther King's civil rights movement? Have we forgotten why returning veterans sometimes were shunned?

Many of the people who went to Vietnam did so in ignorance or moral indifference, just as many of the people who protested did so because it was in fashion. But on both sides, those who *knew* what they were doing were patriots. As in the Civil War, one side fought for liberty, the other for justice. Such a division is tragic, because ultimately the two—freedom and justice—are one; neither can live without the other.

So the future will see photographs of protesters giving the finger to raw recruits, and photographs of dead college students shot down by Nixon's soldiers. It is hard to take these kids (ourselves) seriously, now that we are middle-aged, or to say anything except "a plague on both your houses"—but history will enshrine the moment as it has enshrined the Civil War. After all, a youthful disagreement that results not only in several hundred thousand dead boys, but also in children, women, and old people slaughtered, is serious one way or another. But now that we are old enough to be cool-headed about it, the old bastards who got us into it are long gone, and we sit here with our wounds, our memories, and our corroded middle age.

* * *

Those who lived through the 1960s have a chance at understanding something about the 1860s. War is a constant; suffering is its general condition. When you enlist, you are volunteering to suffer. Perhaps you will suffer for others, but you *will* suffer. Lee's seventeen-mile-long wagon train of wounded in the retreat from Gettysburg provides a view into the nature of soldiering:

> All along the route by which this train made its way, broken wagons and dead and dying soldiers were strewed. The bottoms of the wagons were smeared with blood. Barns and houses were improvised into hospitals. Groans and shrieks of agony filled the air as the wagons jolted on the rough and stony way, while cries and prayers and curses were heard all along that moving line of human woe. Wagons were ditched and teams stalled, and as the roads became blocked the train took to the fields where the wheels sank to the axles in the soft earth. Drivers lashed their horses; curses and profanity abounded; axles were broken; wagons and caissons, and an occasional cannon, were abandoned; and dead soldiers were taken from the wagons to give more room for the remaining in-

mates, and thrown by the wayside. To add to the terror of the scene the Federal cavalry were upon them, and dashes were made here and there along the line and hundreds of wagons with their miserable and suffering inmates were captured.

The vastness of this train, and the aggregate of human agony it contained, has never been understood by the country.

General John Imboden, in charge of the train, wrote later,

Shortly after noon the very windows of heaven seemed to have been opened. Rain fell in dashing torrents, and in a little while the whole face of the earth was covered with water. The meadows became small lakes; raging streams ran across the road in every depression of the ground; wagons, ambulances, and artillery—carriages filled the roads and fields in all directions. The storm increased in fury every moment. Canvas was no protection against it, and the poor wounded, lying upon the hard, naked boards of the wagon bodies, were drenched by the cold rain. Horses and mules were blinded and maddened by the storm, and became almost unmanageable. The roar of the winds and waters made it almost impossible to communicate orders. Night was rapidly approaching, and there was danger that in the darkness the "confusion" would become "worse confounded." . . . It was moving rapidly, and from every wagon issued wails of agony. For four hours I galloped along, passing to the front, and heard more—it was too dark to see—of the horrors of war than I had witnessed from the battle of Bull Run up to that day. In the wagons were men wounded and mutilated in every conceivable way. Some had their legs shattered by a shell or minnie ball; some were shot through their bodies; others had arms torn to shreds; some had received a ball in the face, or a jagged piece of shell had lacerated their heads. Scarcely one in a hundred had received adequate surgical aid. Many of them had been without food for thirty-six hours. Their ragged, bloody, and dirty clothes, all clotted and hardened with blood, were rasping the tender, inflamed lips of their gaping wounds. Very few of the wagons had even straw in them, and all were without springs. The road was rough and rocky. The jolting was enough to have killed sound, strong men. From nearly every wagon, as the horses trotted on, such cries and shrieks as these greeted the ear:

"Oh God! why can't I die?"

"My God! will no one have mercy and kill me and end my misery?"

"Oh! Stop one minute and take me out, and leave me to die on the road-side."

"I am dying! I am dying! My poor wife, my dear children! What will become of you?"

> Some were praying; others were uttering the most fearful oaths and execrations that despair could wring from their agony. Occasionally a wagon would be passed from which only low, deep moans and sobs could be heard. No help could be rendered to any of the sufferers. On, on; we must move on. The storm continued and the darkness was fearful. There was no time even to fill a canteen with water for a dying man; for, except the drivers and the guards disposed in compact bodies every half mile, all were wounded and helpless in that vast train of misery. The night was awful, and yet it was our safety, for no enemy would dare attack us when he could not distinguish friend from foe. We knew that when day broke upon us we would be harassed by bands of cavalry hanging on our flanks. Therefore our aim was to go as far as possible under cover of the night, and so we kept on. It was my sad lot to pass the whole distance from the rear to the head of the column, and no language can convey an idea of the horrors of that most horrible of all nights of our long and bloody war.

* * *

Words kill, and words make alive. When Abraham Lincoln explained the war to the North, he resurrected a Union that otherwise would have been a neurosis or a corpse, and gave it a new birth. The people's acceptance of his explanation was a necessity. And it continues to be necessary with each new generation, because otherwise we will consider his words lies, his reasons propaganda, his speech only a tool. A test for inspired utterance is not only its efficacy at the time, but also its efficacy now.

In the postmodern world we are apt either to freeze inspired words, depriving them of their continuing organic life, or to take them apart until the pieces add up to whatever we want.

Nobody gave us an explanation for Vietnam. The president who might have was shot to death in November 1963. It appears that we are left with a confusing clamor of liars, unconvicted felons, and draft dodgers who were for or against the war trying to run the country right over the hole in our hearts.

In his book *Bloods,* Wallace Terry quotes a Vietnam vet:

> it eats away at your inner being. It eats away at everything you ever learned in your life. Your integrity. Your word. See, that's all you have. Vietnam taught you to be a liar. To be a thief. To be dishonest. To go against everything you ever learned. It taught you everything you did not need to know, because you were livin' a lie. And the lie was you ain't have no

> business bein' there in the first place. You wasn't here for democracy. You wasn't protecting your homeland. And that was what wear you down.

During the 1968 presidential campaign, Robert Kennedy said, "Now as ever, we do ourselves best justice when we measure ourselves against ancient tests." The "ancient test" of the American faith is the Gettysburg Address. For it, the brave men whom Lincoln buried went to their deaths. For what faith did the brave men of the 1960s go to their deaths? Have we kept Lincoln's faith?

* * *

Although I have been walking an old battlefield, I feel that today I have become reacquainted with my own generation. The Civil War, Great War, Second World War—all these have made our world. The direct inheritors of the Great War—the men and women who found the Second World War on their hands—were our leaders during Vietnam. Eisenhower, Kennedy, Johnson, and Nixon were World War II people. Those presidents were contemporaries of my father and mother, who had known First World War veterans and who had heard Civil War soldiers speak on Decoration Days, in cemeteries where their parents' and Lincoln's boys' bodies lay. It is a small world.

In this short time and space, as narrow as a month of chilly days, we can see the grief and confusion that have been dropped into our inexperienced hearts and minds. *Now what?* The question insists as the millennium turns: *Now what?* We can accept the death of heroism, of reason, of humanism and everything having to do with the Enlightenment—good and bad—and with it the death of hope, the death of government of and by and for the people, the death of rights and freedom—for why not? The old ideas are gone, the supports of rights, liberties, and hopes. They all rested upon one thing. Shall we declare the entire month to be an anniversary of the death of God?

> . . . I've talked to chaplains, talked to preachers. . . .
>
> . . . I have read the Bible from cover to cover, I keep looking for the explanation. I can't find it. I can't find it.

* * *

On this anniversary of Ia Drang, I found the grave of Second Lieutenant Hess. The air was unseasonably warm, although the mid-November sun had begun to set behind South Mountain. I was carrying a notebook; after a while I found a place under an old evergreen and wrote some lines.

Elegy Written in the Soldiers' National Cemetery
Gettysburg
For Larry Leroy Hess
2d Lt Co A 1 BN
5 Cav Div
Vietnam

One score years and five, and twelve long days ago,
my father died. I saw his face, I see it still—
and you, the same name, "L. L.,"
died of bullet wounds in Vietnam the same month.
You lie here—I see your stone
two rows down from this evergreen,
white marble streaked drab green
under these fir needles.

I could wonder if my father had another son,
one who went away to wars,
a boy in green he named his name, "L. L.,"
intrepid and bronze-armed,
as brave and smooth-faced as his other son
is rueful and contemplative,
sitting in this twilight—
    a prism of blues, azurean and candy,
    washed with distant chemical mud low near the tree line,
    fingered with torn cotton shreds of grey,
    those clouds the lower down the more
    like Georgia peach, until, touching
    gunmetal South Mountain they burst inefficaciously
    in runny bled red;
    no homeward flocks here but moving headlights
    and always, every second, the dumb drone
    of motors and empty gushes of mechanically swept air;
    tinged cannons up the slope, beneath their trees,
    once bathed some hearth boys' kingdoms in blood,
    rang some inglorious Milton mute,
    struck dead some little
    village Hampdens and ascending Cromwells
    innocent and guilty equally of each other's blood,
    with their stunning, thunderous bucks;
    farther up, below that balsam's wreathy branch
    the Lincoln Speech Monument, its words

facing the other way,
and the wind blows
from the east, sweeping my thin, inky words dry,
musing the branches;
the fragrance of these firs and pines
shunted down across that flat fallow field
(full of tossed and zippered folk)
the field of Pickett's Charge—
it grows too dark to write—
I could wonder if there was another
son, mute in white marble honor.

You knew things I will never know,
or am too old to know. I still say
I was right about the war—
I didn't go—
but you were the better man
because it was harder to be wrong
than right: look at your stone,
and say it isn't so.
Look at me, in olive khaki drab as if I were
in France in 1917—
I look the part, don't I?
Little Round Top with its monuments and statues
rises in the dying sun, and you are here,
and I am here,
together;
but I have only words and you have Death.
This morning at the Trostle Farm,
where Bigelow's Ninth Mass. Battery—
those boys bronzed by splattering metal red,
those glittering, heroic men forgotten—
held the field
just long enough to save the battle
and the army and the nation and our—
no, my—children,
held the field under the bursting air—
I saw someone had left a flag,
the tiny Stars and Stripes stuck
upright on a cannon through some lacquered links
of its ancient chain,
fallen askew—
I straightened it, as I wouldn't
have done for you

back then (you took and did it for yourself),
for those boys, those men,
and on my way here this afternoon
passed by and saw
that our flag was still there.

NOVEMBER 15

A Great Civil War (Virginia Wade)

I might have found a Confederate grave this afternoon. I had been looking for a place where a number of Southern boys had been buried together in a long trench. Those fellows had been mere victims, several regiments of men ordered by incompetent officers into an unreconnoitered attack. In long lines they walked toward a stone wall until, at the last moment, they heard someone somewhere shout an order and a whole brigade of Union soldiers rose up in front of them and fired into their faces. Those Southern boys died by the hundreds for absolutely nothing, and for what Cause?

Nobody else that I know of has found the exact burial site. The written records were not complete or precise. The best technology available has been used to spot the burial site—including helicopter overflights with infrared photography—but has turned up nothing conclusive.

I walked over the ground. The familiar old scent of autumn rose from the rich field that morning. The ground felt soft but firm beneath my boots; it was lush with thick grass and moss. As I looked at the ground, a strange, overpowering electricity filled me; the hair stood up on the back of my neck. I felt that I was standing on the burial trench itself.

Of course, my "find" can never be proved. It is known that the Confederate remains there—meaning only bones and personal items—were all exhumed and sent south a few years after the battle. Digging up the sod would reveal nothing, and would destroy what is left.

There can be no proof, in today's sense. We can find no material object. We have no documentary evidence. We have no conclusive photographic, electronic, technological data. But, as if I had stepped through a rift in time, my body could feel that I was on the place. We have a limited idea of proof, upon which we have become slavishly dependent. We need to think in wider terms about what is real. "Broader and deeper we must write our annals," Emerson said.

The important question is not where were those boys buried, but who were they? Why did they die? Why did they enlist in this great civil war? What design or conjunction led them to that place, and for what purpose, if any? Who were their mothers and fathers, sisters and brothers; who were their wives and children? Was there any consolation for them?

While flying to the British Isles six months before, we saw what appeared to be a darker landmass on the horizon. I pointed it out to my children. Was it Scotland? No. It was a solid layer of pollution in the atmosphere. It is a worldwide shadow we no longer even see from underneath. It is the Shadow of Death.

We have made this shadow because we want money. We made slaves of people because we wanted money, and still do. We are encouraged to value things and people now according to their material worth in the great global market—the vast slave market. Almost daily, perhaps, we do something we feel is wrong, but reason steps in quickly and tells us why we have to do it. It might not be the same act as that which at Chernobyl killed, mutated, and condemned thousands of people and released poison upon all of us, *but it is the same tyrannical principle.* I will get for myself what I want. To get whatever I can is my right.

Most causes can be reduced to this. The Union's could not. That is why "Father Abraham" Lincoln and his children could be heroes.

As I look into the wind that stings my eyes and makes them tear, I think of my children, each of whom I have brought to this place.

Andrew Peter, little boy, not quite yet the Big Fisherman his name promises but already the maker of offbeat jokes and puns, a wordmeister; already an artist who puts his arm around me where I'm sitting and says, "Daddy, live a little." *Not a malicious bone in his body.*

Elizabeth, who had already been street smart and chic at age two, who has hardly ever raised her voice except in comedy; used to make her own language, as leaves "winded away" autumn after autumn; makes it all look easy and said at age nine or ten: "I'll probably have to get a job at the gas station selling cigarettes to burly men." Now she's ready to go away to college. *I know who I am . . .*

Sarah, ten years ago—rolling down East Cemetery Hill, blonde curls and laughter bubbling in the wind. I tried rolling down with her last November, but I am not enough of a child anymore and it was not long before earth, grass, and sky all spun together. She is a philosopher now, asking questions only the faithful can ask. *A freethinker.*

The three grieved when we visited the Jenny Wade House last year. We sat down in that cellar, like the family that loved Jenny, a few feet from where the cheap model of her lay—where her body lay after the accidental bullet found her upstairs in the kitchen. There her family had sat, in the half-darkness, all through July 3, through the massive artillery bombardment, within sound of the immense growl and musketry of Pickett's Charge: the mother, Jenny's sister and her baby, and the body of poor Jenny.

* * *

Through the warm rain of June, steady and soft on the windowpane, a young woman stood watching, some seven score years ago. At an hour past noon, she held the curtain aside with a slender hand. Her sleeves were still turned back; she clutched her apron with a hand still streaked with the dough she had been kneading. A moment ago a party of horsemen had ridden past, the hoof beats muffled and heavy on the soft mud of the street, quick and crowded together rather than orderly. The laughing, yelling, the "*yip, yip*" called by one of them had sent a chill through her and caused a sick sensation in her stomach.

All this Friday morning she and her mother had stayed inside, fighting the mixed rushes of hope and reason, fear and trust, that careened through them with a new dreamlike, nightmare-like immediacy. It did not seem that this could be happening, *to them, here,* even though rumors and news had been running through town for two weeks. Across the mountains, to Greenwood and Chambersburg, Rebel cavalry had come up from the Valley in Virginia. The reports were true.

Those Rebels had struck Chambersburg over a week ago now, sufficient time for the truth to have been sifted from the terrified rumors. It was not so bad as had been feared at first. Cavalry belonging to a man named Jenkins, it had been; it was just a raid.

But first the rumors had made it a full-scale invasion by Robert E. Lee and the whole Confederate army, maybe a hundred thousand hungry, vicious, and uncivilized Southerners. Some of the women in town were saying that even the women down South carried revolvers. Their men, mad with hatred for the North and greedy for everything, would not hesitate to steal whatever they wanted, even young women's virtue, ready enough to kill anyone in their way and commit to flames anything left over.

It had turned out to be nothing of the kind. Jenkins's cavalry was not even a part of Lee's army. It was a loose, half-trained brigade of farmers and mechanics from the Shenandoah Valley who had fought under the dashing Turner Ashby the summer before, when Stonewall Jackson had raged up and down the Valley. Fortunately Maryland, the Potomac River, and the Army of the Potomac stood between Lee's army and southern Pennsylvania.

Still, the residents of Gettysburg were relieved that Jenkins's men had not ranged across to their side of South Mountain. They were a hideous lot—long-haired like witches, each man bristling with as many pistols as he could carry, bowie knives—dressed in filthy rags and outlandish costumes of vagabonds—beards down to their belts, like Jenkins's himself—wild and undisciplined. It was said that Jenkins had graduated from the Law School at Harvard, but his brush with civilization did not seem to affect his men nor mitigate their depredations. They had stolen thirty thousand head of cattle, who knows how many pigs and sheep, and had scoured the countryside for horses. Many farmers west of the mountains would not be able to bring in their crops now, and would inevitably go bankrupt before year's end.

Worst of all, Jenkins's cavalry had ridden down all the Negroes they could find, herding them like animals, whole families, sending them south. Here was where the war revealed its true color. They had even demanded that Greencastle's citizens turn out and round up Negroes for them. Whether the unfortunates were runaway slaves or free Negroes who had lived their whole lives in the North made no difference. Who knows how many had been sent south?

But Jenkins had turned out to be something other than a bold, ruthless leader. Reports said that forty men of Boyd's New York cavalry, who had been escorting supplies coming from the Valley up to Harrisburg, had chased Jenkins from Chambersburg. Nine days ago the Rebels had even left Greencastle and gone back South. Jenkins spooked easily, evidently, for there were no regular U.S. troops this side of Washington.

This young woman's fiancé was in a small Union army in the Shenandoah Valley, so it might not have been with complete relief that she heard of Jenkins's return South. At least while Jenkins was up here, there were fewer enemies down there. But to think that one of those enemies—not a cavalryman, thank goodness—was Wesley Culp, one of their old mutual friends from Gettysburg! Wesley had fought in the Valley last year, one of Stonewall Jackson's troops. The one comfort was that someday the war must end. It could not go on forever.

This young woman's name was Virginia, nicknamed Ginnie or Jenny by her friends and family. Though she lived, not much is known about her. One has to surmise what she thought, that warm, rainy June day. She would have been relieved along with her townspeople when news came of Jenkins's departure, and life would have more or less returned to normal. But Gettysburg was too close to Maryland—and too close to the route up from the Valley of Virginia behind the mountains—for complete comfort. The rumors continued. If there had been one raid, there could be others. Gettysburg had been training a company of volunteer militia, made up of students from Pennsylvania College, young farmers, Gettysburg merchants and their sons.

They had put on their new uniforms and marched out west of town this morning in the rain.

Virginia could hardly have thought of the militia and the events of this past week without a shudder. A few days after Jenkins's return to Virginia, the rumors had been cut through like a knife by Governor Curtin's sudden call for twenty thousand militia. The talk of raids was over. Lee and the Army of Northern Virginia had left their camps along the Rappahannock River, gone west to the Valley; they had crossed the Potomac into Maryland, heading straight for Pennsylvania.

They would not stay west of the mountains, that was certain. Harrisburg was east of the mountains. So were Philadelphia and Baltimore. So was Washington. The only question was, which way would they come? Would they go north, across to Harrisburg? It was hard to believe that Lee did not intend to turn southeast toward Washington—which would bring the Rebel army right through Gettysburg.

Where was the Army of the Potomac? Where were their own boys? They were defending Washington City. The surmise was that the commanding general would not dare to come up to Pennsylvania and risk a battle against Rebels so far away from the national capital—nor would President Lincoln let him. So the towns and people of Pennsylvania were to be sacrificed, while the Union army remained near the fortifications of Washington City. There was no help coming. Gettysburg was in occupied territory, and there was nothing to tame the conquerors.

It had only been a matter of when, and it had been this morning.

Someone had ridden into town shouting news. The Stevens Iron Works this side of Chambersburg was in flames. Next a neighbor came to say the young women must stay inside: Rebels had actually been seen four miles from Gettysburg.

So the militia, including its Gettysburg company, had gone out this morning, but they were a forlorn hope. Ginnie probably noticed that some of the boys were trying to put their bayonets on their muskets as they marched by in the drizzle, and evidently did not know how to do it. They had new uniforms, guns, knapsacks, but knew not what to do with them. You could not call what they did *marching*. Officers cursed and swore at them, but still they went up the muddy street crowding and bumping, starting and stopping in their confusion, not in straight lines at all, looking wide-eyed frightened, like young cattle. When the Rebels come on, they will run. One almost hopes they do.

A couple of hours later the militia boys had come back. Ginnie had seen only a few of them, running down the street. They were no longer carrying their new muskets. She had not noticed any sound of shooting. Most of the boys must have run north of town, through the fields, to get away. So few of them had come past the house. One had knocked at the door but then had changed his mind and run on immediately. And now came the riders.

What Virginia Wade might have seen from her window were cavalrymen of Wright's Battalion, Jones's Cavalry Brigade, belonging to the Army of Northern Virginia. These were not quite like Jenkins's long-bearded, seedy-looking scavengers, though they appeared to be rough enough. Some of them carried long infantry muskets; many others carried as many pistols as they could get, like Jenkins's men; some carried shotguns. They came riding down the street with the easy casualness of experienced riders, full of fun and bravado, brandishing pistols and sabers, riding from one side of the street to another, dressed in every kind of clothing—butternut-dyed trousers and jackets, gray, black or brown trousers, red shirts, blue shirts, checked shirts of all kinds and filthy with dust and sweat; boots to the knee, or flapping shoes; raincoats, dusters; and all kinds of hats, wide-brimmed, plumed, caps, straw hats, brown, black, dirty white—confident, careless, disciplined despite their apparent willfulness, not a thing in the world to make them afraid.

They were young, most of them, and they were men; Ginnie let the curtain fall back into place and she stayed inside.

* * *

Through that afternoon and evening she would get enough news. Some of the older men, the ones who had less to fear from staying in town, had gone to the town center, the Diamond—to see what was going on. They were met there not by cavalry but by the calm, disciplined, orderly regiments of Gordon's brigade of Georgia infantry. They filed along Chambersburg Street far enough back so as to continue out of sight. Companies of gray-uniformed and butternut-clothed men lounged along all sides of the Diamond. Their general, John B. Gordon, was a dignified, imposing officer. Straight as a post, severe-looking but gentlemanly.

Later, the division commander rode into town ahead of the other brigades. Major General Jubal A. Early proceeded to demand from the representatives of Gettysburg's town government a phenomenal list of "requisitions": large amounts of food and supplies for men and horses. Early's Division contained nearly six thousand men. He wanted a thousand pairs of shoes and five hundred hats. He offered to accept, as an alternative, $10,000 in cash—not Confederate money. The citizens of Gettysburg must have felt a mixture of fright, mirth, and consternation. There wasn't anything like that amount of goods or cash in this town of twenty-four hundred, ten blocks long by at most six wide.

Early, a lanky man with a gentlemanly look when he was not hunched up with arthritis, was shrewd, not more ruthless than he needed to be, and smug. (In his memoirs, Early wrote that it was well that the militia had not stayed to fight Gordon's Brigade; otherwise some of them "might have been hurt.") He had shown by destroying Thaddeus Stevens's Iron Works that he was willing to disobey General Lee's orders, flagrantly, when his own intellect and reasoning powers justified it. Sure of himself, articulate—he was a lawyer—and domineering, Early would talk his superior officers into committing two of the greatest mistakes—possibly—of July first. A year later, in 1864, he would throw away a potential victory in the Shenandoah Valley, and his small army with it. And after the war he would divert attention from his own failures by criticizing others. But that was all in the future; today he had everything well in hand.

His troops combed Gettysburg's shops—getting little more than horseshoes and nails. On the north side of town, he discovered two thousand rations in a parked train of about a dozen cars, took them, and set the rolling stock afire. The smoke could be seen by most of the town, and its significance was viscerally understood. The merchants accepted Confederate money for what goods they were required to give up. Some of the Southerners broke into houses, taking what they wanted from the terrified people who had remained inside, stalking through the living rooms and kitchens with their muskets, pistols, and open haversacks. But the most memorable impression was created by Hays's Brigade, whose officers got hold of more than enough liquor in town to get the whole brigade roaring drunk. The liquor was issued to the men and all fourteen hundred took advantage. Hays's Brigade was different from every unit in the Army of Northern Virginia—very different. The brigade's other name was the Louisiana Tigers. They were a rough set by any standards—tough men from Louisiana speaking a language completely unrecognizable to Pennsylvanians. Mustachioed, knife carrying, and swarthy, these foreigners looked and acted particularly brutal, their Creole speech darkly terrifying. They had been bad enough *before* they all got drunk.

Fortunately, the Confederate high command was interested in discipline; furthermore, most of the Tigers were camped north of town. But Virginia Wade and her cousins must have felt frightened and abandoned. Where is our army? Why must they remain in Maryland?

* * *

Early's troops moved out the next morning, but not back toward the mountains. They marched eastward, toward York, on the way to Philadelphia. For four days it was nothing but tense waiting: when will the rest of the rebel army come through? Evidently they did not intend to leave Pennsylvania. The town was surrounded, the citizens knew. Early was in York. More Rebels were in Harrisburg. An unknown number, perhaps Lee's main body, lay at Chambersburg. It is this direction they must come.

On the morning of June 30, Ginnie, or Jenny, Wade might have stood talking with neighbors. With what one witness termed "great excitement," mixed with consternation—what one might call near panic—people passed on the frenzy of news. More Rebels, thousands of them—infantry—had been seen west of town on the road from Chambersburg and Cashtown. It was a brigade, or a division, and they were moving directly this way. There was not much left in town to steal. What frame of mind will these Rebels be in if we have nothing to give them?

Once again many of the men left town, taking horses with them, and whatever they could pack or throw onto wagons in a few minutes. The town's Negroes had long since left. Federal officials, such as the postmaster, might well be arrested and sent south.

What little we know of Jenny Wade allows the possibility that she turned back to the house, determined to carry on with her chores and permitting neither the panic nor the Rebels to stop her necessary work.

The house must be tidied, dinner must be prepared, perhaps bread must be baked. If we are going to be part of Confederate territory, we must still do our duties.

But the sound of horsemen again might have been too much. *When will it end?* Hearing the heavy approach of cavalry coming up the street, she might have thrown her apron aside, heedless of her sister's exclamations, and gone to the door. *When will you people leave us alone? Take your war and go back to Virginia!* As she opens her door, the first horsemen, the head of the column, move past at a trot, a dense, tight column, orderly and quiet, equipment jingling, men in dusty but regular uniforms, carrying short carbines strapped to their saddles, tough men, tanned and riding with the easy tautness of veterans—*men in blue.* She might not have believed her eyes at first. These were not militia at all! These were Union horse soldiers.

Who are you? she calls.

Buford's cavalry, ma'am.

The column picks up, cantering past now—battle-hardened men, not like the ones she had seen last week, and not apt to be frightened by any of them, either—hundreds of them. Her eyes blur. *But where are you from? To whom do you belong? What army—?*

They answer her, some touching their caps, as they pass.

Inside again somehow, she leans against the door, her head back in joy and relief as she barely can say to her tense sister and mother:

Army of the Potomac.

* * *

Heroes save us.

* * *

Virginia Wade was the only civilian who died during the Battle of Gettysburg. The town was occupied by Confederates Wednesday through Saturday, July first through fourth, and as such was a battleground for snipers. While kneading dough on the afternoon of July third, she was struck in the back by a bullet passing through the wall of her sister's kitchen.

The horse soldiers Ginnie saw were living representations of what was passing, riding to the rescue in their splendid toughness that late June morning 140 years ago. Their bodies lie in the Soldiers' National Cemetery in Gettysburg.

* * *

A few days before leaving for Gettysburg this time, I sat beneath an oak beside a clear, blue lake and watched a wedding party gathering for a photo by the shore. It was sunny, deceptively so, for the light came at that slant without heat of late fall, and the water's glitter looked like teeth. The women in the party, waiting for the camera to be ready, shivered and hugged their bare shoulders in formal evening dresses, images of misery. The bride, surrounded by the others, looked somehow as if she were to be sacrificed. All the members of the party—groom, groomsmen, ladies in attendance, minister—all were dressed in black; only the bride was in white. Each man wore a flower—one small red spot upon the breast.

* * *

We are all present. *We are all one family, everywhere, past and present,* I tell my children. But they are not here. I am alone. A father without his children is a pathetic creature.

> Cast me out upon the deep dark sea.
> Let voices make my memories strange.
> Tie me to the mast, but let me see;
> and bring me home again.

What is the past without our children?

Virginia Wade was not a hero of the battle of Gettysburg; she was one of its victims. War is mostly victims. Ginnie could have stood for the whole battle, and all its doomed youth. How can all this tragedy be resolved? How can all these dead young people be accounted for?

The personal nature of war is too easily forgotten. "War means fighting, and fighting means killing." War is not primarily technology and explosions or tactics and supply. It is primarily personal loss. All war is civil war; all battles mean people sit and grieve. This is what Lincoln addressed at Gettysburg. His words reach their full meaning only for those who are paying too high a price. They ask God why, and Abraham Lincoln answers. The question Lincoln addresses is not, what is worth dying for? The question is, what is worth giving up my child for?

NOVEMBER 16

Final Resting Place (Sanctuary)

Identity is an accomplishment.
—Vaclav Havel

The man is still not back. What does he think, no one dies around here? Cemeteries run themselves?

Tomorrow is the beginning of "Heritage Days" in Gettysburg. For two days, people will converge on Gettysburg by the thousands and tens of thousands: tourists, scholars, buffs, reenactors. There will be so many men in Civil War uniforms that it will feel like there is a war on. Motel rooms are booked for fifty miles around. The reenactors will bring their own tents, firewood, cooking pots, campstools: you can already see the watch fires of a hundred circling camps.

It is the 130-somethingth anniversary of the Gettysburg Address. Today is my last chance for two or three days to look around without crowds, and still no cemetery superintendent! It is enough to make a man weep.

All right. So I'm on my own again. The meter is ticking here; I can't stand around with my hands in my pockets. The thing to do is *carefully* inspect all three possible sites.

The "traditional site" is the easiest to see, and tradition itself has made it the most plausible. A tall monument stands at the focal point of the semicircles of soldier graves. That monument has the irrefutability of stone. "Here was given the Gettysburg Address," it seems to say. Where else could the speakers' platform have been?

The new site—or rather, the actual site, or hypothetical site, that is the old site, the original site—for the Gettysburg Address has been argued for persuasively by Ms. Harrison. It is accepted as authentic (and called the "Harrison Site") by no less an authority than Garry Wills in his prize-winning book *Lincoln at Gettysburg.* But controversy exists (or *existed,* if Mr. Wills is correct that "at least this battle of Gettysburg has been won") because of that man named Selleck.

The Gettysburg National Cemetery was set up and dedicated under the supervision of a board of commissioners, one from each state. W. Yates Selleck, a resident of Milwaukee, was the commissioner from Wisconsin. He was *on the speakers' platform with Lincoln.* And he left a detailed description *with a perfectly clear diagram* of where the platform was located. Not where the flagpole stood (which became the site, probably, of the present column monument)—but not the "Harrison Site" up in Evergreen Cemetery, either. The so-called Selleck Site is outside the last semicircle of graves, behind the New York section. The crowd, according to Selleck, all stood on the downward slope north of the graves. Abraham Lincoln stood with the graves behind him, not in front of him.

Present-day authorities dismiss Selleck's description and drawing, but I happen to know that in Milwaukee there is nothing to do but go bowling and tell the truth.

The photographic evidence—one photograph, with another taken from reverse angle supporting it once you accept that first one—shows Harrison to be generally right, however. But can you believe your eyes?

Garry Wills was informed that there were no graves in the crowd's area at the time, but I think that was not the case. Section G, I think it is, lies to the southwest of the Harrison Site, in the path of the procession and possibly underfoot during the Address. How many graves would have been too many, before the authorities would have balked, or the visitors objected? In any case, it cannot be said that there was no problem at all with graves being around the Harrison Site.

There is another problem with the new site, photograph or no photograph. Frank Klement was the premier—perhaps the only—authority on the Soldier's National Cemetery and Lincoln's Gettysburg Address. In his last book, Mr. Klement did not take the Harrison Site particularly seriously. He did not treat the photographs at all. (Perhaps there is good reason. In old photographs, might we not see what we expect to see? Is there something we are not seeing this time?) His doubt concerning the Harrison Site had to do with the rivalry between David Wills, who was in charge of the National Cemetery and the dedication ceremony, and David Conoughy, the owner of Evergreen. Conoughy wanted the new graves to be made in *his* cemetery. He thought Will's scheme was publicity-seeking entrepreneurialism. Correspondence of both men with Governor Curtin is housed in the Park Service's library; it shows mutual distrust, and probably hatred—of the seemingly unreasoning, implacable kind which only family members or neighbors are able to generate. Klement is sure this animosity would have prevented Wills from even considering putting his speakers' platform in his rival's cemetery. The president of the United States and Edward Everett giving their speeches in Conoughy's cemetery? Mr. Klement does not take sides, but he thinks the controversy—largely between the Selleck Site and the Traditional Site—is far from over. Mr. Klement, remember, was a Milwaukeean.

There are other reasons to doubt the Harrison Site. Jacob Hoke, a citizen of Chambersburg, attended the ceremony and says he stood only a few feet from the front of the platform as Abraham Lincoln spoke, and states flatly that the speech was given where the monument now is. Others say the same. Reporters on the scene, claiming that the site gave a panoramic view of the battlefield, walked all over the hill and could have been referring to anyplace up there. Furthermore, they had no idea where the events of the battle actually took place. The reporters disagree, and cancel each other out. But Hoke, who was there and later wrote a good book about the Gettysburg campaign, and Selleck, who was a commissioner and sat on the platform, present strong, if conflicting, cases.

William Frassanito, the expert on Civil War photography referred to in *Lincoln at Gettysburg,* has objected that contrary to what is said in that book, he never has agreed to the "Harrison Site." He believes the speakers' platform was in Evergreen Cemetery, but not at the "Harrison Site."

Perhaps only now would people take a photograph more seriously than written evidence. It is not a simple matter of believing what is before our eyes. The written testimonies are before our eyes, too. But a photograph, vague and blurry in many respects though it is, naturally seems more important to us, the first visual rather than literate people in quite some time in the civilized world. The absence of mediators appeals to us even more, right now: there is no authority involved except ourselves. This is perhaps one unintentional result of Lincoln's speech. I can look at the photograph and make up my own mind. For me, such evidence is supposed to matter more than the testimony of two men who did not look at a distant, vague photograph 140 years later: they were there, in living color, on the spot, and they were not stupid.

At what point do we prefer not to believe Hoke's and Selleck's eyes and brains, and choose our own more distant view?

* * *

On a nice Sunday morning at Oxford last summer, my group of American college students visited a large high-Anglican church for the service. The choir sang an exquisitely lovely anthem, so English that I hardly felt I was in the twentieth century—and then I realized, when they were nearly done, that they were singing the American spiritual "Steal Away."

Plato understood the danger of art: music makes the words. If an African-American song can lose its heritage of oppression by a change of harmonic venue, perhaps any words can be read in more ways than one. (Anyone who has had a book of theirs reviewed knows this.) A popular movie like *JFK* can make millions of people believe a version of history which is almost certainly false. But what Plato might not have liked to admit, I think, is that nearly everything is art.

Everything we know gets selected and arranged in passage through the human mind. Of this the postmodern world is aware with a vengeance. Is there no way to come face-to-face with what *happened?* Is there no certainty founded on something outside the human mind?

Postmodernists answer that if there were truth outside the human mind, we would not know it—and in what sense could we call it truth?

There is something very helpful in this, as a reminder of the limited nature of what we call truth. How nice if postmodernism would prevent war with this helpful reminder. If the deconstructionists could persuade everyone willing to kill for their version of truth that they should not be certain enough to kill, it would be a service. But deconstruction will not change human nature, and what postmodernism does chiefly is make us feel miserable.

Perhaps philosophers have always understood that the problem of human knowledge is how to get it outside the human head. The Irish philosopher Berkeley put the knowledge of "objective" fact—something he also found otherwise inseparable from the human mind—into the mind of God. The Modern World was unable to take Bishop Berkeley's solution seriously. Postmoderns, I suspect, not only do not believe that this problem has such a solution—or any solution, for that matter—but they also might not view this condition of human knowledge as a problem. It is only a problem if you want to preserve some last foothold in the idea of "objective fact."

But we want sanctuary from our own minds. The building in which the text of "Steal Away" was musically deconstructed that Sunday satisfies human need. Our need for shelter goes beyond the physical.

Hadrian's Wall in northern England was one means of protecting us from the barbarians, or from ourselves—or postmodernism might say it was a way of keeping the disfranchised disfranchised. Our coach driver said he loved the Romans: the road along the Wall is virtually the only straight road in Britain. The stones used in Hadrian's Wall, which stretched across England from east to west, were not merely picked up and bundled on top of each other like farmers' walls. They were quarried and cut to uniform size and shape. Most of the Wall is gone now, but farmers' walls in that area contain many rectangular stones, all of a size. Perhaps it shows that good fences still make good fences.

At any rate, how would you like to be building a wall and handling a stone handled and cut by a Roman two thousand years ago? Would it not provoke some silence, and some thought?

Samuel Johnson used a stone on the ground to disagree with the philosophy of Bishop Berkeley. Kicking the stone, he announced, "I refute it thus!" Johnson might have been glib, but quarried stones do have a certain anti-deconstructive force. We have simply forgotten how to use those stones.

A historian would insist that my musings on the stone cut by a Roman are muddled. It is improbable that a *Roman* cut the stone. Local laborers were no doubt compelled into service, and could not steal away without instant penalty. The Wall in the area we visited was manned by the First Cohort of Tungrians, a group of eight hundred Belgians. In addition, Frisian cavalry patrolled the district. Supplementing this core was the basic manpower of the "numerous Hnaudifridi," and of course, where would any of us be without our numerous Hnaudifridi. If these auxiliaries were not real, we are not.

The Wall makes an impossible scene, running across the wide-open undulations of the green north England hills—one of the most beautiful scenes in England, perhaps because the depth of history gives the landscape a quality of mystery and mind. In a way, the Wall makes of northern England a text, that is, a natural text with human overwriting. The strangeness of the text prompts thought about past and present. The stones are there. We are connected to them, and are separated from them.

Hadrian's Wall is real precisely because of its *difference* from us, its strangeness. Berkeley's God knows all about Hadrian's Wall. Therefore it is that God alone who can grant freedom. The intellectual freedom we have as moderns and postmoderns has not enabled facts and objects to move freely out from our *oppressive minds* (there is no other postmodern location), but has connected them to us ontologically—being to being. Such freedom is an illusion. It is as if we have tried to make ourselves Berkeley's God, but without objective knowledge, and we find that we have no freedom to grant.

Across the green, cloud-dappled English landscape that day, military helicopters flew low over Hadrian's Wall like dark, futuristic, mechanical insects, murderous and powerful—partly a hope of defense, and partly an admission of failure. They go freely back and forth across the wall as the Picts and Scots could not. Are they, like the Cohort, mercenary defenders, or barbarians who finally broke through? As if the difference between the two was ever clear. In retrospect, they seem like confused, moronic creatures buzzing around something they cannot get into their heads.

Another sanctuary, hollow in a different sense, is not very far away. Coventry Cathedral's bombed-out shell stands next to the new Coventry Cathedral. The Germans destroyed the old cathedral during World War II, then helped build the new version. That site of contrasting ruin and contemporaneity is an image of history, which tears down one era and puts up another. The impression one gets standing inside the old walls reading a plaque commemorating German help in the rebuilding, is one of futility. Why preserve and study history at all? Is it merely a form of entertainment, or coercion? Our barbarism goes on all the same.

History is a kind of refuge. Also near Hadrian's Wall is the picturesque Durham Cathedral, a lovely and imposing sight atop a high, forested riverbank. In the River Wear, salmon run the dam under the shadow of the old church, still a church after all these years and centuries. Inside lie the bones of one of the ancestors of English learning—one of the greatest of them, called, in fact, "the father of English learning," the Venerable Bede. The Latin inscription identifies the remains: *Haec sunt in fossa Baedae venerabilis ossa.* It is a rhyme that works in English, too: "Here in stone are the Venerable Bede's bones." Bede's *History of the English Church and People* did more than record events; it helped create "the English Church and People" by assuming for them, each and together, an identity. The preservation of that memory, that identity, that structure, was the preservation of a sanctuary. It was a thing set apart, that identity, and a place to come to again and again when enemies clamored and overwhelmed.

Durham Cathedral itself was a sanctuary in the Middle Ages. An applicant, perhaps in trouble with the law, or simply in trouble, knocks at the door. Bells are rung. He is admitted; he is given a black cloak with a yellow cross embroidered on the left shoulder; he is sent into exile carrying a white cross before him. Centuries later, when interest in the Church revived in England with the evangelical movement, the attention of sanctified people was directed outward: the abolition of slavery, amelioration of the effects of poverty and ignorance, establishment of care for the sick and imprisoned. Likewise history. It is a place to go to recall ourselves. But if history exists for us, the living, it is not merely a place of comfort; it exists to recall us to a noble work someone else has begun.

Coventry Cathedral could have been left a ruin. Because it was rebuilt, we might say that it was futile to destroy it. History reminds us, certainly, of futility, just as Wilfred Owen's poetry reminds us of futility—not necessarily the futility of effort, but the futility of evil.

For old Bede, History was a redemption of life. To keep the faith is to try to redeem life from futility.

The modern age questioned whether knowledge can originate outside the human mind; postmodernism makes the implied break obvious, then breaks what is inside the mind into a kaleidoscope of pieces. Modernity meant to liberate us from outside tyranny, but now we are enslaved to ourselves, and in turn we find that chaos, while it has no power to coerce, also has no power to liberate. Evidently that is a power we are unable to seize for ourselves.

In that service back at the church in Oxford, the lector read the parable of the prodigal son. Alone with his regrets in a brave new world of mud, slop, and alien snouts, the young man is roused by his memories. "I will arise and go," he says, and in fact returns home to retrieve his identity. There his father forgives him, redeeming the past and the present. Somewhere in the long-forgotten past we have a home, a place of refuge to renew our strength. Maybe it is only in our heads. But one day, perhaps, some venerable man or woman will help us recall it in the deep heart's core, come to ourselves, and steal away, steal away to freedom.

* * *

Maybe we should dare to hope more than we do. Shelley wrote that hope is not a certainty but a moral obligation. Its opposite, despair, stifles love and imagination—the means of doing good. Despair therefore assures the conditions which give rise to it; hope preserves a condition of *possibility* in which imagination and love might work. Hope is a matter of duty.

On a visit to Cambridge one day, we stopped at the nearby American World War II cemetery. The white markers are laid out on a quarter circular plan, somewhat reminiscent of the Soldiers National Cemetery at Gettysburg. I came upon a man from my own state: "Robert F. Marshall, Wisconsin, SGT 547 Bomber Squadron, 384 Bomber Group." Like Wilfred

Owen—and how many others?—he had died close to a war's end: March 19, 1945. I looked up at the inscription on the long wall in front of the graves: "All who shall hereafter live in freedom will be here reminded that to these men and their comrades we owe a debt to be paid with grateful remembrance of their sacrifice and with the high resolve that the cause for which they died shall live eternally."

What debt do we owe? Perhaps hope. After what they did and gave up, it would hardly do for us to despair, would it? In the presence of these graves one hardly feels the right to indulge in cowardly behavior. These honored dead recall us to our faith.

Did some few ghosts regard us with sardonic, maddened smiles, or grasp toward us to rave their hellish memories? And did some darkly wonder if we mean to march the same mud again?

It is easy to echo Abraham Lincoln's beliefs, but do we have any left of our own? Surely the limits of human knowledge become most visible on the field of battle. Arjuna looks to his divine charioteer, whose answer is, Go forward; do your duty.

* * *

We had an insufferable "guide" for some of these excursions in England—a man who could not get rid of any fact in his head, and who had no discriminatory faculty. Every fact was as important as any other, whether it was when a nearby agricultural school was founded and by whom or that England fought a war against a certain Adolf Hitler, "a great German leader." His facts concerning America were wonders of invention. We learned things about George Washington that no one ever knew before. Once, I looked toward the back of the coach and saw that all the students were either sleeping or tuned in to their headphones. I was the only one listening, and seething. Another good picture of the contemporary world: Nearly everyone tuned in to their own rock music while a few other miserable wretches exchange misinformation and national jealousies.

All right; so be it. Immensely relieved one afternoon to be on an excursion without this airbag, I snatched the microphone next to the driver and commenced disseminating knowledge. "Through the trees to our left you can barely see the estate of Dame Edith Tudds-Buttles, now well advanced in age. Her property encompasses Bews Meadow, the battlefield where Edward XVIII defeated an army of small barons, his forces driving the enemy entirely through the use of Welsh hammers. If any of you are interested in further information regarding this significant engagement, I refer you to the work of Professor Grenville Bleary-Neegles.

Coming up on the right, in fact, is Groton Snigley, the home of the professor's great-grandson." Etcetera.

Americans have always enjoyed making fun of English names and customs and what seem to be self-conscious "airs"—and have gotten their share of ridicule in return. But there is no real rancor in it, except that reserved for Americans who adopt English mannerisms and become genuinely affected. Even Mark Twain cherished his honorary doctorate from Oxford. Of course, he liked to wear the academic gown they gave him around the house. The point is that it comes easy to criticize Oxford's grandiose squalor and its obsolete pretentions, but with what shall we replace it?

In that lovely, civilized Oxford English you still can hear, amid class oppression, unintended comedy, and everything else, that heroic unconcern which the next generation shall need, which humankind has always needed, and which we shall need as long as life on earth remains, with its horror and futility and the frail frame of mortality poised like tissue against chaos and death.

* * *

Now, in the Soldier's Cemetery at Gettysburg, I recall those summer months, and most particularly an evening at Gray's country churchyard. The poet himself is buried there. We stood beneath his old, old yew tree.

> Beneath those rugged Elms, that Yew-Tree's Shade,
> Where heaves the Turf in many a mould'ring Heap,
> Each in his narrow Cell for ever laid,
> The rude Forefathers of the Hamlet sleep.

The English country churchyard where Thomas Gray wrote his elegy is still a peaceful place. Some of the people who live there are shepherds and farmers, like their ancestors who lie under the old gravestones.

> Far from the madding crowd's ignoble strife,
> Their sober wishes never learned to stray;
> Along the cool sequestered vale of life
> They kept the noiseless tenor of their way.

Flocks are still ushered home from the hillside; they flow hesitantly across low meadows streaked with sunset light. Far off comes a shepherd's syllable of command; from a near farm lane, dull bells and the lowing of a plodding herd.

Settling stones with solemn epitaphs still surround the ancient tree where the young man sat with leaves of paper some two hundred years ago. What he wrote on those pages soon became a favorite in England, and before long his verses crossed the Atlantic, reaching even the wilderness of Kentucky, Indiana, and Illinois. The "Elegy Written in a Country Church-Yard" was one of Abraham Lincoln's favorite poems. He quoted it when asked for his life's story during the election of 1860. "The short and simple annals of the poor" would do for describing his youth, Lincoln said. His early years were grim, sad, and grinding, and they would not be of much interest to us—much less would they seem lyrical, as they do now—were it not for the invisible hope and silent promise they contained. But Abraham Lincoln's life was tragic for all that, and he was himself an elegy.

> . . . Melancholy marked him for her own.

In our own turn-of-millennium twilight, frail words reach like lengthening shadows across old graves.

> For who to dumb Forgetfulness a prey,
> This pleasing anxious being e'er resigned,
> Left the warm precincts of the cheerful day,
> Nor cast one longing lingering look behind?

The beauty of Gray's Elegy marked its melancholy upon Abraham Lincoln. From it he learned that an elegy answers beauty with beauty. Such is the source of an elegy's hope; such is the source of its immortality. The elegy draws its grace from the grace of what has passed, transforming it, and to the degree that a new beauty is born, the elegy lasts and the dead shall not have lived in vain.

* * *

I wonder what Mr. Lincoln would have thought of our postmodern era. He was only partly a modernist anyway. He believed in equality, representative government, reason, economic opportunity; but he had a religious temperament, more and more audible as time went on, and he thought the purposes of God transcend our values, actions, wants, and perhaps even our reason. The postmodern idea that there is no transcendent moral universe would strike Lincoln not only as stupid and maybe vicious but also as sad and foreboding. On the other hand, he might have liked having somebody around to remind the Modern World of its limitations, short of staging a World War I, a Holocaust—or an American Civil War.

It has been said that World War I changed the modern mind, but the Civil War did the same things in America fifty years earlier. Lincoln was watching it happen, seeing the bodies buried right at his feet—or was it up behind him? Or was it at some distance down the slope from the speakers' platform? Here we see that the question of where Lincoln actually stood while speaking the Gettysburg Address does become important: it has symbolic significance. In any case, he saw the tall flagpole—saw the high American flag surrounded by corpses. His interpretation, he believed, was worth fighting for and dying for. But were the graves and the dead boys behind him, in his memory? Or were they below him, being in a sense recreated from above by him? Or did he stand right in among them?

The third option, that Abraham Lincoln stood more or less at the focal point of the semicircle of graves, is very appropriately known as the *traditional site.* In Western tradition, which includes the modern tradition, there is a shared location common to the event and to its interpreters. The Gettysburg Union dead and Mr. Lincoln's platform stood on exactly the same ground. Their event was his event. We stand with him and them, all of us together.

If he stood off below them, at the Selleck Site, Mr. Lincoln funneled them into his memory where they were understood and then given to us so that we could see them his way. We the audience, we the people, are below the visionary explainer, who is in turn below the men and events themselves.

Everything is different, and very postmodern, at the Harrison Site—not least because Ms. Harrison attacks the received and the reasoned sites. She places Lincoln at the top, far above the graves. He sees not only them, and not only the battlefield, but the broad panorama from Maryland to South Mountain, "the mighty Alleghenies." Taking all these things into view, he dispenses his interpretation downward to us. He has remade the Union dead, as Wills implies, who remain silent in their long, deep earthen holes, unknowable, and whose actions can never actually be known in themselves. Lincoln recreates them *for* his own purposes *to* us. We also stand above them. They or rather not *they* anymore—are made by Lincoln in our minds where we make what *we* make, therefore ourselves standing above the event (as the literary critic, says the deconstructionist, stands superior to the classic literary text.)

This whole exercise is itself postmodern if it allows the alternatives to stand as they are. But we might dare to say that Lincoln actually did stand somewhere, and not at all three places. If there *is* an objective location on Cemetery Hill where Lincoln stood, then we are not in the postmodern situation as concerns at least this.

But *can* we know where? Can we get ourselves out of the postmodern vestibule of hell? Seekers of Lincoln's speech are like the new physicists: One sees Lincoln like a photon going through a hole in one location; another sees him at another location—and the reader of one or another account accordingly sees him at one or the other place too; and the current interpretation imagines and puts him where *nobody at all says they saw him.*

Selleck says the platform stood behind the New York section of graves. Hoke, who stood a few feet from Lincoln, says the platform is exactly where the monument now stands. Harrison, who was not there, says all the witnesses *meant* the platform stood up the hill from the graves—she deriving this conclusion from technology (photographs), and by playing the texts off against each other and deconstructing them after a fashion. The National Park Service has installed a new marker affirming the Harrison Site, and on low days I find myself almost believing her, too.

The Modern World gave Ms. Harrison the tools with which she has been able to achieve the present postmodern effects. The literary-critical method and the historical-critical method were applied first by German theologians to the text of the Bible. Now, heaven forbid, they are being turned on Gettysburg itself!

Because I find the spectacle of the Modern World devouring itself by the tail to be not only thrilling but appalling, and because I am a freethinker, I will propose, for sake of argument, a *fourth* site. I will not call it the Gramm Site—I don't know how authentic the name is anyway, as applied to me or anything associated however remotely with me; I will call it the Lincoln Site. Why not steal a march on the enemy? Actually, the site I propose (for the sake of argument) is marked by a bust of Lincoln, and behind that the text of the Gettysburg Address. It is a small but very conspicuous memorial to the Address. You see it right away upon coming out of the Visitors' Center and entering the National Cemetery. The first time I visited, I thought this was the place of the Address, and felt like a knothead when I discovered I was nowhere near the site. On second thought, I will call this the Knothead Site.

What does the Knothead Site have going for it? First, my making the mistake twenty years ago shows that the site is a natural. Second, it is handier to the Visitors' Center. You want testimony of eyewitnesses? Selleck says it was off to the side. This is off to the side. Eyewitnesses say you could see all over the battlefield. You can see all over the place from the Knothead Site. You don't want graves trampled? There's room for five thousand people between this site and the graves, easy. As a bonus, the big trees and the gazebo were not there. For ease of approach by the dignitaries' procession, this site cannot be beaten. Most of all, I'm convinced Ms. Harrison *meant* this site when she wrote about the Brown vault site over the fence in Evergreen. Photographs showing the flagpole? You could see the flagpole from there. The cemetery gate? What cemetery gate? The photographs are lousy. They're fuzzy. Who can prove anything by them? In a few years I will need bifocals. Statements by eyewitnesses that contradict details? Shucks, *all* the sites are contradicted! It's the Knothead Site. It feels right. I like it.

NOVEMBER 17

What We Say Here (The Other Address)

While Abraham Lincoln was writing his Gettysburg Address on this day in 1863, another man was rehearsing his own Gettysburg address. The man was Edward Everett, the country's premier platform personality. On the program at Gettysburg, only his speech is billed as the "oration" of the day. The president is simply to make the dedication; that is, give a short formulaic pronouncement officially establishing the Soldiers' National Cemetery. The day was designed around Everett. Asked in September to deliver the oration for an October ceremony at Gettysburg, Everett had said that he could not possibly be ready until November 19. So that day was seized upon and the dedication ceremony was postponed for a month.

Everett needed the time because he put a great deal into his orations. This one would last the usual two and a half hours, and Everett would deliver it all from memory, as was his practice. There would be no reading of a text, no looking down at a sheaf of paper, to interpose between Everett and the audience. He was an expert in the use of voice, inflection, and gesture; a master of drama and declamation; and a gifted writer of literary oratory. The two and a half hours were no tedious imposition upon the audience. The oration would be entertainment as well as ceremony and edification. In those days, people attended speeches and debates, whereas today we sit with our beers at ball games or in front of a television. Everett's Gettysburg oration would be eminently successful with the crowd and the newspapers. It would live up to expectations.

Those people were not airheads, any more than Everett was a mere performer. Yet compared to Lincoln's speech, Everett's is just awful. This is not necessarily to say much, because very little in the way of rhetorical art compares well to Lincoln. Everett, at sixty-nine, was a learned and experienced man for whom the word *distinguished* might have been coined. The presidency of Harvard and a term as secretary of state were among his credentials. He had been one of Emerson's teachers. Nevertheless, his speech would be little noted nor long remembered.

Why did Everett's speech fall and die right after the occasion, and Lincoln's live? Primarily because Lincoln's was alive in the first place. Everett's address is words; Lincoln's is more like a deed. Everett's speech entailed no consequences, whereas Lincoln's entailed the most solemn ones. For Everett's, nothing is at stake; in Lincoln's, everything is at stake.

One is struck by the *static* nature of Everett's speech from the very first words: "Standing beneath this serene sky, overlooking these broad fields now reposing from the labors of the waning year, the mighty Alleghenies dimly towering before us, the graves of our brethren beneath our feet." Everett's eye "ranges over the fields," he "considers," he "comprehends"—and the word *stand* reappears three times. Lincoln's words are simple and active: *do, take.*

Everett's address does not grieve, as it does not move. Two particularly jarring faux pas in Everett's speech betray its inert nature. One is his statement toward the end that the Confederate who "grovels at the foot of a foreign throne for assistance in compassing the ruin of his country" is a wretched being, by comparison to whom "the humblest dead soldier, that lies cold and stiff in his grave before us, is an object of envy beneath the clods that cover him." This is a strikingly careless sentence to inflict on families grieving for their loved ones. Lincoln's painful restraint deals with actual life and death.

Like Lincoln, Everett employs biblical phrases, though for him they are ornaments rather than, as for Lincoln, powerful evocations of profound religious ideals. Everett's last paragraph begins: " . . . let me again, as we part, invoke your benediction on these honored graves. You feel, though the occasion is mournful, that it is good to be here."

Several things make this piece of peroration miserable. One is that, in the shock and grief of the moment, it might not feel good to be there. Another is that Everett is content to pronounce a benediction and drift away, which of course is not wrong or unusual, but it is a world apart from what Lincoln's Address does. The chief item is the biblical allusion itself: "it is good to be here." The words recall the Transfiguration of Jesus in Mark 9:3–5:

> And his raiment became shining, exceedingly white as snow; so as no fuller on earth can white them. And there appeared unto him Elias with Moses: and they were talking with Jesus. And Peter answered and said to Jesus, Master, it is good for us to be here; and let us make three tabernacles; one for thee, and one for Moses, and one for Elias.

Everett's allusion is appropriate, but he does not realize how appropriate. Here on the mount of Cemetery Hill, the dead are transfigured; they have become heroes, immortals in our national pantheon. But in the New Testament story, Jesus has no time for making little shrines or booths to honor the heroes of Israel. His transfiguration is meant to kick his disciples into gear. They do not linger; Jesus brings them down from the mountain and out into the world. Lincoln wants us, the living, to be transfigured, and to get working.

But a writer for the *Providence Journal* gave the chief reason why Everett was memorizing a mere historical footnote on this day. After the dedication ceremony, he asked whether even "the most elaborate and splendid oration" could be "more beautiful . . . than those thrilling words from the President." The *Springfield Republican,* not originally a Lincoln paper, wrote that the president's Address has "the merit of unexpectedness in its verbal perfection and beauty."

* * *

What does it matter, that one speech was better than the other? Are we indulging in mere literary criticism? Was the event at Gettysburg a forensic competition? There was the matter of winning the war, which Everett's speech could not effect. The words we say here, Lincoln knew, could make a life and death difference to the Republic, and to any nation conceived in and dedicated to liberty. To Everett, the speech ultimately did not matter, except to himself as a success or a failure in performance. Lincoln, on the other hand, was transparent in the speech. The Gettysburg Address is filled to the full with purpose: it is a transaction between the dead and the living, between the past and the future, from which the speaker has disappeared. As such, Lincoln's Address was high art.

We might evaluate speeches on the basis of what they achieve. In 1992 a group of black South Africans toured the Kennedy Library in Boston.

Now middle-aged, they were veterans of South African jails, people who had been fighting apartheid for twenty-five years. The library's chief archivist asked them if they remembered Robert Kennedy's four-day visit to South Africa in 1966. To his amazement, five of the South Africans recited parts of RFK's Cape Town University speech.

Kennedy had spoken to his audience that evening about making a newer world of liberty and justice. There were four dangers working against taking the lead in "the introduction of a new order of things":

> First . . . futility: the belief that there is nothing one man or one woman can do against the enormous array of the world's ills. . . .

In reply to this danger, Kennedy asserted that, "It is from numberless diverse acts of courage and belief that human history is shaped." The second danger is "expediency," the idea that "hopes and beliefs must bend before immediate necessities." Against this danger, Kennedy said,

> if there was one thing President Kennedy stood for . . . it was the belief that idealism, high aspirations, and deep convictions are not incompatible with . . . realistic possibilities, no separation between the deepest desires of the human heart and of mind and the rational application of human effort to human problems.

The third danger is timidity; the fourth is comfort.

> Everyone here will ultimately be judged—will ultimately judge himself—on the effort he has contributed to building a new world society and the extent to which his ideals have shaped that effort.

The words had sustained them, they said, through the long, dark years.

NOVEMBER 18

We Have Come to Dedicate (The Visitor)

On November 18, 1863, President Abraham Lincoln arrived in Gettysburg. Up on Cemetery Hill, a speakers' platform stood ready. The digging of graves had been temporarily suspended.

When Abraham Lincoln stepped off the train, the citizens of Gettysburg saw the most recognizable figure in America, and at the same time the most utterly strange. A London *Times* reporter said you could not pass the president on the street without taking notice. He was self-conscious about his face, which many people termed ugly, but which others said could be the handsomest face they had ever seen. "He made such an impression," someone remembered. You were struck by the ugly, sad, dull strength and dignity of this tall man in wrongly fitting, rusty black. At nearly six-foot-four, Lincoln was one of the tallest men of his generation. (The average Civil War soldier was five-foot-seven.) But he looked even taller than he was. His hands and feet (size fourteen) were large, and his arms and legs extraordinarily long. His shoulders and chest were narrow. When he sat, he appeared no taller than anyone else except that his knees stuck up, as if he were sitting in a child's chair.

He was unusually strong. Having spent his youth and early manhood at manual labor, the president could still pick up four hundred pounds, or hold a heavy axe out straight from the shoulder, gripping it with only his thumb and two fingers. He had always known his strength.

When awakened from the "ugly, sad, dull" appearance he assumed in thought or repose, a "miracle" would take place. His amazingly mobile face would come to life, his eyes would light up, and he would be all expression and handsomeness. There is no photograph of this popular Lincoln, because to be photographed for a portrait in those days you had to freeze, head firmly against a brace, and wait for the plate to receive its full impression. No photograph, wrote Walt Whitman, gets the "subtle and indirect" expression of Abraham Lincoln. Another observer said that Lincoln's face is "unfathomable"; one "cannot understand" it. He was "the man nobody knows." His closest associate, law partner William Herndon, once boasted that he knew his partner better than Lincoln knew himself; but he had to admit, finally, "I never fully knew and understood him."

> He never revealed himself entirely to any one man, and therefore he will always to a certain extent remain enveloped in doubt. Even those who were with him through long years of hard study and under constantly varying circumstances can hardly say they knew him through and through. I always believed I could read him as thoroughly as any man, and yet he was so different in many respects from any other one I ever met before or since that I cannot say I comprehended him.

But some things about Abraham Lincoln struck everyone. "Lincoln's melancholy never failed to impress any man who ever saw or knew him," Herndon wrote. "The reader can hardly realize the extent of this peculiar tendency to gloom." People in Gettysburg, watching as the tall man in the tall black hat came up the street to the Wills house, would have noticed this worn, melancholy expression, and along with it they might have remarked to each other upon the black mourning band around the hat.

The president's son had died in February 1862. The affectionate Willie had been like his father—quiet, studious, intelligent. His mother and father had been pushed to their limits by Willie's death, and Lincoln, ultimately, had not been consoled. It seems altogether fitting that at Gettysburg, among the graves of the Republic, the president still mourned his own son.

* * *

There at the Foot of yonder nodding Beech
That wreathes its old fantastic Roots so high,
His listless Length at Noontide wou'd he stretch,
And pore upon the Brook that babbles by.

The Lincoln who steps forth in our imagination is partly a legendary figure. The homespun youth, barefoot, in blousy shirt, props himself on his elbows before the fire and reads perhaps those very lines from Gray's Elegy which were to fit him. His chief readings, he said, and as his own writings witness, were the Bible and Shakespeare. A few years later, a young man in New Salem, Lincoln was described by many as spending all the time he could manage prone with a book. Did he also lie listlessly beside the flowing Sangamon, hopelessly in love with the calm, lovely, and gracious Ann Rutledge?

Hard by yon Wood, now smiling as in scorn,
Mutt'ring his wayward Fancies he wou'd rove,
Now drooping, woeful wan, like one forlorn,
Or craz'd with Care, or cross'd in hopeless love.

When she died, a lasting November came to his soul. That is when, perhaps,

. . . Melancholy mark'd him for her own.

Some modern Lincoln scholars have doubted the Ann Rutledge "legend." Benjamin Thomas, whose work had long been the most reliable one volume biography, is skeptical. Stephen B. Oates goes quite a bit farther, claiming that there is not a "scintilla of evidence" supporting a love for Ann Rutledge on Lincoln's part. Now, what exactly is a "scintilla" when it comes to historical evidence? What we have for most of history are written scraps of paper. Of such scintillas we have quite a few regarding Abraham Lincoln and Ann Rutledge. Most of them are reports of witnesses in William Herndon's biography. David Herbert Donald's authoritative biography (1995) therefore accepts the fact of Lincoln's love for Ann Rutledge, and considers the question of his lifelong devotion to her to be unresolved. *The Shadows Rise: Abraham Lincoln and the Ann Rutledge Legend,* by John Evangelist Walsh (1993) reexamines Herndon's evidence and concludes that the story is true. *Herndon's Informants* prints a number of interviews with Lincoln's friends and acquaintances which support the belief that Lincoln loved Miss Rutledge.

The story for a while was that Mary Todd Lincoln detested Herndon, who despised her in return. It all started when he was introduced to her at a dance, in the course of which the very young man with the best of intentions calamitously praised her ability to dance by comparing her smoothness to that of a serpent. From her flash of indignation then stems the Ann Rutledge story, the recent theory went. As a means of exercising his hatred for Mrs. Lincoln, Herndon, when it came time to give posterity its best eyewitness picture of Abraham Lincoln, concocted a story about an early grief in love so as to show that his great law partner, Abraham Lincoln, could not really have loved such a termagant as Mary Todd.

But that theory assumes a lot about William Herndon. He would have had to have been quite the irresponsible, nasty midget. But that is not what he was. Lincoln himself is Herndon's best character witness: he chose him for his law partner. *Billy,* Abraham Lincoln said before he left for Washington in 1861, *I want you to leave our shingle just the way it is—"Lincoln and Herndon"—and if I come back when this is all over we'll go on practicing law together as if nothing had ever happened.* Abraham Lincoln was secure enough to choose strong personalities for his cabinet; he would not have chosen some insect for a law partner.

Herndon's book itself is a convincing witness. It is a masterpiece of description. Rightly, most of our picture of Lincoln goes back to Herndon. Has anyone surpassed Herndon's description of Lincoln as a public speaker?

> When he began speaking, his voice was shrill, piping, and unpleasant. His manner, his attitude, his dark, yellow face, wrinkled and dry, his oddity of pose, his diffident movements—everything seemed to be against him, but only for a short time. . . . As he proceeded he became somewhat animated, and to keep in harmony with his growing warmth his hands relaxed their grasp and fell to his side. Presently he clasped them in front of him, interlocking his fingers, one thumb meanwhile chasing another. His speech now requiring more emphatic utterance, his fingers unlocked and his hands fell apart. His left arm was thrown behind, the back of his hand resting against his body, his right hand seeking his side. By this time he had gained sufficient composure, and his real speech began. . . . He never sawed the air nor rent space into tatters and rags as some orators do. He never acted for stage effect. He was cool, considerate, reflective—in time self-possessed and self-reliant. His style was clear, terse, and compact. . . . He always stood squarely on his feet, toe even with toe; that is, he never put one foot before the other. He neither touched nor leaned on anything for support. He made but few changes in his positions and attitudes. He never ranted, never

> walked backward and forward on the platform. To ease his arms he frequently caught hold, with his left hand, of the lapel of his coat, keeping his thumb upright and leaving his right hand free to gesticulate. . . . As he proceeded with his speech the exercise of his vocal organs altered somewhat the tone of his voice. It lost in a measure its former acute and shrilling pitch, and mellowed into a more harmonious and pleasant sound. His form expanded, and, notwithstanding the sunken breast, he rose up a splendid and imposing figure. In his defense of the Declaration of Independence—his greatest inspiration—he was "tremendous in the directness of his utterances."

Herndon was not in the business of justifying anything about Abraham Lincoln. His irascibility was directed at exactly those people who were creating myths out of whole cloth. It did not take an enemy of Mrs. Lincoln to see that her husband was unhappy in his marriage. Going on the circuit for months at a time, spending only the odd weekend at home even after the railroads came—otherwise telling his stories in uproarious sessions with the other lawyers on the circuit, riding his plodding horse in the rain, or brooding the long prairie miles in his black carriage: he had no happy home.

Herndon saw firsthand the painful evidences of an unhappy union. This was one of the truths he meant to tell. In the nineteenth century this was tarnish, not legend. But his biography shows that he was not a single-minded, petty cad out to get Mary Todd. He is remarkably fair to her. His descriptions of her, taken on balance, are more favorable than unfavorable. On Herndon's pages we see Mary Todd not as a pudgy paranoid but as a masterful, socially gifted near-genius. This is fair reporting, because Mary Todd must have been one of the smartest people of the age. She had known what Abraham Lincoln knew, when nobody else had known it.

When the young man from New Salem was a recent arrival in Springfield, Mary Todd had for some time been acquainted with a young man named Stephen A. Douglas. The future "Little Giant" was already on the ascendant. Napoleonically dynamic, impressive in bearing and ambition, the cultured, socially adept, educated easterner was a power in state government. Dancing with the man one evening, Miss Todd quickly saw the brilliant career ahead of him—a conqueror who intended to go to the White House. Then the tall, poorly dressed, awkward young man just in from the sticks—Abraham Lincoln, knowing few of the social graces, marked, one would assume, for "homely Joys and Destiny obscure"—came up and said he wanted to dance with her in the worst way. (And that is exactly what he did, Mary said later.) She knew before the evening was over that this Abraham Lincoln, not Stephen A. Douglas, would one day be president of the United States. You and I would not have imagined it.

Her husband came to rely upon Mary Lincoln's ability to judge people's character and abilities, though of course his own sense was what he always came down to. She might not have liked Billy Herndon, but she did not think him a fool or a liar.

Ann Rutledge's grave is in the cemetery at Petersburg, Illinois, where she died, a few miles up the road from Lincoln's New Salem. Edgar Lee Masters's poem is inscribed on the stone:

> Out of me unworthy and unknown
> The vibrations of deathless music;
> "With malice toward none, with charity for all."
> Out of me the forgiveness of millions toward millions,
> Shining with justice and truth.
> I am Ann Rutledge who sleep beneath these weeds,
> Beloved in life of Abraham Lincoln,
> Wedded to him, not through union,
> But through separation.
> Bloom forever, O Republic,
> From the dust of my bosom!

* * *

If you and I are free partly because of someone's compassion born of suffering, then we might be excused for visiting, from time to time, the grave of Anne Rutledge, and also the grave of Nancy Hanks Lincoln in the woods of southern Indiana. From them a deathless beauty was brought forth in the November of Abraham Lincoln's soul.

> Let not Ambition mock their useful Toil,
> Their homely Joys and Destiny obscure;
> Nor Grandeur hear with a disdainful smile
> The short and simple Annals of the Poor.

We go not merely to grieve, but to recall that some do not live and die in vain. We would also be reminded that history rests upon wives, mothers, husbands and fathers, brothers and sisters. They helped to make us what we are. Our lives are conversations with them.

* * *

Deconstruction is a term given to reading a text by way of its inner tensions and contradictions. The critic—if a deconstructionist—considers him or herself superior to the original text, which is nothing more than raw material. The critic plays the text against itself, exploits its inner problems and contradictions, and comes up with a new text.

For instance, take "all men are created equal" as a mini-text. Because it apparently refers only to men, the text contradicts itself in asserting equality of any kind. We can go on, now, to make new "texts" starting from the old one, which our reading has exploded like a kernel of popcorn.

Never mind that *men* used to mean something different from what it means now. This difference—or *defer*-ence, to employ one of the clever puns that deconstructionists especially value because puns themselves show tensions in language—is inevitable from one usage to the next. A meaning in a text is *deferred* until some future reader discovers it, regardless of the original writer's understanding of his/her words.

Deconstructionists admire each other's texts. It does not matter that their turgid, nutsy prose usually produces new texts infinitely inferior to the old ones over which they claim superiority. They have expanded their "work" into all fields of the written word: law, theology, philosophy, history. Everything in these fields is raw material for new texts. Nothing rests on foundations more secure than language itself.

Deconstruction therefore has an apocalyptic feel. Unlike previous methods of misreading, distorting, and exploiting texts, deconstruction denies any authority. There is no objective truth, or God, or law of nature to fall back upon once deconstruction saws off the branch it is sitting on. Nor is there any connection to the past. What we fancied as a connection is only language, and language can be chopped up and scrambled. All there is to history is History (the texts). Nothing escapes the besom of destruction—or deconstruction.

Enter Abraham Lincoln with the Gettysburg Address. The Address can be read as an attempt to manipulate the audience through a deconstructive reading of the Declaration of Independence. That is, the Address's "text" reinterprets, recycles, and reinvents the Declaration's "text" in order to motivate people to win a war. It certainly was Lincoln's purpose to win a war. But is that all? That is, where is Lincoln's text? Is it above us, prophetically (that is, morally) interpreting history and enlightening us as to its meaning? Or is it right among us, a democratic attempt to understand what is happening, offered to equals trying to understand a tragic effort to restore liberty and union? Or is it beneath us somewhere—a "text" to be remade for our own purposes? Where is the platform?

Where has history gone? Well, it was never there in the first place. Written History tells not what was, nor what is, but only what we are saying. The universe has fallen in upon us. We have begun to think that all we can think about is ourselves thinking. Self-consciousness is the only consciousness. There is no Lincoln. There is no Gettysburg Address. There is no equality.

This is where we are, as deconstructing postmodernists. To paraphrase a young officer on Omaha Beach, only two kinds of people are going to stay here: those who are already dead, and those who are going to die. Theoretically, there is no way out. Sheer cliffs, machine guns, and human vulnerability dictate that conclusion. Nevertheless, anyone who wants to live is going to get up and *take those heights.* Hope is not insubstantial: its substance is faith. What broke through the concrete defenses at Normandy was the faith Lincoln defined at Gettysburg.

Let us not think, then, that beauty brings no practical results. Lincoln's Address has lived to defy the evil within us for a century and a half, and will live after we are gone.

* * *

Mr. Lincoln had come to Gettysburg today by a somewhat circuitous route, requiring two trains and six hours of travel. The itinerary had been publicized. Crowds of people who were beginning to love this president gathered at his stopping places. At one of them, a little girl was lifted up to a window of the presidential car. She held out a bouquet of rosebuds, saying, "Flowerth for the prethident." Mr. Lincoln went to the window, accepted the flowers, and leaned forward to kiss the child. "You're a sweet little rosebud yourself," he said to her. "I hope your life will open into perpetual beauty and goodness."

NOVEMBER 19

The Gettysburg Address

During the night it rained, dampening the dusty roads. Then the clouds moved on, and stars emerged in unshrouded heavens. Toward Baltimore and York the horizon paled, and the sun rose clear in a cloudless sky.

Its light shone upon a continuous procession of people approaching Gettysburg on its nine roads. They had started while it was still night, coming in their carriages, Pennsylvania wagons, buggies, farm carts, on horseback, and on foot. Some came out of curiosity, some came to hear Everett's oration, many came to see the president, or to pay their respects to the fallen. Many wore mourning: they were the families of the Union dead. In their thousands, the incoming people were like the armies of July that had concentrated on this town of twenty-four hundred residents. The houses were already filled with guests; in Gettysburg's few hotels, hundreds had slept on floors overnight. Trains arrived, discharging more visitors.

Ward Hill Lamon, the president's old Illinois friend, aide, and bodyguard, arose at dawn. He was in charge of the dedication ceremony and it was going to be a busy day. He ate a hurried breakfast and then walked to the Wills house to see whether the president needed anything. In the town square, a giant American flag had been lowered to half-staff on the sixty-foot flagpole.

Lamon was admitted to Judge Wills's house and was told that the president was already up, talking to John Nicolay upstairs. The presidential secretary had beaten Lamon, stopping by to see whether the president required anything. In fact, the president had made some changes to the last sentence of his speech. All of it except that tenth sentence was written in ink on a sheet of White House stationery, but the conclusion had been penciled on a blue-gray sheet of paper which Wills had given Mr. Lincoln last night. In a few minutes, the two came downstairs. Shortly afterward, Secretary of State William Seward joined the group.

Someone, perhaps Lamon, arranged for the president and secretary of state to be shown a portion of the battlefield, so the two went outside and stepped up into a carriage and were driven away through the town square. Lamon evidently had satisfied himself that the president's escort was sufficient, because he stayed behind to make certain the ceremony's marshals were all present, properly attired, and understood their instructions. Lamon was careful of the president's safety; the big, burly man carried two pistols, two revolvers, and two knives. Lincoln, a fatalist, gave little thought to danger, but he liked Lamon's company. The man was a hard drinker, a brawler, and loved the earthy stories that might provide a former prairie lawyer some escape from the cares of state. The president might have retained Lamon, as some biographers apologetically speculate, on Lincoln's maxim that those who have no vices have no virtues. In any case, Lamon would run a good program today.

The president's carriage turned up crowded Chambersburg Street. Someone probably pointed out to him that the first impressive building, Christ Lutheran Church, whose broad steps ascended on the party's left, had been a hospital during the battle and a chaplain had been shot to death on those steps. They continued up the street, against the flow of people coming the same direction that Lee's Third Corps had poured into town on July first. The presidential party headed for the Lutheran Theological Seminary, near which and on the grounds of which much of the first day of battle had been fought.

At the Seminary, Mr. Lincoln would have stepped down from the carriage and walked a little. From the gentle elevation of Seminary Ridge he would have seen a thousand Rebel graves. Some had been dug into the Seminary lawns; most lay in the fields directly in front of the buildings and off to the north. Many mounds; some boards jutting up from the ground bearing faded penciled inscriptions; some large burial pits. The Southerners had come that July afternoon in lines a half-mile wide and three ranks deep. Until flanked and overwhelmed, the outnumbered Union infantry and artillery here had mown down Lee's troops like grass—and here they lay. Lincoln did not think of Southerners as enemies, not invaders; they were us. We are one nation. The Union boys had died here too by the hundreds, holding Lee long enough for the rest of the Army of the Potomac to come up and secure the hills back on the other side of town. The battle had been won here at the Seminary on the first day, though it seemed like defeat at the time. Lincoln understood such things.

Those boys who had held on and died here lay up on Cemetery Hill now, the hill they had ensured would be a sanctuary for the Union army, and for republican government everywhere. Lincoln would be speaking over their graves, over their bodies.

The group walked on, through the dry stalks and weeds where fragments of clothing and equipment still lay as far as one could see, past the field burials, to a woodlot several hundred yards out from the Seminary. Lincoln stood silently regarding the spot where General Reynolds had been killed. Many thought John Reynolds had been the ablest officer in the Army of the Potomac. Just before Gettysburg, Lincoln had offered him command, but Reynolds had declined. Here is the place where he died. Reynolds had selected this place to fight. He had been waving some of his infantry into a charge when a bullet found the back of his head.

The president was quiet on the drive back to the Wills House. The battlefield affects people now, nearly 150 years later; then, it had been only four months. Mr. Lincoln went to his upstairs room. He must change into clothing appropriate for the ceremony.

At ten o'clock, he came downstairs. The president wore his usual black from hat to boot, contrasted today by a pair of white riding gloves which Mrs. Lincoln must have sent along. People noticed that Lincoln looked serious and melancholy. Even his ride to the cemetery would bear that impression out: he would begin by sitting up stiffly in a dignified manner, but soon forget all except his own thoughts, hunching forward in the saddle and musing abstractedly.

But first he had to get to his horse, held ready for him outside the Wills house, and this was no easy assignment. A crowd waited outside, and as soon as the president emerged from the house, people pressed forward. Someone proposed three cheers, and hundreds of people on York Street and in the square responded heartily. Then they crowded around Lincoln, who now was busy shaking hands. He could not get to his horse.

Lamon stepped forward and bellowed an order for the crowd to move back and let the president through. Lincoln then mounted, but the crowd penned his horse and wore out the president's right hand and arm. Lamon now ordered his marshals forward. These men wearing yellow and white scarves cleared the way for Lincoln, and the procession got under way, amid three more cheers louder than the first.

The procession was impressive. The Marine Band led, followed by cavalry, artillery, a full regiment of infantry, and another band. In a photograph taken that morning on Baltimore Street, the infantry's bayonets gleam in the sun. Behind the military rode the president and other dignitaries, including three cabinet members and nine governors. Behind them came representatives of the eighteen states that had commissioned the Soldiers' National Cemetery; and following behind all came a great crowd of townspeople and visitors.

Lamon had things well planned, because when the military procession arrived at the crowded cemetery the troops moved irresistibly into two facing lines leading from the entrance to the speakers' platform. Thus they made an avenue for the president. When he arrived and dismounted, the waiting thousands went respectfully silent, and all the men removed their hats.

It was nearly noon. Lamon, the master of ceremonies, looked around for the main speaker, who had not ridden with the procession. Edward Everett was fashionably late. He had taken a stroll over part of the battlefield, but he was not out there now. He was in a small tent behind the platform. It seems he had spoken so euphemistically, and with such gentility, about his need for a tent adjacent the platform, that a couple of dignitaries entered it with Everett, and it had been some time before he could get rid of them. His kidneys unburdened and his appearance refreshed, Everett now left his tent. Judge Wills and the governor of New York went down to escort the speaker up the platform steps, and everyone rose. The president shook Everett's hand, the dignitaries sat, and Lamon stepped forward to begin the ceremony.

He read some regrets from officials who were not present, a band played a dirge, then Lamon introduced Rev. Thomas H. Stockton, chaplain of the House of Representatives. Stockton's prayer lasted nearly ten minutes, and while some considered it "a prayer that thought it was an oration," it expressed the grief felt by many who had come to mourn their fathers, husbands, and sons. The president's eye moistened as the minister spoke about the men whose bodies now lay in new graves or waited in coffins for burial: "Alas, how little we can do for them! We come with the humility of prayer, with the pathetic eloquence of venerable wisdom, with the tender beauty of poetry and with the plaintive harmony of music, with the honest tribute of our Chief Magistrate, and with all this honorable attendance: but our best hope is in thy blessing, O Lord, our God! O Father, bless us! Bless the bereaved."

At the prayer's conclusion, Lamon signaled the Marine Band to play the hymn. As the full tones of "Old Hundred" fell and faded, Everett moved to the podium, carefully placed the manuscript to which he would not refer, and began his oration. While Everett spoke, hundreds at the fringes of the crowd (estimated at ten to fifteen thousand) wandered off, either unable to hear or uninterested. Some preferred to walk the hallowed ground and think their own thoughts, say their own prayers. But most listened, and when Everett finished after more than two hours the applause, though not enthusiastic, was polite.

A men's chorus then sang an ode composed for the ceremony, and when they finished, Lamon stood and said, "The president of the United States." Lincoln rose and stepped to the podium. Waiting for silence, he adjusted his spectacles, found that the sun glared off his pages, and put aside the spectacles. Holding the two sheets in his left hand, Lincoln spoke the Address from memory. He spoke more easily than usual, with calm expression, in a tenor voice that could be heard at the edges of the crowd:

FOUR SCORE AND SEVEN YEARS AGO

As an invocation starts a tale, the deep Address begins. The first words work like an incantation; they raise us from our narrow place in time. The years are skimmed by a phrase familiar long ago: our ancestors' time will be our time. The past has been remade, brought forth in both senses: brought into our sight, and given birth.

This antique phrase is elevated like the words of epic poets: *Sing, goddess, of the wrath of Achilles; Offspring of heaven first-born; Arms and the man I sing*—though the mastering spirits invoked are not gods but men; the Our Father here is "our fathers." Who ever knows their father? Up from a mythic, timeless past emerge the mystic unknown figures:

OUR FATHERS BROUGHT FORTH

Named "fathers" like the Old Testament patriarchs or like God himself, but performing the work of a mother, the founders "brought forth" the nation as the New Testament says Mary *brought forth* her firstborn son. This speech will be saturated with biblical thought, language, and cadences—arising from Lincoln's youth in the fertile ground of the old-time religion, spoken to people who knew well the King James Bible and who believed the doctrines of traditional Christianity. Lincoln conceived and expressed political theory in the usage of American Protestantism, not for the first time—it had been done since the Puritans—but uniquely. These "fathers" are mothers. They are not doctors or midwives. The fathers are named fathers, but as spiritual or ideal figures they are both and neither male and female, father and mother. Liberty is the ecstasy, the transport, the *Union*—in a realm higher than things of the material world—out of which came an incarnation, something into the world of things: out of *liberty* and suprasensual ideals working as *persons,* like the Trinity, a supraearthly society or association or *union,* comes an earthly *thing,* an *incarnation:*

A NEW NATION, CONCEIVED IN LIBERTY

Like a growing child, a Savior of humankind, a savior of the other incarnate beings like himself, as the infant Jesus was brought before the Lord ("Every male that openeth the womb shall be called holy to the Lord") in a ceremony of dedication, so the new nation does not live to itself, but is presented *for* something or Someone higher, and the people of the earth are in this way saved:

AND DEDICATED TO THE PROPOSITION THAT ALL MEN ARE CREATED EQUAL.

If Christ is brother to all of us, then we are all brothers and sisters of each other. If America was dedicated to the proposition that all people are created equal, then all Americans insofar as they are Americans, accept that proposition and are, as creatures of God, equal with each other. Insofar as the people remain a nation, that nation belongs to the proposition, as a dedicated child brought to the Lord belongs to Him.

It is not correct that Lincoln included God only late in the Address, and late in its writing. God is there from the first sentence. No one is created, equal or otherwise, unless there is a creator. But the creator, like equality, is proposed—*is in the proposition.* He may be only a hypothesis, but the creator is inseparable from equality. We are equal not by natural right, or by reason's demands, or by human power, but by virtue of the nature of our creation. This is an essential part of the proposition to which we are dedicated. Mysterious, unmanifest except by His arts, God stands behind the revelation/mask of epic and New Testament images. Only *proposed,* the Godhead is not *known* by us; but like fabled Israel we, America, take our chosen identity from Him and apart from him have no unique being. But we have moved an American step from the English Puritan idea of a nation chosen by God, to a nation that chooses God, thereby chooses itself, dedicates itself, takes up its cross and crown, gives birth to itself and in these words themselves keeps conceiving itself.

This American savior of humankind must struggle, like Adam and

Eve outside of paradise must *work*, to *make* this proposition true, to *prove* that it is true, to give birth back to the proposition that gave it birth.

NOW

When the fathers are gone except in the proposition they institutionalized, except in *us*—the time has become real: curt, short, without a mist of archaic or elevated euphemism or euphony—a blunt, hitting word, because in that work and struggle we have been hit, bullets are flying, the test is upon us all in blood:

WE ARE ENGAGED IN A GREAT CIVIL WAR,

Not the fathers, and not the past, but *now, we*. It is impossible that the rest of the Address could simply eulogize the dead, or dedicate a resting place. The present is a tough time, brought here by tough talk, and it is in our hands.

And we are our own enemies. It is not *we* against the South. There are no two countries, only one. It is *we* against ourselves. It is a *civil* war. There is a mysterious purpose, a supervening power like the epic fate or the Christian will of God, but all we can see, by the light God gives us, are the human agencies. The opposition to our proposition might start as principalities and powers above the earth and below the earth, but it is people against people—people who would be kings, people who would be tyrants, people who would be overseers, and people who acquiesce in or gain from their power; these people, ourselves, oppose us: the sin is in us. First within us must be created a clean heart; a right spirit must be renewed. If we are the last, best hope of earth, then our divided house must be set in order, because the people of the world are saved through the proposition only if they give it their *assent*. It is a matter of words, still, and ideas, still, and of spirit and will, though the struggle between assent to or refusal of the proposition is incarnate in a physical, civil war.

TESTING WHETHER THAT NATION

Who asks the questions? Who administers the test? We who are reading Lincoln's words are the judges of whether his listeners passed the test. A fine and unwelcome responsibility—because it implies that we, also, will be judged by our posterity. The Address points toward the future; the little diamond of 272 words bulks itself into the last paragraph, the future tense.

Does the testing come of itself? Is it somehow imposed by the future? Is there a supreme Tester? Is the idea of self-governance naturally tested in a world hostile to the idea? If the latter, then how has the hostility arisen? Perhaps Lincoln believes human nature is corrupt or naturally craven, greedy, and authoritarian. The world operates, by itself, according to the law of the jungle, where power, hunger, and fear legislate. But humanity, if the proposition is true, was not created in that state; humanity has reached its depraved condition unnaturally, through an agency of evil, or through its own free will. The movement toward equality, then, is impelled by divine intervention or by the growing enlightenment of humankind, and the cumulative force of centuries of learning and reason. If humans were created equal among themselves and also given the capacity to choose evil and good, we also have the innate gift of reason to battle against and eventually overcome the will to power, the tyranny of hunger, the slide toward greed. Lincoln's speeches and actions are predominantly reasonable and reasoning. For him the better angels of our nature reason together. If he has properly explicated and extended the original proposition conceived by the Revolutionary generation of 1776, sons of the Enlightenment, then Lincoln, the proposition, the nation itself, are children of the Enlightenment, too. Now, over a century after Lincoln, the Enlightenment ideas are shattering, assailed on both sides by heathen and Christian; now, as a millennium passes, a rough beast has the Enlightenment mind in its hard jaws. *Now* we too are engaged in a great civil war.

OR ANY NATION SO CONCEIVED, AND SO DEDICATED

America is preeminent, not in power, not in wealth, but in example. The savior is a rabbi, a teacher, the truth of whose teachings depends upon the purity, courage, and faithfulness of his life. The savior's authority—the authority of America's example and therefore the power of its proposition over the whole world, tyrant and slave alike—derives from the consent of the governed. If the governed do not consent—if they are not *united*—the nations of the world will not go up to the holy house, for it will have divided into ruin. These truths we hold to be self-evident. How does this war test whether *any* nation so conceived and dedicated can long endure? The longest leap of logic in the Address occurs here. Why must other nations fail where America fails? It may be that the president refers to a *belief* of the other nations: that this American trial will show them all whether political equality is possible. Yet the logical leap still would exist, now in the minds of others. Lincoln is stating, perhaps, a simple truth, whether logical or not: Other countries will not summon the strength to try establishing political equality if American liberty and justice perish.

The president implies a simple statement: *If American equality fails, all potential equalities fail.* They will remain unborn. The other side of the statement is not implied: if America succeeds, all potential equalities (nations conceiving themselves according to the proposition of equality) will succeed. Perhaps some will fail, but not all will fail. America makes no guarantee of success to others. However, its failure would doom others. In asking why, we imply the question: Why has not the failure of others before us similarly doomed America?

The answer reveals a radical assumption: There have been no others. Democracies, republican experiments, yes. But nations dedicated to the proposition that all are created equal? No. Never before. Show me one, Lincoln might say. For him, then, equal justice under the law is prior even to liberty, for the condition of liberty must be equally shared by all. The democracy of previous peoples extended only to some; others were slaves or otherwise disfranchised. There is no liberty, in the American sense, without equality—that is to say, justice. The great postmodern, post-Enlightenment American mistake is to assume the other way around: that liberty is prior to justice. Liberty without justice almost immediately runs to the end of its tether and chokes; it becomes the privilege and power of the few. But justice entails, necessitates, liberty. Where one has power over another, without that other's consent there is not equal justice under the law.

More than this is implied. America *became a nation* at exactly the same time it was dedicated to that proposition. The Declaration of Independence created, out of not merely thirteen entities but out of *more* than political entities, a *new* nation. At that moment what came soon to be called the United States of America was born. Where there was no nation, there now appeared a nation. It was like the universe being created by a statement. Words *made* something. (The Declaration is an Enlightenment document not only in its philosophical assumptions, but also in that people declared *themselves* free, *created themselves* as a nation. No king did it, and God established it only insofar as the nation conforms by its own decision to a general condition made by the Creator.)

There is still more to this proposition, and that is the *basis* for equality. Lincoln's view assumes a Creator. It is not merely a nineteenth-century mode of speech, to say "created equal" instead of, say, "are equal" or "naturally are equals." Lincoln would not have said it differently today. No other nation brought itself into being coterminous with its belief in God who has created people as equals.

The closest is ancient Israel, but only because it came into being around Moses and the Exodus. America alone has combined biblical Israel's theism and the Enlightenment belief in the equality of people.

Lincoln understands the Declaration in more strongly Enlightenment terms than even Jefferson. For Lincoln, the statement of equality is a "proposition"—not an assertion or a "self-evident" truth. The test, therefore, is logical. If the proposition is valid, a nation so dedicated can survive. If there is a contradiction somewhere in the proposition, an invalidity, it will expose itself in the practical, tangible world. The real foundation for the proposition's validity is that it will work better than any other. It is truer than any other. It is an *exclusive* proposition. That is, the alternatives must be false. If it is false that human beings are unequal, then governments trying to operate on that basis must fail. On the other hand, the proposition, *if true, must work.* Equality is not logical or theoretical, but *political.* If we are politically equal, that truth will be shown if nowhere else *politically.*

Therefore, the test of the proposition is imposed, finally, not by posterity or by other nations, but by the logic of action.

Nevertheless, there is a secondary sense in which the nations test our results. As the United States can have a new birth of freedom, so perhaps can other peoples have new births, can rouse themselves and dedicate their countries to this proposition. So perhaps, too, can they be partially reborn, approaching like the United States itself, imperfectly, a proposition that creates teleologically from the future. Thus the disfranchised people of the world, the unjustly handled, watch for hope and inspiration.

Only an Enlightenment manner of thought can so convert a transcendent, logical proposition to the everyday, material well-being of individual people in this world. There is no more accurate apotheosis of the Enlightenment than the Gettysburg Address. It is the most modern thing ever said.

WE ARE MET

The Address is leavened with archaic expressions which heighten the language and separate it from everyday speech, as Homer and Virgil lifted the language of their epics toward the level of their heroic themes: "Fourscore and seven," "brought forth," "we are met," "perish from the earth." Lincoln, like Milton, creates his own language: "our fathers," "altogether fitting and proper," "our poor power to add or detract," "the last full measure of devotion," "a new birth of freedom." Like the language of *Paradise Lost,* the language of the Address sounds familiar because of its ancient echoes—Latin, for Milton, and the Bible for both. However, it is a language no one spoke at the time, or had ever spoken before, or has since. Lincoln has brought forth for this occasion a new idiom.

The rhetorical devices in the speech, carefully worked over the course of long thought and repeated revision, add firmness and life to the ancient echo, but the structure of the speech gestures emphatically toward the future. The shortest paragraph is the first, dealing with the past. The paragraph beginning with "Now" is a little longer. But longer than both is the final paragraph: the unfinished task remaining before us—that this nation, under God, shall have a new birth of freedom—and that popular government shall not perish. The brevity of the speech is likewise aimed at the future: short, direct, memorable, imperative. At no point are we more than two minutes from the war, these graves, the future. This is no time for speeches. The Address is not a speech, it is an act. A new thought, a new language, a new dedication—it punches the future into action.

"We are met" reminds us of our own presence here. No recounting of the battle as history, no eulogizing—a deliberate refusal to dedicate the dead or the ground—the speech places our feet on this hallowed ground. We are one part of the triangle: past, present, future; the heroes, ourselves, those who come after us. Now, what are we going to do about it? These dead are *here;* we are *here;* we are standing on holy ground. Now what? Are we going to make ourselves worthy of our position, standing on the very ground of their example? Will *we* nobly save, or meanly lose, the last best hope of earth?

We are met together. In relation to these dead, we are one. What they did here has made us one grieving family. The words of the Address declare us all children of the same fathers, parents of the same children. In the midst of civil war, all of us here are its antidote: we are one here, now, during this moment, and in this resolve.

We are here to dedicate. It is our intent, our desire; and together only will we ensure the new birth of freedom. "Freedom and Union, one and inseparable, now and forever!"

WE ARE MET ON A GREAT BATTLEFIELD OF THAT WAR.
The name Gettysburg is not given. It is a universal battlefield in a universal war for equality. Nor has "that nation" ever been named. It is one place standing for all places where the test of endurance is met. It was on Cemetery Hill, at Gettysburg, during the Civil War in America that Abraham Lincoln spoke these words in order to strengthen the Union's will to fight and win. But in a larger sense, the place, the battle, the war, the nation, these words, belong to the ages.

The battlefield we are met upon is in the mind or spirit, and the weapons are words. What hearts decide will be played out in flesh and blood. Lincoln wrote that at any time the Almighty, by operating on the minds of men, could have ended the struggle, but evidently chose to have it carried on. Perhaps the struggle could not cease until it was defined. Here, on the field of a battle fought in the middle of the war, as in the climax at the midpoint of a Shakespeare play, the lines of conflict were drawn clearly. Perhaps the war could not be understood for what it was, or what it could be, until it was carried into the North, until it was aimed at the heart of the Union. Now that heart has been illuminated by fire. The nation has finally fought itself to the bone; the beating heart, appallingly frail, frighteningly mortal, is laid bare; it is full of blood.

Equality is mortal. It is in the hearts and veins of everyone in this place, or it does not beat at all. Its dead lie all around us, at our feet; the beating of our own hearts carries the task forward.

We are reminded of where we are. The thought alone inspires and humbles us. Are we worthy to stand where they struggled, died, and now lie? It depends. What will we do about what we know? Their struggle gave birth to this understanding. They may not all have known what they were fighting for, but now, the definition having been fought to light, their acts take on the hallowed purpose: Their future moving back into their present, they died for the proposition that all men are created equal. Our past has been redeemed and sanctified. The illumination that *they* brought forth has done this. History has been rewritten by the issue their deaths defined.

Now the great battlefield and that war are no longer intolerable. Random death, meaningless advance and retreat, the chaos of chance have been replaced by purpose. The tall man whose election started this long war now stands at the center of it, and becomes its voice: " . . . I confess plainly, that events have controlled me." All join, using his words in the great chorus of the Union, which is the only means of equality.

Several Confederates were mistakenly buried in the graves we are met to dedicate. All around, farther out on the battlefield, lie thousands more. Lincoln believed them not to be a belligerent nation, but insurgents within the single nation. Why did they die? Is the Address their perfect tribute as well? No, and yes. There is no vindictiveness in Lincoln, and certainly no nonsense. The Southerners were forces against Union and equality; hence, despite their intentions, they fought against liberty as well. They were wrong. They have to be defeated in order for the world's hope to survive. If they come back into the Union, it can only be as people who repent of an evil.

But in another sense the new birth of freedom is their work, too. Without their challenge in the name of liberty, the nature of liberty would not have been defined. Without their challenge, the evil of inequality, assented to and participated in by Americans on both sides, would long endure. Had they ceased fighting early, the results of the war would be less "fundamental and astounding." The offense must needs come; nevertheless, woe to him by whom the offense cometh.

Neither side has escaped the horror. This field belongs to everyone who does not live a holy life in a perfect world.

The benefits of equality and liberty will belong to any people who choose them. It is not for the Union dead or for the Southern dead to be dedicated or not dedicated; it is for *us* to be dedicated. Not the past, but the future will be consecrated. Anyone North or South can be dedicated, consecrated, hallowed, if they choose to take up the great task remaining before us.

WE HAVE COME TO DEDICATE A PORTION OF THAT FIELD

Or so we think. We are drawn to the ceremony of a great event. The battle itself has become a ceremony, now that it is a past and therefore imagined event. (Even for the soldiers, most of the battle must be imagined, because they saw only a small portion of that field. What they do remember becomes gradually more mixed with imagination.) The ceremony is meaningful, whereas the battle was chaos. Only the perspective of a *will* makes the events meaningful. It is so only within the framework of that will, but we wish to accept some framework that cures the chaos of our relationship to the events. This ceremony afterward perhaps can straighten out the mess of this battle, this war, this fear, this uncertainty, this grief.

But we are in for a surprise. The president will not dedicate a portion of the field, he will assent to no ceremony; he will put the work of meaning upon us. He has taken up the burden of interpretation, but we must carry it away from the battlefield. The future, which is even more chaotic than the past in that it is less known, is illuminated partly by these words; however, it must be brought forth into organized existence by our dedication. The ceremony is for us; it is not an end but a beginning. Only for a moment may we look at that battlefield

AS A FINAL RESTING PLACE FOR THOSE
WHO HERE GAVE THEIR LIVES

This is part of Lincoln's refusal. No "resting place" will be dedicated. This was not a place of rest in July, nor is it a place of rest for us, the living, in November. Even in our ashes live their wonted fires. We must take something from this place, from these dead—take something back to the madding crowd's ignoble strife, to ennoble that strife and to win it. Here they gave their lives; from here we take what they gave: not death but life, not rest but action. What specifically can we take from the lives they gave? Not life itself, of course, for us individually; but somehow in a grand economy their gift, their life, could not be wasted. Action comes from action, and birth comes from life, just as freedom comes from justice. If their gift can be taken up, it must be somehow congruous with what they gave: not dust to dust, but life from life. They are the ones who gave. From action, we must take action if they are not to have given their lives in vain; from dedication, dedication; from life, new birth. Let not dismissive sentimentality mock their useful toil. In us, in our action, they shall not sleep, but wake.

Though he knew his Address would be read by thousands if not millions elsewhere in place and time, and not merely heard by the audience at Gettysburg, Mr. Lincoln emphasizes *here.* He means to bring us all to Gettysburg. The honored dead *here,* lying at the platform's feet, are the firm foundation of these words. The institution in and by which republican government is perpetuated rests on the blood of martyrs—but, like the church, it depends upon a living person. We are brought here, to Gettysburg. Liberty and equality rest upon *their* dedication to the proposition of equality, likewise upon *our* dedication. *We* and *they* come together at the words.

What they did here is passed on to us in, with, and under these words. Farm boys and mechanics, shopkeepers and teachers, sons and husbands and brothers, they did not seek the honor and the glory of their task; neither did they fail to accept the work that was thrust to them. They did not retreat back toward their former cool sequestered vale of life, but in the hands of God rose to shoulder their fine and fatal dedication, and pursued the clamorous tenor of their doom. Therefore ask not for homely joys and destiny obscure; ask rather for one nation, under God, with liberty and justice for all; ask for a just and lasting peace among ourselves and with all nations.

THAT THAT NATION MIGHT LIVE.

The word *that* appears a number of times in the Gettysburg Address. It is particularly important in the final sentence, the syntax of which is not clear unless we understand how Lincoln means the blankly flexible word *that.* (Lincoln's use of *that,* first of all, is an echo of Jefferson's use of the word in the Declaration of Independence: "that all men are created equal, that they are endowed . . .") The speech in this sense interprets itself; it provides its own key, in an unexpectedly small word. The word, except where it is meant to call attention to one specific thing out of all in the class—that nation, pointed out from all nations—means "in order for." It is a briefer form of "in order that" or "so that." These dead gave their lives so that this nation might live.

But Lincoln does not say "this nation," even though he says *here,* intending to be local. He means for the nation founded on the proposition to be considered from a distance. Partly, it is the distance of an ideal. He does not want *that nation* to be confused with *this nation,* because *this* nation is not fully dedicated to equality yet. *That* nation, if we contemplate it from outside and agree that its nature is good and desirable, becomes a task of our decision rather than a mere accident of our birth. It is not a location but an ideal. He wants *this* nation to become *that* nation. It exists in the mind, however much it is physically coextensive with or dependent upon the country called the United States of America. Here is more Enlightenment idealism: The ideal form does not exist anywhere, not even in a realm of ideas, except as it is worked toward and realized. But it is an idea.

The idea's realization is conditional. "Might" means partly "would," and partly "have the chance to." The condition, partially fulfilled by their dedication, partially depends upon our own dedication now, and, if the speech truly "wears well," upon the dedication of those who follow us. Well before its midpoint, the Address leans toward the future.

At this place the Gettysburg Address touches the mystic chords of human life, perhaps arising out of, and gleaming in toward, the unconscious mind. The president speaks of life coming from death. This is an ancient motif of eulogies, resonating with the belief that the dead can nourish our spirits. More pointedly and powerfully, it resonates with the story of a dying god. In Christianity, the sacrificial death of Christ gives followers an eternal forgiven life—but the dying and rising god is a motif known widely in the history of religions. From the god's death comes a benefit, comes life. The Gettysburg Address partakes of this archetype, sharing its mythic power. Its authority and truth are tested by our dedication to it. It is we who are inspired; it is for us, the living, to breathe the breath of life.

What nourishment have these dying soldiers given us? What is the nature of the life they have passed on? Only that life for which they fought and died. That life is described farther on. But first, the deflecting and inadequate intentions of the audience must be put to rest:

IT IS ALTOGETHER FITTING AND PROPER
THAT WE SHOULD DO THIS.

These dead could be like any other dead. To come to dedicate a final resting place is prescribed by custom: it is not larger than the custom. "Fitting and proper" means that dead people's bodies should be buried with ceremony. Meant in ancient times to send the dead away to the place of the dead, the funeral ceremony means at all times to comfort the living. The president did not come to Gettysburg for this. There is a war on; the war has a purpose. You can almost hear the next word coming.

BUT IN A LARGER SENSE, WE CANNOT DEDICATE—
WE CANNOT CONSECRATE—WE CANNOT
HALLOW THIS GROUND.

The modulations are given in ascending order. The substitution of "hallow" for "dedicate" is necessary, for we can dedicate. We can set something aside for an exclusive, designated purpose. But Lincoln must have us think of dedication in another way. The speech turns on a pun, or an equivocation in the philosophical sense: two uses for the same word. The two are related. The center of the speech is poetic: the double use of a word generates a new illumination in both directions, toward both words. To do this, Lincoln must dissatisfy us with our intended uses of the word *dedicate.*

If we came thinking we could hallow this ground, we now feel silly. We quickly throw down such presumption. But we never intended to hallow anything. Either Mr. Lincoln has hornswoggled us, or we assent to having our vision enlarged. Dedication must have not only a larger meaning, it must have a sacred meaning.

It has been thought at many other times and places that ground *can* be consecrated. It has been thought that a pope or a bishop could do this. The Address expresses a deeply ingrained Protestant viewpoint. Here President Lincoln's words reflect not simply the Enlightenment, but the origin of the Enlightenment and of the Modern World: the Reformation. No human, whether by apostolic succession or by ecumenical council, can declare something to be holy. Something can be sacred only self-evidentially. There is no other humanly mediated authority. The Scripture is called holy because of its content, and not because the church has declared it to be so. To whom does the job, the right, the dangerous responsibility of declaring the basis of faith to be the basis of faith belong? It is for us, the living. Similarly, Mr. Lincoln does not declare the ground to be sacred; he declares that the soldiers have made the ground sacred by their acts. If we agree with him, that's that. The idea is more or less self-evident to the extent that we agree with it.

Lincoln's thought is so pervasively religious, and his religion is so pervasively political, that ground symbolizing dedication to the proposition becomes sacred. Salvation is not individual, it is communal: in this Lincoln's view is thoroughly biblical. Further, if there is any separation between religion and politics, one or the other or both are false. If the soldiers' actions have made this place holy, it is only because there is a source and arbiter of holiness, it is only because we are all "under God," and only because the proposition that all men are created equal comes from God.

THE BRAVE MEN, LIVING AND DEAD, WHO STRUGGLED HERE, HAVE CONSECRATED IT

The ground itself can be consecrated—has been consecrated. Places on the physical earth, according to the Address, can become sacred. What does "sacred" mean? First, it means that a place is set aside from the ordinary uses and traffic of the area around it. This is not what Lincoln means, however, because it is the state and national governments, not the "brave men," which declare and protect the separate, specialized existence of the Soldiers' National Cemetery. For the president, this ground itself has a quality—which no declaration or human act after the battle could establish.

The sacredness of holy ground, which it has derived from acts in the past, consists in its power over the future. Were the future not to be affected by their struggle, these dead shall have died in vain. A holy place affects us now, heals us now, and sends us out to do the will of that power which has made the place sacred. A holy place is inspirational. In this sense, the sacred scriptures of the world are sacred. Similarly here, through the medium of words, last July's holy acts will seize us today, and working with our wills, shall exert force tomorrow.

To what extent has the divine nature of sacred acts become humanized in Lincoln's mind? At first it seems that he has entirely appropriated religious language for human, political concepts. If this is true, we have a wily Address indeed, gripping us at our deepest concepts, sounding our most revered resonances, for historical, military, and political purposes. To an extent this must be true. But it cannot be the main idea.

This is so because Mr. Lincoln *reverses* the process that would have meant humanization of religious concepts. He does not say *we* are using *their* acts. On the contrary, we are the ones *being used.* We are not the ones affecting a change over the acts of the past—that is, in the terms within the speech itself. We are the ones *affected.* We cannot dedicate. We are the ones to be dedicated. It will not do for us to think we are in control of events, through our language or otherwise. Something in the soldiers' acts has assumed power over us. We cannot establish anything by what we say here; we can at most try to understand what they did here.

This understanding, like understanding the Bible, involves not conceptualizing but *doing.* "A good understanding have all they that do his commandments." Thus the understanding comes only in the future, with our doing.

The Gettysburg Address was, in Mr. Lincoln's mind, not an act imposed upon the war, but rather his *explication* of the war. Throughout his presidential years, he tried to *understand* what was going on. These attempts were not made apart from his religious consciousness. "Why doesn't the war end?" is always the question, *why doesn't God end the war*? "What is the war for?" is always, *what is God's purpose for the war*? In November 1863, Abraham Lincoln was still working toward an answer. Seventeen months later he was farther along, and his thinking was an acceptance of the mystery of God's will. All he could see to act upon ("with firmness in the right, as God gives us to see the right, let us strive on to finish the work we are in . . . ") was a hypothesis, a *proposition,* that all men are created equal. As both a political and religious foundation for all of this—the political and religious being inseparable—the proposition could not lead the incomparably logical Lincoln to denature the religious content of sacredness.

Furthermore, the president never went beyond his very legal understanding of the will of the people and, even more, the confines of the Constitution, despite his own strong feelings. The prime example of this is emancipation. Though it was Lincoln's "oft-expressed personal wish that all men everywhere be free," he did not abolish slavery until he believed that the only point at which presidential power could be invoked against it had arrived. It was the war power. Only military necessity could justify abolition as a means of depriving the South of human resources. Therefore, slaves could be freed only in rebellious states. Loyal states could not constitutionally have their slavery touched by presidential order rather than by constitutional amendment. Lincoln was criticized for not emancipating earlier, and he has been criticized for not emancipating all American slaves everywhere. But his restraint was not hypocrisy; it was logic—and, no doubt, courage. With the Union saved, and the Constitution not destroyed to do it (its destruction being the practical result of a successful rebellion), there was hope of transforming American society with slavery abolished and equality strengthened. The president believed in doing only the legal and the possible, as power was given him to do so. That power came from the people through the Constitution, and it came from above. Without divine aid, Lincoln had told his townspeople when he left Springfield, he could not succeed; with God's help, he could not fail. That divine help would not be given apart from the democratic will of a people whom the divine will had established.

The speech, then, points its understanding of the Civil War forward. He might state the founding belief in the proposition, but neither proposition nor belief bring about the *meaning* of the proposition and the faith that realizes it: "for just as the body without the spirit is dead, so faith without works is also dead." The essence of the speech is its transmission, not establishment, of Gettysburg's sacredness; that is, the essence of the Gettysburg Address is future work for equality.

It is that work, not men's deaths, that have made Gettysburg holy. *The brave men, living and dead, who have struggled here, have consecrated it*

FAR ABOVE OUR POOR POWER TO ADD OR DETRACT.

The limitations in the Address are the rudder of its exhortation. We cannot dedicate. We cannot consecrate. We cannot even add or detract very much. Ours is a poor power.

The Gettysburg Address implies an understanding of human insignificance. It is the *work* that is great. Those who did this work have been ennobled by it, and by their devotion to it. What *we* might try to add to or subtract from that work, for our own reasons, sums up to not much. Mr. Lincoln did not believe that by thoughts and words he could bend the past to his purposes. His words were not intended to master the soldiers at Gettysburg; his words were intended to follow from their works.

The worst injustice we do comes from neglecting our unimportance. *The Paths of Glory lead but to the Grave.* We die if there is no food; we perish without water or love. We cannot buy away a stroke or heart attack; we spoil like fish in the grave. We are all created equal. *Why should the spirit of mortal be proud?*

Napoleon might not have marched to Waterloo, or waded through slaughter to his throne, had he regarded his bare paunch in the mirror every morning. Tyranny is false glory; oppression is a forgetting of our frame; injustice is a failure of humility. The great proposition is based less upon our power than upon our weakness.

THE WORLD WILL LITTLE NOTE, NOR LONG REMEMBER, WHAT WE SAY HERE, BUT IT CAN NEVER FORGET WHAT THEY DID HERE.

This statement is often taken as modesty, even calculated modesty. Or it is taken as a compliment to the soldiers—which it must be, in part. But the Address is too tight to permit nice compliments for their sake alone. The purpose of the speech is to encourage people to change the future and save humankind; this statement thus must be seen as functional. In order to do so, we must first recognize that it is true. Not that the Address has been forgotten, but that the battle is of prior importance. That is, there could have been no Address without the dead; they give it the power that has launched it into the future. Mr. Lincoln is quite aware of this. He could not have given such a statement as the Address upon an inferior occasion, or upon no occasion. It draws its strength from the regret, shock, horror, sorrow, and doubt of the battle's aftermath. The reality of real people dead, their bodies in these small graves, gives pervasive elegiac urgency to the Address. Therefore, Mr. Lincoln reminds us of *these* dead, *here.* This is no disembodied speech. We feel it because it still carries tragedy, because it still draws upon the dead and what they did here. If the dead are removed from Gettysburg, the life will drain from these words.

The Address does not accept the unity of deed and word. There is no assumption that deed is superior to word, because the proposition is words. Rather, in these circumstances we cannot by words surpass or live up to these brave men's deeds. It is not that we are inferior; it is that the times call for action. Republican government is challenged by arms, by physical force. For the moment, the only value of words is to encourage action.

In this sentence the Address touches most directly, with infinite restraint and power, the note of lament. "It can never forget what they did here." It is the assumption upon which the speech works, this lament. Who does not know what they did here will not understand what we say here, will not take up their work. All the morbid sentimentality of the mid-nineteenth century is gone; the beating human heart remains alone. This place in the Address (though punctuated by patriotic applause at the time) suggests a point of stillness. The Address turns here, around this silent point: timeless, depthless loss, anger, and question.

> . . . all the Air a solemn Stillness holds . . .

As if they wait for an answer; as if the end and vacancy and unjust stop of their lives asks an answer—the blazing hearth no more burns for them, the busy housewife no longer may expect him home,

> No children run to lisp their Sire's Return,
> Or climb his Knees the envied Kiss to share . . .

Why?

In the silence *they* wait for our answer.

IT IS FOR US THE LIVING, RATHER, TO BE DEDICATED TO THE UNFINISHED WORK WHICH THEY WHO FOUGHT HERE HAVE THUS FAR SO NOBLY ADVANCED.

The call is electric and demanding. "The trumpet shall sound and the dead shall be raised, be raised incorruptible!" In us their work goes on.

The signature of life and identity in this world is our work. Lincoln, the central figure, is known like Aeneas for the mysterious role he played: deeply strange, yet deeply perfect. In a republic's fate, we are all the founders and the fathers; and in its life all our lives, individuals still, flow together, while from it we have that life which is particularly human, which is God-ordained: equality, liberty.

The president has surpassed us. There will be no dedication of the cemetery. Our grief will not be ceremonially assuaged. Nor will he allow us to dismiss the dead in peace. Now we are attentive, we are thinking, we are wondering. What did they die for? What *work* do they bequeath to us? Fighting, suffering, dying, and killing are now *work*. It is that idea which redeems them.

The slaughter of Gettysburg was visible around the crowd on Cemetery Hill. Gashed trees, graves mounded by the hundreds. In the clear November sunlight they saw the pattern of the Soldiers' Cemetery—two thousand graves still to be opened and filled. They had read newspaper reports and possibly seen photographs of the dead. Most of all, they had seen the lists. Killing, dying, maiming, crippling. What else was warfare?

It was work. In this cause it was not merely the work of Adam's curse but noble work.

The president used the word "nobly" in another place: this generation shall nobly save, or meanly lose, the last, best hope of humanity. The word is not a common Lincoln word; it is a rare extreme. It carries a chivalric, almost sentimental strain Lincoln seldom sounds. Here is one thing worth high feeling; here is one work that ennobles a matter-of-fact race.

Abraham Lincoln was not sentimental about work. He grew up with drudgery. But work that arises from justice is noble.

Lincoln saw equality largely in economic terms. All persons were entitled to the proper compensation for their work. Political equality ensures this. Without equal rights under the law, a poor storekeeper could not get wealthy or become president, nor could a black man support and educate his family, nor could anyone listed among the short and simple annals of the poor have material hope. Work that creates hope is noble.

The Address is pointed toward hope. Hope may be a transaction between God and the people of this grim world. The fact of existence is work; we are all, to use the terms of the Genesis story, under Adam's curse: "In the sweat of thy face shalt thou eat bread, till thou return into the ground: for out of it wast thou taken: for dust thou art, and unto dust shalt thou return." Nothing is noble in this situation. Only the prospect of rising above it is noble. Only for that prospect do we labor our best, and only for that prospect does labor have meaning. But all human work, like all human life, remains within that bleak framework. We do not make ourselves divine. Were we left on our own, our life would be tragic or futile. Lincoln saw people work and die. If there is such a thing as hope, it must come from higher up. But the Address never leaves this world for the next, any more than it replaces the "sacred" with the "secular."

Hope is the high and excellent call that transforms human beings and human work. A herald of transcendence, it is worth living or dying for. Human institutions, at their best, pattern and mirror transcendent hope. Where there is no justice, and no liberty, there can be no sensible hope. (Hope must be sensible, to the modern mind. Only the possible can properly be hoped for.) But where there is liberty and justice for all, there is hope.

The evidence for this thing unseen, justice, is their work and ours.

In this way we can be transformed for and by the future. This November speech in a graveyard is an instrument of hope.

IT IS RATHER FOR US TO BE HERE DEDICATED

In the giant of American Protestantism, the Baptist Church, the common practice is to *dedicate* a baby in place of baptism. A person is to be baptized only when he or she is old enough to make the decision. Lincoln, growing up where Baptists and Methodists were fighting it out, knew this usage well. In the Address, where the image of birth dominates, this meaning of "dedicate" is intended.

But the Address is immediately, then ultimately, concerned with death. There are six references to death here, four using the words *died* or *dead* directly. The seven reminders that we are *here,* on the ground of struggle and with the dead, reinforce that consciousness. Death is on everybody's mind, of course. The purpose of the Address is to explain this death; it is a kind of theodicy of democracy. The counterthrust is birth: life from death, transformation, reaching a new stage, hope. The frame of the Address places death within the context of life. First the fathers *brought forth;* finally the nation shall have a *new birth* of freedom. Here, in the center of the Address, the word *dedicate* (the sound of it perhaps coincidentally echoing death?), turns the listener's thoughts from death through work to life. A dedicated child is promised, devoted, to God and God's kingdom, pointed toward that higher birth, new birth. The Scriptural verse used by the Baptists as the cornerstone of baptism is Colossians 2:12: "Buried with him in baptism, wherein also ye are risen with him through the faith of the operation of God, who hath raised him from the dead."

This operation, or *work,* is done by the soldiers and by us. Birth is a struggle. We are the nation, the children, whom the fathers brought forth.

As the convert is buried in the water by full immersion and is lifted out a new being, a citizen of an eschatological Kingdom, so we and the soldiers are buried in this struggle, and through the operation of dedication are pointed to a new birth. We are to the new nation—the *essence* of which is liberty, justice, and equality—as the individual soul is to the kingdom of God—the essence of which is God's rule, meaning justice, equality, and liberty from sin, death, and the devil—from all oppression. Through dedication, we enter into eschatological hope, a kingdom or republic that exists only in the future.

The eschatological nature of democracy's hope is what justifies Lincoln in drawing out the meaning of the Declaration of Independence. The perfect republic is not present now, and certainly was not in 1776 when the country had hardly come into being (struggling for birth against the British Empire); just so, the kingdom of God exists in the future, but "at hand." Dedication is evidence for what is yet unseen, but coming into being. This implies a modern view of the linear nature of history and the tendency toward progress in human affairs. This view, also biblical, sees the teleological reality of God and God's kingdom giving meaning to history, past and present. What is imperfect becomes more perfect. The Constitution begins: "in order to form a more perfect union."

TO THE GREAT TASK REMAINING BEFORE US

Why do we work? Why not just forget this "great task" and go about our business of getting and spending? Who gave us this job?

Ultimately, we give this job to ourselves, insofar as we accept it. In a democratic society, the task must be voluntary. Gettysburg was the last decisive battle of volunteers, and the president stands at their graves to impress upon us their example. It is a fight for who we are. As Homer's Odysseus, or Ulysses, fought the tyrant of the seas, the anarchists of the caves, and even refused immortality to regain his identity, so we may choose to be who we are. God made us all equals. We can fight for who we are or we can accept less. We know what we are in this imperfect nation, but we also know what we may be if we choose in "that nation." It is a choice of life or death.

The choice is imposed upon us by those who have taken away our liberty, by those who would deprive anyone of justice. Delivered well after the Emancipation Proclamation, the Address assumes that we fight—if we fight for liberty and justice—for others as well as for ourselves. Another person's equality is part of ours.

This cannot be a selfish task, because pure self-interest argues eventually for the strong taking whatever they can get. It is a *limited* self-interest that the proposition seeks to establish. We are equal politically, meaning we have the same rights, among which are life, liberty, and the pursuit of happiness. We will not all lead the same lives, or all have all the liberties humanly possible, nor all be equally happy. But the *hope* of life, liberty, and the pursuit of happiness is not to be denied. Limitations are mutually placed because it is not *my* rights but *our* rights that are asserted. Rights conflict where desires are uncontrolled; for this reason were "governments instituted among men." But the limits imposed by government must not be tighter upon one than upon another, with respect to these hopes; and they must be imposed only for the purpose of assuring those hopes equally to all. Right government is a means of hope.

This is proper because hope, as a transcendent ennobler of a less than noble race, must have a divine origin. And it is God who has created us equal. Hope is rooted in that creation. Eschatological hope is therefore rooted in our origin. Both alpha and omega are creations of God. The task we accept participates in creation. As it was in the beginning, so may it be, world without end.

Mr. Lincoln saw this idea not theoretically but practically. He had long thought that American republican government must succeed, or the rest of the world would abandon its republican hopes. He understood human nature: we will not be inspired by losers. He wagered that right and might would be the same. In dedicating ourselves to be buried in and with that death which dies for others, we dedicate ourselves to a new life and an imperishable hope. Out of death is brought life. This is God's work.

THAT FROM THESE HONORED DEAD WE TAKE INCREASED DEVOTION TO THAT CAUSE FOR WHICH THEY GAVE THE LAST FULL MEASURE OF DEVOTION

How can the dead be a source of life? This clause connects dedication and devotion. We are to be here dedicated *so that* we may take (Lincoln uses the subjunctive, or conditional, mood, omitting *may*) our devotion from their devotion. It is a specific devotion: *devotion to that cause,* and that cause is the proposition that all men are created equal. Our dedication connects us to that devotion.

There is a trinity of religious concepts underneath the Address. In the beginning there was the fathers. Now the children of these fathers struggle, leaving some of the sons lying dead around us. In the future we will partake of the spirit that animated them. We can be connected to their devotion—we can *take* devotion—from them—in no physical way. Nor does the president mean this as decorative rhetoric. Least of all is he engaging in figurative sentimentality. He wants people really to increase their devotion and win the war—using somehow the devotion of the honored dead.

They are honored, we remember, not because of what we say over their graves, but because of what they did. They struggled. They worked for the proposition and for that government which is dedicated to it. They are honored because of their faith, a faith that was not without works. Faith can be transmitted. It uses words and deeds, but somehow the transaction is spiritual. Proclamation (like the Address and like emancipation) joins with devoted action (like the work of these dead) to generate new birth, new life—hope—in these who see and hear. This generation, an extension of the original creation, is affected by the spirit.

As faith is associated most with the fathers, and unselfish love with the dying sons, so hope is associated with the presence of the spirit. In this November creed of democracy, it is implied that the institution animated by the spirit (of devotion to the proposition)—in Christianity it is the Church; in the Address it is popular government—is the embodiment and vehicle of hope. It is the mystical body of devotion to that cause, and by working for it we are sharing in a transformed life with those who died and with all humanity. The Apostles' Creed is similarly divided into a short, a longer, and a long section, roughly matching Lincoln's motif of past, present, and future as well as, of course, being governed by Father, Son, and Holy Spirit. In the bright if fragile November sunlight, we are subliminally recalled to our deepest beliefs in the midst of our deepest anxiety. The result is comfort—literally, "strengthening much." Comforting is the traditional office of the Holy Spirit. Lest we think to have gone too far with religious implications underlying this political Address, we should remember that the reverse direction also obtains: the doctrine of the Trinity is a political image, full of government, administration, almost with legislative, judicial, and executive branches.

The president, "Father Abraham," is not only acting as prophet and king here; he is also priest. By means of the Address he transmits a transcendent power, during this most solemn and ceremonial occasion, where body and blood and remembrance are sharply, painfully real. As priest, he also comforts. We the people, having lost our loved ones to the cause, are not only strengthened but also consoled. Like Abraham in the Bible, Lincoln originates a new nation, and like a priest he comforts his people.

Abraham believed, and it was counted to him as righteousness. If the nation is to be saved, and through it the world, it will be through the righteousness of faith, or devotion. But faith is not partial devotion. These dead gave their last full measure of devotion. (The phrase "full measure" is from the King James Bible.) The 260 men of the First Minnesota on the second day of the battle knew that the order to charge into a full brigade of Southerners meant the sacrifice of their lives; it meant their deaths in exchange for a few minutes. They leveled their bayonets and went in. From these honored dead we take increased devotion to that cause for which they gave the last full measure of devotion.

THAT WE HERE HIGHLY RESOLVE THAT THESE DEAD SHALL NOT HAVE DIED IN VAIN

Shall not have died in vain, the president says: not *have* not died in vain. When shall they not have died in vain? In that eschatological future, the seal of our hope. Standing on a high point of the Gettysburg battlefield, seeing not only the sad fields of memory but also wheat fields, barns, roads, a town, and the blue mountains to the west, Mr. Lincoln reminds us that we are not a people of geography, race, or nationality, but of an idea. Such a nation, so conceived and so dedicated, cannot long endure without devotion to this idea. Where there is no vision, the people perish.

If that future does not arrive, these dead shall have died in vain. It is as if they await a general resurrection, in the hoped-for kingdom of the people. That kingdom will not arrive without our work.

Therefore let us be dedicated, *so that* we may highly resolve to work for that cause. "Highly resolve" implies what Lincoln called "an oath registered in heaven." A high resolve is elevated above the normal plane of things. To "preserve, protect, and defend the Constitution of the United States" was Lincoln's oath and high resolve. All of us as equals in "that nation," this republic, can have the same oath registered in heaven. Again, Lincoln was not dispensing empty, sentimental rhetoric. He called for an oath to match his, for which he would give the last full measure of devotion.

THAT THIS NATION, UNDER GOD, SHALL HAVE A NEW BIRTH OF FREEDOM

After he had been in Gettysburg one night, Lincoln added the words "under God." (Who would not?) The addition is simply the undercurrent of the Address bubbling up through the surface. If the proposition assumes a Creator, then the new birth which that proposition generates must issue from the same source.

The phrase "under God" is necessary to distinguish one new birth from all the others. It might be safe to speculate that Lincoln was particularly familiar with the tenth chapter of Jeremiah, which, along with the

Book of Job, is one of the two possible sources of the last phrase of the Address. Job might suit the private Lincoln well, but Jeremiah is the public prophet, the anguished voice seeking God and human faithfulness amid the agony of national disaster.

> . . . the customs of the people are vain:
> for one cutteth a tree out of the forest,
> the work of the hands of the workman . . .
> They deck it with silver and with gold . . .
> Silver spread into plates is brought from Tarshish,
> and gold from Uphaz,
> the work of the workman,
> and the hands of the founder:
> blue and purple is their clothing:
> they are the work of cunning men.
> But the Lord is the true God,
> he is the living God,
> and an everlasting king . . .
> The gods that have not made the heavens and the earth,
> even they shall perish from the earth,
> and from under these heavens.

(The rhetorical parallel—"from the earth, and from under these heavens" is a favorite device of Lincoln's. His usage represents not a borrowing from classical rhetoric but a thorough assimilation of Hebrew poetic technique.)

Mr. Lincoln assumes the governance of God. "The will of God prevails," Lincoln wrote. Now, if God is ultimately in control of nations, there will be only two kinds of government: the kind that God ordains—based upon His creating all people equal—and all the rest. Idols all, these other governments are only the work of cunning men. They are silver from Tarshish and gold from Uphaz; purple is the clothing of their rulers. They shall perish from the earth.

This theological essence of the Address sounds strange to us now, but in the mid-nineteenth century Americans breathed the air of Christian theology. Protestants thought in the phrases and cadences of the King James Version of the Bible, and not without having been raised on its concepts. If they understood the idea of being plunged into the death of Christ and raised into new life with Him, it was because they had been baptized in the rivers and creeks of the South and Midwest.

Even the political texts they studied breathed the speech and the assumptions of the King James Bible. Webster's Second Reply to Hayne, a favorite of Lincoln's—in which, among other places similarly, occur the phrases "the people's government, made for the people, made by the people, and answerable to the people"—praises the Federal Union in these terms: "Under its benign influences these great interests [finance, commerce, and credit] immediately awoke as from the dead, and sprang forth with newness of life."

Lincoln's use of biblical language is not casual or merely conditioned: The logic of the Address, not merely its effect, depends upon the beliefs of the prophets and the practice of Christians. The ultimate appeal throughout, stated only here, is to God.

The new birth of freedom, then, is like the new birth of a Christian at baptism: the new life is qualitatively changed from the old life. The man or woman looks the same, but something essential has been transformed. The old life has not been done away with as much as fulfilled in a new key: the personality remains, but it now has citizenship in heaven. Just so, freedom becomes new freedom. Its promise is qualitatively nearer fulfillment. The old person, the nation before now, had freedoms; but there are many freedoms. Freedom itself is now to be reborn onto a higher plane; its original promise is nearer fulfillment. Freedom is transformed because it becomes identified critically more closely with its true nature, as the reborn Christian assumes his most essential identity as a child of God and resident of heaven. His short life is now eternal life. He is oriented toward and by his spirit, and his spirit shall not perish but have everlasting life. So the spirit of freedom, "the proposition that all men are created equal," becomes the orientation, the identity, of what we call freedom now, and this essence shall not perish from under these heavens.

As the renewed spirit orients the believer in the Christian life, the new life, through his conscience, so freedom is governed—held on course, diverted and steered between dangers—by the principle of *justice.* Neither oppression nor anarchy, neither tyranny nor license, are permitted when this principle governs. Justice is the conscience of freedom. As "faith without works is dead," so freedom expires without justice.

It all falls apart without equality, just as it all falls apart without the Creator. Lincoln did not live in our age. To a large extent, he did not live in Jefferson's, either. Nevertheless, Lincoln the lawyer knew the significance of words in a document, and the words are there—how much more important each one is in a *founding* document: "We hold these truths to be self-evident, that all men are created equal, that they are endowed by their Creator with certain unalienable rights. . . ."

The nation was founded upon a belief, and the belief is in God. Lincoln was not changing and extending the principle of the Declaration; he was explicating it, unfolding it, drawing out its implications and its promise in a culture saturated with Christian thinking, if not by Christian behavior. Now we discount the nineteenth century faith of our fathers, those murderous idealists, earnest soldiers, killer angels. They were too naive and too hypocritical for us.

The president spoke of hope: new life, new freedom, under God. It was November—a chill coming on, the sun sinking low in the sky; he meant his words to last. We need them in the bleak midwinter.

The Gettysburg Address is a primary document of that nation now because it brings to light not only the founding promise but also the whole promise of freedom and equality. And that promise is still the last, best hope of earth, still bringing light to the nations. The hope it brings is a political hope and, even more than a political hope, a new birth of freedom under God.

The words were spoken on the nineteenth of November 1863. The Address, Mr. Lincoln, and the soldiers living and dead who struggled at Gettysburg for a new birth of freedom, are given new birth in the hopes of nations, are transformed in the expensive promise *that government of the people, by the people, for the people, shall not perish from the earth.*

Now they belong to the ages.

* * *

The president had been interrupted by applause five times. Now, at the end, the applause was sustained. Someone proposed three cheers for the president, and the crowd responded, adding three more for the governors.

From this point, we are left to our own thoughts. Thirty years later, Ward Hill Lamon wrote that Lincoln had been dissatisfied with the Address, saying it "won't *scour*" (like a plow that fails to shed the soil), and wished he had prepared more carefully. In the 1890s, a near deification of Lincoln occurred. The tale arose that he had composed the speech while riding the train to Gettysburg—being inspired in romantically divine fashion. The listeners, including Seward and Everett, could not recognize this masterpiece, and Lincoln was too modest to think well of it. These falsehoods have enjoyed a long persistence, but there is nothing to them. The very copy of the Address most commonly printed is the "Everett Copy," sent at the orator's request. Everett had written, "I should be glad if I could flatter myself that I came as near to the central idea of the occasion in two hours as you did in two minutes."

Why did Lamon concoct a lie, and eventually believe it? He had not seen Lincoln working on the speech, probably had never seen a draft. How could such greatness have been composed by a normal human being? And he had known Lincoln as a normal human being. Surely such a thing as the immortal Address could have come only as a stroke of inspiration from a divine source. Lamon might have gotten the main idea right. We hold treasures in vessels of clay. And perhaps Lincoln did feel empty, felt it didn't *scour.*

The president sits down, and a chorus and band present another dirge.

> O! it is sweet for our Country to die,
> how softly reposes
> Warrior youth on his bier,
> wet by the tears of his love . . .

After the Address, an anthem for doomed youth. *Dulce et decorum est. . . .* Now the president of Gettysburg's seminary and college speaks a brief benediction, and it is over. But for Lincoln's children—those here dedicated—it has just begun again.

* * *

Perhaps a theologian from the Lutheran seminary stood here and listened to Lincoln's few, appropriate remarks. He may not have been entirely satisfied. "What would Luther have thought? *This America might be conceived in liberty, but we are all conceived in sin.*"

* * *

The crowd dispersed slowly after the procession filed back out the cemetery gate. The president hosted a reception and attended a meeting and a dinner, then at around six o'clock boarded the train. Lincoln's head ached, and for some time he lay across a seat with a wet cloth on his forehead. The thousands left Gettysburg by the ways they had come.

But up at the Soldiers' Cemetery, many who had attended the dedication stayed, lingering among the graves, walking over the sites that had become well known since the three-day-long battle. Some could not yet part from father, son, husband, or brother who would stay up here after the last visitors had gone.

> On some fond Breast the parting Soul relies,
> Some pious Drops the closing eye requires;
> Ev'n from the Tomb the Voice of Nature cries,
> Ev'n in our Ashes live their wonted Fires.

The sun set behind South Mountain, the air grew chill, and the stars came out above. The new graves lay washed in pale moonlight; newly planted trees cast faint shadows. One person remained on Cemetery Hill. A reporter from the *New York Herald* walked alone among the rows. He had little to say in the silence and solitude. "Even the relic hunters are gone now," he wrote.

I understand him—this reporter who lingered long after the words and deed were done. I understand him more than I understand the others who were here a century and a half ago, more than the sources of an evil that made all these graves, or the beauty that had raised up this army which still goes marching on. Who would not

> cast one longing ling'ring Look behind?

But it is better to follow the steps of Mr. Lincoln. It is more important to follow him away from here than to have followed him here: one must come down from the mountain. There is a war on.

NOVEMBER 20

That Cause (Confederate Rose)

Who can understand his errors? cleanse thou me from secret faults.

—Psalm 19

Back in Washington, Mr. Lincoln was sick today, November 20, and getting sicker. I took advantage of this circumstance to slip over to the enemy's side. That is, I hiked across the fields between Union and Confederate lines to visit some Confederate memorials.

On the Gettysburg battlefield today is inscribed another Gettysburg Address. Unlike Lincoln's, these words are addressed not to the living but to the dead. On the base of the pedestal of the Virginia Monument, next to Lincoln's perhaps the most noble memorial on the field, stands the inscription:

Virginia, to her sons at Gettysburg.

This memorial is highly visible from the Union lines across the fields on Cemetery Ridge; appropriately—even as its distance far off in the tree line is also somehow appropriate. The Virginia Monument stands roughly where General Lee watched the advance and retreat of Pickett's Charge, on Seminary Ridge. At 41 feet in height, and with a base of 28 feet by 32.5 feet, the monument is very large.

But it is even more striking than it is large, with its equestrian statue of

Robert E. Lee—a calm figure of alert grandeur. Interestingly, the rider and horse achieve their memorable effect not by exaggeration (like the figure of Jackson and horse at Manassas, both bulging with muscles) or through sentimentality. The figures are highly realistic.

The designer and sculptor, F. William Sievers, went to great pains to get it right. He studied not only photographs of the general, but also the life mask taken in 1869. For Traveller, he studied the skeleton preserved at Washington and Lee University, and searched carefully for a living Tennessee Walker of the right size and build. You look up at the figures, for they stand atop a 10- by 14-foot pedestal 24 feet high. Lee was actually a tall man who looked even taller on his tall horse, because an unusual portion of the general's height was in his long waist. He was the kind of person of whose elevation one was always conscious. Here, on the Virginia Monument, Lee rides the clouds, his lion-like, finely sculpted head against the eternal sky. He is a kind of father alike to us who look up at him, and to the bronze figures in front of him at the base of the pedestal.

In bronze—the metal of Achilles and Hector, Ulysses and Agamemnon—seven representative soldiers of the Army of Northern Virginia are figured. One is a cavalryman, a member of the upper class; he carries the banner of the Commonwealth of Virginia. Two artillerymen stand at the ready, one with pistol and the other with bugle. The sculptor wrote: "The several characters are drawn from various walks of life. The figure to the extreme left, biting off the end of a paper cartridge might well be the average man about town; the next, a mechanic. The bearded figure is of the professional type; and the gawky figure with charging bayonet, a farmer. These four characters are infantrymen." In Lee's army, they have become more than cogs in the wheel of a material economy.

William Sievers, like the composer of "Dixie," was a northerner by birth—Fort Wayne, Indiana, and his studio was in New York. But he had grown up in Atlanta and Richmond, and his first commissioned work had been for a Confederate monument in Virginia. He was well prepared, having studied in Rome and Paris, and his design was chosen over those of forty other artists from across the nation. His research was careful, even down to items of equipment carried by the soldiers and scattered under them to represent the debris of battle.

Reprehensibly, yet representatively, some of those items of equipment are gone—stolen by "collectors" and other vandals. Enacting postmodern historical theory, they have chipped away irrevocably at the past, at living memory, for their own privately selfish ends. The group at the base is not perfect, and this is perhaps also appropriate in its way. The figures are each realistic in appearing to be in battle, but they are not acting in concert. It looks like one of them might be about to club one of the others. The figures are not fighting together, except insofar as they seem to be defending a perimeter. This is typical of Confederates, especially those who resist the idea of a central authority. It looks here as if each is getting in the other's way a little. Yet the overall effect is quite good and, like the figure above, noble.

The figure of General Lee is bareheaded, exposed to the sun. Removing his hat is unexpected and strangely humble. It is the impulse of a man under God, watching the tremendous battle for which he bore responsibility but which was "in God's hands." It is also a gesture of respect toward his soldiers, the salute of a great general to great troops. Its message enacts the monument's inscription: "Virginia, to her sons at Gettysburg."

From Robert E. Lee, such a gesture of affection and respect is the ultimate democratic message, "as old as the Scriptures and as clear as the American Constitution," given by a man who did more than any other American to destroy that message. The case of Robert E. Lee is an interesting one, filled with ambiguity. Some parents confuse their children.

* * *

Robert Edward Lee was born into one of the most aristocratic of American families. The famed "Lees of Virginia" included two signers of the Declaration of Independence and a hero of the Revolutionary War, "Light Horse Harry" Lee—Robert Edward's father. The birthplace of Robert E. Lee, Stratford Hall, looks small if judged by European standards of aristocracy, but Arlington, the Custis-Lee mansion, is one of America's grandest sights when viewed across the Potomac. It is an imposing memorial and the reminder of a threat, both at once.

Robert E. Lee did not get that mansion from his own family. The Lees had fallen on relatively hard times. The only house Robert E. Lee ever owned came from his wife, Mary Custis, a great-granddaughter of Martha Washington. He married into Arlington, lost it immediately at the outbreak of hostilities, and lost it permanently when it was used by the Federals as a cemetery early in the war. After Appomattox, the general needed a job in order to support himself and his family. He was to the manor born, as everyone knew without insult or resentment, but he never really lived in his own house—whether the Custis mansion or a government tent in Mexico, the frontier post of a U.S. cavalry colonel, the superintendent's quarters at West Point, a plain Confederate States government tent during the Civil War, or a house owned by Washington College in

Lexington, Virginia. It is no wonder that his last words may have been "strike the tent!"

Though he was born into a mansion, Lee was, in a larger sense, a self-made man. He had no vices—a result of discipline, probably—but he did have flaws. Today, in a time and place where anything from smoking to not being competitive are thought of as large flaws, it might seem archaic to say that Robert E. Lee fought to control a really great sin, anger. (He was right in taking anger seriously. Cigar smoking never hurt U. S. Grant's generalship, but anger might have worked against Lee at both Antietam and Gettysburg.) Lee also feared a paternal tendency toward irresponsibility. But careful with money, as Light Horse Harry had not been, the son Robert became America's biggest spender of lives during the Civil War. His family and personal associates benefited from his battles of character; his soldiers sometimes lost when he lost. All along, he tried to model himself on a great hero, George Washington, and the extent of his success makes Robert E. Lee a hero to us—to the degree that we ignore the origin of his cause. He succeeded brilliantly in small things, but he lost the war. The war was a question of character. Lee's character has always been central to students of his battles. Did he lose because he was outnumbered and outgunned, or because he did not measure up to U. S. Grant and Abraham Lincoln?

His partial moral success made him a noble man in some respects. A primary mark of noble quality in a person—certainly in the America of Jefferson—is the ability to recognize nobility in others. This Lee did, and tribute from him, because of his hard-won character, was significant tribute. He removed his hat to soldiers more than once during the war, and does it still, as long as bronze can define the gesture.

The sons at Gettysburg are all dead. Lee's tribute is an elegy. It is also an exhortation: affection and respect are more fundamental to equality and freedom than are any law, declaration, or constitution. The troops might be different now.

In the early 1960s, the American public, to the tune of 70 percent, thought the government "would do what is right most of the time or always." By 1992 the figure had fallen to 29 percent. We are "cynical," according to that study. In a country that hosted no Great War in the twentieth century, what excuse have we for being cynical? Cynicism implies a vacuum. It is also a response to ambiguity.

The purpose of American public education used to be clear: to make citizens. A republic depends for its survival upon an informed and judicious constituency. In that sense, our schools were once the last best hope of earth. Now we train draftees for the world market, a mechanism of vast cynicism. Why not? Recent leadership has been confusing.

But if History is largely biography, we might use the heroes and villains of the past to educate our young people in liberty, equality, and the threats to them. Heroism begins with imperfection; therefore we, who are imperfect, can be inspired by heroes. That a person like Robert E. Lee was not all hero does not make him all villain, or vice-versa. Nor does it mean there are neither heroes nor villains. The sons of Virginia at Gettysburg began the war as villains but entered our century as heroes. The Lost Cause myth acquired elements of both fraud and nobility from Robert E. Lee. The Rebellion's squalor, horror, error, and futility would have been unbearable to the losers had they no mythically great figure to stand for some measure of victory after all that loss. Now that purpose has been served well enough, and has run its course. We must relearn the ability to discern heroism. We could use another Venerable Bede to write our history.

I think another reason Lee on the Virginia Monument has removed his hat is to acknowledge the tribute of his men. Soldiers like winning generals; they make us think we are dying and suffering for something worthwhile in the end. But at Appomattox many of Lee's soldiers still adored him, loser though he had become, and that adoration has only increased. His soldiers fought for Lee: this at once praises and condemns him. They admired, respected, and trusted him like a father. They felt he was of a higher order somehow, and he gave them something they could not survive without: hope. Particularly as we judge their cause, it is against their standard that we must measure ourselves as followers, and against which we must measure our leaders. More than that, Lee helps us understand our natures—the imperfect condition theologians traditionally refer to as "sin."

* * *

The Confederate rose, or cotton rose—*Hibiscus mutabilis*—is a flower suggestive of the Christian God. Its trinity of names includes a mysteriously liturgical Latin one which suggests more than one appearance or nature. It is like a pictured rose that hangs in Gettysburg's Christ Church: the Seal of Martin Luther, a rose within a rose. The outer rose bursts red like blood unfolding in water, suggesting God's dismaying passion. The inner flower blooms bright white, symbolizing the beauty and eternity of God. Haloed in gold leaf, both are actually one rose, whose center is a cross.

So the Confederate rose. Had not confused tongues named it, would it be a trinity? Had not our fathers' passions stained it, would it smell as sweet? How could it blossom in such unhallowed ground?

Cotton: the long, low, mournful dirge of the South. Bandanna-covered heads bow under the hot sun; voices moan a litany for freedom. The staple has fixed the world's attention and the Old South's fate. It is the flower of clothing made necessary by shame in the last hour of paradise. Cotton is an emblem of humankind's curse, of labor for the sake of profit from an industry consuming the earth and its people. It was conceived in sin. The cotton rose, like sacred honor, is a sparkling-white filamented fruit that turns in the hand and heat of time to blood.

Confederate rose: an emblem of boys and men who bled the stream of Southern error and sacrifice, its beauty a reminder poignant and recurrent, each summer a fresh heart's wound, a presence of the dead. Sacred history, together with grief and longing, becomes *the past,* each one's story—light turned to blood, present turned to *long ago* and become present again: in this rose we and they are one, two aspects of a trinity—past, present, and to come.

Mutabilis: the moment has two natures, past and present, as well as evil and good. Light ran into blood for them. Their blood has become our light: by it we praise and condemn; by it we are praised and condemned. We are all rebels, more than we know. In us, the mortal sons of the South live on.

Because of what we know and feel for its name, we look at the cotton rose, Confederate rose, *Hibiscus mutabilis,* with sorrow that is honor, conscious of a double loss which makes us what we are. We have reconstructed this flower, calling it a rose, calling by its name the husbands, fathers, sons, and brothers dead long ago. Confederate rose, proud rose. In our naming of it we reveal our incorrigible nature; in our naming of it we take up the power of those in the past to refashion us in their gallant image.

* * *

One day after my second college year, my mother, father, and I went to visit some friends in a nearby town. The others were inside the house; Len and I sat out on the porch. For a long time the only sounds were made by his rocker on the old porch floor, the creak of my wicker chair when I shifted, and an occasional breeze moving through the heavy shade trees. Deep summer silence and peace. Then Len spoke, in a few brief sentences, about the meaning of his life.

"All that makes any difference is how much you've done for people. I haven't done much in my life. Almost nothing."

I could hardly believe I had heard the words correctly. If he had not done much for people, who had? What hope was there for a bump on a log like me?

I had some idea of the good my father had done. He had saved lives, he had relieved pain, he had restored people. His partner and enemy Ernst, for example, had come to him a virtual cripple, unable to work. No one else had been able to relieve his back pain or restore his mobility; Ernst was the first to say so. From early childhood I recalled my father bringing home things he had accepted as payment: two dozen eggs, a cake, bread. I once saw a ledger full of nonpayments, thousands of dollars in that year alone which he would not collect. When people came to him, he treated them.

Unless they were black. I learned this to my mortification and humiliation when I was about thirteen. Both the father and mother of a friend of mine worked outside the home—an unusual thing then, in that suburb—and an African-American housekeeper was in charge during the day. I heard her talking about some medical condition she had, saying she was tired of paying twenty dollars to visit doctors and getting nothing for it. "My dad charges only seven dollars," I volunteered. "And I'm sure he can fix you up in no time." (That would have been his phrase.)

I found out a short while later that she had been refused an appointment because of her color.

After some brooding, I finally asked my father whether he treated people of her color. No. No Negroes. That was that. Slowly I discovered some reasons. He feared that he would lose his white patients. But he feared African Americans even more.

Len had attended the National College of Chiropractic when it still was located on Chicago's south side. One night he had heard gunfire, opened his door, and found a black man on the doorstep in a pool of blood, fatally shot. As a medical student in St. Louis he had been sent to many gruesome scenes. But not every white man treating wounds in black districts comes to my father's conclusion; and surely he had treated violent whites, too. What else was there?

My mother told me that Len used to have nightmares. She would be awakened by his moaning and shouting. He was back in Chicago. My father absolutely never cursed. He did not use even mild euphemisms. The worst he got was cross, and it passed in seconds. But in these nightmares he would curse and swear bitterly, ferociously, always about the (two words he never used:) "damn niggers." What was behind this?

Beginning when I was about ten he slept in my room, and I always feared that I would hear those strange outbursts, horrifying in someone so mild. Who was he, this man who hated at night? Where was he? Why this appalling anger?

Near the end of his life, Len must have wondered why he had lived. The one thing worth living for—helping others—he thought he hadn't done much of. And there had been no compensation. His marriage was bad: both of them had been. At age fifty he suddenly had had a kid to take care of and get in the way, to tie him down and disturb his peace—and to take his wife's side against him. A little echo of the ridicule he got for things he did, said, believed in.

He never enjoyed all the money he earned. It always got flushed into somebody else's pocket. The country itself was getting worse. First there had been the hated Roosevelt (my mother's hero), who "sold us down the river" at Yalta. Then the vulgar Truman. Eisenhower had been all right, but then there was Kennedy, and the boorish Texan, Lyndon Johnson. No hope within, no hope without—and his health was getting worse.

He used to relieve his quiet desperation with humor, but no more. As a child I loved his travel stories, filled with slapstick and self-deprecation, in which he was always the hapless victim of somebody's bizarre or ridiculous behavior. He used to call himself "Brother Grimm." He used to imagine absurdly funny things, like cartoon characters coming to life. But now he was unrelievedly tense, cornered, and I suspect, angry.

He had lost. All along, he had been fighting a lost cause.

His American Dream had been good, but not good enough. Len lost the war against his worst enemy: himself. The nighttime violence had been occurring in L. L. since he was middle aged and healthy. Self-make himself as he might, or do however much good, my father could never escape the fallen angel of his nature. If this mild man without malice could curse and perhaps even kill in the dark streets of his heart, who is without sin? However much we improve our world, we cannot improve our souls. World War I can be read as a confession. The old Adam still lives; our civil war goes very deep. The saints we admire were tortured souls, and the heroes we must follow were sinners.

> O my soul, thou has said unto the Lord, Thou art my Lord: my goodness extendeth not to thee, but to the saints that are in the earth, and to the excellent. . . .

Who will help us escape our nature? *Who will deliver me from this body of death?*

Once, just before dawn, I happened to awaken. Looking across the room, I saw my father's arms uplifted toward the ceiling, toward beyond, toward God. He stayed that way a long time, until after I had fallen back asleep.

* * *

It has been a long, long walk down the row of Confederate monuments and cannons, along the battlefield road into the past and into the narrowing corridor of my father's life. At this point in this grim weather in this gray month, one could slide into melancholy. Fortunately, a positive thought occurs to me, "for so to interpose a little ease": tomorrow I will accomplish what I set out to do here. I will settle the question of where Lincoln stood to deliver the Address. First thing in the morning I'll go back to the cemetery. The caretaker has returned. Maybe I can clinch this thing.

NOVEMBER 21

The World Will Little Note (Futility)

> —O what made fatuous sunbeams toil
> To break earth's sleep at all?
> —Wilfred Owen, "Futility"

With a little work and thinking, a person should be able to figure out whether the Milwaukee man, Selleck, was right about where Abraham Lincoln stood when he spoke the Gettysburg Address. All that is needed are a few fresh ideas, clear logic, and the fortitude to look at things as they really were. Professional historians have understandable limitations. The Park Historian, sadly, probably has an agenda, a desire to make a name by destroying old, accepted interpretations. Of course I cannot say for sure because I have never met her. Called a couple of times to try to make appointments, called to try to arrange a walk-through of the sites. She was busy. Meetings.

But she could meet Garry Wills, famous author of *Lincoln at Gettysburg*. All right. I know I'm nobody in particular. Just a guy.

Before going to Evergreen Cemetery, however, a little spadework needs to be done. First, a little hunt through the Park Service's files so I will know what I am looking at when I get to the cemetery. Most people don't know about these files.

"Nothing in particular," I say to the librarian. "Just want to browse through the files. Kind of interested in the cemeteries." I do not want them to know what I'm up to. These are Park Service people, remember. Very fine people. Know a lot. Very helpful. I respect them. But I'm here to explode a theory concocted by one of their people. I need to maintain a low profile.

Sitting at a tiny table next to the file cabinet at the end of a wing of the Gettysburg Cyclorama Center, I look through a manila file containing pages of unpublished letters, sheet after sheet of clippings. Here is one pertaining to D. H. Buehler and E. G. Fahnestock, two of Gettysburg's leading citizens. (The Fahnestock Building stands near the town square.) The two wrote this letter to Pennsylvania's Governor Curtin not long after the battle in 1863. It seems there was another battle going on. There is going to be a cemetery, but who will be in charge and where will it be? Will it be made in Evergreen Cemetery, owned by Mr. David McConaughy, or in a new place, next to Evergreen, as proposed by Mr. Wills? "The main difficulty" with getting the cemetery established, wrote the two, lay in the "*peculiar relations* subsisting between them"—between McConaughy and Wills. Apparently David Wills and the president of the Evergreen Cemetery Association distrusted, perhaps hated, each other. Each wants the cemetery; each wants to deal the other man out. McConaughy lost the cemetery competition. He saw Wills as an entrepreneur. Wills saw McConaughy, who wanted to buy parts of the battlefield to preserve them, as a developer.

Here is a letter from Wills to Governor Curtin, written March 21, 1864, after the cemetery dispute was over. The bad feelings have not dissipated. It is impractical, Wills says, to have the battlefield preserved by a developer (McConaughy). After all, the fence rails the soldiers used for breastworks have already been dug out by the farmers. The preservation scheme is "visionary and impractical and in fact entirely useless." McConaughy has proposed it for a "selfish & mercenary purpose," despite its fine-sounding name: "Gettysburg Battle Field Memorial Association." Bad blood. How likely would it have been, as Frank Klement points out, that Wills would have stood for the dedication of the Soldiers' National Cemetery being made in McConaughy's cemetery?

But here is something else. A letter from Wills to the governor of Delaware before the cemetery was designed. He says he was "decidedly of the opinion that we should entirely ignore State lines or the appearance of division of States in this sacred project, and bury all together in these grounds as they fell." (Of course most of them fell by state, in their regiments.) It is an entirely fitting and proper idea, though perhaps less interesting to posterity, and making it harder to find individual soldiers. Although Wills won on the cemetery location, he lost on this issue. Perhaps he lost other battles as well. Maybe he objected to the ceremony being held in Evergreen, and got stuffed again. Such possibilities vaguely trouble me.

Here is an old article from *Lincoln Lore* (January 1966) reprinting the official order for the procession: "The military will then close up and occupy the space on the left of the stand, the military leaving sufficient space between them and the line of graves for the civic procession to pass." The writer of the article infers from this that the Selleck Site is correct. It seems Kathleen Harrison and Garry Wills infer the new site from this.

Here is another interesting item. An artist, Joseph Becker, drew a contemporary view. He places the platform—though not exactly where Selleck puts it—*behind* the graves! And near the New York graves! It is a stylized drawing; it indicates no slope at all, which is inaccurate, but it basically supports Selleck!

I knew it. Good old Selleck, aina? *Landsmann.* Here is his file. Selleck drew the site, too. He has carefully marked the spot of the platform. It is behind the New York section, on the northwest side. Oh, oh. That's what he *draws.* What he *says* is, "40 ft. NE of the outer circle of soldiers' graves." He says *northeast*? That's not where he drew the spot. Northeast would be . . . would be. . . . Northeast might be in Evergreen.

Here are some clippings from the Gettysburg *Compiler.* There are several references to the speakers' platform standing "in the center of the cemetery." Now what does that mean? Does it mean the center of the new cemetery, or the old cemetery? It means no Selleck, that's for sure—*if* it is accurate. My stomach feels vaguely upset.

Here is file 10-11. The Associated Press says the platform was on the "highest point of ground." That might mean the Harrison Site. Others report a view of the Round Tops—which can be seen from the highest point, but not from the Selleck Site. Of course, the reporters were spread out; you can see the Round Tops from the Knothead Site, too.

File 10-11 shows that "correspondents consistently referred to the presence of graves in front of the platform." Whitelaw Reid wrote that the speakers' stand "was erected on the spot where the monument is to be built, in front of which are two semi-circular sections with portions set apart for each state." Finally, File 10-15 contains something from the *Adams Sentinel* (a local paper) of July 4, 1865, reporting the dedication of the monument's cornerstone. It is reported as the site of the speakers' platform back in November two years ago. These reports confirm neither the Harrison nor the Selleck Site, but the traditional site!

How many graves were there? Again, File 10-11. Of the eventual total of 3,564 reinterments, only 1,258 had been completed by November 19, 1863. Twenty-four of Ohio's 131, 100 of Pennsylvania's 526, 158 of New York's 866,

4 of Indiana's 80, and so on. Still, a lot of headboards protruded here and there across the new cemetery. The marshals were present to protect the graves.

That is Ms. Harrison's linchpin. The Cemetery Commission would not have wanted, would not have *tolerated,* trampling on the soldiers' graves. I rush out of the Cyclorama Center. Has anyone, *anyone* thought to check around the Harrison Site, to see how many graves would have been trampled there? Ms. Harrison's assumption that those mid-nineteenth-century people would not trample graves is correct—but her assumption has to be carried *all the way.* They would not have trampled civilian graves either. (Except in battle.)

I shall be gallant about this. Ms. Harrison is, after all, a female. As per the mid-nineteenth-century point of view, women ought to be treated kindly and with respect. I will be modest, humble, and magnanimous. When you kick someone in the pants you should be poised, moderate, kind, gracious, attentive to feelings, and maintain respect for their principles and dignity as well as your own.

I arrive at Evergreen Cemetery panting. I walk through the old gate, the famous gatehouse, and proceed respectfully along the lane. I read names well known to anyone familiar with the names of hills, farms, buildings associated with the battle: Culp, Spangler, Trostle.

One does not begin to understand the mid-nineteenth century until one walks through its graveyards. There are so many children. Here is a grave marked "Dear Kate" and "Our Babe" (Catharine, 1848–1853). Another marked "our daughter," 1853–1853. There is John, "aged 5 years."

I begin to circle the knoll of the Harrison Site. To the east and southeast I reconfirm headstones as old as 1767, engraved with old lettering—the "s" still written like "f." To the southwest is a tall monument dated 1859. More to the east, where the crowd would have stood: 1832, 1834, 1854. To the northeast, one from 1855 and one as fresh as February 1863.

To the south of the Harrison "Site," 1854, 1815, 1788—the Revolutionary War veteran. There are many more, including 1836, 1828, and 1802. Many very old graves seem just as high in elevation as the new site's knoll. I stop noting down the actual names because a funny feeling begins to come over me. This is a cemetery, not a museum. These are people, not facts. Here are couples, parents, and children.

On the west and north sides lie many more graves. The north side especially has many old, old grave markers—those full-length gravestones flush with the ground, covering the whole grave, like the ones in Boston and England.

And then I come back around to the final one—the one I had not been expecting. Directly north of the site, where part of the crowd would have been gathered:

Mary Virginia Wade

Here is the confirmation. Her grave—the grave of the only civilian to die in the battle—this one surely would not have been trampled.

The monument itself was not put up until 1901. Ironically, it had not been done by Gettysburg citizens but by the Women's Relief Corps of Iowa. She is buried next to her father and mother.

That last fact I do not yet fully appreciate as I walk slowly back to the gatehouse, where I have an appointment with the caretaker, Mr. Henry, who finally returned yesterday.

He is a fine person, very cordial, knowledgeable, and helpful. Not like somebody else, who did not have time for me. But no more about her. Really, how would it feel to have one's case demolished? And by a nobody; just some guy. The thought struck me that it might reflect adversely on her job, and not merely upon her reputation.

Mr. Henry has been telling me something.

"Say what?" I inquire.

"1855. Evergreen Cemetery was established in 1855."

O, somewhere hearts are happy. *1855?* "How, ah . . . how might that, ah, be?" I ask. *How could this cemetery not be older than that, with all these old graves?*

The graves were moved from churchyards all around the area. There isn't a church on this hill; nevertheless Evergreen Cemetery is one large country churchyard, consolidated postmodern fashion, one century next to another.

"Were the graves all moved here between 1855 and, say, 1863?" I ask carefully. (He probably knows Ms. Harrison, so I should be circumspect.)

"Oh, no. Not at all. Only a few were moved by then."

But there are reports of headstones all over the place during the battle. Only a relative few? I clear my throat and ask, "Where? Which ones?"

In the gatehouse he pulls out some old books recording the dates of some of the reinterments. Many were never recorded. The books prove that most of the graves I had noted were not yet here in November 1863. Ginnie Wade's remains had not been brought up to Evergreen Cemetery by then. First she had been buried in the garden behind the house where she was killed, then moved to the cemetery of the nearby German Reformed Church.

As a historian, indeed, as a Man of Letters, I have three choices. I could fall down. I could go ahead and make up the best argument I could. After all, some of the graves to the east and southeast, in sections B and G, were present at the dedication. But I suppose the officials had had to choose between disturbing several graves in Evergreen and disturbing 1,258 graves of soldiers who had died saving the Republic. I take the third choice. I gulp, and walk purposefully out of there.

> Alas! What boots it with uncessant care
> To tend the homely slighted shepherd's trade,
> And strictly meditate the thankless muse,
> Were it not better done as others use,
> To sport with Amaryllis in the shade,
> Or with the tangles of Naera's hair?

Out of the corner of my eye I seem to catch a headstone with my name on it and the inscription *Semper Asinus.*

But no. I am a hero. In the short space of two hours I have saved a lady's job.

* * *

Walking away, I do wonder whether the trees on the Harrison Site might be too old for a platform to have been constructed on that place in 1863. I also consider the possibility that to pay attention to reporters who said they saw the Round Tops is to be selective; it is to ignore others who said the platform was at another place—and it is to assume the reporters meant you could see those hills from the speakers' platform, though all they said was you could see them from where the reporters were standing. However, when I look at a copy of the photograph, I see the plain sense of the Harrison Site. But much worse, I now began to *feel* the platform up there. Well, I am a citizen of the postmodern world, like it or not.

Ha. With that I destroy postmodernism. By abandoning my own program and submitting to the *facts,* I show that historians can work toward an objective reality. Abandoning smaller game, I have bagged the big prize! Sure.

I walk down through the Soldiers' National Cemetery to cheer myself up.

The trees are grand and beautiful. Eastern hemlock, magnolia bare in deep November, the large gingko, the tulip poplar; and the widest tree, its trunk broad as a house, the beautiful and old, gnarled, elephantine purple beech. Here and there through the cemetery, among and behind the old, old graves, stand summer trees now looking dead and cold: Silver maple, red oak, basswood (named *Tibia americana*), the sycamore maple, sweet buckeye—American like the men whose bodies lie beneath them, themselves of the older century when Longfellow wrote of the village blacksmith and Abraham Lincoln walked to his law office in Springfield, and many of these boys sat dreaming by their fishing holes near home. And then the willow-like weeping beech, its light gray trunk marked with carved names and initials like the headstones where I stood. To one side the black locust, on the other the white pine.

* * *

Preoccupation with the location of the speakers' platform might appear trivial, but it seems to have mattered to Abraham Lincoln. While he was working on the speech, he called in William Saunders, the designer of the Soldiers' National Cemetery. The president wanted to know where he was going to stand.

I wonder what it suggested to him. If there is evidence for the president's location in the Address itself, surely it is the reiterated *here, here.* The president did not say "up there," gesturing behind him; nor did he say "there," pointing past the audience. But internal evidence in the Gettysburg Address supporting the traditional site is a frail reed to lean upon.

Consensus has moved away from the traditional site. History, with its newfound faith in technology, has become very democratic. But in democracy, dissenters have rights—even if they have very little platform to stand on.

Two days after the speech, November 21, President Lincoln remained quite ill. He had begun to feel a bit unwell on the eighteenth, the day he went to Gettysburg. After the speech he felt worse. Today he was diagnosed as having varioloid, a form of smallpox. I am not feeling particularly good myself.

* * *

I return to the library back at the Cyclorama. I am interested in the Rose Farm and so I nose along the shelves until I find "Rose Farmhouse Historic Structure Report, Parts 1, 2." In it are all sorts of interesting facts. The area that includes the Rose Farm had been bought by Jacob Sherfig (changed to Sherfy), a German Dunkard—an Anabaptist. That means—as if there were not enough irony already—the first "owner" of most of the land the second day's battle was fought over was a pacifist. On this Urfarm were to be found, by 1863, the famous farms of Warfield, Wentz, Houck, Weikert, Snyder, Joseph Sherfy, and Rose.

This original Sherfy, or Sherfig, was himself interesting. His parents, Kaspar and Magdalena, had moved to Maryland from Germany. Jacob and his wife Catharine lost their firstborn son, Daniel. He was killed at age six when a horse started, running away with the little boy caught in the harness. His father had had a premonition, "as if one of his children had to be taken which one would he give up." He could not decide. Neither could he banish the thought. He said that "his trusted 'watchers' told him in the spirit that one of his little ones would be taken."

That area would never be far from the old country. Across the Emmitsburg Road, up where the Home Sweet Home Motel now stands, the U.S. Army constructed a POW camp in 1944. Eventually about five hundred Germans were held there, in not uncomfortable quarters. It was reported that the SS prisoners intimidated the others—human nature being what it is. These prisoners harvested fruit for two American canning companies, Knouse and Musselman. Interesting trivia to settle a dismayed stomach.

I go have another look at the copy of the Gettysburg Address in the Cyclorama building. It is the earliest known copy. The second page is written in pencil: Mr. Lincoln was still working on that part of the speech. First he had written, "It is rather for us, the living, to stand here," but crossed out "to stand here" and wrote, "we here to be dedic" (the next page is missing). In that change is something like a revolution, yet appearing so casual.

You can imagine him carefully underlining the word *did* in "what they did here." The copy shows something of how he thought about, and how he delivered, the speech. Looking at those words, one feels that Mr. Lincoln *meant* it. And still, one cannot grasp the fact that he wrote on those very pieces of paper. It is nearly inconceivable. But there they are.

Why is anyone interested in any of this? Fatigue takes over after a while. Why the Rose Farm, why the wording of the Address, why, of all things, the *place* of the Address? I find out later, in Klement's book, that Selleck is less than reliable. He erroneously stated that the Address elicited no loud applause from the audience; he once wrote that the platform was eighteen feet long, and another time twenty—a minor error, certainly. He also reported that the weather was cloudy when the consensus of others is that it was sunny—so sunny that Secretary of State Seward had to sit with his hat over his eyes (but that was during Everett's address; the secretary was probably sleeping). Selleck also wildly exaggerates the crowd of ten thousand as being fifty thousand. Mr. Klement also perpetrates an error. It was reported that "the Marine Band played Luther's hymn 'Old Hundred' impressively," but I think Luther did not write that hymn. Why are these historical questions, errors, corrections worth anything?

One answer is supplied by the inscription on the Florida monument, which I passed on Seminary Ridge yesterday, near where Kershaw's men lined up for their attack on the Rose Farm: "by their noble example of bravery and endurance, they enable us to meet with confidence any sacrifice which confronts us." You need small facts like you need the remembered sound of someone's voice. Facts generate History, but History is greater than the sum of its facts. We hold this truth to be self-evident: that all people are sacred. Therefore, History becomes a sacred story as it is told. A cloud of witnesses who were born, lived, and died surround it on every side.

In the Visitors' Center, in a display case, the Krauth family's Haviland china is displayed. Not one piece had been broken, though it had been used and left about by Confederate infantrymen. Maybe an officer came by and said casually, "Now don't you go breakin' that fine English china, boys." It is our link to them. When we hold these pieces in our sight, those people are alive again. Detail overcomes time. The small facts remind us that history is people—people like you and me.

After I drove away from the Cyclorama and the Visitors' Center on Cemetery Ridge, I happened to stop along an old stone-and-rider fence. Glancing at my outside rearview mirror, I discovered that I was looking down the mouth of a cannon. Words etched across the bottom of the glass said: "OBJECTS IN MIRROR ARE CLOSER THAN THEY APPEAR."

* * *

Perhaps we cannot know where Lincoln stood, but we can find the exact location of the Address. If it exists anywhere, it exists where we are going. Lincoln wanted a moving Address. He wanted it to advance from place to place and from person to person, its truth marching on. It was not to be placed and headstoned. It is rather for us, the living. *Living words for living people.*

So we know *where* the Address is, but do we know *what* it is? We could look at Lincoln's use of the Declaration of Independence in either of two ways. He may have found the tension in Jefferson's text, and exploited it for his own purposes. In such a case, Lincoln would have "deconstructed" the Declaration. (That is the current term; other words might have been used in the past, many of them more accurate and none complimentary.) Or Lincoln "explicated," *unfolded,* the earlier piece of writing. In the first case, Lincoln, the man who held the country together in order to preserve representative government and who emancipated the slaves, was actually another of the oppressors who have always used language as a lever for power. While that idea is fetchingly postmodern, one wants to carry asininity only so far. If Lincoln explicated Jefferson, drawing out the Declaration's implications, then Lincoln was a servant of the text and its spirit. He kept the faith.

The Founding Fathers instituted a Supreme Court to interpret the text of the U.S. Constitution. But the idea of legal authority itself is being shredded by postmodernism and deconstruction, which takes an Occam's Chainsaw to everything. Nothing important is untouched. Loki's hordes are on the border; not one arrow is dull, not one ankle-strap is loose. "None will break ranks," Wilfred Owen wrote in 1918. Has an intellectual twilight of the gods come upon us? Has the wolf swallowed the sun?

If texts have no authority, and there is no objective past or reality, then we are lost at sea. One postmodern historiographer says, "Everything has become contemporary . . . everything has also become history." Must the present be a Charybdis into which past and future are sucked inexorably, in the chaos of individual minds?

Is Western civilization standing face-to-face with a Zen Koan?

Our civilization is spilling into a new era where old certainties are gone. In their place we have not a new age, but the intellectual rubble of the Modern World. For a time we can stand in the mess, bemused; but soon we must build to survive. No replicas of the Modern World will do, however. The more accurate they are, the more quickly they must lead to the same holocaust. We have no good choice but to be dedicated to the work before us, though we do not want the inevitable "long twilight struggle" and we do not wish the inevitable fundamental and astounding results. The war comes. We will be remembered in spite of ourselves.

* * *

Perhaps the term *submodern* should replace *postmodern.* But it is unclear whether the current successor to modernism is merely inferior to it, whether it is merely a degenerate condition. Modernism may be a dead end, its own impiety, materialism, and scientism responsible for the twentieth-century blows to progress and reason. Or, on the contrary, the German wars of that century were caused by antimodern forces: fascism, totalitarianism, paganism, nationalism—and modernism should take courage rather than surrender to the shocks it has survived. In either case, there now exists not only the necessity but also the opportunity to advance beyond the old modernism, call that advance what we may. But to whom shall we turn for leadership? Where are our prophets?

* * *

Mr. Lincoln's children, now back from the sunny day at Gettysburg, knew that memory can be harsh when families and history come together. On this day almost two score years ago—November 21, 1963—President John F. Kennedy called his brother from Dallas to wish him a good day. It was Robert's thirty-eighth birthday.

NOVEMBER 22

A Larger Sense (Dallas and Oxford)

On this date in 1963, President John F. Kennedy was shot. We have the Zapruder film by memory. Each replay is an attempt to unplay, but it always comes out the same. The *New York Times* headline—"President Shot Dead"—was not large enough, bold enough, or blunt enough to overcome our disbelief. We are frozen in the frame just before; the last four decades have been a national neurosis. The United States of America has been shot in the head. We The People have collapsed in roses on the back seat of a Lincoln.

The Kennedy Generation has been preoccupied with his stunning death for all these years, and our children do not even know what they have inherited. America became like a single mind in late November 1963, being exposed to the same shock. The nation was transfixed by the landing of Air Force One, Jackie emerging with blood on her suit; by the shooting of the assassin; and especially by the long funeral, patterned upon the funeral of Abraham Lincoln. The sixteenth president's funeral train passed hundreds of thousands waiting along the tracks; JFK's caisson rumbled through millions of paralyzed minds. In the strange but inexorable logic of trauma, we have become perpetrator and victim, assassin and assassinated. Perhaps this figuratively explains the popularity of Ronald Reagan, an idealist like John F. Kennedy, a wealthy and glamorous actor taking aim at the deepest values of Kennedy's children, slinging slug after slug into the New Frontier. We needed a national psychotherapy but never got it.

We were naive children when bullets struck the president in 1963; the 1950s had been a Never-Never Land. The good side had defeated the evil side in World War II. Things are as they should be. Things are what they appear to be.

The shots in Dallas mutilated those beliefs.

* * *

The year 1961 had seemed to mark a new birth of the Enlightenment. Kennedy appeared to be a paragon of pure reason. His calculations were intellectual. He was, Jacqueline Kennedy later said, "an idealist without illusions." He was able to see the irrational around him—the nuclear maniacism that he both fostered and opposed.

But he was, in a way, a caricature, not apotheosis, of reason. To be unfeeling is not the same as to be dispassionate in judgment. Furthermore, Enlightenment rationality, a descendent of classical reason, is inseparable from moderation. Selfish, neurotically insatiable, craving risk and excitement, Kennedy found himself gifted with charm, charisma, wit, style—and having the powers these gave, used them immoderately. For JFK, liberty meant the ability to do what you want.

Living one deception upon another—the vigorous healthy athlete, the family man, the Pulitzer Prize–winning author—Kennedy was not consistent to the core as was another Enlightenment heir, Lincoln. But he met one requirement of heroes: the Greek ideal of *excellence.*

Kennedy generated hope around the world, and his courage was acknowledged by all who knew him. He thus inspired effort and excellence in others. His engaging smile was intelligent; he seemed to preside from scholastic heights of hurried calm, showing just enough amusement from afar to discontent without discouraging. His voice was like the pleading of a psalm against the finitude of what we are. America became aliened without him.

What had been the alternatives to JFK in 1960? He was, in his own way, the best hope of the times. But raising the hopes of Enlightenment, he was unable to embody or fulfill them; and hope deferred, around the world and at home, unleashed the dormant forces that have always waited for the Enlightenment to flicker out. “The world is different now,” John Kennedy said in 1961. As a man who focused the rays of freedom on himself, he was chief among those who made it so. We loved him for it, and still do.

* * *

Kennedy’s limited idea of freedom became modulated by an understanding of justice because Kennedy did have a conscience: a taut young tough named Robert Kennedy. He was an external conscience, but a conscience nevertheless; and President Kennedy made his conscience attorney general. By championing justice, JFK left a heritage of hope. Richard Goodwin, an aide to Presidents Kennedy and Johnson, wrote: “John Kennedy expressed—in words, in action, in manner—his own belief in America’s possibilities; that we were a nation with a large purpose, a mission . . . It all sounded so fresh and contemporary, but it was a reaffirmation of the idea that was the nation—that had come on the Mayflower.”

Is the idea, the faith, gone? Have we become a nation of cynics? If so, America’s public deaths in the 1960s helped make us that way. They were a miniature World War I. We have had nothing like the Gettysburg Address to comfort us, to give the deaths of the 1960s meaning, and to restore our hope. We are the November 1863 North without Abraham Lincoln’s words. Perhaps we have simply forgotten them.

Since President Kennedy’s assassination, America has walked around, to use Lincoln’s phrase, “like a duck hit on the head.” The sudden, graphically recorded killing of a charismatic young president early in his task by a nervy punk for no particular reason is more than we could deal with—or less. We want a conspiracy if we can get nothing else, because we cannot take randomness. The idea of evil is alien to Americans. We have tried to deny the assassination’s evil by denying the goodness in Kennedy, but this has not worked satisfactorily.

Answers to the country’s deep questions might have been given by our moral leaders. But we buried them in 1968 and went on with our lives. Did we think we could do without hope? The times are catching up. The United States of America has always lived a dynamic, dangerous, courageous life between the way things are and the way things should be.

Eventually it becomes time to stop asking “Why?” and start asking “Why not?” Lincoln’s answer to the question of meaning is to get to work doing good, under God. *Under God* implies a recognition and an invocation. Hope ultimately anticipates the advent of a power higher than our own. Any other hope is destructible.

* * *

He was a great man, thought Lord David Cecil. "You felt you were in the presence—as Samuel Johnson's friends did—of someone who made his contemporaries seem like pygmies." He was not a saint, though many pretend he was.

On November 22, 1963, another man known to his friends as "Jack" died—not in Dallas, Texas, but in Oxford, England. Like Jack Kennedy, this man was a learner, the end of whose days was quite different from most of his earlier life—and much better. Like Kennedy, this man, C. S. Lewis, has become the victim of fantasy, wishful thinking, to the degree that the image of him which many people have is surprisingly wrong; at least it would be unrecognizable if held next to the actual person. And like Jack Kennedy, Jack Lewis represents our transition to the postmodern world.

Lewis, like Kennedy, was of Irish ancestry—but was the real thing, in terms of birthplace. He lived in Belfast until his mother died, when Lewis was only nine. Then the boy was sent away to boarding school in England. Though he "reacted with immediate hatred" to England, and always remained in part an alien there, eventually it could be said of him that "he was in love with Oxford."

His early life, like Kennedy's, was dominated by his father. But in Lewis's case it was a preoccupation of rebellion. To a degree he must have invented a father; Albert Lewis was physically and emotionally distant during most of his youth. "I treated my own father abominably and no sin in my whole life now seems to be so serious," Lewis said twenty-five years after his father died.

Those who think of Lewis as a saintly individual might be more uneasy about sin in the matter of his relationships with two women. At Oxford, Lewis lived for many years with an older married woman. After his conversion, the relationship may well have become celibate, if indeed it had not been so all along. It must also be observed that Lewis was monogamous in this relationship, absolutely faithful even to the old age and death of the lady. Late in life, Lewis entered a relationship with another married woman, this one becoming a marriage after her divorce from her first husband. This relationship became the intense joy of his life. Lewis did not want his readers to shrink from the physical aspect of that joy, as is evident in his book *A Grief Observed.* While he did not regard married sexuality as sinful, neither did he regard himself or his wife as pure. They were, he wrote, "A sinful woman married to a sinful man."

Today, many of Lewis's possessions (including the famous wardrobe) are housed in a shrine-like museum at, ironically, a fundamentalist/evangelical college that would have fired Lewis for his heavy smoking and occasionally heavy drinking, if for nothing else. Lewis's recent biographer, A. N. Wilson, calls this shrine a "world of make-believe." Other Lewis devotees, those following the line of Walter Hooper, who was given the right to edit and publish Lewis's posthumous work, wish to believe in "the perpetual Virginity of C. S. Lewis," a shrine of another kind.

There is even a fanciful, if not disingenuous, apostolic succession of sorts regarding Lewis. Hooper, an American who knew Lewis only during part of the summer of 1963, is described by an American publisher as "a long-time friend and for some years personal secretary of C. S. Lewis." An American professor befriended Lewis's brother Warnie after Jack's death, thereby procuring Lewis's furniture and books for the Midwestern college. The impression one receives is that there was somehow a very special relationship between C. S. Lewis and this academic institution. An American couple that had only slight acquaintance with Lewis has generated a cottage industry out of books spinning off from this relationship. I wonder whether it galls those people to read a statement by yet another writer, Chad Walsh, in his long "Afterword" to *A Grief Observed:* "I suppose I knew C. S. Lewis about as well as any American did." He adds, "I came to feel that we understood each other, that we were friends."

The surest acquaintance one can make with C. S. Lewis is through his books. His literary criticism is immensely erudite and uniquely engaging. His apologetic writings, in which he defends traditional Christian doctrines long out of favor in some educated circles, are likewise unflaggingly interesting, partly because of their intellectual flash, but mostly because of Lewis's winsome personal voice. Two examples of the former, from *The Problem of Pain:*

> Lay down this book and reflect for five minutes on the fact that all the great religions were first preached, and long practised, in a world without chloroform.
>
> If the universe is so bad, or even half so bad, how on earth did human beings ever come to attribute it to the activity of a wise and good Creator? Men are fools, perhaps; but hardly so foolish as that. The direct inference from black to white, from evil flower to virtuous root, from senseless work to a workman infinitely wise, staggers belief.

And now this example of the winning personal voice:

> When Mr. Ashley Sampson suggested to me the writing of this book, I asked leave to be allowed to write it anonymously, since, if I were to say

> what I really thought about pain, I should be forced to make statements of such apparent fortitude that they would become ridiculous if anyone knew who made them. Anonymity was rejected as inconsistent with the series; but Mr. Sampson pointed out that I could write a preface explaining that I did not live up to my own principles! This exhilarating programme I am now carrying out.

Unlike Jack Kennedy, Lewis was unretouched and genuine. I spoke with a woman who, as a teenager, had shaken hands with Kennedy during his 1960 primary campaign. She had never met a more sincere person in her life, she reported. This might strike some as comic, some as ironic, some as entirely true; in any case it testifies to a kind of "charismatic gift." Lewis had little charisma. As Wilson describes him:

> he was in no sense putting on an act. The strange locutions, the shabby clothes, the combination of kindliness and brusqueness, the strong 'personality' but increasing *impersonality* of his conversation and interests, were all part of the same process. It is comparable with the oddness which might visit all our outward appearances if we stopped looking in mirrors. The only contrived thing about it was the initial impulse, which interpreted the New Testament injunction to deny self as to 'live without an image of the self'. The 'image' of C. S. Lewis, which many were to find rebarbative, was not, as they imagined, stage-managed . . .

Even in his appealing apologetic writing, as in person, Lewis seems a little too much the very, very smart boy. He did not mature, evidently, until his relationship with Joy ("How many bubbles of mine she pricked."), and, especially, her illness and death. Indeed, what makes the apologetic works fail is this very immaturity. Here is a seemingly overpowering argument being made by a clever debater. The quality of "seemingly" remains, however, and one gradually realizes that this powerful argumentation might very well be destroyed when someone smarter comes along.

It did, in fact, happen. After writing *Miracles,* his most seriously worked out apologetic work, Lewis and his argument were demolished in a public debate by Elizabeth Anscombe. Lewis was not used to this. He was facile, articulate, overbearing, and even bullying in debate. He would, sorry to say, even lie in order to win. To his credit, he realized what his failure against Anscombe meant, and he changed.

The Problem of Pain, an attempt at explaining how there can be a good and all-powerful God if there is suffering in the world, had provided examples of Lewis's argument technique. Characteristically, he forced readers into choices that—if only one knew more, one feels—one might not have to accept:

> There seem, in fact, to be only two views we can hold about awe. Either it is a mere twist in the human mind . . . or else it is a direct experience of the really supernatural, to which the name Revelation might properly be given.
>
> . . . moral law . . . is either inexplicable illusion, or else revelation.
>
> . . . only two views of this man [Jesus] are possible. Either he was a raving lunatic of an unusually abominable type, or else He was, and is, precisely what He said. There is no middle way.

In his most famous doctrinal book, *The Screwtape Letters,* Lewis uses the cheapest of rhetorical tricks to convince readers of his ideas: he places the opposing arguments in the mouth of a devil.

* * *

But his failure against Mrs. Anscombe opened his eyes to himself. "He came to feel . . . [his books'] method and manner were spurious." He never wrote another book of apologetics.

Though he resisted, intellectually, the literature and philosophy of "modernism"—which we might better call postmodernism—Lewis came to a somewhat postmodern view as to the value of rational argument. It seems he gave up the idea that God and the mysteries of faith, or the nature of the world—or the existence of a supernatural world—could be grasped and convincingly argued intellectually. Reason is not, after all, enough.

He had been reasoned into faith in the first place. As a young man, Lewis had been an atheist. His "conversion" seems to have been a gradual intellectual acceptance of traditional Christian ideas. This intellectual certainty enabled him to write the apologetic books, which are still widely read. But when Joy, his wife, died after a few years of autumnal, ecstatic marital happiness, the intellectual "faith" dissolved in a flash of pain. "If my house has collapsed at one blow, that is because it was a house of cards," he wrote in *A Grief Observed.* From this point, his solutions, or his faith, would have to be more than head deep.

The way had already been prepared. After putting aside religious argument, Lewis allowed his inner nature to flourish. Another crowd of people—perhaps "multitude" would be a more fitting word—knows Lewis not as a literary critic, nor as a Christian apologist, but as an imaginative writer, a writer of fantasy. Children read the Narnia stories with a pleasure one finds amazing, because these books are so roughly written, so unlike the way one ought to talk to children, so adult in their humor and import. It is the compelling stories, the intriguing fantastic humanlike creatures, the strange new worlds, the evil of the evil characters and the decency of the good, which have made the Narnia books classics. Lewis thought that ancient mythology was, in a sense, inspired as a way to set up categories in the human mind, categories now ready-formed to accept the historically factual Christ events and understand their deeper significance. There are stories all around the ancient and Norse worlds about dying and rising gods. When the actual thing came along, thought Lewis, we were ready. So, doing the same thing for children, Lewis wrote *The Lion, the Witch, and the Wardrobe,* in which a great lion not only brings a world into being, but also allows himself to be put to death, then rises to defeat an evil witch.

As to logic, this theory may be a good one, though one wonders about the practical effects of its application. Does it prepare a category, or pigeonhole, for the Christian doctrine, or does it make the Christ story appear to be simply one of many such stories? Its value, perhaps, is to confirm the convinced rather than to convert unbelievers.

The Narnia stories are intriguing, but there seem to be two kinds of voices in them that only sometimes merge. One is the wondrous artist, writing of new worlds, universes brought into being on an achingly lovely yet wild song that lights fresh new stars one by one. This Lewis is able to imagine universes under puddles in a wood, great lost cities in cold red starlight, nymphs and fauns dancing in the first wet snow. But the other Lewis is always there, making an argument.

His space trilogy, especially the first two volumes, *Out of the Silent Planet* and *Perelandra,* are more powerful. Some see the trilogy as watered-down Tolkien, a fantasy without the depth of world in *The Lord of the Rings,* its narrative power, or its artistic unity. The trilogy's last volume, especially, harps on immediate and minor philosophical concerns and complaints of Lewis. But *Perelandra,* a reimagining of Milton's version of humanity's fall, is an arresting book. The descriptions of Venus as a floating, vivid, pastel world are almost breathtaking. When the new "Eve" is locked in mortal argument with the tempter, one sits literally on the edge of one's chair, tense with anxiety. Here Lewis has joined his imagination and his doctrine.

But one must read it at the right time. Read him when you are not interested in explanations of Christian doctrine, and most of his books are unsatisfying. That is why his late book, *A Grief Observed,* is his best. It is written by a man who has "seen the elephant."

I do not refer to Lewis's having been in World War I. (He was even wounded.) But considering his war experience, it may be significant to note in *The Abolition of Man* the lack of irony in his use of a line of Roman poetry. He is describing the difference between those who accept a system of "objective value, the belief that certain attitudes are really true, and others really false, to the kind of thing the universe is and the kind of things we are"—and those who do not accept the idea of objective value:

> When a Roman father told his son that it was a sweet and seemly thing to die for his country, he believed what he said. He was communicating to the son an emotion which he himself shared and which he believed to be in accord with the value which his judgement discerned in noble death. He was giving the boy the best he had, giving of his spirit to humanize him as he had given of his body to beget him.

Lewis writes in a way one can hardly believe an Englishman who taught poetry could talk. Perhaps he had never read Wilfred Owen. He did studiously avoid appreciating, and even reading, much "modern" (postmodern?) literature. Possibly the Great War had not reached him; it was the death of Joy that affected him the way the war had affected Owen.

Earlier in life, Lewis had reasoned that "much of one's philosophy and religion are mere talk." Now, July 13, 1960, Jack Lewis sat next to his wife in Oxford's Radcliffe Infirmary. This time, it was over. A year and a half ago, he had been able to write:

> I have stood by the bedside of a woman whose thigh-bone was eaten through with cancer and who had thriving colonies of the disease in many other bones as well. It took three people to move her in bed. The doctors predicted a few months of life: the nurses (who often know better) a few weeks. A good man laid his hands on her and prayed. A year later the patient was walking (uphill, too, through rough woodland) and the man who took the last X-ray photographs was saying 'These bones are as solid as rock'. It's miraculous.

Her remission was not the only strange thing. There was what Wilson calls the "eerie phenomenon" of Lewis's receiving a painful condition similar in outward effects to the disease Joy was temporarily escaping. But for what? The cancer returned. Lewis said to her, as she lay dying, "If you can—if it is allowed—come to me when I too am on my death bed." That night she died.

"Where is God?" cries Lewis in the notes that became *A Grief Observed.* None of Lewis's apologetics or fantasies approach the force of his anger and despair:

> . . . don't come talking to me about the consolations of religion . . .
>
> "Because she is in God's hands." But if so, she was in God's hands all the time, and I have seen what they did to her . . .
>
> A noble hunger, long unsatisfied, met at last its proper food, and almost instantly the food was snatched away. Fate (or whatever it is) delights to produce a great capacity and then frustrate it. Beethoven went deaf. By our standards a mean joke; the monkey trick of a spiteful imbecile.
>
> . . . How do I know that all her anguish is past? I never believed before—I thought it immensely improbable—that the faithfulest soul could leap straight into perfection and peace the moment death has rattled in the throat. It would be wishful thinking with a vengeance to take up that belief now.
>
> . . . What reason have we, except our own desperate wishes, to believe that God is, by any standard we can conceive, "good"?
>
> Time after time, when He seemed most gracious He was really preparing the next torture.
>
> Reality, looked at steadily, is unbearable.

His book is in part a probing, grieving elegy for his wife, just as Owen's work is an outraged elegy for the pale, betrayed dead, and Lincoln's is a political elegy for those who willingly made their sacrifices. All of them are programmatic, trying to change the world, and all of them without meaning to be so are elegies to the Modern World: each uses the terms of modernism to observe that world's passing. The limitations of each come together: Owen could not change the world; Lincoln could not ward off the irony of the twentieth century; Lewis could not explode reason and then approach mystery without it. But his is the basic question: Why? It implies a loss of God, loss of the traditional Father. Where is He? What is He? Do I have a Parent, or am I a stranger dying in my strangeness? In rational creatures, faith inevitably seeks understanding, for reality remains an impermeable and indifferent lump. Life is a crisis of belief. *Basic human nature conflicts with the basic human condition.*

We are aliens to ourselves. As Lewis says prophetically in *The Abolition of Man*—anticipating the postmodern problem: "If you see through everything, then everything is transparent. But a wholly transparent world is an invisible world. To 'see through' all things is the same as not to see." Reality is resistant.

On July 4, 1994, in Independence Hall, Vaclav Havel, president of the

Czech Republic, made an observation on the Declaration of Independence. It contains the same fundamental insight one reads in the Gettysburg Address: "The Declaration of Independence, adopted two hundred and eighteen years ago in this building, states that the Creator gave man the right to liberty. It seems man can realize that liberty only if he does not forget the One who endowed him with it." Therefore, the first question in American politics is whether God exists.

The second question is: What is God like? Politics is an answer, because politics is practical theology. We cannot assume that God exists only as a donor of our rights. *He who planted the eye, shall he not see?* If we act unjustly, we have invented an unjust god; and we inherit whatever the god of our choice endows us with. To believe God does not exist at all is not a practical option: where there is no God, there are no rights, and no offenses. If rights and wrongs are human inventions, we would have to invent God also. But Lewis knew that the God he experienced in the depth of his grief was no human invention.

* * *

The two died on the same day: President John F. Kennedy and C. S. Lewis. In the previous century, when John Adams and Thomas Jefferson died on the same day, fifty years to the date after the signing of the Declaration of Independence, Americans looked for meaning. In addition to their obvious commonalities, Adams and Jefferson had both served on the drafting committee for the Declaration. The prevailing interpretation of the remarkable conjunction was that God had given a sign of His approval of the American venture. Was it a coincidence, or an event?

Kennedy and Lewis were not even residents of the same country, let alone not being former presidents who had played leading roles in the bringing forth of a nation. Why should one find meaning in their coincident deaths? Aldous Huxley, author of *Brave New World,* died on that day, November 22, 1963, too. So did many other people.

Does it mean anything that Wilfred Owen, John Kennedy, C. S. Lewis, Lt. Larry L. Hess, and two people I knew very well died in the same month that Lincoln gave the Gettysburg Address—though not in the same year? Do coincident events *have* meaning, or do we *give* them meaning? The postmodernist believes they are only given meaning. The traditionalist believes we discover what is actually there. Did Lincoln see what the Union soldiers had died for, or did he *make* a meaning for their deaths?

It is for us to decide. Is there a correct answer, or do we make an answer? This is a test.

NOVEMBER 23

For Us, the Living (Weep No More)

The wan weeds of the fields are dry. The gray sky is a mirror, and all of nature has donned a somber costume. A long month ago, swallows twittered in the gathering twilight and were gone. You cannot roam these scenes of death or walk among the soldiers' white stones without "the passing Tribute of a sigh." How could I begin to understand these Civil War losses if I did not know my own losses? But the price is high. What you want for your mind you sometimes pay for with your heart. And what do you get? Nothing, the postmodernists say.

Political and historical questions feel trivial out here on the battlefield today. They pale and shrink and vanish before personal loss and the question of eternity. How did Lincoln join cause and comfort? But of course, there is no comfort unless there is a cause. That is why we ask "Why?" That is why we devote ourselves to charities and works that the dead had been dedicated to. What cause can be big enough for the absence of someone we love?

If postmodernists are right about knowledge, then questions are as meaningless as answers. Tell that to the bereft families who came to hear Lincoln's speech. "Why?" Let a new Descartes say, *I grieve, therefore I am.*

No one asks for grief. "Drop by drop upon our hearts, against our wills, comes wisdom by the awful grace of God." We can assuage our grief only by our own heroism, and heroism is more understandable to those who know grief. The answer to the Civil War comes from Lincoln, who knew his losses. He was our country's melancholy poet and prophet, a man of sorrows and acquainted with grief.

I carry in my pocket today a bracelet. My mother wore it during the last months of her life—this time last year. A small key used to dangle from it. She has taken the key with her. How shall I ever know the meaning of her life and death? She lived through all of this century plus thirty years, if not herself, then by secondary experience. She was the link between the young men of Gettysburg and my middle age, with the world wars and Vietnam and my father. They are gone with her; how can I ever understand them?

But I begin to perceive that she has left the key after all.

In one thing at least, the postmoderns are right. If I am to understand the meaning of a life and death, I must make that meaning. Yet it will stand only if it was there all along.

* * *

This month's heroes and near-heroes all share a characteristic I had not expected, a characteristic which is a foundation for hope. Wilfred Owen, for example, a shell-shocked, sensitive young man who opposed the war, went back to France. More to become a poet than to become a soldier, he accepted his transformation and offered up the Eucharist of his own blood. To the grotesque horror of his war, he opposed a beauty that will outlast the ghostly trenches in France. Beauty is an intimation of transcendence.

John Kennedy did not accept the sickly body life had given him, and though we may debate the degree of fraudulence in his image, he denied his disadvantages through a kind of excellence. With what he appeared to be and with what he said, he dispelled and dispersed a decade, the 1950s, which needed dispelling because it was a false terminal of the American Dream. Even today, nearly fifty years later, the fifties entrance us like the lotos flower. They seem a bright, clear, prosperous, happy Elysian Field of American history. Imagine how attractive they were then. But neither Lincoln's men nor the GIs of World War II had died in order to make the orderly suburbs and big Chevrolets of the 1950s. *We have to get moving again,* Kennedy said. *We aren't finished. We have only begun.* Yet JFK himself once epitomized that decade.

C. S. Lewis again and again relinquished what he had thought was true, thereby learning more and more about the God who "shatters the gods of old." Each time, he left something behind, like Saint Francis dropping his clothes and walking away from what had been his world. In a material sense, L. L. had done this too, typical of American children of immigrants. The entire country has been made on the principle of abandonment. Leave the old world; build the new. This impulse can be heroic. In this sense, Americans have always expected themselves to be heroes, and have considered the country itself to be a hero. Lincoln carried this principle farthest. He also exhorted his people to be such heroes.

But Lincoln was a man of profoundest paradox. One acquires hope from Lincoln's story, because if one person can rise to the moral and political heights that this former rail-splitter ascended, so can another, if excellence is rewarded justly and chances are given equally. Yet no one was more of a fatalist than Lincoln. Indeed, the religious separatists who began to write America's holy history thought like Lincoln: We are working to build the City on a Hill, a New Jerusalem; in doing so, we are only instruments in the hands of Providence.

The more a hero achieves, the more "the will of God prevails." This is one of the profoundest paradoxes of life, perilously close to the whirlpool of absurdity, grazing dangerously the rock of futility. Who can understand the dangers and steer his way between them? Only Ulysses, Homer's "man of many turns," the sufferer who has kept a watch on man's mortality, who has known the great Achilles and gone with him to the place of the pale dead, who trades time for identity, who braves the monsters of the deep and defies the principalities of the air; the hero who acts under the hand of an unseen God.

* * *

I begin to see what a hero is. I begin to awaken from today's numbness. The key has been in my hand all along.

> Now *Lycidas,* the Shepherds weep no more;
> Henceforth thou art the Genius of the shore,
> . . . and shalt be good
> To all that wander in the perilous flood.

NOVEMBER 24

The Last Full Measure of Devotion (Ulysses)

All philosophy begins with death.
—Heidegger

"In Greece the mind and the spirit met on equal terms," wrote Edith Hamilton in *The Greek Way*, a book Robert Kennedy read and reread after his brother's death. He carried his dog-eared copy around with him; he often quoted from it by memory. On the day he died, the book was found open. The Greeks were different from the peoples around them, wrote Hamilton:

> None of the great civilizations that preceded them and surrounded them served them as a model. With them something completely new came into the world. They were the first Westerners; the spirit of the West, the modern spirit, is a Greek discovery and the place of the Greeks is in the modern world.

They brought reason to all human experience, yet the greatest hero of the Greeks, Homer's Odysseus or Ulysses, was not only supreme in reason. He had a great, indomitable heart. Realizing that mental acuity was not enough, he opposed his courage to the uncanny and mysterious forces standing between him and who he was—the epitome of the modern hero: rational, skeptical, intelligent; but he was also, and primarily, human, a sufferer—"a man of many turns" Homer calls him. At the end of his odyssey he found his place among and for others. The Modern Age is in its November now, but Ulysses has become a hero for more than one time and one place.

* * *

This morning, all is quiet along the Potomac. I have driven down to Washington from Gettysburg. Arlington National Cemetery lies spread across the lawns of the Custis-Lee mansion. The shadows from a lowering sky pour across the headstones, lingering and releasing them rank after rank. The last flood of sunshine rests upon Robert Kennedy's grave.

Sometimes his seems to be the smallest and the least conspicuous of all the monuments in this fifty square miles of monuments: the Washington obelisk; the Jefferson rotunda with its rational, elegant reflecting pool; the Lincoln memorial; the eternal flame for John F. Kennedy; and up the hill, the columned mansion. John and Robert Kennedy are buried in Robert E. Lee's front yard. The Civil War was about whether this nation had to be just, or whether liberty could be a self-sufficient principle. In this sense, the war was still on a hundred years later. It has not ended yet. Truly, the universe is no modernist; there is no respect for chronology. What fits together comes together. Behind the high marble figure of Abraham Lincoln across the river miles away, these three are joined: John Fitzgerald Kennedy, his brother Robert Francis Kennedy, and though not entombed here, Robert Edward Lee. They watch behind the Great Emancipator's back, across a Jordan from his alabaster city. The general is represented by empty rooms, where all was accustomed and ceremonial, where folly finally into folly came. But the president even now cannot be murdered with spots of ink. And Robert forged faith, hope, and charity in the dark smithy of his soul. These two brothers were the last Romantics. They were Lincoln's children.

* * *

The National Democratic Convention in 1964, the summer after John Kennedy's death. The forlorn figure of Robert Kennedy at the podium, looking alone although surrounded by thousands of cheering and applauding delegates. His melancholy face. The grieving man enduring an unending ovation. He stood there minute after minute, and fascination with the charming president turned to sad affection for the stunned younger man. He raised his hand hesitantly to quiet the applause, failed, smiled sadly, tried to say "Mister Chairman," and was drowned by applause time after time, for twenty-two minutes. Toward the end of his short speech he quoted Shakespeare, applying the words to his brother:

> When he shall die
> Take him and cut him out in little stars
> And he will make the face of heaven so fine
> That all the world will be in love with night,
> And pay no worship to the garish sun.

The quotation, supplied by Jacqueline Kennedy, can be read ambiguously now, its potential of suggesting America's infatuation with the darkness of John Kennedy deferred until well after 1964, but then it was poignant beyond expression. The feeling was not artificial. Robert Kennedy, according to Arthur Schlesinger, had always been characterized by "abiding melancholy." After Dallas, he had been "haunted" by an Irish ballad:

> Sheep without a shepherd;
> When the snow shuts out the sky—
> Oh, why did you leave us, Owen?
> Why did you die?

* * *

But many Americans hated Robert Kennedy by 1968. He had given himself entirely to his brother's success, doing what was necessary all the time, driving people, threatening people, acting the tough kid brother's part, swinging the hatchet whenever necessary, calculating, shrill, and most notoriously, "ruthless." Everyone who met him liked Jack; Bobby was in the back room doing the dirty work. John F. Kennedy believed you had to lose votes to get votes, make enemies to win friends; and it was Bobby who kept most of the enemies. He could not be cool, urbane, "graceful," like his brother. He was the passionate Kennedy. He was awkward and full of fight, a roughneck in the service of the courtly king of Camelot.

But then his reason for ruthlessness was snuffed out and his own personality developed. Robert Kennedy was late in forming his own identity—like the Ulysses of Homer, becoming himself only at the very end of the story. Some young people could sense the alienation of a man suddenly *outside,* without a role, needing to find who he was and a reason for living.

Robert Kennedy looked and acted like a rebellious student, with his long hair and teenage smile, his youthful idealism and childlike sense of right and wrong. His slight appearance enhanced this effect; he was five-foot-ten but appeared smaller. Nevertheless, RFK was no adolescent, boyish though he certainly appeared. And he was serious to a degree hardly felt today. He had something in common with the generation of the 1860s, when Abraham Lincoln ran for president, and half the nation made use of colored slaves, and one section would make war, and the other section would accept war, and war came.

To many who were coming of age in the 1960s, Robert Kennedy was the Bonnie Prince, the rightful king challenging the usurper, Lyndon Johnson. His was a rebellion against evil to restore the right—the perfect crusade for young people: a revolt for fairness and goodness and justice. Kennedy was a rebel with a cause. Here appeared to be the audacity of Robert E. Lee and the moral grandeur of Abraham Lincoln, with Saint Francis of Assisi added in. Such was Robert Kennedy, brushing back his tousled hair and smiling bashfully; he was one of us, more so than we were ourselves.

His early characteristics remained strong: "moralistic, gloomy." He was the religious Kennedy, going to Mass every Sunday, with an innate Catholic discipline. He was "the Christian," "the believer," the Kennedy who had "soul." He believed in "making a contribution." He believed in service, sacrifice, and responsibility, and he had a strong, if overly contrasting, sense of good and evil. Second youngest of the driving Kennedy clan, and not a born athlete, he had become intensely competitive in order to survive. In school he had played football despite his relatively small size. Later he would do things like finishing a fifty-mile hike and rafting the Colorado River. In 1965 he climbed Mount Kennedy, among the first party to do it. Almost exhausted but nearing the top, as he said later, "I only had three choices—to go down, to fall off, or to go ahead. I really only had one choice." And Jacqueline Kennedy said of him, "He has the kindest heart in the world."

He was like "a character in a novel," someone said after interviewing him. There was more depth and conflict in him than one is accustomed to in politicians. He was, wrote his friend and aide, Jack Newfield, "constantly at war with himself." He once said that he probably would have been a juvenile delinquent or a revolutionary had he not been born a Kennedy. He was not only "shanty Irish," but also one of the "dark Irish" with the "rebellious Irish streak." Blue-collar workers sensed that about him; he was one of them, too.

Newfield remarks at the dramatic significance of the changes in Kennedy's face after Dallas. To understand this man required "a literary imagination." As such, he became "myth" and "symbolism."

After his brother's assassination, "awareness of death conditioned every minute of Kennedy's life." This set him apart from others. He learned about the absurd, says Newfield, a postmodern understanding, but, with Camus, he knew that there are things to be done with this understanding. ("Kennedy and Camus in '68" read the occasional poster at Kennedy rallies.) Kennedy's wisdom became a wisdom of action. The assassination of the president gave RFK his name, but what he did in response gave him his identity.

His knowledge of the absurd, which made him think of the constant possibility of his own untimely death, also enabled his notable sense of humor to flourish.

> Early in 1967 [Newfield recalls] Kennedy flew to Albany for a series of meetings with county leaders. About 11 A.M. the "Caroline" landed at the Albany airport, which was windblown, deserted, and blanketed with freshly fallen snow. As Kennedy was getting off the plane, he suddenly waved to the empty airport, and clasped his hands over his head in the boxer's salute, as if there were actually thousands there to greet him.

A year later, during the Indiana primary, he had to make a dash from the shower to answer a telephone call. Wrapped in a towel and dripping, his hair matted in all directions, he proclaimed to the three people in the room, "Make way for the future leader of the free world." There was something of the rebel, something "anti," in his humor, and a refusal to assume his own importance. One evening at the beginning of his presidential campaign, Kennedy flew back to Washington on a commercial flight:

> At 8:45 P.M., Robert Kennedy, a slouched, rumpled figure, began walking through the oddly deserted new American Airlines terminal. He was alone, and carried under his arm a copy of Shakespeare's *Love Sonnets,* which he had read fitfully on the flight back from New York.
>
> He looked around, and could not see his driver, and said to a few stray reporters, as if trying to dictate their morning leads for them, "The hero returns . . . "
>
> Kennedy . . . looking lost, walked through the automatic doors, where a stewardess directed him to a limousine the airline had secured for him.
>
> "How many with your party?" the stewardess asked with professional warmth.
>
> "Just me. I'm alone," Kennedy answered, getting into the limousine.

The affection he called forth combined with mythological qualities: "his long hair, his nickname of Bobby, his trip to South Africa in 1966, his relationships with Lyndon Johnson and his brother, his compulsive confronting of death in river rapids, mountaintops, and Amazon jungles." Norman Mailer described the "existential hero":

> central to his time, a man whose personality might suggest contradictions and mysteries which could reach into the alienated circuits of the underground . . . a hero can capture the secret imagination of a people, and so be good for the vitality of a nation. . . .
>
> . . . a hero embodies his time and is not so very much better than his time, but he is larger than life and so is capable of giving direction to the time, able to encourage a nation to discover the deepest colors of its character . . . a man who has lived with death.

Campaigning in Indiana in 1968, he tried to explain to an audience of unsympathetic listeners at Purdue University what it was like to be an Indian child growing up on a reservation. His ability to identify with others, often noted, brought him so far into the experience of such a child—which he had witnessed on a visit to a reservation—that "When he got back to the campaign plane, he sat alone by the window for half an hour, tears in the corners of his eyes, the familiar ravaged look on his face, unapproachable."

Kennedy's compassion displaced political ideologies. Coming up from a coal mine in Chile in November 1965, he said, "If I worked in this mine, I'd be a Communist, too." The people he loved understood Kennedy's compassion and considered him different from other politicians.

> One afternoon early in 1967, Kennedy and his Senate colleague Jacob Javits were visiting a tenement on the Lower East Side. The customary clot of children was waiting on the sidewalk when a late arrival asked what was happening. One of the children, about a ten- or twelve-year-old Puerto Rican, answered, "Senator Javits and Bobby are inside the house."

* * *

After his brother died, Robert Kennedy, despite retaining fundamental elements of his nature, moved along a continual process of change that seemed to accelerate right down to the end, when it seemed during those last days in California that he had finally found who and what he was. He appeared to be less taut than before. He quoted his brother less and enacted JFK's characteristic gestures less, even confessed that his brother (and he) had been wrong about some things. With Lyndon Johnson and Vietnam virtually removed, Kennedy had found his cause and his essential constituency. He had become, in Arthur Schlesinger's words, "Tribune to the Underclass." But his identity, as with Homer's Ulysses, was less a discovery than an achievement.

Kennedy's process of change produced what Newfield calls "the shock of unrecognition": people who met RFK were startled by the difference between the man they had spoken with and what they had expected him to be. Only a year or two after 1968 I met a political consultant who had been acquainted with virtually all the well-known figures of the sixties at one time or another. Of course I asked him about Robert Kennedy. He said, "Robert Kennedy was a son of a bitch." I suppose he was. The question is, when was "was"? Kennedy, by acts of will and heart, made of himself something he had not been.

The public did not follow his complex inner odyssey. Robert Kennedy remained, in 1968, a "magnet for hate." He took an inordinate number of unjust criticisms and attacks without answering. His rival for the Democratic nomination, Eugene McCarthy, seemed to have a talent for mean sarcasm and vicious remarks. But Kennedy was trapped by his own past and the reputation he needed to live down. He had to avoid appearing "ruthless." In addition, he was "basically introverted" and emotional, and as such did not have the natural ability to deflect, counter, and publicly belie personal attacks as his brothers could. In private, he could dispel some of the charges. One morning at home, after taking the newspaper upstairs to Ethel, he came back down and said to a friend, "That's my good deed for the day. Now I can go back to being ruthless." Once during the last campaign an aide who had fallen asleep at work woke to find Kennedy putting a blanket over him. The aide looked up and mumbled, "You aren't so ruthless after all."

Occasionally he could handle a liability in public. Having been accused of carpetbagging during his New York senatorial campaign, he said at the Women's National Press Club Dinner, "I can't tell you how happy I am to be here representing the great state of . . . ah . . . ah . . . " The Kennedy name and the Kennedy money were always issues. At Skidmore College in 1967, Kennedy spoke of the costs of running a campaign in large states like New York: it was impossible without the help of either a famous personality or enormous sums of money. But, Kennedy said, "As an unknown, virtually without funds, I was, of course, an exception."

He never won over the middle-class liberals, the intellectuals. (Arthur Schlesinger, the well-known Harvard historian, had been an acquisition of John Kennedy.) Back in the fifties, Robert had worked briefly for Sen. Joseph McCarthy. Kennedy entertained some of his father's basic conservatism; nevertheless, his working for McCarthy was in large degree a matter of family loyalty, even Irish loyalty. The fact that Kennedy soon quit and worked against McCarthy was not remembered, except perhaps as disloyalty or opportunism. He had been one of the best attorneys general ever, some thought, bringing "justice" back into the Justice Department, working for racial equality, but it was easier for liberals to remember what a tough chief law enforcer he had been. Many liberal students stayed against him during the '68 campaign, often showing up at his rallies to shout challenges and insults.

The high emotions of the time resulted in what was then called the "lightning rod" phenomenon. James Reston, writing in the *New York Times,* said on April 24, 1968:

> There is a very large body of anti-Kennedy voters in this country these days. . . . You can't even ride with the Irish cabbies in Boston without hearing some vicious remark about Bobby's policies or his person. . . . The opposition to him is personal, almost chemical, and sometimes borders on the irrational.

He did not take popular positions. His salient position had been opposition to the war in Vietnam. When he gave his March '67 speech against Johnson's bombing policy, only 24 percent of the American public opposed the bombing. For many liberals, he had spoken out too late—even though he had come out against the war as early as 1966. It is easy to understand McCarthy's animosity toward Kennedy, who entered the presidential race after McCarthy's strong showing in New Hampshire. But RFK had made the decision before the primary. Kennedy, whose hostility toward Lyndon Johnson was well known, had felt he could not challenge Johnson until the race had been thrown open. Eugene McCarthy's reaction to what he perceived as an interloper, however, became very personal. Almost twenty years after the campaign, the former Minnesota senator told me that Robert Kennedy had "no integrity."

Robert Kennedy thought Gene McCarthy would make a bad president. "What has he done for the poor?" was Kennedy's question in private. McCarthy's issue seemed to be Vietnam, only Vietnam, and he did not appear to be emotionally connected to it. In addition, he seemed, especially to the energetic Kennedy, to be "indolent." To Kennedy, McCarthy's worst fault was that he was "not moral." That is, according to Newfield, McCarthy would speak in favor of something on television, and then vote against it during closed session.

Kennedy was not a real "pol," like his brothers. He could not put aside his emotions about people, and his judgments about right and wrong could not be suspended outside the Senate or after campaigning hours. An outstanding campaign manager for his brother, he was not capable of making the right moves for himself. "Politicians generally made him up tight and bored him," Newfield recalled. "He once told me, 'You know, there aren't ten politicians in the whole state [New York] I like and trust.' "

His emotions and his black-and-white moralistic nature prevented his being able, as was the likeable Hubert Humphrey, to garner delegates by wheeling and dealing, promising and shoulder slapping. "The normal faked cordiality among warring politicians [was] impossible for him." As president, he would have had trouble with Congress. "Maybe my personality just isn't built for this," he said on May 30, 1968. That was during the California campaign, where he was continually mobbed by intense, frantic crowds that crushed around his open car just to get near him, to touch his hand, to get one of his cufflinks or a PT-109 tie clasp.

* * *

In November 1967, Robert Kennedy's book *To Seek a Newer World,* titled from a favorite passage in Tennyson's "Ulysses," was published. In it, he says: "First is the danger of futility, the belief that there is nothing one man or one woman can do against the enormous array of the world's ills—against misery and ignorance, injustice and violence. Yet many of the world's great movements, of thought and action, have flowed from the work of a single man. A young monk began the Protestant Reformation . . . and the thirty-two-year-old Thomas Jefferson . . . proclaimed that all men are created equal."

His book (largely written by Adam Walinsky) expresses an Enlightenment combination of idealism and reason in its call for hope and courage. He knew better than most people that this point of view, so consistent with his brother's, was subject to the absurdity of the post–World War I world. His understanding of that was not merely academic, not merely literary. Yet he believed, somehow, that absurdity does not necessarily entail futility. If there is anything he leaves us except seared hope, it is that belief. "In any event," he concludes, "it is the only way we can live."

* * *

The intensity of feeling for Robert Kennedy went beyond celebrity enthusiasm or infatuation. Cesar Chavez, leader of the farm workers in California, said that the feeling for Kennedy "was a phenomenon that can't be explained. . . . I don't think that I'll ever live to see another public figure [do it]." Robert Kennedy, said that Rev. Hector Lopez, was "the last of the great believables." Peggy Noonan, who later wrote speeches for Presidents Reagan and Bush, said: "to have been young and heard his hopeful call, to have known there was a politician who didn't like the greedy and stupid but preferred in fact the modest and even strange, to have seen him exhort people and insist we can do better—to have seen that and lived through those days is to keep, always, a sense of excitement about the possibilities of American life. It was moving, and unforgettable. Which is why so many of us who grabbed for his hand will never let go."

He was "a man who had just discovered another dimension of injustice, pain, and human folly," wrote Elie Wiesel. "Battered by destiny, he wanted to show his solidarity with victims everywhere." Prophets, Wiesel points out, are never on the side of those with power: "I read his speeches, the ones before and the ones after. The ones before the murder of his brother are often pragmatic. The ones delivered afterwards are strikingly lyrical and sometimes prophetic: they move you deeply."

Those speeches are often surprising. On November 26, 1967, he was booed by an audience at the University of Oklahoma for speaking against the student draft deferment. On one such occasion he asked how many were for the deferment. He got an overwhelming affirmative chorus. When the noise died down, he asked, "How many of you are for the war?" The crowd gasped at their own perfidy, then cheered Kennedy. Such confrontations were not rare. Addressing eight hundred medical students in Indiana, Kennedy was heckled, then challenged with questions regarding his wish for medical care for the poor. "Where are you going to get all the money for those federally subsidized programs you're talking about?"

"From you," Kennedy retorted. Then, stepping toward his audience, he continued:

> Let me say something about the tenor of that question and some of the other questions. There are people in this country who suffer. . . . You are the privileged ones here. It's easy to sit back and say it's the fault of the federal government, but it's our responsibility too. It's our society, not just our government, that spends twice as much on pets as on the poverty program. It's the poor who carry the major burden of the struggle in Vietnam. You sit here as white medical students, while black people carry the burden of the fighting in Vietnam. [Cries of "We're going!" interrupted here.] Yes, but you're here now and they're over there. The war might be settled by the time you go.

He was hissed and booed. At the end of the speech one student rose and said, "a lot of us agree with what you are saying," and there were cheers and applause.

> In . . . Indiana, a state filled with conservative, rural, and small town people who (except in Gary) could be expected to be hostile, many listened to Kennedy. One observer said about farmers in another rural state, "In Nebraska I saw the way he related to people who had nothing in common with him at all. . . . He certainly wasn't a farmer. Yet, there was a kind of communication between him and . . . leather-skinned, very hard working people. Very traditional values . . . they probably didn't like . . . antiwar demonstrators. Outside of Omaha, they might not have seen a Negro in their lives . . . the people who would be the *last* people in the world you would imagine Robert Kennedy to have any relationship with, who really had not come to scream and to yell and cheer, but to listen. And he got through. . . . It really taught me a lot about him."

About his campaign in Indiana, Kennedy said: "The people were fair to me. . . . They gave me a chance. They listened to me. I could see this face, way back in the crowd, and he was listening, really listening to me. . . . I loved the faces here in Indiana, on the farmers, on the steelworkers, on the black kids." Nevertheless, RFK had remained "brooding and lonely" in Indiana.

Kennedy believed that American power could "make the difference in helping the world survive," but by carrying on the Vietnam War, we were "throwing our men, our dreams, our power" away. After RFK's March 1967 speech on Vietnam, the president of the United States told him, "I'll destroy you and every one of your dove friends in six months. You'll be dead politically in six months." A year later, Johnson's threat had not been fulfilled, but 70 percent of the public still approved of the war effort. A friendly newspaper columnist told Kennedy that some of his nonpartisan friends felt "compelled to regard Bobby Kennedy as a traitor to the United States."

In March 1967, he had said: "Three Presidents have taken action in Vietnam. As one who was involved in many of those decisions, I can testify that if fault is to be found or responsibility assessed, there is enough to go round for all—including myself." But even if "this war was not our doing, and is not our fault, still it is partly our responsibility." Then he made a characteristic appeal:

> It is difficult to feel in our hearts what this war means to Vietnam. . . . All we say and all we do must be informed by our awareness that this horror is partly our responsibility; not just a nation's responsibility but yours and mine. It is we who live in abundance and send our young men out to die. It is our chemicals that scorch the children and our bombs that level the villages. We are all participants.

He continued with what was a prime concern of Martin Luther King Jr.: "It is diverting resources which might have been used to help eliminate American poverty, improve the education of our children, and enhance the quality of our national life."

In an interview on November 26, 1967, Kennedy asked, "Do we have the right here in the United States to perform these acts because we want to protect ourselves . . . ? . . . [To] feel it when we use napalm, when a village is destroyed and civilians killed . . . is also our responsibility . . . if this country is going to mean anything."

He went on to state what he considered to be the meaning of America: "we love our country for what it can be and for the justice it stands for and what we are going to mean to the next generation."

* * *

If "our ideal of America is a nation in which justice is done," there was enough to blight that ideal in the late sixties. Visiting a migrant workers' camp in upstate New York in 1967, Kennedy walked past a farm owner's shotgun and entered an old bus that housed three families:

> It was filthy and the odor was overpowering. Inside, they found children covered "with unhealed scabs and flies."
>
> "Bobby's hand began to shake from . . . rage," Newfield recalled. "It was like watching a man going through a religious conversion. Then an old, bent Negro woman wandered into the bus, and Bobby, on instinct, reached out to touch the back of her neck."

After a hearing on rural poverty in Mississippi, Kennedy wanted to visit the people the hearing had been about.

> They went from shack to shack, listening to men long out of work, without skills or prospects, and parents trying to keep their babies alive on rice, biscuits, and gravy left over from old surplus handouts. . . .
>
> Evers remembers one shack with "no ceiling hardly. The floor had holes in it, and a bed . . . black as my arm, propped up with some kind of bricks to keep it from falling. The odor was so bad you could hardly keep the nausea down. . . . This lady came out with hardly any clothes on, and we . . . told her who [Kennedy] was. She just put her arms out and said 'Thank God' and then she just held his hand."
>
> *Des Moines Register* writer Nick Kotz, accompanying the group, watched Kennedy, who had seen "a child sitting on the floor of a tiny back room. Barely two years old, wearing only a filthy undershirt, she sat

rubbing several grains of rice round and round on the floor. The Senator knelt beside her.

"'Hello . . . Hi . . . Hi, baby . . .' he murmured, touching her cheeks and her hair as he would his own child's. As he sat on the dirty floor, he placed his hand gently on the child's swollen stomach. But the little girl sat as if in a trance. . . . For five minutes he tried: talking, caressing, tickling. . . . The baby never looked up."

Evers remembered that "tears were running down [Kennedy's] cheek, and he just sat there and held the little child. Roaches and rats were all over the floor. . . . 'How can a country like this allow it?' [Kennedy asked him.]"

In 1968 Kennedy told an audience:

> These are our responsibilities. If we cannot meet them, we must ask ourselves what kind of a country we really are; we must ask ourselves what we really stand for. We must act—and we must act now.

According to a Pulitzer Prize–winning writer for the *New York Times*, "it was Bobby Kennedy who seemed to embody the fusion of religious and political ideals." Peter Edelman, a law professor who was Kennedy's legislative assistant from 1965 to 1968, calls Kennedy's legacy "a real politics of values." Kennedy believed in equality, justice, and democracy—traditional values for an American. But he believed in them passionately. "He fought evil wherever it surfaced," wrote Xavier L. Suarez, mayor of Miami in 1993. But Suarez had something a little more personal to say, having dated Kennedy's daughter Kathleen: "I will always think of him as one of the best fathers I ever met."

In Scottsbluff, Nebraska, Robert Kennedy said that American history "is in large measure the redemption of the faith of the Founding Fathers." The Fathers were aware of a "root fact of American life: that we all share in each other's fortunes. . . . It is this sense, more than any failure of goodwill or policy, that we have missed in America." Only with this awareness restored can we become, he said, "the last, best hope of man."

There was only one hope left to many Americans after April 1968. Hosea Williams, who had been an aide to Martin Luther King Jr., wrote of that time:

> We felt as long as Dr. King lived, he would lead us to higher grounds. . . . But after he was killed, it left us hopeless, very desperate, dangerous men. I was so despondent and frustrated at Dr. King's death, I had to seriously ask myself . . . Can this country be saved? I guess the thing that kept us going was that maybe Bobby Kennedy would come up with some an-

> swers for this country. . . . After Dr. King was killed, there was just about nobody else left but Bobby Kennedy. I remember telling him he had a chance to be a prophet. But prophets get shot.

* * *

So much hope flourished that spring, despite the nightly news of Vietnam and amid the seeming callousness and brutality of society and government. There could be something better than the indifference of the suburbs, the smoldering of the inner cities, the crew-cut hostility of the town and countryside. Bobby Kennedy was campaigning in California, surrounded by crowds of crazily happy people—black, Hispanic, white—mobbing his convertible, reaching toward the candidate in his white shirt sleeves, big Rafer Johnson or Rosey Grier holding him inside the car, arm around his waist, as the people reached at him, pulled at him, wrung his hands. Is it too good to be true?

At the hotel ballroom after he had won the California primary, he told his happy supporters, "We are a great country, an unselfish country, and a compassionate country."

He was reaching to shake the hand of a Hispanic kitchen worker when the shot was fired right behind him. As his enraged friends wrestled with the shooter amid lights and cameras and recorders above him, Kennedy lay on the floor, a deep, deep pool of blood enlarging under his head.

Out in the ballroom people screamed, moaned, covered wet faces with their hands; young men pounded walls in anguish. "Not again? *Not again!*" Kennedy's senatorial press secretary said, "There were a hundred people in that hotel who would have gladly taken that bullet for Bob." Even at McCarthy headquarters, students in their red, white, and blue decorated straw hats sat and cried. Back in the kitchen after they took him out, his blood still glistening on the floor, someone noticed a sign on the wall: "The Once and Future King."

In the morning he was gone. The doctors had watched in grim astonishment as his incandescent heart had continued to beat, hour upon hour, long after the brain was dead.

* * *

On Fifty-first Street in New York City, outside Saint Patrick's Cathedral, people had been gathering all Thursday night and Friday morning. They continued to come all day Friday, and into the night. At the funeral on Saturday, Jacqueline Kennedy was there, Coretta Scott King was there, with so many people in speechless grief more than in shock, for they loved him. On television we heard Edward Kennedy repeat, with a sudden clarity and pitch of voice that sounded strangely like his brother's, one of Robert Kennedy's favorite statements, from George Bernard Shaw: "Some men see things as they are and ask, Why? I dream things that never were and say, Why not?"

He was a "good and decent man," the remaining brother said with difficulty, "who saw war, and tried to stop it; who saw wrong and tried to right it; saw suffering, and tried to heal it." The congregation sang "The Battle Hymn of the Republic." Then the long course of the funeral train, like Lincoln's; and like Lincoln's funeral car, Bobby's was watched by thousands and thousands waiting along the tracks as it passed.

Jack Newfield concludes his memoir of Robert Kennedy:

> Now I realized what makes our generation unique, what defines us apart from those who came before the hopeful winter of 1961, and those who came after that murderous spring of 1968. We are the first generation that learned from experience, in our innocent twenties, that things were not really getting better, that we shall *not* overcome. We felt, by the time we reached thirty, that we had already glimpsed the most compassionate leaders our nation could produce, and they had all been assassinated. And from this time forward, things would get worse: our best political leaders were part of memory now, not hope.

For Newfield, Robert Kennedy's assassination had the effect of World War I.

But Kennedy himself had entered the postmodern disillusionment, as if he were representative of all of us, and had come out the other side—not with answers but with his sleeves rolled up. He went about doing good. When he returned from his trip to Mississippi he telephoned people he knew and asked them to send boxes of food and clothing to specific addresses (Kennedy had noted them on slips of paper.) And he tried to become president. "It is from numberless diverse acts of courage and belief that history is shaped." Faith itself is evidence for things unseen.

The American faith is a unique and defiant paradox of religion and politics, of compassion and optimism, of naivete and pragmatism, of bold presumption and understated humor, of youthful unselfishness that wills above all to give freedom and justice to posterity—America's and the world's. The American faith seeks a newer world, and what it does not find it makes. We face a greater challenge than any previous generation of Americans because we believe that right does not prevail, that goodness is not rewarded, that life is unfair. What will we do? Will we conform to this world, or seek a newer world, making it as we go along? We have learned that we will fail in this attempt. We may choose other paths. They are all ignominious.

Like the sun of an old year, the Enlightenment settles below the horizon. Solid shapes of a known world become shadows. Arthur Schlesinger's biography of RFK concludes by reporting the following incident:

> The train arrived in Washington. Night had fallen. . . . The pallbearers, not sure where to place the coffin, walked on uncertainly in the night. Averell Harriman finally said to Stephen Smith, "Steve, do you know where you're going?" Smith said, "Well, I'm not sure." Then Smith said, "I distinctly heard a voice coming out of the coffin saying, 'Damn it. If you fellows put me down, I'll show you the way.' "

* * *

You would be threescore years and fifteen. What would this world have been with thirty-two years more of your life? From you we might have learned the practicality of hope, a way through and beyond this gray mirrored no-man's land we've thought ourselves into, this "postmodern" world. Darkness and the short days come. This we know, though the old moon still shines. All years run down; all shall sleep a cold sleep. All shall settle in the dark.

A prophet sees beyond the years, sees an advent in God's very absence, burns with expectant love, lives by faith. A prophet gives flesh to the promise of justice and hope.

You climbed your brother's mountain in the cold; you came back down and your face shone like Moses' with the divine image. You loved the nonexistent, the worthless, the poor, the nobodies and nothings of this world, who could not vote or contribute to campaigns. The children, and children's children—the world to come. The greatest heroes love the unborn. Surely that is a divine image.

Like the saint whose name you bear, you abandoned everything to become an instrument of God's peace. You made yourself new, then tried to renew the world. Mercy burned through despair. You loved us.

You might as well have preached to the birds, for all we listened, for all we did. But we remember your voice as the long day wanes. It joins the great appeal, made down the generations: Abandon everything but love and faith and hope, leave behind the evil that your elders wish you to inherit; follow me. And generation after generation, children of a coming kingdom hear it, the echo of a living word:

NOVEMBER 24

Come, my friends,
'Tis not too late to seek a newer world.

* * *

That odyssey ended in 1968. Now, here, the last brown leaves have fallen, strewing Bobby's grave. The sun is low down the sky; "the frost gleams where the flow'rs have been." Solitary fragments of frozen dew lodge in the letters of words carved into stone:

> Each time a man stands up for an ideal, or acts to improve the lot of others, or strikes out against injustice, he sends forth a tiny ripple of hope, and crossing each other from a million different centers of energy and daring those ripples build a current which can sweep down the mightiest walls of oppression and resistance.

Robert Kennedy's words are not guarded. They are not nuanced with irony; and in an era when even the young sound old, his convinced idealism sounds painfully childlike. They should, because he had painfully made himself young again. The pragmatic, ruthless Kennedy had gone back into the womb of his soul. He emerged a better man. He remade himself by emptying himself. He lived for his work, and his work was good. It has not changed the world, but he knew that the best he could do was try to improve what he could, starting with himself. He was well acquainted with evil and absurdity. He decided to live "as if," to make a Pascal's wager with his life and act as though goodness is the only investment that never fails. He knew it was work for greater hands than his, and that it would not be completed in his lifetime, or in a thousand years; but he remade himself in the echo of his brother's words: "Let us begin."

NOVEMBER 25
Unfinished Work (JFK)

Monday, November 25. The streets of Washington are black and gray. All the world is black and gray through the small television in 1963. Muffled drums beat the death march slowly and incessantly. A man has been killed, and the world mourns: this was the president, this was our president there on the caisson. Its slow wheels rumble along the pavement. On the coffin a flag covers the dead, stiff and rectangular, not like a flag in the wind—it is a flag in the cold, a flag in the mind: all the waxen horror under it, all the mystery, all the fragile, blasted hopes of dark faces along Pennsylvania Avenue; these go into the young mind and will never come out again. "Why?" Bobby Kennedy sobs that night, and a friend outside his door overhears. "Why, God? *Why? Why?*"

* * *

Our grief and horror have become essential to us. In one way or another we will certainly pass them on, but not as we know them, for only to our generation are they immediate. The death of our president is something this generation has in common with the generation of the 1860s, the generation of the Civil War and Abraham Lincoln, but it also shows how we most differ. Our different griefs divide us.

People have noted without quite knowing what to think, that there appear to be several striking coincidences, or parallels, between Abraham Lincoln's death and John F. Kennedy's. For example, Kennedy's secretary, whose name was Lincoln, suggested that he not go to Dallas, just as a man named Kennedy warned Abraham Lincoln not to go to the theater. It is even more striking when one discovers that it was not Evelyn Lincoln who had strong misgivings about the president going to Dallas; it was her husband, "Abe."

Evelyn Lincoln reports having more than once a "strange, unexplainable feeling" as the President prepared for the trip to Dallas. Coincidences, premonitions, and the like have always interested *primitive* peoples because they seem to show that a higher power controls human events. This is reassuring, and it implies that events make sense. We can abide not knowing all the answers to our questions, just as long as we believe there *are* answers somewhere.

Interest in coincidences and premonitions is alien to the modern world, to the world of the Enlightenment in which we were raised. John F. Kennedy certainly would have scorned it. We associate such pop-paranormal stuff with California. Furthermore, many people reject the Lincoln-Kennedy coincidences because they suggest a kind of equality, or parity, between the two. It is agreed that Abraham Lincoln was a great man, but there is no such agreement with regard to John F. Kennedy. Kennedy possessed great abilities and great weaknesses; his character contained at least one great virtue and one great vice.

If courage, as Robert Kennedy said, is the primary virtue because it enables all the others, then John F. Kennedy had a great share of the primary virtue. Receiving the last rites of the Roman Catholic Church at least four times, and living more than half his days in great unacknowledged pain, according to his brother, John Kennedy dashed ahead with "the full exercise of his powers along the lines of excellence" nevertheless. Even Richard Nixon, back in the fifties, lamented when it seemed that "brave Jack Kennedy" was going to die—again.

The courageous do not collect cowards around them. One could hardly think of a scene in ancient or modern history equal in tragic nobility to Jacqueline Kennedy walking between the surviving Kennedy brothers behind the caisson carrying her husband's body. Her veiled face shows a Greek-like beauty: elevated dignity and sorrow. This was the young woman who three days before had stood with her husband's blood and brain matter on her suit watching a new president taking his oath of office on Air Force One. In the car with her husband falling against her she had exclaimed, "Oh Jack, Jack! What have they done to you?" At the funeral she was neither indifferent about a philandering husband nor too sedated to plan a ceremony that expressed, dignified, and ennobled a nation's grief. When she bent down and instructed John Jr., three years old that day, and he stiffened into a salute to his father's coffin, the hearts of that generation were torn beyond repair.

It was, in a sense, staged, but nevertheless authentic. Such was the paradox of Kennedy's presidency. As a great Civil War writer, Bruce Catton, wrote, "What John F. Kennedy left us was most of all an attitude." You could call the attitude *hope.* A president who inspires hope, who "wrenched us out of ourselves and compelled us to meditate about the whole that is greater than the sum of its parts," has done something extraordinary, something worthwhile and great. On one hand, the hopes given to African Americans and millions of other Americans—and to millions around the world who believed that America was leading a struggle for freedom and equality everywhere—these hopes were based on show, on style, pose, and role-playing. But in 1960, a presidential candidate could have posed a very different pose.

Catton says America "turned some kind of corner" during the Kennedy years, and "almost without our knowing it, one era came to an end and another began." John F. Kennedy symbolized that moment of change. It is an error to separate symbol from reality. One reason it is an error is that the new era coming, though JFK probably little knew it, was postmodern.

John Kennedy was the quintessential modern man. People remarked at Kennedy's cool, intellectual "detachment," his faith in reason and technology, his lack of religion. At American University in 1963, Kennedy said, "man can be as big as he wants." This is a modern, Enlightenment idea. If, as Garry Wills claims, America is "the first child of the Enlightenment," then John F. Kennedy was also in a way quintessentially American. Thus he captured our imagination and the world's.

But one might raise a fundamental criticism of John F. Kennedy: He was a man who never was in love. That was his worst illness, a true Achilles' heel. An all too obvious result (lamentable because it reflects our preoccupations) was his addiction to bedding women. This did not create an image for American men to copy at the time, because almost nobody knew about it, but it has caused trouble for politicians, and therefore for us, ever since. And it did have at least three deleterious consequences for his presidency and for the United States. One was that the Kennedys were unable to oppose J. Edgar Hoover's campaign to discredit Martin Luther

King Jr. Hoover had too much on JFK. This, claims Garry Wills, "makes a mockery of any talk that John Kennedy's sexual affairs were irrelevant to his politics." Secondly, his dalliances took him away from his duties—and the man with the black briefcase—at times that could have turned disastrous. That, it would seem, is malfeasance. Thirdly, the macho ideal might have got the world into nuclear war.

During the October 1962 missile crisis, the alternative that Excom (the president's executive committee) never seriously considered was to do nothing. But the international perspective, as expressed to Kennedy by David Ormsby-Gore, was that the United States was not entitled to total immunity from nuclear weapons any more than was the rest of the world. The missiles were not a threat, for reasons since detailed by, for example, Wills. We outgunned the Russians in nuclear terms 17:1. Finally, most important, the missiles were defensive in nature for reasons Kennedy would not tell the public: The administration had agents in Cuba trying not only to overthrow Castro but also to assassinate him. The Russians agreed to put the missiles in to defend Cuba, but

> To the American public, this step looked unprovoked, mysteriously aggressive, threatening. . . . There was no way for Americans to know—and, at that point, no way Kennedy could bring himself to inform them—that Cuban protestations of purely defensive purposes for the missiles were genuine. We did not know what Castro did—that thousands of agents were plotting his death, the destruction of his government's economy, the sabotaging of his mines and mills, the crippling of his sugar and copper industries. We had invaded Cuba once.

But Kennedy would not even permit it to appear that he would trade U.S. missiles in Turkey (right on the Soviet border) for the removal of the Cuban missiles—even though he had his brother assure the Russians we would do it. By forcing the public humiliation of the relatively moderate Khrushchev, Kennedy was playing a very dangerous game with all of our lives. He was not willing to tell the truth to save us.

But of course Kennedy was working in the early 1960s, not in 2000. The American people, ignorant or not, were not prepared for Russian missiles in Cuba, justified or not, five minutes away rather than twenty-five. In Kennedy's defense it must also be said that he resisted his military advisers. He was appalled by their casual, to him crazy, attitude toward the use of nuclear force. In this there is a fundamental sanity, in fact decency, which we are not usually prepared to accord a philanderer. At one point he said that if he were to do as the Joint Chiefs of Staff said we should, none of us would be left alive to tell them if they turned out to be wrong.

There is a second aspect to this. In the beginning of that crisis, virtually all sentiment, including the president's, was for an air strike to destroy the missile sites and, if possible, warheads. Only one person spoke indefatigably against a sudden, overwhelming mission of hundreds of U.S. planes droning in at dawn over the Cuban people. Dean Acheson, one of Kennedy's Excom members, thought Robert Kennedy was an "inexperienced fool" to go on comparing such a strike to the Japanese attack on Pearl Harbor in December 1941. After a couple of days, a hard-headed Republican, Douglas Dillon, finally came around, realizing that Robert Kennedy thought we had fought World War II for *ideals,* which we would absolutely betray by a sneak attack on Cuba. According to Wills, Robert Kennedy "always had a lively moral strain in him," and Excom was saved "from acting as recklessly as the Bay of Pigs advisors had" by "one man":

> For two days the President pushed for assurance that an air strike would work, and no one of sufficient weight was opposing him—no one but Robert . . . the happy outcome of the missile decision, that outcome—to the extent that it was happy—was the single accomplishment of Robert Kennedy.

This is true as far as it goes, but one more name should be mentioned: John F. Kennedy. He could have taken the other advice.

Again, it must be remembered that the United States in 1962 would not have accepted Wills's point of view. (Wills himself says that the country never really became liberal, even after the martyrdom of Kennedy and Lyndon Johnson's landslide victory over Barry Goldwater in 1964.) Kennedy's freedom of action was limited not only by his own deceptions—lies, one might say—he was also governed by some realities which held him at least partly within his era. Nikita Khrushchev played the missile crisis incredibly tough, considering how little hardware he had. Though perhaps history will ultimately credit *Khrushchev* for averting nuclear war in 1962, we could have easily done much worse than had John F. Kennedy in the White House.

Of course, the results were mixed. Kennedy's humiliation of the Soviets resulted in their arms buildup, which helped impoverish and crack up the Soviet Union, but which also made the world much more dangerous—as it still is, overstocked as we are with nuclear, chemical, and biological weaponry. Furthermore, "his real legacy was to teach the wrong lesson, over and over," says Wills. That "lesson" is that the United States should make conciliatory gestures, or be willing to negotiate, only after the other side has been in one way or another defeated, in one way or another shown who is boss. This, an extension of the macho attitude, has had consequences in Vietnam and since. What would Lincoln have done, we might wonder.

Which brings us back to the idea of comparing the two presidents, and to the weakness in Kennedy's inability to love. One could mention that perhaps in the last months of his life he had come to value his wife and children more—a view that even the highly critical Thomas C. Reeves comes to in *A Question of Character:* "Once more it appeared that Jack's ability to empathize, to care as well as think about others, was growing beyond his earlier, more self-absorbed detachment." During the missile crisis, the president found it important to be with his family in the evening; but according to Richard Reeves he did not stop his philandering even at the end. However, there are other elements in Kennedy's story.

One is his dedication to freedom. In June 1963, during his famous visit to Berlin, Kennedy looked over the Berlin Wall into East Germany. A witness, seeing him turn and step back down, said, "He looks like a man who just glimpsed hell." To a man who loved liberty in 1962, East Berlin was hell. (What would his expression be while walking through an inner city in America, as his brother did, today?) It would be perverse to see the libertine only, and lose sight of the lover of liberty.

There is another partially redeeming love, which perhaps only people who have been there, or are descendants, would understand. In June 1963, all his advisers had told Kennedy that a visit to poor, politically and internationally insignificant, tiny Ireland would be a waste of time. But he overruled them all; he simply *wanted* to go. His secretary reported that in Ireland, "All the cares of the world had suddenly gone from his shoulders." It was an unselfish and heartfelt, entirely exemplary love, somewhere in a green corner of his mechanical heart; and if from all the lies, vanity, faithlessness, selfishness, pride, and coldness he is saved by some kind spirit reaching down for Jack Kennedy, it is an Irish spirit; and may it be as kind to us all.

* * *

One might have a darker picture of Jack Kennedy, a black-and-white profile with lurid highlights: an irresistibly charismatic man of wealth, power, and appeal, who used his advantages for pleasure and ambition. The so-called fathers of our nation seem to have rejected this type of leader. For all his intelligence, John Kennedy was not an intellectual, and for all his coolness and detachment, JFK was a servant of desire. The Enlightenment fathers had an aversion to their own son, this dark thing sprung partly from their minds, but with elements of an old earth still clinging to him.

John Kennedy drew his power from the people. It did not remain with us; we surrendered it to him. We were infatuates. The rest of the world hoped charismatic power did issue from democratic power; for them it appeared that a Jefferson could become this shining demigod. They would not have lined the Champs-Elysées for Abraham Lincoln.

The two, Abraham Lincoln and John F. Kennedy, bore certain resemblances to each other. For each, it seemed that the thing he was made for was to be president. Neither was distinguished as a legislator; both came to the office with what we might call abysmal inexperience. Both made the times their own, so it seemed, and afterward they seemed to have changed the times. Lincoln, however, admitted, "events have controlled me."

Both reached office through the forces of their eras, but each had a gyroscope inside which was also a source of energy. William Herndon said that Abraham Lincoln's ambition was like a little engine that never rested. For Kennedy, "the only qualification for the most powerful office in the world was wanting it."

"No one ever knew John F. Kennedy, not all of him," said his close acquaintance Charlie Bartlett. The same was said about Abraham Lincoln: he was a man nobody knew. Both men won acceptance and admiration through their intelligence and humor—attracting crowds of men (there was the element of being the "man's man" about both of them, according to their times and places) but becoming really close to none. Perhaps this is true about many who move into positions of great power. Such power is an uncanny thing. When coincidences pertaining to the two presidents are brought up, perhaps we need not think the two are being compared personally. Perhaps if there is meaning at all in those coincidences, it is due to their place within a national story arranged by a power whose purposes, reasons, and plans are unknown to us. Perhaps only Lincoln would have accepted this.

The two have become known for what they said. Of course, Lincoln wrote his own speeches; Kennedy did not. Today, Kennedy's sound "tinny," to adopt Garry Wills's term. Lincoln's words have grown and deepened with the years. Kennedy's inaugural address, memorable as it is, seems a self-conscious attempt to say notable things. Lincoln's words, made for their utility at the time, have slowly unfolded their profound beauty.

We have been held and transfixed by death and beauty in John F. Kennedy. Such is the high fascination of classic tragedy. With Lincoln, the beauty is invisible to the eye, and grief at his death remains grief and not fascination. As we go deeply into Lincoln's story, we are not transfixed but transformed. We are not made brittle, but something inside awakens and flowers and becomes stronger. With one we are touched by a demigod outside us; with the other we sense a spirit within. Through their similarities, profound differences show.

* * *

The two presidents dealt with the evil of power differently. Lincoln saw and acknowledged guilt in all of us. God has given us, both North and South, this terrible war in response to our complicity in injustice: We all have drawn material advantages from slavery, Lincoln said in April 1865, and now the ledger must be balanced for us all. The military power of the United States is to be used penitentially, in the awareness that this necessary evil stains whoever uses it.

For John F. Kennedy, the distinction between good and evil seems to have been a rational, rather than a moral, one. More fundamentally, "irony was as close as he came to a view of life." Everyone knows his summary statement: "Life is unfair." Irony is a postmodern stance—not, as for Wilfred Owen, a tool or a weapon, a knife meant to expose evil for what it is. That things are only what they appear to be is, in a way, the essence of postmodernism: our *worldview* is the world itself, to the extent that we can know it. Perhaps that postmodern notion was the philosophical position, insofar as a nonreflective person has a philosophical position, of John Kennedy. For Kennedy, freedom is the human ability to satisfy desire. For Lincoln, freedom is a divine endowment. The best use of human power, for Kennedy, is to secure rights; for Lincoln the purpose of power, based on the original power of God, is to maintain right.

* * *

The Declaration of Independence states:

> We hold these truths to be self-evident, that all men are created equal, that they are endowed by their Creator with certain unalienable Rights, that among these are Life, Liberty, and the pursuit of Happiness.

Lincoln echoed the "that . . . that" structure of the Declaration in his conclusion at Gettysburg to show both continuity and transformation: "Ye have heard it said of old, but I say unto you."

The speech that John F. Kennedy was to have delivered in Dallas on the twenty-second of November 1963 also plays off this pattern:

> We in this country, in this generation, are—by destiny rather than choice—the watchmen on the walls of world freedom. We ask, therefore, that we may be worthy of our power and responsibility—that we may exercise our strength with wisdom and restraint—and that we may achieve in our time and for all time the ancient vision of peace on earth, good will toward men.

The paragraph is filled with irony. It is a kind of prayer, to be read by a man who apparently had little to do with prayer. (His wife said during the campaign that it was unfair for him to be criticized on account of his Catholicism since he was such a poor Catholic.) There is a gratuitous echo of Lincoln's second inaugural address in the words about achieving a peace for all time—gratuitous because we had not just come through a momentous war. Consistent with his campaign tactics, Kennedy was employing high rhetoric to instill an impression of crisis. As with Lincoln, there is biblical language, but here it is not part of the text. It is, rather, a familiar passage brought in from outside. Still, it was almost the season of Advent, and perhaps the "peace on earth, good will toward men" from Saint Luke's Christmas story belongs more than first appears. After all, the essence of JFK was hope. But what kind of hope can be brought forth by someone who does not love?

If the Kennedy presidency was somehow redemptive in America and the world, and if John Kennedy is to be redeemed in historical memory, it is because of hope. Likewise, if his presidency and person are to be condemned, it would be because that hope was dishonest or misdirected.

What was the hope that JFK inspired? According to his secretary, that hope was based upon his demonstrating that "we could expect more from ourselves," and that "America's too-long-delayed promises [could] come true." He himself showed that the Greek ideal of happiness could be achieved: " 'full use of your powers along lines of excellence.' . . . He reminded us that the greatest of the promises of America is that here all of us should have the right to do the same."

This sounds very much like Lincoln, who believed that each person should be free to work the best he can and enjoy the fruits of his labor. The key difference is in the Greek ideal of excellence. For Kennedy, the American Dream consisted in giving chances. There was no fairness involved, for "life is unfair," and the way he achieved his own success was unfair. Give as many chances to as many people as possible without depriving the strong and the excellent of their big chances—that was, it seems, behind Kennedy's ideal. (It sounds eerily like something Ronald Reagan might have appreciated.) For Lincoln, life was ultimately fair, if mysterious, because the reality across which history is stretched is a moral universe, with God above. Therefore, the kind of chances given in the political and economic realms must be equal. In Lincoln there is a sense of justice based upon a just universe. In Kennedy's view one sees characteristics of postmodernism, but one wonders whether postmodernism will be able to withstand either the demands of power or the requirements of justice.

One is tempted to believe that Kennedy's hope and promise were intoxicating illusions. If Lincoln was wrong about this being a moral universe in the hands of God, then his hope was illusion, too. One cannot always prove a hope to be real or illusory, but if one chooses to hope rather than to despair, one must also choose one's hope.

Rights and equality have been in tension since the founding of the United States. They naturally conflict because individuals' strengths and weaknesses are not created equal. While governments are instituted, ideally, to compensate for such disparity, strong elements within government and society will conflict, not only with each other but also with the weak. The strong will assert their rights, and the weak will be deprived and oppressed unless equality is regained.

Rights can be asserted in successful representative government only within the limits placed by equality. Justice is therefore the overriding factor, the initial and constant condition. When John F. Kennedy died, many African Americans felt that they had lost a friend. It is well for us to remember that in the context of the 1960s, he was such a friend—that is, by contrast to the alternatives. Martin Luther King Jr. did not entertain illusory hopes about Kennedy, but neither did he expect more, or as much, from others. From today's perspective, Kennedy seems insincere and insufficient. But again, he could have made *other* choices; he could have failed to support the civil rights movement, and he could have decided not to go on television to tell the American people that racial justice was an issue of right versus wrong that is "as old as the Scriptures and as clear as the Constitution." It is hard to believe that Kennedy's decisions were motivated only by political considerations. John Kennedy did love freedom.

Still, JFK sounded quite different from Robert Kennedy and Martin Luther King Jr., who were motivated by dedication to justice and who loved their people, like Lincoln. John Kennedy struck brilliant notes; his brother and King struck deep chords.

The two generations, Lincoln's and Kennedy's, appear to have differed along similar lines. The Civil War generation chose duty over happiness, and the 1960s generation has been choosing happiness over duty. But I am a member of that later generation, and I still have hopes that, despite the evidence of the 1980s and 1990s, we have it in us, and in our children, to choose duty. That choice was present in many Vietnam War soldiers, as well as in many Vietnam War protesters.

Memories of the Kennedy years are youthful ones of sunshine and idealism, and they are memories of darkness, violence, and grief. They bind those of our generation to each other. The grief is partly for ourselves. Many Americans detested Kennedy then as now. He was controversial then as now. Thomas Reeves quotes an aide as saying—referring to Kennedy's practice of slipping away from the officer who carried the U.S. nuclear warfare codes to disappear for liaisons—that the Soviets "could have bombed us to hell and back" before the president would have been found. Kennedy exposed the nation's highest office to blackmail by his affairs with Marilyn Monroe and others.

But my skepticism regarding John Kennedy is reasoned rather than felt. Even reasoning, however, I am not sure that I would prefer us to have had any of the alternatives to John F. Kennedy in 1960. Anyone growing up in those times must still be left with some emotions, whether dark or bright, about JFK. When I reread the book *Four Days,* full of photographs pertaining to the assassination and funeral, I still feel sick and disoriented. When I see film of him or hear that voice again, I feel that unique clutch of hope and grief. For me, after all the revisions and revelations and reevaluations, he is still President Kennedy. As Pierre Salinger said that November, "We will laugh again, but we will never be young again."

* * *

It is ironic that the World War II generation—exemplars of duty, sacrifice, and responsibility—created the generation of the 1960s, known for self-indulgence and irresponsibility. Those who saved democracy and worked for posterity raised a generation of Californians. John F. Kennedy was therefore a much more exact representative of his generation than most GIs who had fought in Europe and the Pacific would have wanted to admit. Like them, he sincerely espoused the most sacred public beliefs of America; and like them he created my generation. The sixties began with words about bearing every burden, and ended by baring everything. Perhaps Wilfred Owen identified the great, destructive fraud promulgated by Kennedy and consumed by us: *dulce et decorum est.* Kennedy charmed us into thinking that it is sweet and seemly—glamorous—to live for "that nation" of liberty and equality. But it is not so. The heroic generation knew it, had seen it: the world war had been horrible, however necessary. Now, we find it difficult to do anything that is not sweet and seemly, because our first public hero joined service and pleasure in our imaginations. We are living a lie. When work and glamour were split by those bullets in Dallas, we took the glamour and ran. We had been spoiled. Liberty had become a playboy's toy. We think that what does not please, we need not do; and to sustain the illusion of pleasure's importance, we are willing to draw the future, and posterity, into the same black hole with the past. Everything is present—a present for us.

This is a harsh statement, and like most generalizations, it has limited validity at best. Bobby's legacy is counterevidence. The degree to which he still convinces our minds and moves our hearts is the degree to which we may retain our self-respect and convey hope. We still know the difference between right and wrong, and between present and future; it is just that for us, these distinctions are hard. Whatever else we are or are not, compared to our mothers and fathers, we lack Lincoln's larger sense of things.

Though our generation still does not know what to do with its memories of John F. Kennedy, we are secure in our admiration of Jacqueline Kennedy. The soft-spoken, acute Jacqueline was one of the rare public persons who proved herself to be as great as her fame. Courageous and strong, like Ulysses she had been to hell and came back whole. What JFK's memory cannot achieve in us, Mrs. Kennedy's might, for we know what she did with her fame: she mastered it. To raise her children well became her most important goal. She was an intellectual, cultivated and artistic. The cultural elevation of Camelot came from her, a woman who would read a book per day, knew the history of art, and had brought classical music to the White House. Many Americans, fed on the candy glamour of Hollywood, misunderstood Jacqueline's beauty to mean mindlessness. Yet somewhere in our hearts we saw more than stylishness in her. Though in different degree and kind, we were all hurt by the same hurts; she and we suffered the same November. Her pain was the hardest and her behavior was the noblest.

She was an incisive judge of persons, as those who faced her calm, penetrating stare testified. So it is not impossible to accept her testimony concerning John Kennedy, as we would accept the intelligent, cultured Mary Lincoln's admiration of Abraham Lincoln as being instructive. Despite all the callous unfaithfulness she endured, Jacqueline loved Jack and admired him, and wished his legacy of hope to survive. His achievement, insofar as she can testify to it, must have been an honest one. Together, John and Jacqueline Kennedy summoned America to an aristocracy of excellence, an aristocracy not of the wealthy but of the beautiful and brave.

* * *

John F. Kennedy's last speech continued after "good will toward men":

> That must always be our goal—and the righteousness of our cause must always underlie our strength. For as was written long ago:
>
> "Except the Lord keep the city, the watchman waketh but in vain."

The aspect of irony which postmodernists neglect is its appropriateness. Appropriateness implies meaning. An individual, whether a president or a character in a play, might not know how fitting his words are in a larger sense, but such ignorance does not signify that there is no larger sense. All of us are in the position of a limited, ignorant character in a Greek play, unable to see beyond our moment on the stage: that is the human condition. Like it or not, we must take something on faith. Either we accept the idea that our limited view *is the world* as an article of belief, or we believe that a wider, outer universe really exists. How either belief is carried out can be said to constitute our faith.

After the assassinations of the 1960s, we emerged into the split light of the postmodern era, having lost considerable faith in politics, history, and the outside world in general. That world included public heroes, the very idea of which we came to distrust. "Public hero" became a phrase that carried a sound of irony, if not sarcasm. "The hero returns," RFK said in this vein. But because our instincts are insufficient for survival, humans shall be taught, like it or not. If public figures are discredited, we shall learn our lessons from private figures. So be it; let us look closer to home if we must. Our parents teach us before we even think of rejecting them. We must learn our faiths from somebody.

If the twentieth century has taught us that we are not *Homo sapiens,* rational creatures, it has confirmed that we are *Homo fides,* creatures of faith. If we are free in any large sense, we are free to choose our faith. There are bad ones and good ones.

* * *

"All of November was a bad time for him," a friend said of Robert Kennedy. Newfield wrote that RFK "was never to recover fully from the trauma of Dallas." Just as he landed in Indianapolis for a campaign stop in 1968, Robert Kennedy was told of Martin Luther King Jr.'s assassination. A journalist sitting opposite Kennedy on the plane wrote: "He just broke down. It was unbearable to watch him, to know he was thinking about his brother getting it the same way. I don't want to go through that again." He refused to cancel his scheduled appearance before an African-American crowd, even though the Indianapolis chief of police warned him not to appear, and the police escort left him just before arriving at the scene of the speech. No other white man in America could have done what he did that evening, telling the horrified crowd of Dr. King's death, and saying:

> we have to make an effort in the United States; we have to make an effort to understand. . . . What we need is not division . . . what we need is not hatred—what we need is not violence, but love and wisdom, and compassion towards one another, and a feeling of justice towards those who still suffer within our country.

What other politician would have or could have quoted Aeschylus to the crowd from memory?

> In our sleep, pain which cannot forget falls drop by drop upon the heart until, in our own despair, against our will, comes wisdom through the awful grace of God.

* * *

For over thirty-five years this date, with its public solemnity and its confusion, has stirred the angel of grief that waits upon memory. The gray streets of Washington and the numb gray faces, the persistent tolling of the drum, the sharp, dry sound of caisson wheels on pavement—these memories remain and cannot be assuaged or answered. Time does not soften them. But a closer grief has come to put that day of 1963 into a more distant past. Today one year ago, Ruth's funeral—Ruth, the daughter of Ingeborg, who had come from Norway to die young; the niece of Karl, the young Norwegian who found himself in Pershing's American Expeditionary Force in 1917; Len's wife—my mother. In this loss I typify my generation, which is moving through middle age. Once more we are being united by our griefs.

On this day is the funeral; on the next is a long drive to that western Wisconsin cemetery where her parents are buried. How do we accept the unacceptable? How do we make sure our honored dead shall not have died in vain? What have they given us, and how shall we use it? How can the forever unfinished be finished?

Today was the anniversary of a public committal; tomorrow is the anniversary of a private one. One day the World War II generation is remembered; the next day my generation looks again into the mirror. The distance from modernism to postmodernism is one rotation of the earth. Fortunately, the earth does not stop there. Though it seems that November will last forever, memory assures us that a new season will come, that dry weeds will be transfigured under snow. "If Winter comes, can Spring be far behind?" So concludes the last poem I read to Ruth Margaret.

NOVEMBER 26

Shall Not Perish (Beautiful and Brave)

> A soul, living from a great depth of being, awakens in us by its actions and words, by its very looks and manners, the same power and beauty that a gallery of sculpture, or of pictures, are wont to animate.
>
> —Emerson, "History"

One year ago today, a spray of pink roses lay in the sun atop a cherry-wood casket in the old cemetery. Not the old cemetery here in Gettysburg, but in the small western Wisconsin town where Martin and Ingeborg are buried. The new grave, their daughter Ruth's, had been opened that morning.

The night before, I had brought out a box full of old photographs to show to Ruth's grandchildren. The photographs were the best means I could think of for telling them who Ruth had been, as far as I knew. By themselves, the photographs were not much. They were few; the great majority of the roughly two hundred pictures were of other people. The other limitation was that I had to identify and explain the photographs—a circular process based on my surmises, which though in this case might be the best in the world, convey the bias and misconstructions of an only son. So I was telling them in part who I was; I was also trying to tell them who they were. But more important, I was telling them something about who they could be.

That white cardboard box from what was once Milwaukee's best department store held everything Ruth saved by way of history, except for a few documents such as her father's immigration papers, kept in a leather folder in her bureau. The photographs were not organized; I organized them, as postmodern historians say one must. There were only two written documents in the box, and almost none of the photos bore identifying inscriptions of any kind on their reverse sides. I relied on memory to identify images I had not seen in thirty or forty years. Out of these I imagined her life.

A narrative only seems to be continuous. The best short story or novel or historical account has the appearance of life's fluidity only because our imagination animates what is selected and told. For this reason it could be said that I do not know my mother, and presented merely a fictitious verbal text to her grandchildren. Nevertheless, I did know something. Though sacred histories are based upon imperfect knowledge, they are necessary. That evening's photographic elegy contributed to my children's identities, as the Pilgrims and the Gettysburg Address contribute to the sacred story that makes America. As I told Ruth's story, I realized that her history is the story of the entire Heroic Generation, and that she held the key to heroism itself.

The oldest photograph is not of Ruth but nevertheless is the proper place to start: it is of her mother, Ingeborg. The small, sturdy portrait is from a studio in Elverum, Norway, taken in about 1905. It shows a woman probably in her twenties. She wears black, with a fine white lace shawl. A long, thin gold chain drapes almost to her waist. Her face is full yet delicate, her expression calm and faintly remote. Her hair, long but gathered turn-of-the-century style, was very light brown, almost blonde. This I know because there is, after all, another source of history in Ruth's bureau: two books. One is Ingeborg's Bible, which contains a lock of her hair clipped by someone, perhaps Martin, after Ingeborg died of tuberculosis in 1917.

The other book is a small journal, also in Norwegian. Ingeborg kept this when she took her two small daughters to Norway in about 1913. Some of its pages are scribbled over with Ruth's attempts to do what her mother was doing.

I met Ingeborg's nephew in Norway, back in 1972. He told me their grandfather was a railroad executive. The family's social and economic standing had been high. But Ingeborg had fallen in love with a blacksmith—my grandfather—who worked for the railroad. Perhaps there is more to this part of the story, and to the history of the man who worked as a blacksmith in America, but I do not know it. I do know his tastes, which were always simple. His manner was always kind, open, and generous. He was a very practical man, always dismissing worries and grief with the observation, "Well, there's nothing I can do about it." He was extremely frugal, impaling the stub of his cigar on an ice pick and smoking it down until it nearly burned his lips—strong as coal—and at the rate of one per week, relit and stretched across four or five days. His bedroom was the size of a closet, white-walled, and contained six items: the bed, a small nightstand, Ingeborg's picture, a large photograph of his two living daughters, a box of cigars, and an ashtray he had gotten free at the Oslo Tavern in town. (Shaped like a bathtub, it contained a pink, nude, somewhat chubby young woman posed to support a cigar. Around the bottom it said, "Put your hot butt in my cool tub." That item, memorable to a young boy, did not survive Ruth's examination of the house upon Martin's death.) Once, and once only, I awoke in that house to beautiful, strong baritone singing outside. I could not imagine who it was. It was the laconic, musing, reflective Martin, who spent his days in his chair—outside when possible, such as that summer morning—thinking and remembering. His wife died when he was forty-one; he lived another fifty-four years. When asked why he did not remarry, he always answered, "I would never find another lady like Ingeborg."

This was the man Ingeborg married and left her home in Norway for. If he was firmly down-to-earth, she was just as sure of the impracticalities. He had come to America first, found a job smithing in the railroad shop, rented a room, and went back to Norway for his betrothed.

I saw that upstairs room which was to be their apartment when I was looking to buy a house in that town some years ago. I sat down on the bed there and tried to picture one of the only stories I have ever heard about Ingeborg—told to me not by Ruth but by a friend of the family. When she arrived at the top of that narrow stairway and saw the little room, Ingeborg refused even to unpack her trunk. He must find them a better place.

She must always have grieved for her home and family, and for Norway. She took Ruth across the ocean at age four, along with the infant Lula, leaving her husband for over a year. Her father must have sent the ticket. She did come back. They lived in the rear section of the lower floor of a two-story house, the last on the street and nearest to the railroad tracks—an ironic reminder of her father's life in Norway and her husband's labor here in America. "Tramps" getting off the boxcars used to chalk a mark in front of that house for those who came after: here lives a person who will pity you and give you food.

In those days, surviving tuberculosis was largely a matter of will. In my experience only the Irish come close to the love a Norwegian immigrant has for the old country. In the late fall of 1917, American doughboys were getting on the troopships; the Great War was grinding its appalling toll. One morning after Martin had reluctantly gone to work, Ruthie went into the quiet bedroom where her mother Ingeborg lay. *Kjaere Ruth;* dear Ruth. Quietly Ingeborg told Ruth to go and get her teacher. Ruth ran out and down the alley. Her fourth grade teacher, who lived a few houses away, had not yet left. She followed Ruth to the corner house, and when they came inside the room, the teacher said they must find someone to fetch her Papa. "Your mother has left this world, Ruth."

Ruth remembered that at the funeral, Martin took her five-year-old sister Lula up in his arms and said, tears in his eyes, "Look at Mama, Lula; you will never see her again."

And Martin bought a plot near the row of Civil War graves, and said good-bye to his lady that November. It would not be quite correct to say that Ruth never saw her mother again. The day they came to transport Ruth to the TB sanitarium, she saw her mother in the room; and for a moment Ingeborg stood behind the minister when Ruth and my father were married. In these things I only say what was told to me. Ingeborg was always with Ruth, who, in a sense, declined to accept the death of that lady.

I think the earliest photograph of Ruth was taken at about age ten. She poses with her beloved little white poodle, her only companion for a while, because Martin sent her and Lula to live with his sister's family in Minneapolis. He must not have believed that he could raise two girls by himself. In any case, he may not have been able to see through his grief very well. He visited his daughters every weekend, but spent much of the time with his brother-in-law at the local tavern. He did not become a drunk, however; he was too frugal and too practical for that. And he intended to bring his daughters back.

The photograph of Ruth and Toodles shows a girl with furrowed brow, a motherless child. Another photograph shows Ruth and her cousin Min pulling a cart with Lula and cousin George riding. It too pictures a serious face. The months stretched to years. Ruth entered junior high school. She was confirmed in Minneapolis with her cousin. In the formal photograph, the pastor seated straight and serious amid his confirmands, everyone is sober. One is tempted to think they had all learned their Nordic theology and were suitably stoic about the claimed benefits of salvation. Ruth, however, is not merely sober or even morose. She has a penetrating stare, quietly angry and resentful. She would have been thirteen or fourteen.

She had "seen the elephant," as Civil War soldiers would have put it. In her own way, she had felt the First World War soldier's barbed wire, machine-gun fire, and mustard gas. Many children lost their parents in those years—by the thousands during the influenza epidemic near the close of the decade, if not by the war—and many young men had entered the apocalypse of the Western Front. And nearly all of us have figuratively lost our parents, in that the solid old beliefs of previous generations were shot away during the last hundred years of the old millennium. But the question is: What then shall we do?

There is a photograph taken by Ruth at that time. On the back, in the young girl's careful hand, is the name, "Mrs. Fairbanks," and under it, "Jordan Junior High School, Summer 1923." No other photographs from that time are preserved. To the very last days, Ruth knew from memory lines and lines of Longfellow, Emerson, Whittier, Bryant—and not merely because children then were made to memorize interminable stretches of the Schoolroom Poets (though it was far from being a futile activity, as Ruth proved.) Mrs. Fairbanks gave Ruth her love of those poets, and of literary art. At age ninety, Ruth could still remember lines from Keats and Shelley and Browning and Tennyson, moments from Shakespeare, and passages from Milton.

"If eyes were made for seeing / Then Beauty is its own excuse for being." Only days before her death, Ruth heard and understood long readings from Emerson's essays and his *English Traits.* The English, he said, have a stout and understated courage that pervades all they say and do. He might have been describing Ruth, though no one noticed it until her last year or two when—her family having moved a thousand miles away because of a temporary job of her son's—she dressed herself every day in one of her long, elegant dresses, and nearly blind and deaf, made her way without cane or walker, slowly and painfully, to the retirement complex's dining hall, frail as straw flowers, always having a gracious word to say to anyone she encountered on her way. The courage had been there all along. From her mother had come refinement and idealism, and from her father the practicality to find a way to survive. Ruth had determined not to sink. It was the bar Mrs. Fairbanks held out that she chose to grasp. The photograph of the teacher on the steps of Jordan Junior High School shows a slim, carefully dressed woman in her thirties, with short blonde hair. She appealed to Ruth, perhaps because of something Ruth found in her that reminded her of Ingeborg. Evidently neither Ingeborg nor Mrs. Fairbanks accepted the world as it is. Neither did Ruth. From the "greatest that has been thought and said" Ruth might also have known, as evinced by her life, the words Cervantes gives to his strange hero, Don Quixote. It is one of the greatest sentences in all literature: "I know who I am, and who I may be if I choose."

Ruth had learned that human nature is not proof against death, that the world does not make sense nor is it fair, that we do not know answers to the questions which matter most, that we are "poor, bare, forked animals." It is not necessary for a young girl to be taught the ideas and lingo of postmodernism to be convinced of these things. Ruth understood the human condition. "I know who I am." She was a motherless child, raised speaking the language of immigrants, poor and from a small town. And she chose to be none of these. "I know who I am, and who I may be if I choose."

While Don Quixote was not a realist in the paltry sense, he lived a reality that ultimately impressed the most reliable of those around him as being the profoundest sanity. He lived as a resident of the Golden Age. He was brave and went about doing good. Though not healing the sick or raising the dead, he made farm girls into princesses and ignorant peasants into disciples who would govern a new world. In short, we have learned in this century who we are; now it is up to us to choose what to be. The world will remain futile and absurd and gory on its own terms, but what will we be? We may decline to be conformed to the world we know, and instead be confirmed in the world we imagine. We can choose our parents and we can choose our world. If we would change our unchanging world, let us first change ourselves.

It comes not without a price. The anger in Ruth's face on that confirmation day would never leave her, nor would an ever-increasing guilt that started perhaps with her mother's death, and was encouraged by the corrupted version of Lutheran theology which had been taught since the generation after Luther. But no one would know this price because Ruth chose to maintain, as my cousin wrote to me, "an unfailingly gracious demeanor under all circumstances." No one knew, that is, except her son, who lived in the same house with Ruth for many years and heard the moaned fury and despair that came through the walls of her room from the place of her nightmares. But character is evaluated by the waking hours. Our most significant dreams are those we choose to fulfill.

The one direct description of Ingeborg that Ruth would offer was that she had refined taste and made beautiful things. Surely Ingeborg's courage in the last hour—indeed the last years—of her life made a profound and indelible impression upon Ruth, as did her love of beauty. These two things, courage and devotion to beauty, are unlike the world and the human nature we know, but we may choose them.

The world would not cooperate with Ruth, however. It would try to kill her.

The next photograph was taken with her sister Lula. The younger is of junior high school age; Ruth must be sixteen or seventeen. Both are slender but robust. And they are together in a way they had not been since Ingeborg's death. Martin had brought them back.

One of the two written pieces in the white box is the tag from a Christmas gift, saying, in English, "To my dearest Ruth, from Papa." The other is older. It is a letter in Norwegian, written on gilt stationery that one would think had been Ingeborg's. The letter consists of one sentence, and it is about Ruth coming home.

The homecoming did not begin ideally, however. When Ruth saw the tiny house without indoor plumbing that her father had been able to buy, she cried, as Ingeborg might have. The house was so small that Martin and several of his friends used logs as rollers to move it back from the street and over the cellar Martin had dug for it. They used old winter coats and rags to give some insulation to the walls. It had two bedrooms; later Martin would build a tiny back porch and add another bed for use in summertime. A small white shed stood behind a little garden plot. Martin had constructed it from boards off retired railroad cars.

The two sisters worked hard, cooking and cleaning as well as going to school. They filled the icebox and stocked the tiny pantry (which eventually became a bathroom) as money would permit. Ruth remembered her father leaving to chop wood up north when he was laid off work temporarily, and going away in the summer to cook for railroad work gangs. He became an excellent cook, and Ruth never much relished anyone else's culinary efforts, least of all her own. Manual labor and cooking she would shun all the rest of her life, both being things not done by the kind of person she wished to be. Once, as she stood abstracted during dishwashing time, Lula upbraided her. "They also serve," Ruth replied from one of Milton's sonnets, "who only stand and wait."

Ruth's sense of loss was never assuaged by a happy family life. Indeed, her early memories are of desolation. Of course she remembered her years in Minneapolis as being very unhappy, though she never spoke ill of her cousins or the aunt and uncle who had taken their two nieces in. What little she was willing to recall about those years tended to be ambiguous, such as her uncle making beer in the bathtub during Prohibition, or her cousin George's charm and intransigence. The little dog had been killed in the street sometime early in those years. Even Ruth's earliest memory was of a loss. On the voyage to Norway, a boy had taken the muff her mother had given her for the trip and thrown it into the ocean. Did she remember her other sister, the small child who had died of scarlet fever? Yes, she did.

Her graduation picture shows a fresh, open quality that would later become beauty. "I was in awe of that beauty," a friend told me last November. "She was the most beautiful woman I have ever known, more beautiful than a movie star. Yet she was always kind and gracious, never aloof or cold." The young graduate penned a strange note on the back of the portrait—for the photograph had been a gift for Martin—oddly formal: "To Papa, without whose presence today my Graduation Day would not be complete." Was she proper and formal because Mrs. Fairbanks had taught her to be? But Mrs. Fairbanks must have drilled into her students the proper use of time and tense. Did Ruth give the photograph to Martin that morning, feeling that she had to prompt him to attend her graduation ceremony? Surely he would have intended to come. Yet between the two there was always both devotion and a kind of distance—something very peculiar and hard to understand for non-Norwegians. She had lost her father when she had lost her mother, not only in having to move away from him but also in the distance or reserve he seems to have displayed in the casualness and unsentimentality of his regular, faithful visits. She sentimentalized him; she also moved away from him, never long visiting the small town once she had left it.

Perhaps these voids where she needed love provided good practice, for she was about to form some of the strongest, longest, and deepest emotional ties of her life, most of which were to end tragically. The next photograph is of two couples. Ruth and a friend also named Ruth pose with their dates. America has entered the Roaring Twenties: the young women's dresses have become shorter, the hair is tightly curled and waved and also shorter; the stockings are white silk. It is the middle twenties still—no flapper attire, boas, or bobbed hair, but the old era is gone. The young men look happy; the girls are sober and are striking attractive poses. The other Ruth is with the person whom she will marry—I recognize him. I would know her as a middle-aged woman, always sweet and considerate almost to a fault. What I did not know as a child, of course, was that the friend we were visiting had a strange and unbelievable interior life. She would claim to have business dealings of colossal values with Mafia men, and to have dangerous and deadly adventures—she, who lived in a modest residential neighborhood in Minneapolis with her blue-collar husband. True, she led a demanding and exhausting life, adopting and raising a disabled child. (If she is not now among the blessed, who shall be?) But the Ruth I knew better, my mother, consistently refused the consolations of fantasy. She may never have been as happy as the friend of her youth, but she would not relinquish her knowledge of reality. She knew her enemy. If she rejected the idea of becoming the wife of a blue-collar worker on a residential street in Minneapolis, then she would not fall into that life and merely escape it in her mind. What she could change in the everyday world, she would.

But attending to the photograph, one notices instantly that the healthy figure of the earlier photographs has changed terribly. Ruth is as thin as a wire clothes hanger. She has been going to the university, which is perhaps where she met the other Ruth. Few women, of course, went to any university in 1927. Still fewer of these were daughters of immigrant blacksmiths. But Martin worked for the railroad, the old Chicago-Northwestern that terminated in the Twin Cities. His daughter could ride free. Certainly she could not afford to live in Minneapolis; she rode the trains several hours, several days per week. It was a strenuous regimen. She studied literature for two years. Eventually her weight dropped to less than ninety pounds, ghastly for a young woman of five-foot-seven. It was tuberculosis. She became so weak that she could not rise out of bed. Certain that she would go there to die, the doctor ordered her to the State Sanitarium in Wales, Wisconsin, near Milwaukee. Martin loaded his old car with Ruth's things. A friend of theirs, Lula, and father and daughter made the ten-hour drive to the southeastern corner of the state. Once again it was good-bye: maybe for years, and maybe forever.

One more glance at that portrait of the two Ruths and their escorts. The standing Ruth, my mother, has a gentle expression on her face. She holds what must be pink roses—not dark enough for red, not white, and clearly not yellow. But there is a firmness in her gentle expression. The chin is soft but while not exactly *set*, is firm. Ruth would spend five years at the sanitarium. Few people who remained there anywhere near that long came out alive. Those years served as her university and as her time in the trenches surrounded by death, and when she came out she knew for certain not only who she was, but who she was going to be.

The five years in the "State San" were Ruth's equivalent of a combat soldier's life in the army, with some differences. At State San, it probably took more courage, and the odds were worse. Those five years were longer than the Civil War or World War I. While others her age were at home or in college, Ruth lived in a plain barracks with a row of comrades—but again there was a difference. Soldiers' barracks are heated. Fresh air, and plenty of it, was the theory on TB treatment at the time—an improvement over earlier practice, but only partial. Windows were left open during the Wisconsin winter nights. Of eight photographs from State San, only one is not from the last two years, and that one is probably from the third year, judging by the hair style and the relative fullness of Ruth's face. It is the only photograph in which Ruth and her friends do not appear in normal clothing; she and another young woman are wearing hospital gowns. You can see only the collars of the gowns, because both young women are wrapped in blankets. But both are smiling.

Like soldiers, the young women made their own grim fun and developed their own slang. On those cold winter nights, each woman was given a large ceramic hot-water bottle to take to bed with her. The girls called them "pigs." (Probably the pigs kept the girls from freezing early in the night, and then vice versa.) The women of the barracks produced their own newspaper, in the editorial tasks of which Ruth figured prominently. They put on dramatic productions. One of the pictures shows a troupe of nine young women, dressed in costumes complete with bandannas on their heads, plus Ruth, front center in normal attire, possibly their director, choreographer, or narrator. In another, from the same—last—year, three young women pose in a mock-dramatic, happy triangle out in a summer meadow.

There is only one solo photograph: Ruth in 1932, with hat, dress, purse, and heels, probably the day of her release. Until then, she had not been alone. All the photographs are of groups of as many as forty, and most (including the forty) are carefully inscribed on the backs with full names. The inscriptions show a new handwriting. Ruth had learned a calligraphic script that she used for the rest of her life. She wrote with a blotter under the lines, creating letters perfectly even and symmetrical while full of flourishes and elegance. She would go back under each line and draw in the tails and punctuation. Perhaps at this time also Ruth changed her middle name to Margaret, a name of elegance and substance, unlike her original small-town common name. It is clear that she did not put on airs, however; she is always surrounded by friends in carefree, sometimes clowning poses. The friends I knew who survived State San were all down-to-earth and practical even as they were tasteful and dignified. Ruth's best friend shortly after she left the San was a plain girl with a heart of gold. "Margaret" simply conformed to who Ruth was choosing to be. It was the Anglicized form of Ingeborg's sister's name, Margit.

But I said there were no photographs from the first years at the sanitarium. The girls did not look too good when they first arrived. As in a field hospital, they were sorted into categories as to their chances of survival. Ruth was put into the lowest. After a while, she was moved up. But all the photographs of those happy young women are photographs of people who have tuberculosis. Many are under sentence of death. Like a photograph of an infantry platoon, each pose is marked by a sense that images—faces, bodies, names—will disappear. Here no retreat from the front was possible. There was no rotation out of the trenches for rest and relaxation, no going into winter quarters or going home on furlough. Victory or death. The shells came in always, day and night. Tomorrow, the bed next to yours might be empty; tonight, your close comrade might die. And it came strangely without sense, and ones you were sure would survive often did not.

As is common with war experience, the years at State San were Ruth's central years. Never would life be so intense, never would she be surrounded by friends of exactly this kind, who shared terror and the chances of life and death. Friends she made there were friends for life. There was always a unique closeness and an understanding among them, which could not be interrupted by time nor lessened by distance. "We were soldiers once, and young."

There are two other photographs taken at the State Sanitarium, both very small, one of a young man in a suit, the other of the same man, the same day with a touch of snow on the ground, arm-in-arm with Ruth. She told me that once she had intended to marry a minister. It was clear from what she said that he had been the man of her heart. They did not get married; he died of tuberculosis. Here, in this white box of photographs, the night of her funeral, I had found him. Written on the front of the photograph of the two of them is the single word *Fidelitas.*

> Let not ambition mock their useful toil,
> Their homely joys, and destiny obscure;
> Nor Grandeur hear with a disdainful smile
> The short and simple annals of the poor.

His suit is somewhat ill fitting, of course, for in those days—the Great Depression—a minister would as likely have been paid with eggs or promises as with money. He looks healthy and solid: Who would know there was an incoming shell with his name written on it? He is the Anne Rutledge of my mother's life. I do not know his name. I suppose it could be found, along with his origins and schooling, perhaps even letters. But I have no desire to know more about this young man who could have been my—or somebody's—father. His greatness is in Ruth's heart, and in that word: *Fidelitas.*

> No farther seek his merits to disclose,
> Or draw his frailties from their dread abode,
> (There they alike in trembling hope repose),
> The bosom of his Father and his God.

Perhaps she chose for the rest of her life to be what she had wanted to be for him. *Who would not sing for Lycidas?* She was herself an elegy.

* * *

How Ruth survived those five years it is hard to know. As her doctor said when she was eighty-five, "If you survived tuberculosis back when they didn't do anything for it, you were tough." We come with our nature and get what our parents give us. Beyond that, what? Drop by drop upon our hearts by the awful grace of God comes wisdom.

Ruth learned her life's lessons, bad and good, at State San. There she learned to take not one thing on faith. She distrusted everything—though she never showed it—especially life. A soldier learns this on the front line. There are no guarantees. If you do not take hold of your life, but instead wait for a miracle or sit back and hope for change, death will come first. Miracles might occur, but it is of their essence that they cannot be predicted or expected. God tends to side with the larger battalions. If faith means anything, it is what you are and what you do, not some idea or an attitude of waiting.

I think she admired the godly more than she admired God. She certainly did not trust Him. This point of view is not a formula for happiness, it does not meliorate guilt, and the only chance it has of coping with fear is to overbalance it with despair. All of these describe Ruth under the visible surface. Behind the pink walls and counters of her kitchen and the Italian figurines beside her white, gold, and pale-blue furniture—beneath the perfect photogenic smile, she was a frank realist: Realist enough to survive, too realistic to be happy. People loved the pleasure of her company. She was a presence of beauty they knew they would be more desolate without; she was to them a living rose. The unique, deep beauty of the rose comes from its acquaintance with grief.

It would be unsophisticated to think of Ruth as being false, just as it is sophomoric to insist that civilization is only a sham, a denial of what we really are. Civilization is an act. It is also a choice, and we are creatures with will. It is only paint, but we can paint the Sistine Chapel. When Ruth determined to survive, whether or not in words or thoughts, she set to work on a composition of her own choosing.

The message might have got through to her long ago, though against her will, that her mother had not survived because she had been too much the romantic, too much the idealist. Pure idealists are ineffective. Don Quixote himself, who only thought he knew what he was, is laughable in his powerlessness to change the world, tragic in his inability to survive. Pure idealists are fools, just as pure realists are jerks. The trick is to *choose* your idealism. This is what Lincoln did. This is what the signers of the Declaration of Independence did. The Declaration forms the American faith because it shows us not what we are, but what we have determined to become. The Constitution, in its checks and balances and total distrust of lopsided power, deals with what we are. Ruth survived tuberculosis because of her constitution; her leaving for the city instead of returning to her hometown was her declaration of independence.

She paid a high and continual price for her declaration in guilt and redirected anger. But, in the words of a combat hero at Omaha Beach who, after some natural hesitation, walked through a minefield to rescue a wounded officer: "It was the kind of behavior I expected from myself." Yet once more it was good-bye—not only to her father and sister, but to the best friends she had yet made, and perhaps to a grave somewhere nearby. *She gained from Heav'n ('twas all she wished) a friend.* Good-bye to the friends laughing in front of the barracks in winter; good-bye to the only certainty she ever had of being loved and to the last friends she ever wholly trusted. A friend who had been discharged a year previously had found Ruth a job and an apartment in Milwaukee. *Tomorrow to fresh woods, and pastures new.*

* * *

She made new friends: Louise, kind and honest and good-hearted as ever a person was; Dorothy, an artist, strong and faithful; Lillian, who understood that as with all beautiful people, the essence of Ruth's beauty was not physical but, in the character sense, moral. There would be Ellie—cheerful, refined, understanding, devout—Dolores, Lou, and the dozens of people she happened to sit beside while having lunch or waiting for transportation and with whom she struck up natural, happy, and brief conversations. Were she to be judged by her friends alone, Ruth would be among the happy. But always there was an image of the past, such as one captured in a photograph of her State San friend Barbara, taken off the coast of Monterey: a young woman in shadowy profile at a railing, the golden sun setting behind her, and she forever beautiful and hopeful and young.

It was well that she made new friends, for she needed them. The old ones continued to die. In my childhood alone, three of her best friends died: Gertie, laughing and cheerful and always a semi-invalid; Hazel, serene and compassionate; Marcie, worn to nervous agony by pain. Even her sister Lula, though not until Ruth was eighty-five. We flew down to Florida, and my mother never shed a tear nor said a word. To live was to grieve; by then she had had plenty of practice. Her husband and her father had died within a year of each other. Grief was not for others to see; it is for your room, your heart, your sleep. A photograph of a Norwegian uncle makes this easier to understand. Unlike the sensitive-mouthed Martin and his sister Olga (looking severe enough, nevertheless, in her wire-rimmed glasses), this uncle looks positively frightening. His eyes are as colorless and penetrating as those of a ghost in an Icelandic saga. His mouth is a steady, strong line. His chin is like a rock beside a northern fjord. The Germans were fools to invade Norway.

While my mother gave the impression of freshness, she was never again completely healthy. She required bed rest for two or three hours every afternoon. Like JFK, she concealed her physical weakness through her middle years. Later, she learned to "enjoy poor health" as another way of trying to fill the emptiness or mask the longing that always lingered. The most beautiful photograph of her, possibly excepting her wedding portrait, was colored by the photographer. Her blouse is peach, her cheeks mildly pink; her eyes are shining, and the bright but not overstated smile gives an impression of easy energy. Eventually she herself worked at a photographic studio, retouching and coloring portraits.

For a while, she had had rather poor employment. While cleaning a house in Fox Point, later to become a high-toned suburb of Milwaukee, she looked around. She admired more than the house and its contents. Fox Point was quiet; fresh Lake Michigan air sharpened the senses; the grounds of the house were lush with lilac and flowering crab. On the long bus ride home to the south side of Milwaukee—an area populated by factory workers and mechanics, Poles and Germans—she decided that someday she would live in Fox Point.

The story of her engagement and marriage is quickly told, though not as quickly understood. She knew two men, Ernst and Len. One was a native German, the other the son of Germans but who never spoke the language again after he left home. The first worked in a knitting factory; he was large-boned and hale, as lively and sensitive as a child, a man who would cry when he heard Beethoven played on Sunday in a park. Len was a young chiropractor, slight and shorter than Ruth by three inches, dapper, and rather handsome. Ernst was solid rather than handsome, and though he harbored the kind of German soul that loved Brahms and Goethe, he was a knitter and would always be a knitter. Len had the soul of a mystic—a bad prospect for a romantic realist—but he was a professional man of sorts. Ruth chose Len.

Her choice was not as cold as I have made it sound, nor as neurotic as one might expect of a semi-invalid who married a physician. The wedding photographs are elegant. Len, the "free thinker," and the shell-shocked Ruth did not put on a church wedding. Instead, the ceremony was held in a formal room of the best hotel in the city. Ruth's dress was long and embroidered and the train filled the steps the couple posed upon. A portrait of the bride shows a profile as fine as any; she resembles Ingrid Bergman, without the vulnerability, but sweeter. The Nazis were a year away from invading Norway, and Pearl Harbor was two and a half years ahead. All hell was about to break loose.

At first the couple appeared to be happy. There are several photographs. In one, they pose sitting on the grass with Martin, beside his garden. In another they sit in swimsuits next to Martin's little house. (Len looks like the unhealthy one, skinny as a whistle.) In another, they are outdoors again, in a meadow, each with an arm about the other. She has her shoes off, and the two appear to be the same height. She never posed standing next to him in heels. They are sensitive about his height, and she does not want a photograph to look bad. They do appear to be happy in these photographs. In some, they pose outside or within their Wisconsin Avenue apartment, from which she regularly walked twenty blocks to the nicest stores, and met Len at his office at eight in the evening. From there they went to dine, typically at a restaurant in one of the small hotels nearby. Another difference between Len and Ernst was that while both worked hard, Len worked all the time.

Ernst always remained in their lives. They had mutual friends, and about ten years after Ruth and Len married, Len invested $50,000 in a knitting mill, making Ernst his partner and putting him in charge. The three dined together twice weekly. Some years after Len's death, Ernst finally—or again—proposed marriage to Ruth. She laughed at him. This shows several things. One, Ernst and Ruth had not had some kind of liaison all along, but rather a normal German-Norwegian relationship. Two, Ruth had fully assimilated the identity she had imagined years back, at the sanitarium. Three, Ruth could be pretty hard.

She should have been the one to handle Ernst in business matters. She had become a good passive aggressor by that time and could run circles around most people without their knowing it, especially Ernst, who was devoted to her. As it turned out, Len was the vulnerable one. He had no instinct for fighting. Ernst's belligerence outraged and terrorized him. (Though a native German, Ernst had served as a reconnaissance scout in Patton's army, one of the men who were not *at* the front, but *in front of* the front.) Len's health went down, and he could no longer try to work his way to happiness. But this gets ahead of the story. Len had invested because Ruth was expecting a baby.

Now, Ruth and Len were developing something like a Norwegian-German relationship of their own by then, as I surmise, but Ruth saw herself not simply as the wife of a professional man, dressing well and creating a tasteful household. She was to be a mother; there was to be a child. Ingeborg had not been merely a refined lady; she was Ruth and Lula's mother. Ruth too would be a giver of life. Once again, however, the circumstances of life turned their gun barrel directly at her.

"If you have a child, the probability is that you will die," the specialist told her. (She did not consult Len on medical matters, evidently; or else he was shrewd enough to remain neutral on this one.) Ruth was having a TB breakdown. They had been married nearly ten years. Len was fifty, Ruth was forty. She went to another doctor.

There was little or no question in her mind as to what she would do; she simply needed a doctor who would help her. The next doctor told her the same thing as had the first. After I do not know how many doctor visits, she found a man named Featherstone who sized her up and told her to go ahead. That name, Featherstone, could well apply to Ruth. She was getting frail again, she would not be able to nurse the baby or even bring it home for months. In the first photograph of Ruth holding the baby, she is wearing a surgical mask. In the next, some months later, her smile is absolutely brilliant.

The moral of this story is that "living the life you imagine," as Thoreau phrased it, is not a question of fantasy or merely a matter of decoration. It is a very practical thing, with consequences of life and death. The world will little note nor long remember that without Ruth's imagination and courage you, Reader, would not be reading this; but I can never forget that without her cold bravery I would not be alive.

A hero is a giver of life. To each of us, a parent can be a hero. But however heroic they seem to me, Len and Ruth were not heroes in the large sense, the public sense. One remained decent and compassionate in an angry world; the other defied darkness and set a light in her own house. While they were not national heroes, they have taught me what national heroes are. A public hero gives life to his or her public. For Lincoln, his Union soldiers living and dead gave life to the Republic—gave it a new birth, in fact. To many of my generation, John Kennedy gave a rebirth of hope in the American promise to blacks and whites. At the same time, C. S. Lewis faced the mysteries of the universe and interpreted them to us, as Wilfred Owen had interpreted our nature through the decency and beauty that could characterize us if we choose—writing his elegies to that possibility before the very muzzles of the machine guns. None of these heroes was perfect. On the contrary, each was a representative of human nature.

But a hero makes a decision: This is the kind of behavior I shall expect from myself. And by example, the hero tells us, "This is the kind of behavior I shall expect from you." If we make someone our hero, his or her expectation becomes our own. The twentieth century has shown us what we are; we need heroes to show us what we can be. Such people are not liars or delusionaries. They offer us something like Pascal's "wager argument": the truth might lie in either direction, but in which direction do we choose to travel? Which possibility do we choose to enact? In what world do we wish to live? If the universe is not actually reasonable or decent, we have lost nothing by being reasonable and decent because nothing matters anyway. If the world does conform to our ideals rather than our condition, then we have everything to gain. Choosing the reality we desire is really a very practical choice, the only practical choice.

Well, the kid brought forth by Ruth turned out to be what she wanted in some respects, though any attempt to fill a vacant marriage with a child is fraught with tragic consequences. He never cried—a Norwegian in the making. And, born as ignorant as he was, he could be given a good course in the finer things in life without interference from notions of his own. He looked like Ruth and he looked like Len, but he naturally loved the Norwegian woman (the friend who had ridden along to State San years ago) whom Ruth called from her hometown to take care of him during the first five years of his life, when Ruth was more or less bedridden. So, as she said good-bye one by one to her friends, Ruth could not be sure whether the one sure thing, her son, loved her more than he loved someone else. It became a sad and unhealthy contest with no winners, but in the end Ruth probably understood in the Nordic way what did not need saying with words.

Ernst told me that the only time he knew Ruth to have been happy was when her son was small. One photograph from that time, in which Ruth is between a couple of clowning four-year-olds, shows her smiling with nearly the same simple happiness as in the State San photos. Of course, the other four-year-old is the daughter of a State San friend—the friend taking the picture. Another photo from that time shows Ruth standing before a row of store windows reflecting only shadows and light. She looks profoundly alone and uncertain, but somehow expectant.

Two photographs at Christmas span five years. Ruth and Len had moved from their apartment to a house in Whitefish Bay, one suburb short of Fox Point. Each year Ruth picked out a tree and ordered it flocked white and delivered. One year the ornaments were pink balls, the next blue, alternating. The tree would have no lights, except that two small spotlights were trained upon it when the curtains were open. In the first photograph, Ruth sits on the arm of the chair where her son's nanny is seated, and the boy, aged two or three, sits on the floor. (I am told he referred to himself as "the boy.") Ruth's smile is frozen for the camera. In the next photograph the nanny is gone, the boy sits on the arm of Ruth's chair, and Ruth smiles warmly and naturally. The folds of her red dress are spread across the front of the chair. It is a grayish-pink wing chair.

Forty years later, the chair was in her room at Luther Manor Residence. We have a photograph of her seated there again. She is frail and has shrunken considerably: the top of the chair is not level with her chin but with her forehead. In that last photograph, she wears a long dress and glasses. She looks not at the camera but away, still alone and expectant.

In old age, she abhorred having her picture taken. "What a pretty lady," a woman who regularly saw her in church said she always thought, but Ruth did not see the work of years as being pretty. "A *pretty old* lady," Ruth might have corrected. But she did the best she could. Her room contained the bed, dresser, and nightstand that had been bought for the Whitefish Bay house—blond wood, French provincial. The lamps were the same ones; some of the pictures on the wall were from the old living and dining rooms, too. People who came in felt the orderly beauty of the resident; she had transferred some of herself from the aging body and face to things that changed more slowly.

Not having the means or opportunity to become the artist she might have intended to be when she first set off for the University of Minnesota, and then never caring to go back and start over, she made everything around her artistically deliberate. Once designed, a room did not change. Artistic composition is largely a matter of selection and arrangement. Her great work of art was herself. However, even the conjunctions or separations of her friends were made with artistic deliberation. Some of them, quite unlike each other, never met; others were introduced and joined by her. Each friend and acquaintance felt herself to be among and within an artistry evident only in its happy results. That is why her mere presence gave something beautiful and imperishable to people. She seemed incorrigibly impractical, but like monks and nuns in monasteries and cloisters, she maintained the universe. In her faithfulness to her art she echoed that greater faithfulness elsewhere which moves the sun and all the stars.

> *Fame* is no plant that grows on mortal soil,
> Nor in the glistering foil
> Set off to th' world, nor in broad rumor lies,
> But lives and spreads aloft by those pure eyes
> And perfect witness of all-judging *Jove;*
> As he pronounces lastly on each deed . . .
>
> (*Lycidas*, 78–83)

Sometime during the 1950s, the portrait froze. Perhaps Ruth considered it finished. In this decade, she had achieved all she had imagined. The same might be said of the United States of America. As individual as Ruth was, she had lived the pattern of her generation, and in looking at her photographs one sees a portrait of America.

The 1950s were the American decade. The country had been involved in World War I only distantly, so the shock which had stunned Europe was not felt immediately here. Ruth and her generation had been only children then. The depression subjected Americans to a grueling, life-and-death contest for survival, during which people learned to trust and help one another, but during which all resolved not to let it happen again. Then came World War II, threatening what America had imagined itself to be. This life-and-death struggle was for identity as well as for physical survival: the Second World War tested whether this nation or any other nation conceived in liberty could endure against the disciplined forces of totalitarianism. America won its battles and emerged into the bright, clean, orderly world of the 1950s. But was this what had been imagined?

To one way of thinking, it was. The greatest visible difference between the fifties and all previous decades in America was prosperity. Ruth's generation created suburbs and in record quantities built houses to fill them. Americans constructed the interstate highway system, and made enough money for nearly every family to buy a car in which to cruise it. The menial labor of earlier decades became an enemy. It too was vanquished by American industry: ranges, washing machines, dryers, refrigerators, dishwashers, power lawn mowers—all conveniences which became necessary. Television was invented to fill the new, though perhaps elusive, leisure time. Television severely narrowed the country's vision and subjected its imagination to the commercial energies for which television was an expression. In the 1950s, America came to believe that its dream was being fulfilled materially.

That is exactly Ruth's story. Her smile did not change much after the mid-fifties, and it has a professional, standard quality. She had achieved material security, comfort, and convenience in the suburbs. Now, in better health again, she did not begin a serious study of art, though she did take lessons in Rosemaling—Norwegian painting. Literature remained the quantity established by Mrs. Fairbanks; Ruth read no more literature after mid-decade. Instead of books, she bought beautiful things for her home—made by other people. Many of the pictures on her walls were of musicians or dancers performing. None of them was an original.

She would have spent more than Len earned had he not refused to allow her to have a checking account. Even so, such necessities as food were ordered from department stores, and after the departure of her son's nanny, who cooked, meal preparation followed a path of convenience. Cooking and other work were shunned in the convenience of uncertain health. Materialism bought a kind of indolence, which really rested in the imagination.

It is a commonplace to observe that the 1950s only appeared to be bright. Perceptive critics saw not only stagnation during the fifties, they also saw a dangerous and tragic undertone of racism and fear. So when John Fitzgerald Kennedy came along and addressed all three problems—two positively and one negatively—it is no wonder that some imaginations were once again stirred. But he could not have done it had he not represented the material, glamorous victory for which America had settled.

Ruth's inner life suffered from stagnation of the imagination. She remained where she was. She did not become involved in the community, even the schools. It was a stubborn turning inward. Her will remained as strong as ever, but the goal seemed to have been achieved, and her considerable strength was now turned to defense and preservation.

The former Ruth was harder to see. Those photographs of joyful days with good friends at State San would have looked strange to many of her new acquaintances, because now Ruth was becoming more and more silent. The inner torments were getting louder. Identity is more than mere makeover. To achieve identity, one must forgive the past. "A house divided against itself cannot stand." *Never forget.* For a time Ruth, like America in the fifties, had outrun her past.

It could be said that the nightmare quality of the 1960s was really the unconscious 1950s made conscious. America had not improved its soul, and it is to the credit of many 1960s protesters that they realized the country had been following an illusion rather than the dream. Many of the young did not settle for a material fulfillment of the nation's promise. The American Dream is a dream of intangibles—liberty, justice, equality—and one need not accept tangible measurements in place of more permanent, if invisible, realities. The members of the counterculture did not reject materialism merely because they felt secure; they wanted to keep a faith that they sensed their elders had broken.

Unfortunately, as is typical of young rebels, many rejected the values of their parents wholesale: all of them, not only their infatuation with convenience and security and *things.* Those other values had outlasted the depression and denied the world to fascism. They would be needed again. We saw our parents indulge; we had not seen them fight. We did not understand what heroes are. With the immaturity of youth, we cast the world into our own version of the black-and-white fraud we saw the 1950s to have been. But heroes are heroic in part against their own imperfection. Some of us wanted saints even though we rejected the God who makes them. As for Ruth, though her imagination was expiring, her character was still in place and robust. The identity she had made, she would not surrender. Her greatest achievement was still to come.

She did make it to Fox Point. A photograph of her there shows her dress again spread across, in front of, and beside her—a careful composition. Outside large windows, lilac and flowering crab blossomed each spring. Her kitchen was all pink, her living room all white and blue. For her church, she painted a perfect copy of Martin Luther's Seal: a cross within a heart within a rose. It still hung on a wall there the last time I visited, looking oddly alone. And Ruth lived alone in that house, excepting brief interludes, for twenty years after her husband died. It was the only place, she said, where she ever felt at home.

From the first months in Fox Point, Ruth went to church every week. She quietly made sure that her son got to Sunday School, and she placed in his hands the best book in the world. Her money went into offering envelopes. Carefully, elegantly, she lettered all the confirmation certificates each year. Her imagination partly revived. The beauty of her own life had reached its limits, but an infinitely greater beauty was intimated in the religious faith she began to rediscover, with however much reserve.

After leaving Fox Point, she lived with her son and his family, in pink rooms containing her blond furniture. She ceased making things, having partially lost her sight, but she listened hour after hour to classical music, sitting in her grayish-pink wing chair. To her last days, she listened to church services on her radio, and received communion in her room from one of the pastors of Fox Point Lutheran Church. Somewhere she again found the courage that exceeded stubbornness and transcended physical survival.

In her hospital bed, exhausted and only intermittently conscious, she woke up to find that an oxygen tube had been looped from ear to ear beneath her nose. "What the hell is this?" she said almost inaudibly. (Long ago she had picked up a subterranean vocabulary appropriate to nautical pursuits—but no obscenities, just the standard old blasphemies that sounded particularly sharp from a person of her gentility. No one except family ever overheard them.) She had signed a statement prohibiting any artificial prolongation of life. But the nurse bent over her and said, "It will help you breathe better." The longtime tuberculosis patient looked at her and nodded. "Okay," she said quietly.

Outside, the nurse asked, "Has she always been so sweet?" I thought a moment. She could be quite definite. "Yes," I said.

We are complex. One trait does not cancel another. Even now she was pleasing us as best she could. As I sat beside her, she would fall asleep, and wake forgetting anyone was there. "O Lord, O Lord," she began to moan during the last couple of days. So the boy, fearing that she was fearing the deepest fear, bent over her and asked, "How do you feel?"

"I feel okay," she said each time, and there was no more moaning until she fell asleep.

Len had spoken of fear in the last hours; Ruth would not. Wishing to comfort me, she denied her fear, like an officer in battle. A good soldier learns to accept fear, knowing that fear can be managed. To deny fear in such circumstances is not evasion but courage. But Ruth had plenty of plain, raw bravery, too. It was not the ignorant, youthful kind of the new recruit; she had looked death in the eye many, many times. When the doctor told her that kidney failure is fatal, she simply nodded that she understood. When I told her, a few weeks later, that without dialysis she would lapse into a coma in a few days, she did not blink.

Perhaps soon I can stop writing about war. I have wanted to know how people act under pressure, and why they do what they do. Walt Whitman wrote that he had visited tens of thousands of soldiers wounded and dying in Washington hospitals, and that not one of them had cried out in fear or failed to face the end steadily. I no longer need to read about Civil War soldiers, those young men whom Ruth had seen as old men parading on Decoration Day. I have seen what I was looking for in my own mother. We are a pampered and self-indulgent generation, but our parents were a heroic generation and they have taught us enough to pass to our own children. The world will not end because we were foolish, because for a while we believed that reality is not reasonable and enlightened and so we should not be that way ourselves, or because we believed for a while that courage is only for the deluded. We will be remembered in spite of ourselves. Our parents' generation braved the physical and moral tests of the Great Depression and World War II. It is for us to face the theoretical, ideological tests created by our forebears. We can still nobly save, or meanly lose, the last best hope of earth.

John Keats wrote a line that brings us as close as we can come by our own efforts to goodness, to truth, and to God: "A thing of beauty is a joy for ever." Those words of another tuberculosis sufferer—a young man as marked for death as Wilfred Owen—do not mean merely that we ought to act like ladies and gentlemen, despite our natures, instead of like louts. It means that we can decide that the dead shall not have died in vain, and that some things shall not perish from the earth. Ruth decided that Ingeborg would not perish. That decision was a brave one. To make it might have been necessary for survival, but to keep it converted original bravery into daily courage. Her kind and beautiful mother did live on, despite Ruth's anger, confusion, poverty, and fear: Ingeborg's graciousness and generosity with imperishables lived on in someone who had decided to make those virtues her own. Character is a work as well as a gift, and hope is an achievement of faith.

A hero is excellent, though not perfect. "If thou, Lord, shouldest mark iniquities, who shall stand?" Now, especially, when we are conscious of our flaws and inadequacies and perfidities to the point of boredom, it is well to remember by looking at our forebears that heroes conquer their venality. It is not enough merely to be excellent and reprehensible at the same time, like JFK. A hero conquers weakness. Each of us fights a war, and it is of practical and eternal value never to surrender. "I know who I am, and who I may be if I choose." Courage is the way to beauty. Beauty is the best we have; it is the image of God.

Ruth's mind remained clear until she lapsed into a coma. A few hours from the end, as I sat near the bed in the old wing chair, a nurse came in and asked, "Are you all right?" I nodded. I looked at my mother. I can never lose her. A thing of beauty is a joy forever.

NOVEMBER 27

Highly Resolve (Thanksgiving)

It seems my father never entirely gave up buying educational records for his intransigent patients. The evening before my birthday in 1961, Len brought home a long-playing album called *The Union.* From another room, I heard an unfamiliar voice. Coming into our pink kitchen, I saw a record turning on my portable phonograph—an actor reading the Gettysburg Address. Following that came a hymn written on the occasion of Abraham Lincoln's proclaiming Thanksgiving a national holiday. It was November 1863.

* * *

Thanksgiving can be a bleak and lonely day, regardless of whether the atmosphere is the usual bare, gray late November, or whether it is brutally bright with washed blue sky and piercing sun. Last year, Thanksgiving came right after we returned from that cemetery in western Wisconsin. Even after funerals you must eat. You sit in a church basement following the interment and a committee provides food; people might bring casseroles to your house; or you might go out to a restaurant you used to visit.

And then Thanksgiving comes around. But much of the world would eagerly accept the pan scrapings from the American national binge, so it would be perverse to complain about Thanksgiving dinner. In any case, there is an order of the day: "You shall keep the festival of booths [that is, thanksgiving] . . . when you have gathered in the produce from your threshing floor and your wine press. Rejoice during your festival . . . you shall surely rejoice."

This directive in the Book of Deuteronomy established the thanksgiving feast for ancient Israel. No doubt the Pilgrims, whom we credit for our Thanksgiving Day holiday, were observing this Old Testament exhortation. It is virtually a command: not only give thanks for harvest, but also "rejoice." Those early New England religious people, the "Pilgrim Fathers," would be grieved and outraged that this biblical holy day which they were so careful to preserve in the New World is now chiefly a secular festival. It is no longer the solemn, rejoicing feast of gratitude to the Lord God commanded in Scripture. Equally grieved, though perhaps not as surprised, would be the originator of Thanksgiving as a national holiday in the United States. In 1863, the president set aside a specific day in November as a national day of thanksgiving. After recounting the successful work of the Union's armies and navies, Mr. Lincoln, following King James Bible usage, wrote,

> No human counsel hath devised nor hath any mortal hand worked out these great things. They are the gracious gifts of the Most High God, who, while dealing with us in anger for our sins, hath nevertheless remembered mercy. It has seemed to me fit and proper that they should be solemnly, reverently and gratefully acknowledged as with one heart and one voice by the whole American People. I do therefore invite my fellow citizens in every part of the United States, and also those who are at sea and those who are sojourning in foreign lands, to set apart and observe the last Thursday of November next, as a day of Thanksgiving and Praise to our beneficent Father who dwelleth in the Heavens. And I recommend to them that while offering up the ascriptions justly due to Him for such singular deliverances and blessings, they do also, with humble penitence for our national perverseness and disobedience, commend to His tender care all those who have become widows, orphans, mourners or sufferers in the lamentable civil strife in which we are unavoidably engaged, and fervently implore the interposition of the Almighty Hand to heal the wounds of the nation and to restore it as soon as may be consistent with the Divine purpose to the full enjoyment of peace, harmony, tranquility and Union.

Lincoln wanted the whole country to be grateful to God, and wanted the people to rejoice in their gratitude. Now, would those 150,000 families with a freshly dead man in a soldiers' cemetery somewhere, or simply shoveled under Virginia's bloody soil, have been able to muster gratitude, much less joy?

I think they would have tried. Perhaps a young son or daughter would have cried out against it. "How can we pretend to rejoice? Our father is *dead*! You can thank God if you want to, but I am not going to be a hypocrite." "Now, Son," a bleak mother might answer, "we must do our duty as your father did his. The ways of God are unknown. As the president said last summer, we are to thank God in trouble and in prosperity. Saint Paul commands it." "Who is Saint Paul to me, Mother?"

But no, he would not have given a 1960s retort. He would have said, "Yes, Mother," and lowered his eyes. Feelings in the 1860s might have been similar to ours, but people tried harder in those days to observe the civilities.

And giving thanks in grief or trouble is a civilized practice. It is not natural; it is not even necessarily logical. It must be learned, and that chiefly through example. Perhaps it is not so much a conscious experience of God being kind that enables this exercise to take hold. Perhaps it is the eventual realization that fortune and misfortune are unclear, sometimes downright absurd, concepts. At least in the short run.

For example, Deuteronomy includes slaves in the command to celebrate and rejoice: "Rejoice during your festival, you and your sons and your daughters, your male and female slaves, as well as the Levites, the strangers, the orphans, and the widows resident in your town."

In the New Testament, which claims that in Christ there is neither Jew nor Greek, male nor female, slave nor free, we are exhorted to give thanks in all things.

There is something about History in all this. As to the Pilgrims, the picture we all rightly cherish includes bright orange pumpkins, fall colors, buckled shoes, autumn school days. It is an imaginary picture of the feast in the Kingdom of God, however that vision is worded in humankind's various traditions. Perhaps it is all right, at least partly, if we see no irony in that picture, complete as it is only with the Indians gathered around. After all, the Native Americans and Europeans feasting together in peace is the essence of the image. (Gratitude to God is somewhat, but by no means entirely, forgotten in this.) The image is perhaps a handed-down guilty memory on the part of a people who, after all, did not want to be fighting and exterminating another people. It is a poignant picture, fraught with horrific foreshadowings—which sentimentalism brutally covers up, because that is the job of sentimentalism—foreshadowings of the Europeans getting on their feet and, no longer needing the Native Americans, blasting hell out of them from the Atlantic to the Pacific, until now their meager descendants are warehoused out of sight like mental patients and criminals, in corrugated shacks and on the hard-packed earth of reservations. But to deprive children of the hope imaged in the glad, peaceful tableau of the first Thanksgiving is to inflict upon them the I-know-more-than-you-do abuse of adolescent disillusionment. The tableau is one of mature adults. That those who followed after were, and are, less mature and less civilized, is another story to be told.

Stories use their raw materials unsentimentally, and they in turn become material for new stories. The process is both practical and aesthetic. For example, the Bible that formed the basis for the Pilgrims' quest for freedom is peppered with uncritical references to slavery. But only the most abject literalist would claim that because the Bible does not denounce slavery, slavery should be permitted again. No, we erase what we no longer want, though now and then we revive bits of knowledge for our own reasons. The writing of History, like the writing of Theology, takes care of these things. All things are assimilated into the way we live now; we have learned the shorthand of forgetting. Conservatives try to resist it, and liberals try to direct it, but change bears all things along like an ever-rolling stream, and the old ways go out with the wash.

To the modern mind, this is good. But the idea of the stream being progressive rather than merely rolling is in question now. *Time, like an ever-rolling stream, bears all its sons away.* History is in doubt, and with it the reality of the past. Do we make that reality ourselves? Will anything last?

Lincoln might agree that we make any reality the past has. The work so nobly advanced at Gettysburg, he implied, would disappear without our work. His poetic rendering of the meaning of past actions has made them into a particular kind of history, which has *made* the present. Past and present merge in the foreground of Lincoln's words, but only because of the story they are embedded in.

If identity is an accomplishment, as Vaclav Havel says, then part of the accomplishment of a people is to construct their story. Israel created itself out of a historical story of deliverance from bondage in Egypt. As the Hebrews' nationhood developed, so did the story, taking on ever larger dimensions until it transcended national purposes and became a "salvation history" pertinent to humanity at large. The story held Jews together through two thousand years of dispersion and holocaust, and has unified

Christendom as well. Such stories are indeed powerful. As individuals, we want to know our family histories. As a nation, we get our identity from the American story. Like the Venerable Bede's *History of the English Church and People,* our story is a place to come to. Our story is home; it is who we are.

But the story not only reminds us of who we are, it points us toward what we should become. Our American story is a salvation history, containing moral and spiritual dimensions; its essence relates to the acts of God. Lincoln elevated a story of personal grief into the national salvation history, which became a point of hope for "any nation so conceived."

No story works with formative power unless it is beautiful. This is the secret. We are surrounded by a cacophony of stories clamoring for our attention. Only the beautiful ones last. The Greek myths are still told. Children still listen to the story of Moses, the story of Ruth, the story of the Nativity. The Pilgrims sharing their first Thanksgiving in the New World with the people who helped them survive in that world is a story of graceful beauty. Grim as it is, the Civil War is an irresistibly suggestive, panoramically beautiful story. Lincoln's log cabin boyhood, his emergence into the national troubles, his practical wisdom and eloquence, his melancholy and compassion, his humor, and his mysterious and profound destiny all create a story whose beauty moves us strangely. These stories are ours, and they are worth more than the gold in Fort Knox. They intimate a reality beyond our perception. Where their beauty comes from is hard to say. A sculptor shapes the clay, but its warmth has not come from her hands. A poet has written his words but knows their spirit was given by the heavenly muse. I think we should take a moment's time out and give thanks for these valuable insights.

* * *

One evening after my father and I had dined alone, I went into the bathroom to shave, getting ready for a date. (My loyalty, I guess, went only so far.) My father came in, and we talked—the only time I remember—about girls. This meant, of course, only a sentence or two from me, and not much more from him. But the sentences counted.

"One evening in St. Looey I sat on a doorstep with a young woman. She was a poor girl. I've always regretted . . . "

Not much to go on, but at least it is direct testimony, unlike the Anne Rutledge possibility. But no glorious, shining republic bloomed from the dust of this poor girl's bosom. Only regret, lasting regret.

Time, like an ever-rolling stream, bears all its sons away.

My father might have developed a sort of savior complex; perhaps that was one of the appeals of that poor girl. My mother presented some of that appeal, with her pulmonary fragility and the vigilance it demanded. There is also a tendency in some insecure persons to choose someone to take care of, and thereby remain superior to. But if that was the plan, it backfired. Ruth was not to be ruled.

I do not know anything about the situation with Len's first wife. After learning from a family friend that my father had been married before, I went to the courthouse and looked up the divorce proceedings. Len, no doubt, had regretted the marriage first, but she was the one who filed. You needed grounds in those days, and her grounds were bad treatment through bizarre behavior. Seems the younger L. L. drove her beyond the limit with strange talk about spiritualism, astrology, and other aberrations, along with walking the streets alone at all hours of the night. He acted mighty peculiar. Afterward, my father saw to it that she was taken care of financially, I was told.

So he was unfortunate in the love and marriage department. His main energy was directed into his work; his will to work was a little engine that never rested. But that did not touch the empty spot.

What had been the difference between my father's first unhappy marriage and his second? I had been the difference. Today I understand him for the first time. Children are nourished by sacrifice; tomorrow comes from today's dying.

My father gave me his duty and died in despair. He simply traded his chance at happiness for mine, and faced the consequences. He would have been happier without a wife who did not like him and a son who did not understand his sacrifice. A month after he died we received a letter from the president of the National College of Chiropractic, a man who had known L L. "Dr. Gramm was a totally good and noble man," the letter said. "There was not an ounce of malice, of selfishness or deceit in him, and although his sufferings were long and extended . . . " Not only long and extended, but more complicated than anyone knew. What use can one make of such a gift?

* * *

Last night I made a long nocturnal drive in order to be home for Thanksgiving. Tonight I drive back. The month has become an obsession, and I must finish out these last days in Gettysburg. In the middle of the night I enter a quiet battlefield and drive up to the Soldiers' National Cemetery. I am far too tired to get spooked, so I park and tramp in. Gangway, ghosts: my hollow eyes are bright. I am here to give thanks.

To Mr. Lincoln, who spoke somewhere near these graves, I am grateful for a country with a soul. I see that we are joined together—we citizens of a nation, any nation; we are joined together whether we know it or not, wish it or not. In our union with all citizens we are vulnerable to everyone's weaknesses and we benefit from everyone's strengths. "We all share in each other's fortunes." What we are has come in part from our country. Homer's Ulysses, returning home from Troy, correctly identified himself as Nobody until he reached his native shore. He was a Greek; he was an Ithacan; he was a king, son, husband, and father—but he had been none of these things away from his land and family. He gave up an offer of immortality to regain himself. What good is all the time in the world if you have lost your soul? This wandering soul in us has taken an identity at birth. It is human; it is specific. Abraham Lincoln has conferred upon us the essence of our nationality. I would be someone else without him. I would be a slaveholder and a slave; I am a Confederate by instinct.

I am grateful to Robert Kennedy. I wonder whether without him I would be here, alive, today—breathing, standing on the hallowed ground at Gettysburg under this ancient, sturdy tree. My children would not be born. *As a boy during that fall of 1962 I looked up at the evening sky expecting it to rain missiles. I did not know it might have been your voice that stayed them. Even less could I have known that you saved us with idealism; you prevented war because you accepted the soul that Lincoln gave you. You insisted that there be a difference between America and the base desires of the human will. You kept your brother from doing something stupid and wrong in the fall of 1962. Six years later you did something more. You gave the people you had saved an inspiration, a breath of life from somewhere higher. Justice and mercy, freedom and equality: You made them live again, gave them a human face, a voice, gave them seriousness and energy, and clothed them in the love we had for you. All this we who remember you can pass to our children, in whatever form the hope you gave us takes in us. The knowledge that hope can be worked for, we take from Abraham Lincoln, as you gave him to us; and we can give it to our children.*

If we are dedicated to our children. This *dedication,* my father and mother taught me.

He and Ruth put Gettysburg and the Address into my mind, like the One who "putteth eternity into the mind of man."

I make a personal thanksgiving here tonight, full of the bitterness of repentance, looking at these pale headstones. These are the graves of all our days. I cannot thank anyone by intoning litanies; it would be an irony and an insult. Work needs to be done.

NOVEMBER 28

These Honored Dead (Elegy)

> At the core, the American citizen soldiers knew the difference between right and wrong, and they didn't want to live in a world in which wrong prevailed. So they fought, and won, and we all of us, living and yet to be born, must be forever profoundly grateful.
>
> —Stephen Ambrose

I have slept infuriatingly late, considering my resolution to work today. I must get out and use what is left of the dry weather. There is to be snow tomorrow. Moisture pushing up from the coast will slide over a cold front dropping down from the northwest. Today one would not believe it. The air is unseasonably warm and earthy. You can smell the soil. Fields I walk through give up a faintly rotten aroma, the summer's straw ploughed halfway under and turned a humic brown.

Seeking higher ground, I hike up to Cemetery Hill to try to determine where the photographer had planted his tripod just before the dedication ceremony in November 1863. I carry a good copy of the photograph showing part of the crowd with the Evergreen Cemetery gate in the background. Perhaps there is still some chance that the photographic evidence might be inconclusive, or lead in a new direction.

I start at the "traditional site" and walk down and away, behind the rows of graves. The Evergreen Cemetery gatehouse is completely visible in the photograph, but from where I am now standing it is hidden by the slope of the hill. The photographer could not have stood here, downslope from the traditional site.

I walk slowly up the aisles between state plots of graves until I reach a point where I can see the old cemetery gate. In the photograph, the hill cuts off just the bottom of the gatehouse. Near the Speech Memorial, the level seems to correspond. I can see all of the gate except the very bottom. The gate is actually a gatehouse: its arch connects two living spaces. At the time of the Address, the cemetery keeper and his family lived in the place. Today one side is lived in, part of it being used as the cemetery office. The other side is now a garage. In either century—and, one might say, in either millennium—the cemetery gatehouse is an unmistakable landmark.

So, this is how far up the hill the photographer unlimbered. But did he set his tripod here, or somewhere to the right or left—and if so, how far? Fortunately, the sun is out now and then. It is early afternoon, about when the photographer had made his exposure, and of course this date is within several days of the 1863 photo. In the old picture, the sun is shining and has made distinct patterns of light and dark. You can orient yourself by the angle of sunlight striking the arch of the gate. I move to my left. Wrong way. To the right: closer.

I pass behind the column monument, walking southward, in the direction of the Knothead Site. At the plot containing graves of unknown soldiers, marked by numbered square stones, the light in the photograph begins to correspond to what I see. Walking this way and that, I finally find a place where the curve of the hill and the angle of the gateway in sunlight seem to match the photograph exactly. He and I are seeing the gatehouse in exactly the same light. I am quite a few rows back, in the section of numbered squares. The photographer had anchored himself firmly in the Unknowns.

The crowd, then, must have been assembling up the hill, on the other side of the wrought-iron fence, which had not been there in 1863. At first, the camera position suggests the Harrison Site for the speakers' platform. But the crowd is a little too far up for that. They are gathering over that spot itself. The sound of people talking rises. A row of mounted soldiers begins to file up from the south entrance; you can hear the horses plod and whinny. From the town and the roads to the south and east, people stream up toward the hill as if they were spirits. So the Union army had gathered on this hill in July. Postmodernists tell us there is no exact, real past, only what is in our heads. Sometimes the sophomoric nature of postmodernism becomes especially clear.

The current evidence builds a fairly solid wall of probability around the conclusion that Abraham Lincoln stood somewhere in Evergreen Cemetery when he delivered the Address. But something there is that doesn't love a wall. Anyway, the time of the Address is more important than the place, the time being the present. And sometimes the truth in postmodernism becomes especially clear.

The cemetery gate is as sure an astronomical clock as Stonehenge. Were it to remain standing three thousand years hence, people might conclude that the structure had been built to mark a specific time of year. When the sun's noon rays shine directly through the arch without casting a shadow onto either half of the gatehouse—really a reliquary—that is the time of the year, late November, when, according to legend, the famous Gettysburg Address was given, supposedly composed by Abrum the President, but actually the work of a series of redactors, and corrupted by centuries of scribes.

Will the Address still be known in three thousand years? Who will be reciting it with a sigh, somewhere ages and ages hence? The cemetery gatehouse will be an indecipherable mass of buried brick dust then. The column monument will be crumbled and scattered. Even now, the Union graves contain little more than bone fragments, perhaps filmy shreds of cloth, buttons rusted to crepe. No evidence at all will remain. Time's passage makes new places of the places we know. What mute, inglorious Lincoln will shuffle across this hill in this, a different country then, when three thousand Novembers have dropped their leaves to dust?

November itself shall remain, but known by another name. Already the month is out of time. It is no longer the ninth month. Two Caesars, themselves dust for two thousand years, displaced the month. We do not even know the time we live in, what its true name is, except that this cold portion is next to last. Whatever is to come, this, now, gives way before it; we, here, mark the ending of what was.

November, the ending. Who would not cast one longing, lingering look behind? But for what? The songs of spring and summer have been sung from sky and trees by creatures so light and mortal as to seem immortal; they are gone. Where are they? Indeed, where are they? For late autumn has its beauty, too. This is a solemn month, solemn in the high old sense: stately, significant, cold and sad only at the surface. This month sighs the acute beauty of time expiring: November dies on the wintry wind.

Some of these graves, even today, are adorned with little flags or flowers. Apparently some still mourn these dead. All across the Gettysburg battlefield, monuments and markers are decorated, further memorialized, with flowers, flags, coins, and even notes.

But I have never seen flowers at the Speech Memorial that stands at the south gate of the Soldiers' Cemetery. I walk there now, through the rows of graves, under the great old trees, now bare. Here, between the old and new soldiers' cemeteries, between Civil War and Vietnam, a horizontal arch cups bronze tablets embossed with the words of Lincoln's speech. In the center stands a bust of the Great Emancipator. No flowers here, only the speech. No fitter, grander, more poignant memorial could remain. Still, a little sentiment would be fitting, a rose for Mr. Lincoln.

* * *

In *America in the Gilded Age,* Sean Cashman writes that Abraham Lincoln's death was "a political disaster of the first magnitude for the United States." The 1860s and 1960s were idealistic eras, charged with great passions and wounded by divisions, led by heroes; both eras were black with danger, cost, and tragedy because of evils in society and because of hopes Americans rose to fulfill; people believed in and lived for something more than themselves; both eras were followed by "gilded ages"; both generations saw their presidents killed. But have we more in common than that? How much of a disaster for *us* was April 14, 1865? Who, and what, did *we* lose?

William Herndon wrote about his partner, "Sometimes it appeared as if Lincoln's soul was fresh from its creator." Like the greatest of heroes, mythical or historical or both, Abraham Lincoln was the summary and expression of his people and times, yet he was also undeniably unique, "an original." Judge Davis, who knew him long and well, remarked that Lincoln "*thought* for himself," which is undoubtedly a rare quality. While on one hand Lincoln, according to Herndon, constantly calculated the possible, "His ideas were odd and original for the reason that he was a peculiar and original creation himself." One of his secretaries, John Hay, wrote, "As, in spite of some rudeness, republicanism is the sole hope of a sick world, so Lincoln, with all his foibles, is the greatest character since Christ."

His law partner believed the true lesson of Lincoln's life is that "real and enduring greatness . . . must rest upon character." But Herndon did not think that all of us should expect to be great statespersons. "Real and enduring greatness" is the condition each of us wants, by one name or another; some might call it "happiness," others "salvation."

But, of course, Herndon meant historical greatness. If that "rests upon character," then something is being said about those who judge greatness. Napoleon, for example, was a great man, though not a good man. If we judge him therefore to be not genuinely or meaningfully great, it is because *we* believe goodness is preferable to glory; it is because *we* think there are such things as right and wrong. If John F. Kennedy "never thought of the world as a moral place," yet his speeches and decisions aroused in us a hope based upon our sense of justice, of good, and of right, then we can admit that a greatness in the American people, and in the peoples of the world, was sounded and called forth. Though it was the people more than the president who transcended meaninglessness and despair, surely this is an element of greatness in a leader, to call forth greatness in others.

Herndon, clearly, was not thinking of "character," in this abstract sense. What he meant in part was that Lincoln was consistent. Joshua Speed, another of Lincoln's friends, said, "there was entire harmony between his public and private life." The essence of that harmony was Lincoln's legendary, but actual, honesty.

Herndon thought there were four leading elements in Lincoln's character. The first was reason. Lincoln was, Herndon said, the "strongest man I ever saw . . . [in] reason and logic. . . . The office of reason is to determine the truth. Truth is the power of reason, and Lincoln loved truth for its own sake. It was to him reason's food."

The second element was conscience. Herndon called it also "love of the just." Mary Lincoln said her husband was the "kindest man" she ever knew. But conscience is both kindness and truth. "He was a good man, an honest and true one," said Mrs. Ninian Edwards. Another friend, Leonard Swett, said "that kindness never abrogated or beclouded his judgement." In the fields and courts of Indiana and Illinois he had seen human nature thoroughly; his reading had given understanding to this experience. He achieved an elevated point of view: "He never judged men by his like or dislike for them," Swett concluded. "Honesty was his polar star," Herndon wrote:

> In the grand review of his peculiar characteristics, nothing creates such an impressive effect as his love of the truth. It looms up over everything else . . .

"He searched and comprehended his own mind and nature thoroughly." Only with such an understanding could he achieve the ultimate goal of conscience:

> he approximated as nearly as human nature can, . . . "Do unto others as ye would they should do unto you."

(It should be remembered again that Herndon, an irascible man, wrote his biography in outrage at the pious Lincoln portraits being written in his day. Herndon's purpose was to present the man he knew, "warts and all.")

The third characteristic was understanding. He "comprehends the exact state of things and determines their relations, near or remote." Intense thought, Speed said, was the rule for Lincoln and not, as with most of us, the exception. He was a "great student." Lincoln reached his decisions slowly, after profound brooding. "He read less and thought more than any man in his sphere in America," Herndon wrote.

What good are reason, conscience, and understanding to those who have no heart? What use to gain the whole world and lose one's soul? The last characteristic Herndon identifies as heart. "Deep thinking is attainable only by a man of deep feeling," Coleridge said. From his birth mother, Nancy Hanks Lincoln, after whose death the boy Abraham began trying to prevent the petty cruelties he saw all around him; from his beloved "Mama," Sarah Bush Lincoln, to whom he said he owed all he ever would be; and from what mystery?—Abraham Lincoln received the compassion, strength, humanity, and love which Herndon calls heart. "He was never cold," said Lincoln's sister-in-law; his was "a nature as tender and poetic as any I ever saw."

> "With malice toward none, with charity for all."
> . . . the forgiveness of millions toward millions . . .
> Bloom forever, O Republic,
> From the dust of my bosom!

"The glory of Mr. Lincoln's power lay in the just and magnificent equipoise of head, conscience, and heart." "True to nature, true to himself, he was true to everybody and everything around him. . . . He could be false to no one." We cannot spare any truth. Thus when Abraham Lincoln was assassinated on Good Friday in 1865, we were struck by a disaster from which we have not yet recovered.

The *New York Times* reported on a study that found Americans to be less interested in social programs in recent years. We are more inward, more angry, more self-absorbed, and less compassionate. Perhaps we have lost an understanding, in Lincoln's words, of "*whence* we came, *where* we are, and *whither* we are tending." If we want to find a way out of postmodern despair, we might look for Mr. Lincoln.

* * *

Postmodernism, with its denial of objective truth, was bound to remain only a theory for just so long. Soon enough it had to work its way into our body politic and become a practical matter for us all. If, as I wrote most of these pages, we had a president with no sense of the truth as a real thing, perhaps it is because the postmodern idea has permeated us until it comes out at the political apex.

A postmodern idea is that we have only language. There is no objective reality out there to which language refers. There is no truth that is not merely a linguistic construct. Language, in turn, is nothing but a tool we use to get or do what we want. No matter that some postmodernists want to stop the use of language as a lever by which some people oppress others; a deeper menace is the underlying idea that the objective world and objective truth do not exist (other than as language events). It might be as difficult to disprove this idea as to prove that other people beside ourselves exist—but the questions are: How do we want to live? What do I want to be? Will I live as a person who does not believe in truth, or as a person who does?

If the president of the United States becomes a political pustule of postmodern theory, then what are we to expect? If he or she is benevolent, and works for the material benefit of all of us, can we rest easy? Upon such an assurance rests a prop for tyranny, under which one can rely only on the intentions of those with power. It is less risky to hold that certain truths are self-evident, and to act on that basis. And to compel government to act on that basis. *If the foundation be destroyed, what can the righteous do?*

Lincoln's heroes, the Founding Fathers, distrusted human nature as much as does any postmodernist, but they went the postmoderns one better: they included themselves in that distrust. The U.S. Constitution is a very practical document, in which little is left to the intentions of anybody. The Constitution and the U.S. government were instituted to protect our rights on the assumption made in the Declaration that such rights really exist; and they really exist because God endows us with them. If this was true beyond being a verbal contract, then it remains true. Truth is of central importance, and here we see how valuable Abraham Lincoln was, for whom "truth was his polar star." The idea of truth itself, despite fanatical misuses of it, is more valuable than any short-term benefits doled to us by people who believe in no polar star. Rights, of course, can be taken to selfish extremes as far as power permits, and here is where goodness must accompany truth. That is why the loss of Abraham Lincoln is a loss "of the first magnitude."

* * *

We may look upon Lincoln's dead as our own dead. They are a Great War's soldier and poet, whose elegies to the world he saw coming to a brutish end prove his own rejection of brutishness, and which, in their courage and beauty, remain proof against the futility they lament. They are brothers calling out hope to the hopeless and a year of freedom to the captives of time—demanding liberty for the prisoners of place and chance, of poverty and race. They are the nameless soldiers and protesters of Vietnam. They are the unknown mothers and fathers of an uncertain generation. They are Lincoln's children.

* * *

> Yet once more, O ye laurels, and once more
> Ye myrtles brown, with ivy never sere . . .

Once more, as in every passing year, we remember the laughing, melancholy stranger, deep with genius, who made himself new. "I was once a hired laborer, mauling rails, at work on a flatboat, just like any poor man's son." He knew who he was, and who he could be—under God.

> I claim not to have controlled events, but confess plainly that events have controlled me.

What he had lived his life to say, only the dead at Gettysburg had given him the right to say, and the time and place to say it.

Again and again, floodwaters gather; the footing beneath us shifts and sinks. But Lincoln will never really have left us as long as we remain dedicated to the proposition that "all men are created equal." He is ours.

> Henceforth thou art the genius of the shore,
> . . . and shalt be good
> To all that wander in that perilous flood.

No marble monuments will outlast the words that called forth the genius of Lincoln's people. The goodness in them will not end; it already runs in the stream of bravery and beauty that outlives wasteful war and defies the absurdity of questions we cannot answer. "There was no flabby philanthropy about Abraham Lincoln," wrote Charles A. Dana. "He was all solid, hard, keen intelligence combined with goodness." Lincoln was the last of his kind, and first of another. Like the month of November, he arrives in melancholy but calls up expectation, opening a door of hope as he departs.

> With malice toward none; with charity for all; with firmness in the right, as God gives us to see the right, let us strive on to finish the work we are in. . . .

NOVEMBER 29

Under God
(Winter Saturday)

My restless spirit never could endure
To brood so long upon one luxury,
Unless it did, though fearfully, espy
A hope beyond the shadow of a dream.
—Keats

One of C. S. Lewis's colleagues said about Jack's death, "Never was a man better prepared." Since his conversion, of course, Lewis had believed in "the absolute reality of the supernatural world." In this his intellect and imagination worked together; his arguments and his fantasy books are alike luminous with the assumption of a dimension, or dimensions, other than this one. Lewis thought that an inability to believe was "primarily a failure of the *imagination.*" By imagination Lewis did not mean indulgence in wishful thinking—sound exercise of the intellect should limit that—but rather imagination is what allows us to break out of the enclosed world we think we live in.

The intellect cannot do that. For all his antimodernism, Lewis was, in a sense, prophetically postmodern. In *The Abolition of Man* he proposed "a new Natural Philosophy, continually conscious that the 'natural object' produced by analysis and abstraction is not reality but only a view." He decried "the fatal serialism of the modern imagination—the image of infinite progression which so haunts our minds."

Lewis's postmodern hints are surprising because his intellectual conservatism seems incompatible with anything characteristic of his century.

Lewis's modern and postmodern nuances are best seen in what he did on November 29, 1954—a salient day in his life and career. His beloved Oxford had chosen not to promote him. The rather objective biographer, A. N. Wilson, explains Oxford's action this way: "It was not his failure to be a good graduate supervisor which cost him an Oxford chair, it was *Mere Christianity* and *The Screwtape Letters:* the fact that he wrote them, and the far more damaging fact that millions of people . . . wanted to read them." In his way offending the "prevailing orthodoxy" of Oxford, Lewis was "exiled, in some sense, for his refusal to toe the line."

Cambridge knew his value as a scholar and teacher, however, and had not felt the jealousy to which close association can give rise. This more conservative university became a congenial home for Lewis during the rest of his career, though he maintained his house in Oxford, staying in Cambridge only on weekdays during the teaching terms.

His inaugural lecture in November 1954 is noteworthy for two reasons especially. One is that he presented himself as a "dinosaur . . . representing a vanished age, an absolute set of beliefs, a wholly outmoded way of looking at the world." He was a rebel against the Modern World. But despite his intentions, his rebellion did not take the form, entirely, of premodernism. The key is that he presented *himself.* His inaugural presentation, instead of being a removed, traditional academic lecture, introduced the lecturer personally. That was pure Lewis. His literary criticism is so readable because it presents *Lewis,* with his peculiar enthusiasms and insights—in his inimitable language. Likewise his apologetics: they are interesting because they come to us on the voice of Lewis talking. Even his Narnia books are *Lewis* talking to children, and to the adults reading to them. The personal approach is characteristic of both modernism and postmodernism. Modernism discovered the Self, and postmodernism is all too aware that whatever is presented mixes with the person who presents it. The scientist watching and reporting makes the electron jump one way rather than another; the historian makes a History that is really part of himself or herself. Far from lamenting this state of affairs, or even merely reporting it, the postmodern theorist makes capital of it, reinforcing his theories by sticking his bleary face against your nose. So Lewis, rebelling against the modern age while being very much part of its confidence in reason, becomes an instrument of that age's destruction, himself becoming less and less a throwback to an earlier time than a popularizer of an age to come among the very people most interested, they would think, in resisting it.

His conscious alternative, however, was not a postmodern one except in that it was a partial rejection of the modern. He did not foreground all knowledge, historical or scientific; he believed in a background, a supernatural background, for the most important things we know. He rejected the idea that language "is always to be mixed up with the thing it attempts to signify." His idea of objective value rests on a belief that the origins of value are supernatural. Starting on our own, we would not come up with the conviction, for example, "that a man should . . . work for posterity." We could not invent a new system of values, says Lewis, any more than we could invent a new primary color. This system upon whose basics the great religions and philosophies East and West have always agreed "is not one among a series of possible systems of value. It is the sole source of all value judgements." Only this central system overrules rulers and ruled alike: "A dogmatic belief in objective value is necessary to the very idea of a rule which is not tyranny or an obedience which is not slavery." Neglecting this system, which Lewis chose to call by an Eastern name, *Tao,* generates consequences quite visible to us today: "We laugh at honor and are shocked to find traitors in our midst."

But it was probably not Lewis's belief in a supernatural world, evidenced by an objective system of necessary values, which prepared him so well for death. He had believed these things most of his adult life. Nevertheless, according to Wilson, "Like many (most?) religious people, Lewis was profoundly afraid of death. His dread of it, when in the midst of life, had been almost pathologically obsessive." But "towards the end, this changed." Now he could meet a colleague for lunch, both knowing that it was farewell, and impress the other man with his utterly genuine calm, unselfish courtesy, and complete absence of fear or self-pity. What had happened?

His wife had taught him how to die, and so how to live. Her death shattered his notional beliefs about God, the "house of cards" he had built, as a modern man, with his smart, reasoning intellect. Like Owen's Great War, Joy's death was Lewis's wardrobe doorway out of the self-enclosed Modern World. An important element of Hebraic faith is that God is invisible: "Since you saw no form when the LORD spoke to you at Horeb out of the fire, take care and watch yourselves closely, so that you do not act corruptly by making an idol for yourselves."

For a while, *A Grief Observed* appears to be another failure. After storming against God, "hitting back," as Lewis put it, he returns to the old apologetic impulse, even saying, "Feelings, and feelings, and feelings. Let me try thinking instead." He tries to say that, like a dentist, the good God will hurt us the more inexorably He means to do us good. He reverts to the old, forced "either-or" pattern: "Well, take your choice. The tortures occur. If they are unnecessary, then there is no God or a bad one." This is another suspicious argument, like the old ones, because to make this choice we have to assume what we wanted most for him to prove. We will agree that pain is necessary because we want to think of God as good.

But finally, Lewis leaves the old apologist behind. He has outgrown him. Wisdom has come by the awful grace of God. Lewis now believes that God is "incomprehensible and unimaginable." If he chooses the good God, it is no longer through logic, but by faith. It is not a cool, objective choice; it is a soul-felt, determinative choice, a declaration of himself.

Something has happened. More than anything else, it must be the resistant, indefinable reality of love. "You'll try to come to me on my deathbed?" he had asked Joy.

> "Heaven would have a job to hold me; and as for Hell, I'd break it into bits." She knew she was speaking a kind of mythological language, with even an element of comedy in it. There was a twinkle as well as a tear in her eye. But there was no myth and no joke about the will, deeper than any feeling, that flashed through her.

His grief was "like a long valley, a winding valley where any bend may reveal a totally new landscape." One bright day, "after ten days of low-hung gray skies and motionless warm dampness," his spirits brightened, and in a flash of memory less clouded by sorrow, he received, through "something (almost) better than memory; an instantaneous, unanswerable impression" of her. While "to say it was like a meeting would be going too far," it was qualitatively different from any other kind of experience—especially different from remembering or wishful thinking. It was, perhaps the kind of knowledge firmer than any other knowledge, the kind of unsentimental fact that you would face a firing squad for, without any fear. It was not a spiritualistic experience, as generally understood:

> Meet is far too strong a word. I don't mean anything remotely like an apparition or a voice. I don't mean even any strikingly emotional experience at any particular moment. Rather, a sort of unobtrusive but massive sense that she is, just as much as ever, a fact to be taken into account.

Such an experience is "quite incredibly unemotional." But it is grounded in love.

Tennyson described an analogous experience in the climactic moment of *In Memoriam:*

> And all at once it seemed at last
> The living soul was flashed on mine.

Lewis's experience of Joy, Stephen Smith's enigmatic experience of RFK, Harold Owen's finding his brother sitting in his cabin, my knowing the presence of my father, Ruth's seeing her mother, Lincoln's dreams, all came to modern people from somewhere outside the Modern World. Lewis says his idea of God was a "risky extrapolation from a very few and short experiences here on earth." A real experience, not merely of another human being who had died, but of God Himself "would probably blow all one's ideas . . . into smithereens." It is all right that the postmoderns are dispelling the modern illusions that we call knowledge, for, as Lewis says, "All reality is iconoclastic."

> Images of the Holy easily become holy images—sacrosanct. My idea of God is not a divine idea. It has to be shattered time after time. He shatters it Himself. He is the great iconoclast. Could we not almost say that this shattering is one of the marks of His presence?

"Probably half the questions we ask" are nonsense.

> Reality the iconoclast once more. Heaven will solve our problems, but not, I think, by showing us subtle reconciliations between all our apparently contradictory notions. The notions will all be knocked from under our feet. We shall see that there never was any problem. And, more than once, that impression which I can't describe except by saying that it's like the sound of a chuckle in the darkness. The sense that some shattering and disarming simplicity is the real answer.

Lewis's concluding pages on love, as it turns into mystical union with God, shares with the end of the *Divine Comedy* and the "perennial philosophy" of mystics a resolution that moves beyond any dogmatic creed. As Joy turned her gaze toward God, as Dante's Beatrice and his Blessed Virgin turn their gaze to God, so Lewis finally anticipates the soul coming face-to-face with that Love which moves the sun and all the stars.

* * *

Today, November 29, the battlefield is closing like a book underneath a soft cover of snow, sinking under a silent ocean of infinitesimal stars.

I park the slippery car near the chapel on Seminary Ridge; I want to make one last visit to the Old Man.

There is nothing whiter than the seminary in wintertime. Here the steady feather's touch of wind has rubbed the bricks with snow until a sugary glitter lodges in the masonry. Walls are mortared with snow. Bending close to the rough clay, I can see the sun refracted through each flake and grain: in each white fallen wheel gleams all the colors of the universe.

The chapel is more reverent this morning after a night's snowfall. Even the square shoulders of Old Dorm are softened, curving toward the undulating blanket at its knees, and the cupola where the officers watched is bending.

The most delicately etched and colored stained glass lights the chapel; like frost the outlines of Reformation leaders, scriptural figures, and lilies lace the reaching panes. Those who struggled for the faith look airy, distant thoughts abstract their faces, glowing wrinkles of ice sparkle through their backs. The pews, the beams, the window frames are white, mottled with blue-gray light from pale walls and windows.

Holy, placed apart, still and swept by snow.

A groundsman nudges the chapel with his key.

The huge bronze block of Martin Luther glowers, or sleeps. The cannon watching him are draped, sleeping. Down around the sitting Luther I see, smell something. Fragrance of metal. Pink, faintest pink, glowing through the snow. I see it rise around the chapel, spreading. The fields are red! I feel the murmur of the barest wind, tiny as the Star of Bethlehem.

On Confederate Avenue, I cross the Fairfield Road. Cars are tender on the snow. Cold. Down from the ridge, fields freeze deeper. Fence posts gather in their arms and shoulders; here and there a branch cracks. Shadows stretch to ghosts.

A low stone wall covered by a mile of snow. Cannon stooping at their marks. Bare white. There, the fighting men of North Carolina. One points squinting toward the Union lines, snow on his finger.

I walk slower now. I can see him high in the gray sky, Robert E. Lee, gazing evenly over the field. The sun is turning his gray back to gold. His look is lifted over Cemetery Ridge, over all the rest of Pennsylvania. Silent as a father, he watches when the sun slides down behind, when all is black, when the sun returns and lights his face. The rock he steeples says, "Virginia, to her sons."

A silent silver fighter needles evenly northward in the pure cold sky. Stillness.

You would not think this place would still have so much blood in it. Everything I see is sleeping on a sponge of blood. I imagine the end of it all: Sheep with glinting teeth grazing on the ridge, through the Chapel, leaving hoofprints filling up with blood.

This is the season of the Star that emanated into Bethlehem, cool and peaceful like a snow of energy. Perhaps here would be a good place to wait and see if it will prick the curtain of the firmament, letting in a flood of light.

I turn to look, but the soldiers are gone. Snow glints.

A melting crease has trickled into ice along his back. My neck is stiff from looking up. Time to go back. The sun is so low my shadow wants to stretch away from me.

I can track myself back in the snow; the little wind has hardly bent the printing.

The North Carolinians cluster in the evening, the hurt man's finger still pointing, its shadow worming toward Cemetery Ridge. A dream of snow burns on my tongue. Throw down the fat guns. Rise. Go.

It seems farther to go back. These cannon look like empty bottles cracking in the cold; black holes battling the Star. I march on.

My tracks untrickle to the crossroads. Traffic has slushed the intersection.

Seminarians dodge the cold from dorm to library. Sculpted in cold bronze on the chapel lawn, Martin Luther muses a new Reformation, snow by snow, hope by hope, light from light. Of the Father's love begotten, a new world is at hand. Luther's children sleep in the moody drifting of the snow, dreams kicking in the heaps. The seminary watches here, a snowy bushel on a hill, silent, settled like the snow, the snow itself pink shadow, North Star glinting on the steeple's crown.

NOVEMBER 30

New Birth
(Advent)

> Now the Lord said to Abram. . . . I will make of you a great nation. . . . and in you all of the families of the earth shall be blessed.
>
> —Genesis 12

> For this reason it depends on faith, in order that the promise may rest on grace and be guaranteed to all his descendants . . . those who share the faith of Abraham, for he is the father of all of us. . . .
>
> —Romans 4

I am on my way to Christ Church this morning, my last day in Gettysburg. The month has felt like years while I was in the midst of it, but like only hours now at the end. Perhaps time is a fiction of consciousness. Was I here thirty days this month, or have I been returning through years of Novembers? Either the postmoderns are right or I am growing older: the present gets wider all the time.

I have come to the town center early, for a last lingering look at the Wills House, where Abraham Lincoln stayed in November 1863, and where he added two words to the Gettysburg Address. On the sidewalk in front of the old building stands a metal sculpture representing Lincoln talking in a friendly way with a startled and pleased modern tourist. The man is obviously a dad, complete with tennis shoes; no doubt the wife and kids are waiting in the van. I do not care if the idea is sentimental; it is exactly the kind of conversation we need.

Take one page from this morning's paper. It contains a story about the murder of a fourteen-year-old boy named Terrell. He was bright, affectionate, and studious—like Lincoln's son Willie. Growing up in one of our neighborhoods where there is little hope for an African American, Terrell nonetheless resisted the gangs. Raised by a strong, affectionate grandmother with vigorous religious faith, the boy had been determined to make something of himself, Lincoln-like. An eighteen-year-old fellow who had a quarrel of some sort with him walked up to him on the sidewalk, pointed a revolver at his heart and fired. "Why him?" sobbed another boy. "Why not me instead of him?" It could have been. A hundred fifty boys and girls fourteen and under had been murdered in Chicago during the first nine months of the year. Is "The Star-Spangled Banner" becoming an anthem for doomed youth?

One of us should be that metal dad in tennis shoes talking with Mr. Lincoln on the town square, because there are some questions we need to ask him. Unfortunately, we do not have the man himself any more; all we have is the historical record. That record we must use. We cannot afford the elliptical havens of doubt and forgetfulness; our children are being murdered in the streets. We need to remember our fathers and mothers in order to remember our children.

The consequences of absolute doubt are becoming dangerous. True, one should not be too certain that we actually know what we know. Between fact and fiction runs an imaginary boundary that is itself fiction. In my vignette of Virginia Wade (November 15) I deliberately composed an erroneous scene. I had the young woman living on the wrong street; in fact, the troopers did not pass her house. Even the trooper's answer, "Buford's cavalry, Ma'am," was very unlikely. He would have given the number of his regiment: "Fourth Indiana," or whatever. Fiction can be written for the sake of truth, and in this case I needed the cavalry to dramatize Ms. Wade's emotions. Emotions made the war. The intangibles of right and wrong gave it meaning. Facts come in all varieties. It is altogether fitting and proper that postmodernists tell us there is no such thing as objective truth, apart from human personality.

But in a larger sense, there must be fact and truth more solid than our thoughts, and independent of us. It does not require a leap of faith to believe that a universe existed before we arrived. "Know ye that the Lord, he is God: it is he that hath made us, and not we ourselves." Postmodernists can explain everything but themselves. As to Ms. Wade, I have sat in the cellar where her body lay; I have put my finger, verily, into the hole where the bullet came through the door.

* * *

Pausing before the church, I notice fragments of unmelted snow along the letters on the Chaplain Howell memorial at the steps. On the right-hand page of the open metal Bible two verses in raised letters wetly reflect the sun. The top one, from Psalm 18, reads: "He delivereth me from mine enemies: yea, thou liftest me up above those that rise up against me." The rest of the verse isn't quoted: "thou hast delivered me from the violent man." Surely whoever designed the memorial must have been aware of the irony. It is well placed. You cannot enter a church without crossing this little problem.

The other verse is from Hebrews 2, presumably referring here to Chaplain Howell: "He being dead yet speaketh." Speaketh what? That religious faith is ironic, or that it is evidence of something invisible? That the need to believe is stronger than reason, or that reason cannot contain heaven and earth? Religion can tell us whatever we wish. Psalm 18 was one of Stonewall Jackson's and Robert E. Lee's favorites: "He teacheth my hands to war . . . thou hast girded me with strength unto the battle." I think it is one of my favorites, too: "He made darkness his secret place." It is a long psalm.

I enter the sanctuary and take a place near the back. The pews are overlaid with red cushions. As the organist plays, I remove a green hymnal from the rack in front of me. Several ribbons of different colors are bound into the book—the Lutheran order of service is a bit complex. The first hymn will be "O Come, O Come, Emmanuel."

Today is the first Sunday in Advent; more people should be here. But I suppose this large sanctuary was built for the nineteenth century. Still, I have known some people who would not miss church to save their souls.

I trust that a good many Christians happen to be elsewhere this morning. Christians are not those who believe a certain creed or refrain from selected pathetic vices of humankind. They are not simply the liberals or conservatives or evangelicals. Christians are those who decline to accept the demise of Christ. They believe that goodness never ends.

It is worth coming to church today if only to sing the venerable Advent hymn:

> O come, O come, Emmanuel,
> And ransom captive Israel,
> That mourns in lonely exile here . . .

Its solemn tones should not be mistaken for grief. The medieval plainchant tune, *Veni, Emmanuel,* accumulates power and eventually conveys a profound joy, the joy of expectation:

O come, thou Rod of Jesse, free
Thine own from Satan's tyranny;
From depths of hell thy people save
And give them victory o'er the grave.
Rejoice, rejoice! Emmanuel
Shall come to thee, O Israel.

But we have been waiting a long time. Generations have trod, have trod, have trod—and now lie beneath the sod. How long will this waiting game go on? What are we waiting for?

The Church awaits the greatest hero of all: God. All heroes are excellent, but the New Testament God does what is impossible even for God. He becomes not God. Advent's expectation is a yearly invocation of that heroism, that creative unselfishness greater than our poor power to add or detract, that ultimate freedom which makes a new world because it is a new God who speaks it into being. The death and resurrection of Christ is an earthly pattern and image of the new birth of God, who makes the Self He imagines, "who gives life to the dead and calls into existence what does not exist."

This is the hero for whom the Church continues to wait. Humanity is God's unfinished art. Goodness is not perfect. These guilty Lutherans are optimists who have not arrived. But they believe.

They believe in the greatest hero's power and they trust his intentions. Hence this continuing expectation, this belief that something good is going to happen. What turns this belief into faith is a willingness to act upon it. One wagers oneself on the belief that goodness never ends. In this sense, all the faithful are saints, heroes of the Church, microscopic Christs in a massive world. The waiting must go on forever, because time cannot contain the answer, yet if time has any meaning, it is as the medium for that great expectation.

Greatness is a lamentable necessity in an unfaithful world, a world where not all people love each other as themselves. Therefore a hero must be great. But where everyone is good, no one would need to be great. Goodness is the most practical behavior in the long run.

Political and battlefield courage are within our power. Complete goodness is not. Therefore the Church awaits the Kingdom of God, and Advent is an expectation that prays.

O come, thou Dayspring, come and cheer
Our spirits by thine advent here;
Disperse the gloomy clouds of night,
And death's dark shadows put to flight.

It is a paradox, but to the Church, expectation and effort are the same. How shall we work the work of God? *This is the work of God, that ye believe . . .*

The pastor of course preaches this morning about expectation, though not exactly in these words. It is his job to exhort, but ultimately we learn, we are moved, and we act, not by argument but by example.

* * *

I met a man named Stephen a few years ago when I spoke on Gettysburg at a Civil War Round Table. In the course of our conversation I learned that he had served in Vietnam. Every day he was in country, he carried a letter his father had written to him from Iwo Jima. The father, a Marine Corps major, wrote his young son:

> This is a letter that I want your mother to save for you until you are older if perchance I never return. Death is not an easy thing for anyone to understand but every life shall one day end and should that day come for me before I can return to live with you remember that only the body can be taken and I will still be. You both shall know your father better as you grow and know yourself better. I can never be dead, because you are alive. . . . I don't expect you to understand these things but I know you will remember this—that nothing good ever ends.

The major died one month to the day before the Japanese surrender.

"Nothing good ever ends." By being always faithful to that belief, the soldier had shown his son what *semper fidelis* means. Is not that faith the basis of hope? The hero I know is not the major, of course. It is his son. Stephen had been a conscientious objector opposed to the Vietnam War. As a Methodist minister, he could have stayed home, but he volunteered to serve as a medical corpsman. He told me from the wheelchair he has been confined to for more than thirty years that he had been wounded while serving. He had followed his father's footsteps to where they ran out, and then went in the direction they pointed. A son of the heroic generation, Stephen equals or surpasses the courage of anything in that or any other generation. That is well, in view of this generation's extraordinary task of finding and keeping faith in a faithless world. Perhaps things are not as bad as we had thought; perhaps it is not fixed and fated that our generation shall live and die as cowards.

A hero acts upon the hope of heroes. We can learn from our parents; we can choose the letters we carry; we can keep the faith.

* * *

Soon after his death, Abraham Lincoln was compared to Christ. The assassination taking place on Good Friday, his martyrdom for "setting the captives free," his unselfishness, his eloquence, even his having no comeliness and, "despised and rejected" like the Suffering Servant of Isaiah 53, being the most vilified of all American presidents—the comparison was all too facile, and maybe in view of his skepticism regarding Christ's divinity, downright ironic. In *The American Religion: The Emergence of the Post-Christian Nation,* Harold Bloom writes, "The American Christ is more an American than he is Christ." He means not Abraham Lincoln, though the thought suggests itself, but rather the object of popular worship in America. The comfortable and entertaining "gospel" of some religious entrepreneurs might be what Bloom has in mind. The Christ of the gospels and of Saint Paul is, in Juergen Moltmann's phrase, "the crucified God." This is not an American concept.

We have believed in the wrong myth. Our Lincoln is more Hollywood and Madison Avenue than it is Lincoln. Our "Lincoln" is the rags-to-riches American: the poor boy who worked his way to the presidency. But this myth has become a false "gospel" of power and glory. The inevitable fact of the historical Lincoln story is that this successful rags-to-riches man was assassinated. Furthermore, he was never really happy, especially not at the pinnacle of his so-called success, in the White House. Who of us would trade places with him? I preach Lincoln, and him assassinated.

So, just as World War I might offer a dark window to the story and meaning of our era, and the dead at Gettysburg might reveal the foundations of the American experiment, so the person and work of Abraham Lincoln might illuminate a vision of *whence* we came, *where* we are, and *whither* we should be tending. We will all die, and many will die unhappy, but the significance of one's life can be found in the goodness it has given to others. Such goodness shall not perish. The myth or sacred history of Lincoln unites us with the meaning of every person's life. If what I think of him sounds uncritically elegiac, it is an elegy that to our generation is in no sense consolatory. We must *do better,* as John and Robert Kennedy often said, or the work of noble note which Lincoln's dead, and ours, so expensively advanced will be wasted on us, the spoiled, ungrateful children who let liberty and justice peter out in our own land, in our own house. We might be asking too much of an American story, but seeing it the other way is asking too little. Only an America that becomes "that nation" of the Gettysburg Address—a nation of liberty, equality, and justice—is worthy of its saviors and its martyrs.

* * *

The pastor tells the congregation which members are ill, who is having operations, who has been killed or injured in car crashes. It is fitting to do that in this sanctuary, where the wounded and dying lay, their blood staining this floor, in July 1863. The Civil War raised basic human questions. Those whose sons and husbands were killed asked "Why?" and it was God whom they asked. Lincoln's genius in the Gettysburg Address was to funnel the religious question toward political action, and to do it without blanching the political statement or the original religious impulse. He did this not as a wily propagandist but as a person who integrated religion and politics in his own life and thought. Just as the call to sacrifice was political, so the pledges of liberty, equality, and rights are religious.

One of America's peculiarities is that it has always committed itself to the future. Faith is desire to give to the future; the gifts vary, but that desire is constant. Faith is a mystic cord that binds past to future. Some seven score years ago, Abraham Lincoln told his Americans that they were a generation who could nobly save, or meanly lose, the last best hope of humankind. Now we have decided that "noble" is a ridiculous word; self-servingly we suggest that the word can be pernicious. Of course it is well to be suspicious of words, and to weigh them carefully.

Freedom and *justice* and *equality* seem very fragile; they might be mere inventions, like unicorns and leprechauns. As such, they would rely on their inventors and enjoyers for their reality. Only as long as people agree to live "as if," agree to live by invented, figmentary principles like "all people are equal under the law" and "liberty is a right which all people possess inherently," can the group proceed on such bases. But as soon as someone, like the child in the fable about the emperor's clothes, stands up and says, "They don't really exist," and the people say "Amen," then these things—really not *things* at all—would vanish. If the evidence of our actions shows that words do not refer to anything, they are weightless, meaningless, even pernicious.

Once Locke and Rousseau and others proclaimed the idea that humans have "natural rights," things we are born with like eyes and ears. Yet ever since the Holocaust we have understood that rights could become as nonexistent as street address, profession, possessions, family, and life itself, once somebody with power decided to take them away. The Nazis snapped their fingers and all these things vanished for six million European Jews.

Postmodernism claims that all human knowledge, history, law, and rights are mere language about language, and that history tells not what was, nor what is, but only what we are saying. They are like a joke we are all in on—or used to be in on—or like a great stage play which now postmodernists and cynics and dictators tell us was only a tale told by an idiot. If we awaken from this shared dream, the dream will vanish, leaving not a rack behind.

It is no mistake to call the American identity a faith, because like other faiths it is essentially religious. The rights we believe in have no reality apart from the God we rely on. There can be no "unalienable rights" unless we are endowed with them by a God in whom we trust. The problem of liberty and equality and rights is a problem of theology. Imagine Abraham Lincoln sitting in this church.

I wonder whether Mr. Lincoln would have wanted to visit Gettysburg again at all. Why seek the living among the dead—or the dead among the living? But the solemn, musing visit to a place of the past appealed to Lincoln's nature. An early literary performance of Lincoln's was, like the Address, elegiac. It was prompted by his return, in 1844, to his boyhood home in Indiana, "where my mother and only sister were buried." He walked the old fields and woods, visited the old cabins. These new impressions combined with memory, the "midway world" which is part joy and part pain, to leave a residue of melancholy:

> I range the fields with pensive tread,
> And pace the hollow rooms,
> And feel (companion of the dead)
> I'm living in the tombs.

Lincoln felt at home with this sort of thing. "Why should the spirit of mortal be proud?" So reads Lincoln's favorite poem.

> . . . we are the same that our fathers have been;
> We see the same sights that our fathers have seen;
> We drink the same stream, we feel the same sun,
> And run the same course that our fathers have run.
> . . . .
> 'Tis the wink of an eye—'tis the draught of a breath—
> From the blossom of health to the paleness of death,
> From the gilded saloon to the bier and the shroud
> Oh, why should the spirit of mortal be proud?

The poem, Lincoln told a visitor to the White House, was "continually present" with him.

The fact of the November cemetery remains. The facts of the Great War and other postmodern horrors remain. We too live in a world of

November; we too are companions of the dead, "living in the tombs," haunted by legions of our own demons. *O come, Emmanuel.*

We cannot afford to be foolish or mistaken in our hope. We expected a better world, a world of less pain, a world of justice and equality, to arrive in one day, in one month, in the life of one administration—in the life of one Enlightened Age of humankind. We have expected God's work here on earth to be truly our own. But we have learned, drop by drop upon the heart, that our work is imperfect. "The old, unredeemed and unchanged world of suffering, guilt and death is not capable of demonstrating the new creation," writes Juergen Moltmann. Our hope must look toward the star in December.

* * *

So the congregation walks forward, row by row, to receive the bread and wine of communion. We kneel at the rail, a lay person gives us a wafer of bread and says, "The body of Christ, given for you." The pastor gives us each a sip of wine and says, "The blood of Christ, shed for you." Then he lifts his hand over us all, saying, "Now may the body and blood of Christ strengthen and preserve you unto eternal life."

As I walk back to my pew, I realize that this is what I came here for. Grieving, I was looking for new life. I thought I was looking for the place where Lincoln stood to give the Address, but I was really looking for the heroism he eulogized. I wanted to discover heroic life. And here it is. *A hero strengthens and preserves us. A hero gives us life.* To do that, the hero becomes a new person, emptying himself or herself, for us. Every hero is a saint; every saint is a hero. Bread and wine, flesh and blood, are transformed: "a light to lighten the gentiles, and the glory of thy people."

* * *

The lay assistant begins the seemingly interminable "Prayers of the Church." These are a litany of requests, and a litany of remembrance for those who have died. Though we look for the Living God this first Sunday in Advent, surely we are seeking him among the dead.

But our lives are a constant struggle between the living and the dead, and a constant communion. We move among a mighty fellowship. The dead ensure that the living remain who they are, but the living constantly give up their happiness and their lives for those who do not exist—and by these I mean not only the dead, but those yet to come. The dead want us to do what we do not want to do. But to ignore the dead is to forget who we are. We wrestle with the spirits who bless us. In any case, the dead have put us where we are.

Therefore we must learn to choose. Some of the dead would have taken our liberties, denied us our rights, even would have killed us. Others of the dead gave us life. "We are your dead," they all say. "We are yours, and you are ours. We have all made you who you are." The deep moans round with many voices. But we are not helpless. The dream of America believes that we are not completely controlled by our fates, and we need not remain who we were born to be. We have one power over the dead: we may choose among them.

The heroes we choose show us who we may be. So, as the woman at the podium in front says, "We thank thee for those whom we now name in our hearts before thee," and gives us silence, I say the names *Ruth, Len, Mr. Lincoln, Bobby, JFK, Professor Lewis, Wilfred Owen.* Like the windows of the seminary chapel, the windows of memory are engraved with the blessing figures of our heroes, delicate and beautiful as snow, transmitting the divine light to us. Our grandparents—our Martin and Ingeborg—like Lincoln's Founding Fathers, watch from afar. The star we see in our dark night, it is their light. It is the light of the world.

* * *

When Abraham Lincoln pulled the cork out of the Gettysburg Address, it was not only union, emancipation, and VE-Day that came out. The last one out was a little deconstructionist with beret, pencil moustache, and broom, sweeping up everything ahead of him.

Like *The Tempest*'s Caliban, we have awakened from our Enlightenment worship of human beings.

> What a thrice-double ass
> Was I to take this drunkard for a god,
> And worship this dull fool!

Now we are engaged in a great civil war, testing what we shall make of ourselves. It is a war between doubt and faith. Faith seizes upon the invisible and makes it solid. Invisibles outnumber visibles. What we would be, we have to choose.

Faith takes us a step beyond what we believe. That is well, because as Goethe says, "Doubt of any sort cannot be removed except by Action." Faith is our work, even as it is a divine gift. November is the alien work of God, a work that must truly be our own.

The heroic character is formed by the nature of its vision. Robert Kennedy never received an answer to his question, "Why, God, *Why?*" And Abraham Lincoln believed God to be inscrutable. But neither Abraham Lincoln nor Robert Kennedy believed that God's unknowability or the world's apparent absurdity were excuses for inaction, or that they invalidated visions of a newer, better world. The beliefs of the ignominious are temporary. If one is brave and true, one gives tomorrow a goodness that never ends. The American faith can be like Adam's dream: he awoke to find it true. We are children of a dream.

* * *

Now for the last hymn. Because it is "contemporary," I do not recognize it, though its monotony and sentiments are familiar. Like postmodernism, this hymn is all surface. It is a shabby place to start, but we do need to make our own music. Let us begin. This is for all the saints.

This building is still a place to remember heroes, to imagine the past, and to draw strength for meeting and making the future. The greatest heroes, in their own ways, are saints: imitators of God.

> And let the beauty of the Lord our God be upon us;
> and establish thou the work of our hands upon us;
> yea, the work of our hands establish thou it.

The last hymn has been sung and the benediction given. We process out in disorderly expectation, our common pains and hopes brought out here to the steps in the gray wind. November is over; today is the first day of Advent.

* * *

On November 30, the *Washington Star* ran a brief report concerning the president's illness, by which he had been partly incapacitated since returning from Gettysburg. ("Now I have something I can give everybody," he had remarked.)

> President Lincoln is much better to-day, and will be able to resume his office duties to-morrow or next day.

Time to get back to work.

APPENDIX I
Modernism and Postmodernism

This book deals somewhat with "modernism" and "postmodernism." To the modern mind, today's world is disorienting because the familiar world, the Modern World, is ending. This book is partly an elegy for a world gone with the wind. The modern mind understood the world through the eyes of its intellectual parents, people in whose image the modern viewpoint was made: Plato, Aristotle, Moses, Jesus, Mohammed, Thomas Jefferson, Abraham Lincoln. The Judeo-Christian, Muslim deity held it all together, albeit in a *discordia concors,* a harmony of discordant elements.

But postmodernism thinks of reality not as an underlying harmony but as the clamoring discordant elements themselves—only. The kaleidoscope consists of bits and pieces and a tube: there is no underlying portrait or map. This applies not only to the "external world," but, more decisively, to the Self, which was the central concern and feature of modernism. In postmodernism, both the subjective Self and the objective outer world are replaced by language. The object is gone, and the subject is gone. Only the social and linguistic kaleidoscope remains. (While in this text, *November,* there could be a modern Self wandering through the time and space of November, history, and Gettysburg relating everything within himself, in another sense—postmodern—there is no Self here, only a series of chapters somewhat interlinked linguistically.) To modern minds, which have grown up on beliefs in purpose, meaning, and perhaps even in an overall Designer, the kaleidoscope idea is extremely disturbing; and the loss of Self is completely disorienting.

While postmodernism is just what its name implies, a temporary phase between eras with no proper existence of its own, it has become necessary to deal with it somehow because we are temporary, too, and might not outlive it. We are both modern and postmodern. We project ourselves into cyberspace; we respond to blitzing collages of video images; we have become the variety we believe in. Day to day, we are disorder itself. Our lives happen with the apparent randomness of today's bombing in Jerusalem following yesterday's Super Bowl, preceding tomorrow's flood in the Philippines—and history as we live it seems to be exactly what somebody once said it is: "just one damn thing after another." But we also still believe that thirty days make a month.

* * *

Postmodernism is useful in providing a critique of modernism, a structure which has failed us. Postmodernism can give us a few of the reasons why.

One of the chief concerns of modernism—not surprisingly—is itself. The Modern World, or movement, or mentality, has ceaselessly investigated its own nature and its origins. The era that brought us humanism, with its interest in the human being to the exclusion, in effect, of a Creator, has focused on itself to the extent, perhaps, that its focus and its subject have dissolved. "When you see through everything, everything is invisible."

What is modernism? Because this age has worked hard to define the term, one must not expect the result to be unanimous, or simple—or perhaps one should not expect a result at all. In *The Culture of Interpretation,* Wlad Godwicz says, "Modern thought is characterized by the fact that humankind no longer thinks of itself as the emanation or creature of a superior being or as part of an external nature, but rather as becoming." This is not to say that we are seen as becoming something planned, unless planned by ourselves. Here is a product of a leading element in modernism: humanism.

Humanism attempts to free human beings from their former masters: ignorance, political tyranny, religious authoritarianism, cultural desolation, economic poverty. On the other hand, it subjects everything to the human intellect. This leads to the "objectifying" of everything, and everyone, that Heidegger saw as characteristic of modernity. Everything is made an object of knowledge in the Modern World, and the idea is to intellectually "grasp," or control, whatever comes into view. This gives us "knowledge" in the modern sense.

If we are becoming, then progress must be the dynamic of history. Indeed, there is a dynamic; things do not stand still in relation to humanity. History is a drama, or a narrative, telling the story of humankind's progress. Modernism's progress is intellectual, economic, political, social, even—believe it or not—spiritual. (For modernists, the drama and narrative refer to a reality that is in the process of becoming or developing; for postmodernists, the drama and narrative are only texts.)

Along with progress comes what some see as "the supreme value of modernity," the New. The New, however, is always rooted in the foundations of modernity, the root elements, so that the New tends to be renewal, rebirth, renaissance—hence our preoccupation with the nature and origins of modernity itself: we seek justification or legitimization for our new ideas. This is an ancient, not modern desire. Amid the insecurities of newness and progress, we want stability. We certainly want to stay within the Modern World. When we modify the present, it is "by means of a critical return to the past."

Not only knowledge, but *thought,* progresses, and does so "from enlightenment to enlightenment in history." (Thought is only textuality, a system of signs, in postmodernism—free-floating software.) Modernism is dependent upon enlightenment, which is really an idea of how we know things, or of what knowledge is. It is also dependent upon *history,* as something which can be known and which has a movement consistent with the idea of human progress. The modern mind thinks of knowledge as something to grasp and rely upon like objects of sight as opposed to what is out of sight, and thinking of history as events whose progressive story we can know. When either of these two ways of thinking gets fouled up, becomes doubted, the modern mind is in crisis.

Capitalism is also associated with modernity. The rise of capitalism has been associated with two distinctly modern events happening at about the same time: the early industrial revolution, and the Enlightenment. Both depend upon writing. Though "language is indeed central to Western modernity," it is specifically the written word that enables skills, experience, and knowledge to be passed on to the potential work force. The inefficient, one-to-one relationship of master and apprentice is bypassed. Knowledge and production explode, we all begin to live better and better: *voila!* the Modern World. (But postmodernism returns to, and stays with, the writing, or textuality, itself. There is no world, except the system of signs and the social matrix.)

All this passing on of knowledge and goods presupposes a uniformity in human beings. But against this presupposition the French postmodernist, "deconstructionist," Jacques Derrida, opposes the idea of *difference.* This means at least two things. (Postmodern literary theorists are fond of puns, which show something of the limitations and power of language.) First, postmodern theory tries to recall the differences around us. It sees humans as tyrannized by thought and language which attempt to bring us all under one standard. (It would seem, however, that postmodernism has no means for defining or objecting to "tyranny.") Likewise, the former objects of knowledge are not really objects of knowledge; they are other than we, and our proper relation to them cannot be as masters over that which is grasped. This claim might seem to contradict contemporary physics, which believes that things we know are manipulated by our mere observation of them—but actually the message here is that we do not really know anything which we make into an object of that knowledge.

The other meaning of *difference* is much more virulent toward modernity because it questions its very foundation. This meaning plays upon the word *defer*—to postpone, or put forward, or carry forward or away. A piece of writing, according to Derrida, is not a frozen vehicle, structure, or declaration of meaning. There is always a tension between the purported meaning of a text and the meaning demanded by its grammar, syntax, and vocabulary. (More difference in the first sense here.) But grammar, syntax, and vocabulary constantly change—and even in "dead" languages such as Latin the understanding related to these elements changes. So to read a text means to become aware of the gap between the text's intentions and its language, which is beyond the text's control. Perhaps an example could be the difference between Jefferson's idea of *man* as it appears in the text of the Declaration of Independence—"white, propertied"—and Lincoln's: white or nonwhite, propertied or nonpropertied. A further difference exists today, when *male* is no longer part of the definition of *man* as the term is used in our founding political document.

Lincoln's Gettysburg Address could be seen as either an *explication* of the Declaration (a modernist thing to do) or as a *deconstruction* (postmodern), depending upon whether *we* see the difference between Jefferson's concept of men and Lincoln's as a potential, or as a gap. To think that our use of language determines the choice is already to be in postmodern territory, whether we know it or not and whether we wanted to be here or not. (In this, the Gettysburg Address is both modern and postmodern.)

The final point is that in the postmodern world, a text is no longer authoritative. With texts goes history; with texts goes knowledge. There is nothing in the background of texts; everything is now foreground.

* * *

"We can presume that autumn has come to Western historiography," writes F. R. Ankersmit of the University of Groningen, the Netherlands, in an article entitled "Historiography and Postmodernism." People might think that the *writing* of history could come to an end without breaking many hearts. Of course, we would still have history itself, spread out behind us, stolidly intact, should we ever for some reason or whim decide we wanted it. But that is the very thing postmodernism denies. We do not have history anymore. Nothing is there, laid out behind us, *nothing.* The only history we have is all around us, here, now, in the form of language. What postmodernism gives us in place of history is language about language. To use Ankersmit's comparison, history is no longer thought of as a trunk with various branches, but as leaves—leaves only, no branches, no trunk, but leaves only, and the leaves are falling.

History has no vertical dimension, no past—no *historical* dimension, as moderns are used to thinking of the term "historical"; it is all horizontal, all spread out around us. "What remains now for Western historiography is to gather the leaves that have been blown away and to study them independently of their origins . . . what is important is no longer the place they had on the tree, but the pattern we can form from them *now.*" I think one adjustment needs to be made to Ankersmit's metaphor: the whole tree business should be out. Leaves imply a tree, but postmodernism denies the tree. We cannot infer a tree, or a past, from the leaves: The objects we find do not connect to anything we can know for sure, and if they connect to each other at all it is only as we connect them. What we have is not leaves of a tree but leaves of notebooks—*pages,* that is, and history is a vast shuffle novel where we can make the pages relate to whatever pages we want, or write. This sounds perhaps like a deplorable idea, if not merely ludicrous—but it is the very serious and tough claim of postmodernists that, like it or not, this is the way it is. We have been fooling ourselves up until now.

Ankersmit sees this theory or realization as an occasion not for despair but for hope: "Postmodernism . . . draws our attention to the modernists' vicious circle which would have us believe that nothing exists outside it. However, outside it is the whole domain of historical purpose and meaning." Assuming, of course, that postmodernism is right; otherwise we have *put ourselves* precisely outside, or beside, any real historical purpose and meaning. The idea is that modern historiography has invented an essence called "history," and we are chained to that construct we have invented. Postmodernism faces the fact that it's all a construct, and so frees us from the "past"—a fiction—which has enthralled us.

Postmodernism "poisons the well"—a term used by philosophers to describe an argument that denies all the resources that might be used against it. Postmoderns, however, insist that they have not poisoned the wells; they have simply *discovered* that all the wells have been poisoned—or rather *are* poisoned. That is, *try* to find anything in the past. Take my problem with the location of the Gettysburg Address. The new, officially accepted location is supported directly by no witnesses. The argument for it is language about language; that is, it is pure interpretation, which like postmodernism takes all accounts with equal aloofness and regards its own conclusions to be as valid as, or more valid than, the language of eyewitnesses. (There is, one should mention, photographic evidence—but photographs are ultimately vulnerable to postmodern analysis also. Postmodern theorists would say every photograph is a falsification because it is a representation, a slice made into reality, producing something new.) The photos used to be considered evidence for the monument site; now they are seen "clearly" for the first time, after 130 years, to be evidence for the new site.)

This is not to say that I could casually propose my own site, say at the Speech Monument. The reason, for postmodernism, is not that my site can be refuted on reliable objective grounds. The reason my site will not work is that it does not work, it does not get *put to work:* with little argument to support it, my site does not engender further language about the question; it is not very useful in the ongoing world of interpretation. (Perhaps a cyber site would fix this.)

So where was the site, really? We can ask this question—why not?—but any answer is only what some might *think* to be an answer. There is no "really." The question is a kind of mistake, like asking "Which apple is more gorillas?" Some questions, according to the old logical positivists, are impossible; they have no answers. These were called "category mistakes." Today's postmodern theorists are linguistic nominalists for whom there is nothing outside language anyway.

In the matters which concern us most deeply and painfully we often ask erroneous questions, or, for postmodernists, questions referring to nothing outside language. Nobody cares a very great deal where Abraham Lincoln stood when he delivered the Gettysburg Address. The subject, however, raises a question we really do care about (even if we thought historiography is not for us): *Can we know* where he really stood?

Meaningless question! say the postmodernists.

This is not merely frustrating, it shakes us to our very foundations. If we cannot know this, what can we know? The question of what we can know is fundamental to everybody. Knowing what we know is something we have been trained to not live without. If there is any evidence that modern Western culture influences us profoundly, this is it.

If there is evidence that the *past* influences us directly, this is it.

* * *

Art, or poetry, and the past merge in the present of our reading.

Poetry is the foundation of history, says Hayden White in *Metahistory,* a landmark work in postmodern historiography, or theory of history. Everyone who looks at the past, says White, brings to the viewing a "linguistic protocol." This "protocol" is like a grid, or colored glasses, which "prefigure the historical field." We collect the "facts" of history according to the pails we bring with us into the field. We have already chosen the pails before we go berrying. Furthermore, the pails and the data are like the child's toy of shapes and cutouts, by which an assortment of solid shapes can be put into a hollow container, only by fitting the shapes through correct, corresponding holes. So, we go out onto a battlefield, let us say, with a covered pail that will accept squares and triangles, but will not allow circles to drop in—and the squares and triangles have to be of certain sizes.

The pail, White might say, is the "linguistic protocol" we have in the first place. There are at least four possible pails, and they correspond to "the four principle modes of poetic discourse." These are four modes of artistic comprehension that have been fairly consistent since the first human writing. From here, we construct *narratives* of historical events, according to *plots.* There are also four basic, or archetypal "plot structures." (In this, significantly, White follows the work of a literary critic and theorist, Northrop Frye.) These are romance, tragedy, comedy, and satire. We also *interpret* these plots according to one of the several ways humans tend to see truth.

But it all goes back to whether we see the field with a *tendency to connect things* and *see the relationships of things* as either "metonymic" (one thing suggests another, as "reading Lincoln" means reading things written by Abraham Lincoln), "synecdochic" (the part suggesting the whole or the whole suggesting a part, such as "That ain't no militia, that's the Army of the Potomac!" referring directly to only one unit of that army), "metaphoric" (one thing thought of as another, to suggest likeness or analogy, such as "the *thunder* of the cannonade"), or "ironic" (the actual meaning is different from what is said, such as World War I now being called "the war to end wars").

Writing a historical narrative is not, then, simply to string out "the facts." It is to "encode" a story (which must take one of Frye's several literary forms) with the way you see things in the first place. There is no "objective" history in the sense of it being *independent* of who writes it and reads it. We are "indentured" to the language we use for history; therefore "history" is indentured to language. History, it might be observed, is not exactly a *slave* to language; the postmodern idea is that the two work together, one and inseparable.

This means that no explanation of events is always and everywhere valid. That would be possible only if explanations followed purely and objectively from facts as "four" follows from "two plus two." But we do not agree on what genuine facts are, and we do not agree on how to relate them, much less what methods and theories should be used to derive their meanings. In short: "By constituting the historical field in alternative ways, they [historians discussed in *Metahistory*] implicitly committed themselves to different strategies of explanation, emplotment, and ideological implications by which to discern its true 'meaning.'" It is no use arguing for more "realism," because there is no agreement on what is realistic (a word implying artificiality in the first place), or, as White says, there is "a host of conflicting 'realisms.'"

The contemporary academic way of looking at history tends to be ironic, says White, but this approach has been under attack. Modern—or shall we say incipiently postmodern—historiographic thinkers, many of whom are not professional, academic historians, White points out (he mentions writers like Malraux, Yeats, Joyce, and Wells, and philosophers like Jaspers, Heidegger, and Sartre, along with professional historians), attack the ironic view because of its "inherent skepticism" and "moral agnosticism." However, the alternative visions proposed by such challengers are preferred on *moral* or *aesthetic* grounds. That is, there is still no idea of an objective truth, an objective collection and interpretation of facts. White refers to Kant's statement that we may conceive of history "as we please, just as we are free to make of it what we will." (This is another case of postmodernism being latent in modernism—here in the thought of an Enlightenment philosopher.)

White closes by saying that "recognition of the Ironic perspective provides the grounds for a transcendence of it." This is so because "If it can be shown that Irony is only one of a *number* of possible perspectives on history, each of which has its own good reasons for existence on a poetic and moral level of awareness, the Ironic attitude will have begun to be deprived of its status as the *necessary* perspective."

That might be all right as far as it goes, if you do not like irony, or believe that the essence of human life on earth is something other than irony. On the other hand, it might be the most profound irony of all. The only way, ironically, of getting irony to mop itself up is to show that *anything* can have *more than one* alternative meaning to the way it might seem (to somebody)—which itself is the essence of irony. This, in turn, ironically, undercuts the moral and aesthetic bases for attacking the ironic viewpoint in the first place. Leaving us with, of course, the postmodern world.

APPENDIX II
Lycidas

Yet once more, O ye Laurels, and once more
Ye Myrtles brown, with Ivy never sere,
I come to pluck you Berries harsh and crude,
And with forc'd fingers rude,
Shatter your leaves before the mellowing year.
Bitter constraint, and sad occasion dear,
Compels me to disturb your season due:
For *Lycidas* is dead, dead ere his prime,
Young *Lycidas*, and hath not left his peer:
Who would not sing for *Lycidas*? He knew
Himself to sing, and build the lofty rhyme.
He must not float upon his wat'ry bier
Unwept, and welter to the parching wind,
Without the meed of some melodious tear.
    Begin then, Sisters of the sacred well,
That from beneath the seat of *Jove* doth spring,
Begin, and somewhat loudly sweep the string.
Hence with denial vain, and coy excuse,
So may some gentle Muse
With lucky words favor my destin's Urn,
And as he passes turn,
And bid fair peace be to my sable shroud.
For we were nurst upon the self-same hill,
Fed the same flock, by fountain, shade, and rill.
    Together both, ere the high Lawns appear'd
Under the opening eyelids of the morn,
We drove afield, and both together heard
What time the Gray-fly winds her sultry horn,
Batt'ning our flocks with the fresh dews of night,
Oft till the Star that rose, at Ev'ning, bright
Toward Heav'n's descent had slop'd his westering wheel.
Meanwhile the Rural ditties were not mute,
Temper'd to th'Oaten Flute;
Rough *Satyrs* danc'd, and *Fauns* with clov'n heel
From the glad sound would not be absent long,

And old *Dameatas* lov'd to hear our song.
But O the heavy change, now thou art gone,
Now thou art gone, and never must return!
Thee Shepherd, thee the Woods, and desert Caves,
With wild Thyme and the gadding Vine o'ergrown,
And all their echoes mourn.
The Willows and the Hazel Copses green
Shall now no more be seen,
Fanning their joyous Leaves to thy soft lays.
As killing as the Canker to the Rose,
Or Taint-worm to the weanling Herds that graze,
Or frost to Flowers, that their gay wardrobe wear,
When first the White-thorn blows;
Such, *Lycidas,* thy loss to Shepherd's ear.
Where were ye Nymphs when the remorseless deep
Clod'd o'er the head of your lov'd *Lycidas*?
For neither were ye playing on the steep,
Where your old *Bards,* the famous *Druids,* lie,
Nor on the shagy top of *Mona* high,
Nor yet where *Deva* spreads her wizard stream:
Ay me, I fondly dream!
Had ye been there—for what could that have done?
What could the Muse herself that *Orpheus* bore,
The Muse herself, for her enchanting son
Whom Universal nature did lament,
When by the rout that made the hideous roar,
His gory visage down the stream was sent,
Down the swift *Hebrus* to the *Lesbian* shore?
Alas! What boots it with uncessant care
To tend the homely slighted Shepherd's trade,
And strictly meditate the thankless Muse?
Were it not better done as others use,
To sport with *Amaryllis* in the shade,
Or with the tangles of *Neaera's* hair?
Fame is the spur that the clear spirit doth raise
(That last infirmity of Noble mind)
To scorn delights, and live laborious days;
But the fair Guerdon when we hope to find,
And think to burst out into sudden blaze,
Comes the blind *Fury* with th'abhorred shears,
And slits the thin-spun life. "But not the praise,"
Phoebus repli'd, and touch'd my trembling ears;

"*Fame* is no plant that grows on mortal soil,
Nor in the glistering foil
Set off to th'world, nor in broad rumor lies,
But lives and spreads aloft by those pure eyes
And perfect witness of all-judging *Jove;*
As he pronounces lastly on each deed,
Of so much fame in Heav'n expect thy meed."
O Fountain *Arethuse,* and thou honor'd flood,
Smooth-sliding *Mincius;* crown'd with vocal reeds,
That strain I heard was of a higher mood:
But now my Oat proceeds,
And listens to the Herald of the Sea
That came in *Neptune's* plea.
He ask'd the Waves, and ask'd the Felon winds,
What hard mishap hath doom'd this gentle swain?
And question'd every gust of rugged wings
That blows from off each beaked Promontory.
They knew not of his story,
And sage *Hippotades* their answer brings,
That not a blast was from his dungeon stray'd,
The Air was calm, and on the level brine,
Sleek *Panope* with all her sisters play'd.
It was that fatal and perfidious Bark
Built in th'eclipse, and rigg'd with curses dark,
That sunk so low that sacred head of thine.
Next *Camus,* reverend Sire, went footing slow,
His Mantle hairy, and his Bonnet sedge,
Inwrought with figures dim, and on the edge
Like to that sanguine flower inscrib'd with woe.
"Ah! Who hath reft" (quoth he) "my dearest pledge?"
Last came, and last did go,
The Pilot of the *Galilean* lake.
Two massy Keys he bore of metals twain
(The Golden opes, the Iron shuts amain).
He shook his Mitred locks, and stern bespake:
"How well could I have spar'd for thee, young swain,
Enough of such as for their bellies' sake,
Creep and intrude and climb into the fold?
Of other care they little reck'ning make,
Than how to scramble at the shearers' feast,
And shove away the worthy bidden guest;
Blind mouths! that scarce themselves know how to hold

A sheep-hook, or have learn'd aught else the least
That to the faithful Herdman's art belongs!
What recks it them? What need they? They are sped;
And when they list, their lean and flashy songs
Grate on their scrannel Pipes of wretched straw.
The hungry Sheep look up, and are not fed,
But swoln with wind, and the rank mist they draw,
Rot inwardly, and foul contagion spread:
Besides what the grim Wolf with privy paw
Daily devours apace, and nothing said;
But that two-handed engine at the door
Stands ready to smite once, and smite no more."
Return *Alpheus,* the dread voice is past
That shrunk they streams; Return *Sicilian* Muse,
And call the Vales, and bid them hither case
Their Bells and Flowrets of a thousand hues.
Ye valleys low where the mild whispers use
Of shades and wanton winds and gushing brooks,
On whose fresh lap the swart Star sparely looks,
Thrown hither all your quaint enamell'd eyes,
That on the green turf suck the honied showers,
And purple all the ground with vernal flowers.
Bring the rathe Primrose that forsaken dies,
The tufted Crow-toe, and pale Jessamine,
The white Pink, and the Pansy freakt with jet,
The glowing Violet,
The Musk-rose, and the well-attir'd Woodbine,
With Cowslips wan that hang the pensive head,
And every flower that sad embroidery wears:
Bid *Amaranthus* all his beauty shed,
And Daffadillies fill their cups with tears,
To strew the Laureate hearse where *Lycid* lies.
For so to interpose a little ease,
Let our frail thoughts dally with false surmise.
Ay me! Whilst thee the shores and sounding Seas
Wash far away, where'er thy bones are hurl'd,
Whether beyond the stormy *Hebrides,*
Where thou perhaps under the whelming tide
Visit'st the bottom of the monstrous world;
Or whether thou to our moist vows denied,
Sleep'st by the fable of *Bellerus* old,
Where the great vision of the guarded Mount

Looks toward *Namancos* and *Bayona*'s hold;
Look homeward Angel now, and melt with ruth:
And O ye *Dolphins,* waft the hapless youth.
    Weep no more, woeful Shepherds weep no more,
For *Lycidas* your sorrow is not dead,
Sunk though he be beneath the wat'ry floor,
So sinks the day-star in the Ocean bed,
And yet anon repairs his drooping head,
And tricks his beams, and with new-spangled Ore,
Flames in the forehead of the morning sky:
So *Lycidas,* sunk low, but mounted high,
Through the dear might of him that walk'd the waves,
Where other groves, and other streams along,
With *Nectar* pure his oozy Locks he laves,
And hears the unexpressive nuptial Song,
In the blest Kingdoms meek of joy and love.
There entertain him all the Saints above,
In solemn troops, and sweet Societies
That sing, and singing in their glory move,
and wipe the tears for ever from his eyes.
Now *Lycidas,* the Shepherds weep no more;
Henceforth thou art the Genius of the shore,
In thy large recompense, and shalt be good
To all that wander in that perilous flood.
    Thus sang the uncouth Swain to th'Oaks, and rills,
While the still morn went out with Sandals gray;
He touch't the tender stops of various Quills,
With eager thought warbling his *Doric* lay:
And now the Sun had stretch't out all the hills,
And now was dropt into the Western bay;
At last he rose, and twitch't his Mantle blue:
Tomorrow to fresh Woods, and Pastures new.

—John Milton, November 1637

APPENDIX III

Elegy Written in a Country Church-Yard

The Curfew tolls the Knell of parting Day,
The lowing Herd wind slowly o'er the Lea,
The Plow-man homeward plods his weary Way,
And leaves the World to Darkness, and to me.
Now fades the glimmering Landscape on the Sight,
And all the Air a solemn Stillness holds;
Save where the Beetle wheels his droning Flight,
And drowsy Tinklings lull the distant Folds.
Save that from yonder Ivy-mantled Tow'r
The mopeing Owl does to the Moon complain
Of such, as wand'ring near her secret Bow'r,
Molest her ancient solitary Reign.
Beneath those rugged Elms, that Yew-Tree's Shade,
Where heaves the Turf in many a mould'ring Heap,
Each in his narrow Cell for ever laid,
The rude Forefathers of the Hamlet sleep.
The breezy Call of Incense-breathing Morn,
The Swallow twitt'ring from the Straw-built Shed,
The Cock's shrill Clarion, or the ecchoing Horn,
No more shall rouse them from their lowly Bed.
For them no more the blazing Hearth shall burn,
Or busy Houswife ply her Evening Care:
No Children run to lisp their Sire's Return,
Or climb his Knees the envied Kiss to share.
Oft did the Harvest to their Sickle yield,
Their Furrow oft the stubborn Glebe has broke;
How jocund did they drive their Team afield!
How bow'd the Woods beneath their sturdy Stroke!
Let not Ambition mock their useful Toil,
Their homely Joys and Destiny obscure;
Nor Grandeur hear with a disdainful Smile,
The short and simple Annals of the Poor.
The Boast of Heraldry, the Pomp of Pow'r,
And all that Beauty, all that Wealth e'er gave,

Awaits alike th' inevitable Hour.
The Paths of Glory lead but to the Grave.
    Nor you, ye Proud, impute to These the fault,
If Mem'ry o'er their Tomb no Trophies raise,
Where thro' the long-drawn Isle and Fretted Vault
The pealing Anthem swells the Note of Praise.
    Can storied Urn or animated Bust
Back to its Mansion call the fleeting Breath?
Can Honour's Voice provoke the silent Dust,
Or Flatt'ry sooth the dull cold Ear of Death?
    Perhaps in this neglected Spot is laid
Some Heart once pregnant with celestial Fire,
Hands that the rod of Empire might have sway'd,
Or wak'd to Extacy the living Lyre.
    But Knowledge to their Eyes her ample Page
Rich with the Spoils of Time did ne'er unroll;
Chill Penury repress'd their noble Rage,
And froze the genial Current of the Soul.
    Full many a Gem of purest Ray serene,
The dark unfathom'd Caves of Ocean bear:
Full many a Flower is born to blush unseen,
And waste its Sweetness on the desart Air.
    Some Village-Hampden that with dauntless Breast
The little Tyrant of his Fields withstood;
Some mute inglorious Milton here may rest,
Some Cromwell guiltless of his Country's Blood.
    Th' Applause of list'ning Senates to command,
The Threats of Pain and Ruin to despise,
To scatter Plenty o'er a smiling Land,
And read their Hist'ry in a Nation's Eyes
    Their Lot forbad: nor circumscrib'd alone
Their growing Virtues, but their Crimes confin'd;
Forbad to wade through Slaughter to a Throne,
And shut the Gates of Mercy on Mankind,
    The struggling Pangs of conscious Truth to hide,
To quench the Blushes of ingenuous Shame,
Or heap the Shrine of Luxury and Pride
With Incense, kindled at the Muse's Flame.
    Far from the madding Crowd's ignoble Strife,
Their sober Wishes never learn'd to stray;
Along the cool sequester'd Vale of Life

They kept the noiseless Tenor of their Way.
Yet ev'n these Bones from Insult to protect
Some frail Memorial still erected nigh,
With uncouth Rhimes and shapeless Sculpture deck'd,
Implores the passing Tribute of a Sigh.
Their Name, their Years, spelt by th' unletter'd Muse,
The Place of Fame and Elegy supply;
And many a holy Text around she strews,
That teach the rustic Moralist to dye.
For who to dumb Forgetfulness a Prey,
This pleasing anxious Being e'er resign'd,
Left the warm Precincts of the chearful Day,
Nor cast one longing ling'ring Look behind?
On some fond Breast the parting Soul relies,
Some pious Drops the closing Eye requires;
Ev'n from the Tomb the Voice of Nature cries,
Ev'n in our Ashes live their wonted Fires.
For thee, who mindful of th' unhonour'd Dead
Dost in these Lines their artless Tale relate;
If chance, by lonely Contemplation led,
Some kindred Spirit shall inquire thy Fate,
Haply some hoary-headed Swain may say,
"Oft have we seen him at the Peep of Dawn
Brushing with hasty Steps the Dews away
To meet the Sun upon the upland Lawn.
"There at the Foot of yonder nodding Beech
That wreathes its old fantastic Roots so high,
His listless Length at Noontide wou'd he stretch,
And pore upon the Brook that babbles by.
"Hard by yon Wood, now smiling as in Scorn,
Mutt'ring his wayward Fancies he wou'd rove,
Now drooping, woeful wan, like one forlorn,
Or craz'd with Care, or cross'd in hopeless Love.
"One Morn I miss'd him on the custom'd Hill,
Along the Heath, and near his fav'rite Tree;
Another came; nor yet beside the Rill,
Nor up the Lawn, nor at the Wood was he.
"The next with Dirges due in sad Array
Slow thro' the Church-way Path we saw him born.
Approach and read (for thou can'st read) the Lay,
Grav'd on the Stone beneath yon aged Thorn."

The EPITAPH.

Here rests his Head upon the Lap of Earth
A Youth to Fortune and to Fame unknown:
Fair Science frown'd not on his humble Birth,
And Melancholy mark'd him for her own.

Large was his Bounty, and his Soul sincere,
Heav'n did a recompence as largely send:
He gave to Mis'ry all he had, a Tear:
He gain'd from Heav'n ('twas all he wish'd) a Friend.

No farther seek his Merits to disclose,
Or draw his Frailties from their dread Abode,
(There they alike in trembling Hope repose)
The Bosom of his Father and his God.

—Thomas Gray, 1751

APPENDIX IV
Anthem for Doomed Youth

What passing-bells for these who die as cattle?
    —Only the monstrous anger of the guns.
    Only the stuttering rifles' rapid rattle
Can patter out their hasty orisons.
No mockeries now for them; no prayers nor bells;
    Nor any voice of mourning save the choirs, —
The shrill, demented choirs of wailing shells;
    And bugles calling for them from sad shires.

What candles may be held to speed them all?
    Not in the hands of boys but in their eyes
Shall shine the holy glimmers of goodbyes.
    The pallor of girls' brows shall be their pall;
Their flowers the tenderness of patient minds,
And each slow dusk a drawing-down of blinds.

—Wilfred Owen, 1917

APPRECIATION

Thanks to Lynelle Gramm, Sarah Gramm, Stephen C. Turner, Mary Brown, Lisa Crawford, Annette Thompson, and Heather Schepperley Owens for critically reading the manuscript. Rolland Hein provided valuable help on C. S. Lewis and Tom Martin on postmodernism. Serene Worth helped prepare the typescript. David Madden believed. The J. Omar Good Fund and the Aldeen Fund provided money for time in Gettysburg.

NOTES ON THE SOURCES

EPIGRAPH

"The Gettysburg Address" (Everett Copy), in *Collected Works of Abraham Lincoln*, vol. 7, ed. Roy P. Basler (New Brunswick, N.J.: Rutgers University Press, 1953), 21.

NOVEMBER

"Lycidas": Merritt Y. Hughes, ed., *John Milton: Complete Poems and Major Prose* (New York: Odyssey, 1957), 116–25.

"Men call'd him Mulciber": *Paradise Lost,* ibid., 209–469.

"The world is . . . different now" (JFK's inaugural address): Theodore C. Sorenson, *Kennedy* (New York: Harper and Row, 1965), 245.

NOVEMBER 1: ALL SAINTS

"Hell is hopelessness": Juergen Moltmann, *The Theology of Hope* (New York: Harper and Row, 1974), 32.

"Another order concerning the draft" and all subsequent information pertaining to President Lincoln's daily activities are taken from Earl Schenck Meiers, *Lincoln Day by Day: A Chronology 1809–1865* (Dayton, Ohio: Morningside, 1991).

"The $300 commutation" order: Basler, ed., *Collected Works of Abraham Lincoln,* vol. 6, 553–54.

"confessed the power of the law": Shelby Foote, *The Civil War: A Narrative* (New York: Random House, 1963), vol. 2, 637.

"every ward of every city": ibid.

"civil unrest all across the North": ibid., 636.

"struck in the forehead": Gregory A. Coco, *On the Bloodstained Field* (Holidaysburg, Pa.: Wheatfield Press, 1987), 13.

"you form you own conclusion": ibid., 14.

"ironic view of everything": Richard Reeves, *President Kennedy: Profile of Power* (New York: Simon and Schuster, 1993), 22.

NOVEMBER 2: L. L.

"Chrysostom": Moltmann, *Theology of Hope,* 23.

"a few appropriate remarks": Frank L. Klement, *The Gettysburg Soldiers' Cemetery and Lincoln's Address* (Shippensburg, Pa.: White Mane, 1993), 10.

"overstep the bounds of life": Moltmann, *Theology of Hope,* 19.

"Camus": quoted in ibid., 23.

"Somebody said that it couldn't be done": "It Couldn't Be Done," by Edgar A. Guest, in *It Can Be Done: Poems of Inspiration,* ed. Joseph Morris and St. Clair Adams (New York: A. L. Burt and George Sully, 1921).

NOVEMBER 3: PEN AND SWORD

"Lincoln's life was cold": William Herndon and Jesse W. Weik, *Herndon's Life of Lincoln* (New York: Da Capo, 1983), 483.

"I would love him more if he were home more": ibid.
"returned to his guest": Thomas Reeves, *A Question of Character: A Life of John F. Kennedy* (Rocklin, Calif.: Prima, 1992), 244.
"less profile and more courage": ibid., 140.
"personal aggrandizement": Herndon and Weik, *Herndon's Life of Lincoln,* 427.
"coached by Jacqueline": Nigel Hamilton, *JFK: Reckless Youth* (New York: Random House, 1992), xxiii.
"hope seeking understanding": Moltmann, *Theology of Hope,* 33.

NOVEMBER 4: LYCIDAS
"244,000 British": John Keegan, *The Second World War* (New York: Viking, 1989), 71.
"19,000 killed": Martin Middlebrook, *The First Day on the Somme: 1 July 1916* (London: Penguin, 1971), 263.
"1,250,000 killed, wounded, and missing": S. L. A. Marshall, *World War I* (New York: American Heritage Press, 1964), 259.
"743,000 killed in the war": Martin Gilbert, *The First World War: A Complete History* (New York: Henry Holt, 1992), 541.
"wastage": Paul Fussell, *The Great War and Modern Memory* (Oxford: Oxford University Press, 1975), 41.
"rum ration": ibid., 47.
"300,000 German and French": Alistair Horne, *The Price of Glory: Verdun 1916* (New York: St. Martin's, 1962), 327.
"two and one-half million young men were dead": Marshall, *World War I,* 291.
"Ivor Gurney": Fussell, *Great War and Modern Memory,* 74.
"war of conquest": Huburtus Prinz zu Loewenstein, *Deutsche Geschichte* (Munich: F. A. Herbig, 1976), 493. (*Fuer dieses Buch danke ich meine Intensivkurs Studenten, Justus-Liebig Universitaet Giessen: Gaby, Traute, Susanne, Annette, Sabrine, Patrick, Eike, Dagma, Heike, und Alexander.*)
"termed a 'myth' for good reasons": ibid. 489.
"Germans lost the war because of two things": Marshall, *World War I,* 163.
"yarns": zu Loewenstein, *Deutsche Geschichte,* 494.
"air of over-adultness": Jon Stallworthy, *Wilfred Owen* (Oxford: Oxford University Press, 1974), 29.
"Keats was ever-present": ibid., 47.
"worshipped Keats": ibid., 53.
"Rosetti": ibid., 57.
"I know I shall be killed": ibid., 261.
"unseen voices": ibid., 69.
"To eastward, too": John Stallworthy, ed., *Poems of Wilfred Owen* (New York: Norton, 1985), 175.
"This is the Path of Glory": ibid., 177.
"Up half-known roads": ibid., 149.
"Muse, yews": ibid., 161.
"A Tear Song": ibid. 120.
"a fine, heroic feeling": John Bell, ed., *Wilfred Owen: Selected Letters* (Oxford: Oxford University Press, 1985), 207.
"expressionless lumps": ibid., 208.
"a certain sublimity": ibid., 209.
"no better place": ibid., 213.
"mud and thunder": ibid., 211.
"gnashing of teeth": ibid., 215.
"spiritual cold": ibid., 210
"seventh hell": ibid., 213.

"nearly broke down": ibid.
"servants don't do Sentry duty": ibid. 214.
"the more terrific bombardments": ibid.
"The Sentry": Stallworthy, ed., *Poems of Wilfred Owen,* 165.
"the Narcissus do enough": Bell, ed., *Wilfred Owen,* 316.
"still find them sitting there": ibid., 217–18.
"shuddering down the sky": ibid., 237.
"we lay up against a railway embankment": ibid., 238.
"left off writing in the middle of a word": ibid., 239.
"Cock Robin": ibid. 242.
"he stood up and cursed them": ibid., 245.
"Wilpher d'Oen": ibid., 262.
"highest of jinks": ibid., 252.
"vile language": ibid., 268.
"disastrous dreams": ibid., 274.
"reputation of gallantry": ibid., 282.
"so outlive this war": ibid., 304.
"eucharist of their own blood": ibid., 302.
"sympathy for the oppressed": ibid., 306.
"way of spending Sunday": ibid., 286.
"liable to collapse": ibid., 315.
"ebbing tide": ibid., 308.
"desperate desire": ibid., 300.
"a vast, dreadful encampment": ibid., 306.
"unreluctant": ibid., 345.
"I came out in order to help these boys": ibid., 351.
"Strange Meeting": Stallworthy, ed., *Poems of Wilfred Owen,* 125–26.
"suddenly was not there": Stallworthy, *Wilfred Owen,* 25–26.
"nothing should be said": ibid., *26.*
"I must not now write": Bell, ed., *Wildred Owen,* 351.
"behaved gallantly": Stallworthy, *Wilfred Owen,* 279 n.
"my senses are charred": Bell, ed., *Wilfred Owen,* 352.
"under France": ibid., 167.
"no possible negotiation between crime and right": Stallworthy, *Wilfred Owen,* 273.
"eight and one-half million dead": Gilbert, ibid.
"Dulce et Decorum Est": Stallworthy, ed., *Poems of Wilfred Owen,* 117.
"Christ is literally in no-man's-land": Bell, ed., *Wilfred Owen: Selected Letters,* 246–47.
"Spring Offensive": Stallworthy, ed., *Poems of Wilfred Owen,* 169.
"high places": Owen refers here to the places of sacrifice of ancient times. See ibid., 171 n.
"poets must be truthful": ibid., 192.
"no na-poo": Stallworthy, *Wilfred Owen,* 281.
"the most arrant, utterly soldierly soldier": Bell, *Wilfred Owen,* 350.
"deep cursing": Stallworthy, ed., *Poems of Wilfred Owen,* 179.
"all but two were killed or wounded": Stallworthy, *Wilfred Owen,* 285.
"James Kirk": ibid., 285.
"Marshall was shot down": ibid., 285–86.
"You're doing very well, my boy": ibid., 286.
"a certain smile": Moltmann, *Theology of Hope,* 24.
"Anthem for Doomed Youth": Stallworthy, ed., *Poems of Wilfred Owen,* 76.

NOVEMBER 5: THE SPIRIT OF MORTAL
"contradictions": Moltmann, *Theology of Hope,* 337.

NOVEMBER 7: GOODBYE

"Lorena": Irwin Silber, ed., *Songs of the Civil War* (New York: Columbia University Press, 1960), 134–36.

NOVEMBER 11: ARMISTICE DAY

"the day Wilfred Owen was born": Stallworthy, *Wilfred Owen,* 287.

"We were lying off Victoria": ibid., 287.

NOVEMBER 14: IA DRANG

Losses at Ia Drang: Joseph L. Galloway and Lt. Gen. Harold G. Moore, *We Were Soldiers Once . . . and Young* (New York: HarperCollins, 1992).

24th Michigan, 2nd Wisconsin casualties: John W. Busey and David G. Martin, *Regimental Strengths and Losses at Gettysburg* (Hightstown, N.J.: Longstreet House, 1986), 239.

"The time was 1965": Galloway and Moore, *We Were Soldiers,* xix–xx.

"I can't find it": Wallace Terry, *Bloods: An Oral History of the Vietnam War by Black Veterans* (New York: Random House, 1984), 28.

"what I had done was wrong": David J. Regan, *Mourning Glory: The Making of a Marine* (Greenwich, Conn.: Devin-Adair, 1980), 168.

"in the back ward at the VA hospital": ibid., 171–72.

"All along the route": Jacob Hoke, *The Great Invasion* (Gettysburg: Stan Clark Military Books, 1992), 478–79.

"Shortly after noon": ibid., 484–86.

"ancient tests": C. Richard Allen and Edwin O. Guthman, eds., *RFK Collected Speeches* (New York: Viking, 1993), 325–26.

NOVEMBER 16: SANCTUARY

Vaclav Havel, quoted in *New York Review of Books,* March 5, 1998, p. 46. Trans. Paul Wilson.

NOVEMBER 17: THE OTHER ADDRESS

"Standing beneath this serene sky." For the text of Everett's speech, see Klement, *Gettysburg Soldiers' Cemetery.*

"But a writer for the Providence Journal": David Herbert Donald, *Abraham Lincoln* (New York: Simon and Schuster, 1995), 465.

"The *Springfield Republican*": Carl Sandburg, *Abraham Lincoln: The War Years,* vol. II (New York: Harcourt, Brace, and World, 1939), 463.

Robert Kennedy's Capetown Speech: see Allen and Guthman, *RFK Collected Speeches,* 237 ff.

NOVEMBER 18: THE VISITOR

"A London *Times* reporter": Richard Current, *The Lincoln Nobody Knows* (New York: Hill and Wang, 1958), 2.

"such an impression": ibid., 4.

"hold a heavy axe": Herndon and Weik, *Herndon's Life of Lincoln,* 471.

"amazingly mobile face": Current, *Lincoln Nobody Knows,* 4–5.

"subtle and indirect expression": ibid., 5.

"unfathomable": ibid., 6.

"never fully knew and understood him": Herndon and Weik, *Herndon's Life of Lincoln,* 468.

"cannot say I comprehended him": ibid., 470–71.

"Lincoln's melancholy": ibid., 473.

"when he began speaking": ibid., 331–33.

"scintilla of evidence": Stephen B. Oates, *Abraham Lincoln: The Man behind the Myths* (New York: Harper and Row, 1984), 12.

Herndon's Informants: Douglas L. Wilson and Rodney O. Davis, eds., *Herndon's Informants: Letters, Interviews, and Statements about Abraham Lincoln* (Urbana: University of Illinois Press, 1998).

"Ann Rutledge": Edgar Lee Masters, *Spoon River Anthology* (New York: Collier Books, 1962), 229.

"Flowereth for the prethident": Donald, *Lincoln,* 463.

NOVEMBER 19: THE GETTYSBURG ADDRESS

Information used in the account of Lincoln's activities on the morning of November 19 is from Klement, *Gettysburg Soldiers' Cemetery.*

NOVEMBER 20: CONFEDERATE ROSE

Virginia monument: David G. Martin, *Confederate Monuments at Gettysburg* (Hightstown, N.J.: Longstreet House, 1986), 21–25.

"the figure had fallen to 29 percent": *U. S. News and World Report,* November 15, 1993.

NOVEMBER 21: FUTILITY

"the two men, now rivals": Archives, Gettysburg National Military Park, File 10-15.

"an artist, Joseph Becker": ibid.

"file 10–11": ibid., 4–5.

"Whitelaw Reid wrote": ibid., 5.

"nearby German Reformed Church": Cindy L. Small, *The Jenny Wade Story* (Gettysburg: Thomas Publications, 1991), 38.

"a pacifist": "Rose Farmhouse Historic Structure Report," pt. 1, Archives, Gettysburg National Military Park, 13.

"famous farms": ibid., 6.

"one of the little ones would be taken": ibid., 5.

"Selleck is less than reliable": Klement, *Gettysburg Soldiers' Cemetery,* 134–35.

"everything has become contemporary": F. R. Ankersmit, "Historiography and Postmodernism," *History and Theory* 28, no. 2 (1989), 137–53.

For the term "submodernism," see Moltmann's essay in Juergen Moltmann, Nicholas Wolterstorff, and Ellen T. Charry, *A Passion for God's Reign: Theology, Christian Learning, and the Christian Self* (Grand Rapids, Mich.: Eerdmans, 1998.)

NOVEMBER 22: DALLAS AND OXFORD

"reaffirmation of the idea": Richard N. Goodwin, *Remembering America* (Boston: Little, Brown, 1988), 237.

"contemporaries seem like pygmies": A. N. Wilson, *C. S. Lewis: A Biography* (New York: Fawcett Columbine, 1990), 207.

"in part an alien": ibid., 22.

"in love with Oxford": ibid., 74.

"I treated my own father abominably": ibid., 114.

"a sinful woman married to a sinful man": C. S. Lewis, *A Grief Observed* (New York: Bantam, 1961), 49.

"a world of make-believe": Wilson, *C. S. Lewis,* xiv.

"perpetual virginity": ibid., xvi.

"personal secretary of C. S. Lewis": ibid., 30.

"as well as any American": ibid., 93.

"world without chloroform": C. S. Lewis, *The Problem of Pain* (New York: Macmillan, 1962), 16.

"if the universe is so bad": ibid., 15.

"exhilarating programme": ibid., 9.
"in no sense putting on an act": Wilson, *C. S. Lewis,* 147.
"how many bubbles of mine she pricked": Lewis, *Grief Observed,* 3.
"Elizabeth Anscombe": Wilson, *C. S. Lewis,* 213–14.
"even lie in order to win": ibid., 209, 244.
"only two views we can hold about awe": C. S. Lewis, *Problem of Pain,* 20–21.
"moral law": ibid., 22.
"no middle way": ibid., 24.
"method and manner were spurious": Wilson, *C. S. Lewis,* 215.
"gradual intellectual acceptance": ibid., 110.
"house of cards": ibid., 42.
"the City Ruinous": C. S. Lewis, *The Silver Chair* (New York: Macmillan, 1953), 130–31.
" 'Look here!' said Scrubb": ibid., 62.
"inside of an ant-hill": ibid., 127.
"the kind of things we are: C. S. Lewis, *The Abolition of Man* (New York: Macmillan, 1947), 29.
"when a Roman father": ibid., 31–32.
"studiously avoid appreciating": Wilson, *C. S. Lewis,* 161.
"mere talk": ibid., 123.
"it's miraculous": ibid., 278.
"eerie phenomenon": ibid., 269–70.
"if it is allowed": ibid., 281.
"Where is God?": Lewis, *Grief Observed,* 4.
"consolations of religion": ibid., 28.
"in God's hands": ibid., 31.
"monkey trick": ibid., 19.
"anguish is past?" ibid., 49.
"our own desperate wishes": ibid., 33–34.
"preparing the next torture": ibid., 35.
"reality, looked at steadily": ibid., 32.
"if you see through everything": Lewis, *Abolition of Man,* 91.
Vaclav Havel at Independence Hall: *Vital Speeches,* August 1, 1994, vol. 60, 613.

NOVEMBER 24: ULYSSES

"In Greece the mind": Edith Hamilton, *The Greek Way* (New York: Norton, 1964), 34.
"the place of the Greeks is in the modern world": ibid., 15.
"When he shall die": quoted in Arthur M. Schlesinger Jr., *Robert Kennedy and His Times* (New York: Ballantine, 1978), 718.
"abiding melancholy": ibid., 667.
"announcement of candidacy": Allen and Guthman, *RFK Collected Speeches,* 321.
"moralistic, gloomy": Jack Newfield, *Robert Kennedy: A Memoir* (New York: Bantam, 1969), 28.
"the believer": ibid., 33.
"sense of Good and Evil": ibid.
"only one choice": ibid., 126.
"character in a novel": ibid., 28.
"at war with himself": ibid., 21.
"delinquent or a revolutionary": ibid., 4.
"literary imagination": ibid., 29.
"myth and symbolism": ibid., 28.
"awareness of death": ibid., 50.
"learned about the absurd": ibid., 4.
"boxer's salute": ibid., 53.

"future leader of the free world": ibid.
"Just me. I'm alone": ibid., 258–59.
"his long hair": ibid., 29.
"existential hero": quoted in ibid., 30.
"I'd be a communist, too": ibid., 38.
"Unapproachable": ibid., 40.
"Senator Javits and Bobby": ibid., 41.
"found who and what he was": ibid., 303.
"Tribune to the Underclass": Schlesinger, *Robert Kennedy,* 837.
"magnet for hate": Newfield, *Robert Kennedy,* 21.
"ruthless": ibid., 22.
"introverted": ibid., 23–24.
"Now I can go back to being ruthless": Bill Adler, *The Robert F. Kennedy Wit* (New York: Berkley, 1968), 118.
"the great state of . . . ": ibid., 20.
"an unknown, virtually without funds": ibid., 122.
"large body of anti-Kennedy voters": quoted in Newfield, *Robert Kennedy,* 292.
"24 percent . . . opposed the bombing": ibid., 145.
November 26, 1967, interview: Edwin O. Guthman and Jeffrey Shulman, *Robert Kennedy in His Own Words* (New York: Bantam, 1988), 406ff.
"McCarthy dwelt almost obsessively on Kennedy": Schlesinger, *Robert Kennedy,* 972.
"What has he done for the poor?": Newfield, *Robert Kennedy,* 253.
"indolent": ibid., 35.
"not moral": ibid., 212.
"there aren't ten politicians": ibid., 155.
"the normal faked cordiality": ibid.
"maybe my personality": ibid., 309.
"First is the danger of futility": Robert F. Kennedy, *To Seek a Newer World* (New York: Bantam, 1967), 232–33.
"the only way we can live": ibid., 235.
"a phenomenon that can't be explained": Allen and Guthman, *RFK Collected Speeches,* 206.
"last of the great believables": ibid., 309.
"to have been young and heard his hopeful call": ibid., xxix.
"they move you deeply": ibid., xxxiii.
"such confrontations were not rare": ibid., 341.
"cheers and applause": ibid., 343.
"It really taught me a lot about him": ibid., 383.
"the people were fair to me": Newfield, *Robert Kennedy,* 297.
"brooding and lonely": ibid., 286.
"make the difference in helping the world survive": Allen and Guthman, *RFK Collected Speeches,* 289.
"politically dead in six months": ibid., 290.
"70 percent . . . approved of the war effort": ibid., 312.
"a traitor to the United States": ibid.
"Three Presidents": ibid., 292.
"we are all participants": ibid., 293–94.
"It is diverting resources": ibid., 294.
"If this country is going to mean anything": ibid., 303.
"undermined in Vietnam": ibid., 304.
"the enemy is brutal and cruel": ibid., 310.
"forever rest on our national conscience": ibid., 311.
"children starving in Mississippi": ibid., 332.

"a nation in which justice is done": ibid., 204.
"It was filthy": ibid., 202.
"How can a country like this allow it?": ibid., 200–201.
"we must act": ibid., 354.
"fusion of religious and political ideals": ibid., xxix.
"politics of values": ibid., xxxii.
"one of the best fathers": ibid., xxxvi.
"In Scottsbluff, Nebraska": ibid., 372.
"root fact of American life": ibid., 372–73.
"best hope of man": ibid., 374.
"our gross national product": ibid., 329–30.
"only a cleansing of our whole society": ibid., 360.
"prophets get shot": ibid., 363–64.
"the poor are not liabilities": ibid., 370.
"moral energy": ibid., 365.
"in danger of dissolution": ibid., 377.
"a better liberalism": ibid., 389.
"the new politics": ibid., 390.
"we are a great country": ibid., 402.
"a hundred people in that hotel": Newfield, *Robert Kennedy,* 345.
"imperfect savior": Allen and Guthman, *RFK Collected Speeches,* xxxviii.
"numberless diverse acts of courage": ibid., xlii.
"now I realized what makes our generation unique": Newfield, *Robert Kennedy,* 348.
"I'll show you the way": Schlesinger, *Robert Kennedy,* 983.
The reader is referred to the excellent biography by Evan Thomas, *Robert Kennedy: His Life* (New York: Simon and Schuster, 2000).

NOVEMBER 25: JFK
"her husband, 'Abe' ": Evelyn Lincoln, *My Twelve Years with John F. Kennedy* (New York: David McKay, 1965), 365.
"strange, unexplainable feeling,": ibid., 369.
"most of all an attitude": Bruce Catton, *Four Days* (New York: UPI and American Heritage Magazine, 1964), 3.
"one era came to an end": ibid., 3,4.
"a man can be as big as he wants": Reeves, *President Kennedy,* 514.
"first child of the enlightenment": Garry Wills, *The Kennedy Imprisonment: A Meditation on Power* (New York: Pocket Books, 1981), 285.
"makes a mockery": ibid., 37.
"immunity from nuclear weapons": Reeves, *President Kennedy,* 384.
"missiles were not a threat": ibid., 268–69.
"not only to overthrow Castro": ibid., 261.
"To the American public": ibid., 268.
"attitude toward the use of nuclear force": see ibid.
"if they turn out to be wrong": ibid., 379.
"inexperienced fool": ibid., 378.
"sneak attack on Cuba," ibid., 386.
"single accomplishment of Robert Kennedy": Wills, *The Kennedy Imprisonment,* 278.
"never really became liberal": ibid., 221.
"the wrong lesson": ibid., 296.
"self-absorbed detachment": Reeves, *Question of Character,* 4-1.
"just glimpsed hell": Reeves, *President Kennedy,* 535.
"wanted to go": ibid., 532.
"gone from his shoulders": Lincoln, *My Twelve Years,* 345.

"only qualification was wanting it": Reeves, *President Kennedy,* 14.
"No one ever knew John F. Kennedy": ibid., 19.
"irony was as close as he came": ibid.
"such a poor Catholic": Donald Spoto, *Jacqueline Bouvier Kennedy Onassis: A Life* (New York: St. Martin's, 2000), 139–40.
"expect more from ourselves": Lincoln, *My Twelve Years,* 370.
"the right to do the same": ibid.
"could have bombed us": ibid., 244.
"drug therapy": ibid., 296.
"never to recover fully": Newfield, *Robert Kennedy,* 18.
"sense of the absurd": ibid., 52.
"all of November": ibid., 18.
"he just broke down": ibid., 51–52.
"police escort left him": Schlesinger, *Robert Kennedy,* 939.
"we have to make an effort": Newfield, *Robert Kennedy,* 52.
"through the awful grace of God": ibid.

NOVEMBER 26: BEAUTIFUL AND BRAVE

"a soul, living from great depths of being": Carl Bode, ed., *The Portable Emerson* (New York: Viking Penguin, 1946), 123.

NOVEMBER 27: THANKSGIVING

"festival of booths" Deut. 16:13–15, *The Bible: New Revised Standard Version* (New York: Oxford University Press, 1989).
"no human counsel": Basler, ed., *Collected Works of Abraham Lincoln,* vol. 6, 496–97.
"rejoice during your festival": Deut. 16:14 (NRSV).

NOVEMBER 28: ELEGY

"At the core, the American citizen soldiers": Stephen E. Ambrose, *The Victors: Eisenhower and His Boys: The Men of World War II* (New York: Simon and Schuster, 1998), 351.
"political disaster": Sean Dennis Cashman, *America in the Gilded Age* (New York: New York University Press, 1984), 3.
"fresh from its creator": Herndon and Weik, *Herndon's Life of Lincoln,* 475.
"thought for himself": ibid., 417.
"peculiar and original creation": ibid., 476.
"greatest character since Christ": ibid., 417.
"real and enduring greatness": ibid., 467.
"never thought of the world as a moral place": Reeves, *President Kennedy,* 107.
"entire harmony": Herndon and Weik, *Herndon's Life of Lincoln,* 421.
"reason's food": ibid., 481.
"love of the just": ibid., 481.
"the kindest man": ibid., 413.
"honest and true": ibid., 411.
"never abrogated or beclouded his judgement": ibid., 430.
"never judged men by his like or dislike": ibid., 431.
"his polar star": ibid., 481.
"love of the truth": ibid., 487.
"do unto others": ibid., 484.
"relations, near or remote": ibid., 482.
"great student": ibid., 421.
"read less and thought more": ibid., 477.
"petty cruelties": Donald, *Lincoln,* 27.

"never cold": Herndon and Weik, *Herndon's Life of Lincoln,* 411.
"Bloom forever": Masters, *Spoon River Anthology,* 229.
"just and magnificent equipoise": Herndon and Weik, *Herndon's Life of Lincoln,* 484.
"false to no one": ibid., 421.
"less interested in social programs": *New York Times,* September 22, 1994.
"whither we are tending": Basler, ed., *Collected Works of Abraham Lincoln,* vol. 2, 46.

NOVEMBER 29: WINTER SATURDAY

"My restless spirit": *Endymion,* I, 854–57, in *John Keats: Complete Poems,* ed. Jack Stillinger (Cambridge, Mass.: Harvard University Press, 1978), 85.
"never was a man better prepared," Wilson, *C. S. Lewis,* 293.
"absolute reality": ibid., 151.
"failure of the imagination": ibid., 135.
"only a view": ibid., 89.
"fatal serialism": ibid., 90–91.
"refusal to toe the line": ibid., 246.
"dinosaur": ibid.
"mixed up with the thing it is meant to signify": ibid., 277.
"work for posterity": Lewis, *Abolition of Man,* 54.
"new primary color": ibid., 57.
"sole source of all value judgements": ibid., 56.
"obedience which is not slavery": ibid., 54–55.
"we laugh at honor": ibid., 35.
"profoundly afraid of death": Wilson, *C. S. Lewis,* 293.
"since you saw no form": Deut. 4: 15–16 (NRSV).
"let me try thinking instead": Lewis, *Grief Observed,* 41.
"no God or a bad one": ibid., 50.
"incomprehensible and unimaginable": ibid., 27.
"heaven would have a job to hold me": ibid., 88.
"like a long valley": ibid., 69.
"motionless warm dampness": ibid., 52.
"a fact to be taken into account": ibid., 60.
"momentarily facing my own": ibid., 85.
"And all at once": Tennyson, *In Memoriam,* XCV 35, 36, in *Literature of the Western World,* vol. 2, ed. Brian Wilkie and James Hurt (New York: Macmillan, 1992), 950.
"into smithereens": Lewis, *Grief Observed,* 82.
"all reality is iconoclastic": ibid., 77.
"marks of His presence?": ibid., 76.
"the real answer": ibid., 83.

NOVEMBER 30: ADVENT

"fourteen-year-old boy named Terrell": *Chicago Tribune,* September 8, 1994, sec. 1, p. 10.
"the American Christ": Harold Bloom, *The American Religion: The Emergence of the Post-Christian Nation* (New York: Simon and Schuster, 1992), 25.
"my mother and only sister": Carl Sandburg, *Abraham Lincoln: The Prairie Years* (New York: Harcourt, Brace, and World, 1926), 310.
"I range the fields with pensive tread": ibid., 311–12.
"Why should the spirit of mortal be proud?": ibid., 308–10.
"continually present": Current, *Lincoln Nobody Knows,* 8.
"the old, unredeemed and unchanged world of suffering": Moltmann, *Theology of Hope,* 173.

"Caliban": *The Tempest, The Riverside Shakespeare* (Boston: Houghton Mifflin, 1974), V.i.296–98.

On Lincoln's belief that God's inscrutability is not an excuse for passivity, see Allen Guelzo, *Abraham Lincoln: Redeemer President* (Grand Rapids, Mich.: Eerdmans, 1999), 420.

"And let the beauty of the Lord our God": Psalm 90:17 (KJV).

"resume office duties": Meiers, *Lincoln Day by Day,* 222, 224.

APPENDIX 1. MODERNISM AND POSTMODERNISM

"its own nature and its origins": Wlad Godzich, *The Culture of Literacy* (Cambridge, Mass.: Harvard University Press, 1994), 248.

"rather as becoming": ibid., 57–58.

" 'objectifying' of everything": ibid., 255.

"supreme value": ibid., 249.

"critical return to the past": ibid., 248.

"from enlightenment to enlightenment": ibid.

"capitalism": ibid., 254.

"language is indeed central": ibid., 18.

"uniformity in human beings": ibid.

"differences in the universe": ibid., 19 ff.

"autumn has come," Ankersmit, "Historiograpy and Postmodernism," 137–53.

"what remains now for Western historiography": ibid., 150.

"linguistic protocol": Hayden White, *Metahistory: The Historical Imagination in Nineteenth-Century Europe* (Baltimore: Johns Hopkins University Press, 1973), 426.

"the several ways humans tend to see truth": ibid.

"encode . . . indentured": ibid., 430.

"what methods and theories should be used to derive their meanings": ibid., 429.

"discern its true 'meaning' ": ibid., 431.

"host of conflicting realisms": ibid., 432.

"free to make of it what we will": ibid., 433.

"if it can be shown that Irony": ibid., 434.

APPENDIX 2. *LYCIDAS*

Lycidas, in Hughes, ed., *John Milton,* 116–25.

APPENDIX 3. ELEGY WRITTEN IN A COUNTRY CHURCH-YARD

"Elegy Written in a Country Church-Yard": Thomas Gray, M. H. Abrams, et al., The *Norton Anthology of English Literature: The Major Authors* (New York: W. W. Norton , 1996), 1253–56.

INDEX

Kent Gramm is program director of the
Seminary Ridge Historical Preservation Foundation
and author of *Gettysburg: A Meditation on War and Values*
(Indiana University Press, 1994) and
Somebody's Darling: Essays on the Civil War,
forthcoming from Indiana University Press.
He has taught at colleges and
universities in the United
States and Germany.